WE ARE
AT WAR

WE ARE
AT WAR

THE DIARIES OF FIVE
ORDINARY PEOPLE IN
EXTRAORDINARY TIMES

SIMON GARFIELD

EBURY
PRESS

This edition published in Great Britain by Ebury Press 2006
First published in Great Britain in 2005

10 9 8 7 6 5 4 3 2 1

First published by
Ebury Press
Random House
20 Vauxhall Bridge Road
London SW1 2SA

Random House Australia (Pty) Limited
20 Alfred Street, Milsons Point
Sydney
New South Wales 2061, Australia

Random House New Zealand Limited
18 Poland Road, Glenfield, Auckland 10
New Zealand

Random House (Pty) Limited
Isle of Houghton
Corner of Boundary Road & Carse O'Gowrie
Houghton 2198
South Africa

Random House UK Limited Reg. No.

www.randomhouse.co.uk

A CIP catalogue record for this book is available from the British Library

All photography © Getty unless otherwise stated.
Adverts on Page 28 & Page 302 © Advertising Archives

Cover Design by Two Associates
Text design and typesetting by Textype, Cambridge

ISBN 9780091903879 (From January 2007)
ISBN 0 091903874

Papers used by Ebury Press are natural, recyclable products made from
wood grown in sustainable forests

Printed and bound in Great Britain by Cox and Wyman Ltd, Reading, Berkshire

Contents

Introduction

'It is splendid,' Christopher Tomlin wrote in his diary on 14 July 1940, 'to know so many buggering Nazis are down.' Tomlin was a religious man, and Sunday 14 July was a day of fasting. He allowed himself cigarettes, but struggled to afford them. His work as a writing-paper salesman brought in barely enough to buy food and cover his family's mortgage. His brother was in the RAF, his father unemployed. He was in his late twenties, and he was about to be called up.

We know from Tomlin's diary that several other things happened on that day. The Battle of Britain was under way, and Churchill did his best to rally spirits in a speech (Tomlin judged the address a 'grand enervating rag-chew', and was disappointed with the prediction that the war might last until 1942). On the same day there was a radio broadcast describing a victorious RAF engagement over the Channel. For Tomlin this was 'an unexpected delight' and he wanted 'more please!' But then a doubt crept in. 'I must confess I'm nervous of this diary being in authorities' hands. It might get me a year or at least 6 months.' He had reason for concern: people were being fined and threatened with prison for expressing despondency, something Tomlin had done often in previous entries. In addition, the threat of invasion had not yet passed.

His diaries survived, and did not land him in trouble. We are the beneficiaries of his endeavours. Each month, despite the rise in postage costs documented in his journal, Tomlin sent his opinions to Mass-Observation, the organisation established a few years before to record the lives of ordinary people. In January 1940, Tomlin explained the appeal: 'The reason why I am keen on Mass-Observation is because it wants to know and inform, tell all classes about the emotion, acts, thoughts and struggles of the ordinary or

1

"average" man and woman. Too many articles and books are on high-flown subjects, there are none about the prosaic things of everyday.'

The bulk of Mass-Observation's work was made up of answers to questionnaires ('directives') and diaries maintained by people whose opinions had rarely been sought before. In the summer of 1937, a few months after M-O was born, it already described itself as a 'movement'. One of its many leaflets described how 'intellectuals find it hard to express themselves [but] observation comes naturally to people who are living in the thick of work-a-day existence. Among our best Observers are a mechanic, a coalminer, a waiter, a clerk, a housewife (middle-class) and a housewife (working-class).'

The initial ambitions of M-O's three founders – Tom Harrisson, Charles Madge and Humphrey Jennings – were both grand and modest. They announced a desire to construct 'an anthropology of ourselves', a science of the everyday, something that would demonstrate the impact of society on the individual. It wasn't specifically a class issue, but one of accessibility and visibility; those who took part were not generally in positions of power, much less influence.

The modesty of their ambition was revealed in the observers' first descriptive task, to explain what was on their mantelpiece; mantel-pieces, the founders believed, displayed unexpected clues about religion, superstition, personal tastes and the entire life of the home. After this exercise, and for more than a decade, hundreds of people who did not make their living from writing agreed to commit their thoughts to paper; most had never written for public consumption before.

On the eve of the war, those who had previously mentioned their ormolu clock and grandfather's ashes were presented with a sterner task: to record their daily activities as frequently and fully as possible. Almost 500 people contributed something, although many wrote just for a few weeks. Those who wrote consistently, cogently and engagingly contributed to what is now universally regarded as a unique and invaluable record of quiet lives transformed by events far beyond their control.

I first came across Mass-Observation at school, and then again some years later while researching a book about British wrestling. M-O had composed a special study of this strange pursuit, finding in it the perfect framework in which to explore its fascination with working-class leisure and elusive worlds. The study was written up as an essay and, like much of the organisation's early published work, I found it to be a rather dry and detached account. But I hadn't yet encountered the raw material.

In 2002 I was invited to look around the M-O archive at the University of Sussex, and it was to be the first of many visits. There, in the Special Collections department of the library, among the Virginia and Leonard Woolf papers and the Rudyard Kipling note-books, was the most extraordinary display of broad humanity. I had visited the archive (which, predictably, is dutifully and imaginatively maintained despite inadequate funding) with the vague aim of composing a book that would combine some of this writing. The resulting work, *Our Hidden Lives*, was similar in format to the present volume: five diaries interleaved to provide a very personal picture of a significant period in our history. The period covered 1945–48, that dark time in which Britain struggled from victory to prolonged hardship. When I first examined the M-O diaries I believed that there was probably little to add to the extensive studies of the Second World War, and I purposely chose a less-travelled path. But then I looked again.

It is the personal accounts that will always fascinate us most. The allure lies in the minutiae and incidentals, the factors that Arnold Bennett once called 'the interestingness of existence'. The unexpected juxtapositions provide another delight. The five diarists selected here have been chosen for their diversity of employment, location and domestic situations, and for their contrasting styles of writing and personal interests. When the war begins they are aged between 28 and 41, but they are not a representative sample of anything; they are far more important than that.

Christopher Tomlin uses his diary as an adjunct to his church confessions. We learn of his strained relationship with his father, the pressures of debt, his admiration of his brother, his growing feeling of helplessness in what he sees as the bungled prosecution of the war. Many times we read of his attempts to cheer up his customers on his daily rounds, just as the conditions for his writing paper business deteriorate. His fear of invasion may seem slightly comical to us now, when our most enduring image of 1940 remains Corporal Jones in

Dad's Army exhorting us not to panic. But for Tomlin the threat is very real. 'Germany will invade us on Friday!' he writes in mid-July. On the Friday in question he reports, 'No invasion yet!' and then, because normal life is all we have, he adds that he has begun to use hair pomade. 'I don't know why I use it now; I pride myself on not caring two hoots what I wear or look like. Mother is responsible for whatever neatness speaks for my dress. I'm bohemian.' Shortly afterwards he takes his medical exam for enrolment in the RAF, and finds that he cannot touch his toes. The following day, as he awaits the date of his posting, we find him doing bending exercises.

In addition to Tomlin, there is Pam Ashford, 37 when the war begins, a secretary in a coal exporting firm in Hope Street, Glasgow, living at home with her mother and brother, a member of the Soroptimists, a self-confessed hoarder, a perceptive and secretive correspondent of brisk office life (introducing Miss Carswell, Miss Crawford and the indefatigable Miss Bousie, whom our diarist regards, with much justification, as providing superior entertainment to anything available in the music halls). Ashford's Glasgow presents an informative vantage point of the unfolding crisis. The preparatory activities that concern the citizens of other big cities – the gas-masks and air raid drills – immediately acquire a comical air. But Ashford's involvement in the war is anything but remote. Her client list changes dramatically as the conflict unfolds, and she wonders about the fate of her friends in Germany and Holland. Her brother Charlie is an important figure in Scottish air defence, and both of them come from a naval family anchored in Portsmouth and Plymouth. She is touched so deeply by the sinking of the *Royal Oak* that her colleagues have difficulty comprehending her emotions. But the readers of her diary will have no difficulty. Her father built the ship, and it was the custom for wives and daughters to hammer in an early rivet. She describes the honour of having a place in the fleet. 'And now my name has gone to the bottom of the deep blue sea.'

Then there is Eileen Potter, 41, forever groping her way through dark London, a keen tennis player and sword dancer, an evacuation officer for the London County Council. Many have written of the departure of children and mothers from the capital, but there are fewer accounts from the administrator's viewpoint, and fewer still of the chaperone's. We are familiar with the heartbreak of departure and 'strange country ways', but we hear less of the children who have seldom travelled on a moving vehicle and are sick all the way to Somerset. Potter's painstaking chronicles of these journeys from London amplify the worth of Mass-Observation: in more formal and broader histories the details are included as illustration, but here the details sketch the big picture.

One evacuee is Tilly Rice, mother of three, married to a distant man at the Home Office, writer of short stories, fan of her local brewery, beginning the war in Port Isaac. Here she is safe and bored, longing for something to start in earnest. She returns to her home in Surrey in time for the bombs, and her children provide a soft-hearted glimpse of what it was like to have such thrilling adventures.

Readers of *Our Hidden Lives* will recognise the fifth diarist, Maggie Joy Blunt, a freelance journalist in her late twenties living on the edge of Burnham Beeches not far from Slough. Blunt begins her account in December 1939, a little later than the others. She is worried about her brother in Suez and dreams of a new European order, but her domestic concerns are commonplace: the procurement of food and cigarettes, the conduct of her lodgers, the physical and mental health of her friends. She is disappointed by her slothfulness, yet her writing has left us an eloquent testimony of an active mind stopped in its tracks.

This book runs from the days preceding the declaration of war to the midst of the Blitz in October 1940. Unedited, the five diarists' entries for the period account for about 1,400 pages and half a million words. Inevitably my selection has been influenced by what particularly captivates, intrigues and surprises me, and by the entries that advance the narrative in the most fluent way. I have tried to highlight links and themes as well as contrasts, and to most fairly represent the writers' true intentions throughout. At the end of the book I have attempted to find out what happened to the diarists as the war developed and their lives continued.

Throughout the period none of the diarists mention any feedback or other correspondence they may have had from Mass-Observation. There was no contract with the organisation, but from the early documents we may surmise there was a vague agreement that their real names would not be used. I have found them pseudonyms, but all other details are unchanged. Every so often, all the diarists question the nature of M-O and their contribution to it; they admit it takes considerable effort to maintain this additional task in their lives. It is rare for an observer to have written continuously from the beginning of the war to its conclusion – real life tended to get in the way. In mid-May 1940, returning from a Sunday afternoon stroll, Pam Ashford wrote, 'I felt dead tired and crawled along. If my great-grandmother had kept a diary on the Eve of Waterloo and recorded all the trivialities that I put into mine on the eve of this terrible battle that is coming, well I should think she was daft.'

Rather, I believe we should be immensely grateful. We are used to thinking of the first ten months of the Second World War as 'the Phoney War', a period in which we sat in the park looking up at the sky. The diarists compare it to time spent in the dentist's waiting room, or playing a final game of tennis as the clouds darken. But we may see from these diaries that the early phase of the war was not a period in which nothing happened. As Maggie Joy Blunt attests, it was a time in which nothing and everything changed; we learn how the country prepared itself for terrible eventualities, and how varied were the opinions as to who was to blame. Despondency merges with elation, and the moods of our correspondents swing many times in the course of a day as updates reach them from abroad. The gloom of a sunken vessel is relieved by a Valentine's card; depression and flu evaporates with a meal of boiled rabbits.

Each diarist has their own system of news retrieval, a combination of BBC bulletins, press reports and newsletters, and the occasional snippet from those involved abroad. They are more suspicious of authority than respectful of it; regularly their intuition keeps them a step ahead of the Official Version.

We may learn the following: how to handle a stirrup-pump; what doesn't happen when a barrage balloon explodes; what a Soroptimist does; what Hitler's eyes were like; how poor radio comedy was and how Tommy Handley was not the comic genius of his generation; how the Canadians were the butt of jokes even in 1940; and how, when a printing firm explodes, Christmas cards are scattered all over a neighbourhood. We may also learn how much a second-hand Royal typewriter is worth at a time of hardship; what a 'lounge' was; what became of Italian ice cream shops; how Del Monte ground coffee in vacuum tins, supposed to last for ever, is an utter failure, whereas Nestlé Café au Lait has a long life of usefulness; how *sal volatile* (smelling salts) and Kruschen fix many personal problems; how popular were pixie hats; and why Churchill was not always regarded as the man for the job.

We read how people wondered what to do if the Nazis launched a genuine attack during air raid practice; why so many listened to Lord Haw Haw; how many people thought it would be useful to learn German; how batteries became the gift of choice; how the desire for a United States of Europe gathered force; how identity cards became a serious issue for debate; how awkwardly relieved people were when the first raids began; how canned puffin was not such a distant prospect; and how much was known about the concentration camps.

We join the diarists at a time of uncertainty, but we leave them at a time of resolve. They surprise us just as they surprise themselves. In September 1940, Pam Ashford observes that we are approaching dangerous times, but she is eager to confront them. 'What a great thing it is to have been born in the 20th Century,' she notes. 'This supreme moment in the nation's history did not come in my great-grandparents' time, it is not something lying in wait for my great-grandchildren, but it is here in *my* time.' And now, in our time, we may truly understand what it was like.

Chapter One

THE HOLIDAYS

Thank goodness the children left in time: evacuation at Ealing Broadway,
1 September 1939.

'At the National Gallery we decided to move every picture out of London to various places of safety. We chose places in the west of Britain which were not at all likely to be bombed and which had big halls and rooms where all the pictures could be arranged in such a way that we could inspect them easily and see that they were not coming to any harm.

We decided to take the pictures there by rail rather than by road because it really is much smoother and more certain. The only difficulty was that three of our biggest pictures would not go through any of the tunnels, even if slung quite low on the lines on what is called a well-waggon, and to meet this difficulty a member of our staff who is a mathematician thought of that old idea which used to be such a nuisance to us at school, called the theorem of Pythagoras, and he constructed a case by which these big pictures were tilted slightly on their side and the upright part of the case was just low enough to pass through all the tunnels.'

Sir Kenneth Clark on the BBC Empire Service, 29 August 1939

* * *

23 August 1939 Germany and USSR sign non-aggression pact. **25 August** Britain and Poland sign a Mutual Assistance Treaty; British fleet mobilises. **1 September** Germans cross border into Poland and annex Danzig; the start of the black-out and civilian evacuations from London. **3 September** Britain, France, Australia and New Zealand declare war on Germany.

THURSDAY, 24 AUGUST 1939

Eileen Potter
Evacuation officer in west London, age 41
The outbreak of the crisis finds me at Stratford-on-Avon, attending the summer school in folk dancing, and working for the advanced examination in country dancing. Unlike some of the students, I read the paper every day, and am not unprepared for the development of the crisis.

I notice territorials on the way to the station with kit, and think our turn will come soon. In the evening I go to the Memorial Theatre Conference Hall for an evening of folk singing and dancing. Someone says, 'There is a telegram on the notice-board.' I look and find it is for me – 'Report at once for duty.' Return to my digs and decide to travel by the first train next morning. I pack, arrange a taxi, and then return to the Conference Hall and cancel my arrangements for taking the exam. By this time dancing is in full swing and I decide to stay and finish the party, feeling rather like Drake playing bowls on Plymouth Hoe.

FRIDAY, 25 AUGUST

Eileen Potter
Leave Stratford by 7.32 a.m. train. A still, misty, peaceful-looking morning, very few people travelling. I arrive at Paddington at 10 a.m., leave my suitcase in the cloakroom (after being searched for possible bombs) and proceed to my office at the London County Council [LCC] nearby. I find my colleagues drinking tea and talking. Our instructions are to 'stand by' for evacuation work.

SATURDAY, 26 AUGUST

Eileen Potter
Spend the morning and early part of the afternoon standing by. I have my hair shampooed and set, not knowing when there will be another opportunity.

MONDAY, 28 AUGUST

Eileen Potter

Report for evacuation duty, together with six of my colleagues, at the Divisional Dispersals Officer's office, Kensington. One of us has a car, and is kept on duty for messages. The rest of us do office work and interview helpers who have volunteered to escort mothers and babies to the country. A man on the staff appears to be somewhat overexcited by such a sudden influx of female colleagues, and makes facetious jokes, and something is said about alleged complaints about his language and behaviour. We all feel, under pressure of work, that our language is becoming stronger and our manners less polite.

TUESDAY, 29 AUGUST

Pam Ashford
Secretary in coal shipping firm, Glasgow, age 37
In the office a certain amount of 'merriment' prevails in regard to first-aid equipment, gas masks, incendiary bombs, etc. (like the 'We shall all do the goosestep' attitude of 1914). People regard gas masks askance.

The public morale is immeasurably higher than at the black points in the September crisis last year. Mr Mitchell (my boss), who has been spending a holiday at Millport, returned today, which is a day earlier than he was due. He believes the war will last 10/20 years. Miss Carswell openly says 'she has the wind up'. Everybody else agrees that if we show Hitler we are afraid, he will press his point. Noon dialogue between Miss Bousie and me:

Miss Bousie (about 55): In the back of my mind I feel it won't happen. It is too colossal. I woke up last night at three and had such a lovely feeling of calm.

I said: Strangely enough I am not suffering my nerves as I did [during the Munich crisis] last September.

Miss Bousie: I was calm then, but I have had the jitters this time.

I: I have a religious kind of feeling. We must put our trust in God.

2.30: Mr Mitchell on returning from the Exchange announced that 'everyone at the Exchange expects war. It is needed to clear the air.'

I showed Mr Mitchell the carbon of a letter I typed to my Dresden friend on Friday. Ostensibly it consisted of a description of the way sporrans are made (she asked me about this once). I signed it, 'With fondest love, your affectionate friend, Edith.' I added a postscript asking her to give Mr Mitchell's best wishes to Herr Jacob (her boss). We know enough about Herr Jacob to know that he has a cosmopolitan mind and dislikes the intense nationalism in Germany today.

On the way home I bought an electric torch and battery, and looked at stuff for ARP [Air Raid Precautions] curtains for the dining room. It would cost at least £1 to darken. I think I will wait and see what happens.

Eileen Potter

Two of us lunch in Kensington High Street. It is a lovely day and everybody is going about their normal business, wearing summer frocks and looking very calm. Somehow the thought of war seems far away, and we joke about the evacuation, saying what a waste of work it will be if it never comes off.

WEDNESDAY, 30 AUGUST

Eileen Potter

Slightly increased pressure. There has been a rumour that evacuation is to take place tomorrow, but this is definitely denied later in the afternoon.

Pam Ashford

I was so tired that I slept heavily from about 11.30 till 5.30. It is strange that although I am a victim of insomnia generally, I have never had an entirely sleepless night over this crisis. From then till 7.30 thoughts of defending our home against fire were running through my head. In the ante-room between the bathroom and the hall we have shelves stacked with hundreds of old periodicals. I think I will remove them to the cupboard in the dining room.

The boats that we are loading at Glasgow are to sail, although many charters have been cancelled. Thirty Glasgow 'puffers' (boats of 110–120 tons) engaged in the Glasgow/West Highland trade have been commandeered to take supplies to those parts for the Government. I am mystified to know what supplies the Government can want to send there.

Absent-mindedness and poor memory seem rife. All the morning Mr Mitchell has been asking me questions, the answers to which would normally have been quite well-known to him. Mr Mitchell and I both find the same thing, that the strained atmosphere has upset our sense of time. An hour seems like a day, and a day like a week. The month of August seems to have lasted for decades.

Afternoon: calmness prevails everywhere. Miss Gibson who has charge of the bookkeeping for our depot at Govan says that people are not stocking to any remarkable extent. Sandwich-men wearing tin helmets and respirators are parading the streets advertising that ARP wants volunteers.

It is said that the Government schemes for evacuating children are much hindered by parents changing their minds. Those who said they would look after their own arrangements now want the education authorities to take their children away, and vice versa.

Mr Mitchell came back from the Exchange (2.30) confident that there will be no war, pointing out how unnecessary it was. He spent most of the afternoon trying to dissuade me from my policy of stocking household requirements.

There is no doubt that the tension is subsiding in the City this afternoon. Everybody is saying the same thing: 'There won't be a war.' Personally, I think it is premature.

After work I bought a second electric torch and battery, and told the assistant I was setting up everyone in the house. He advised me to bring all our old cases along quickly, as battery supplies are to be rationed.

I then went across to Arnott-Simpson's and examined the ARP curtains. Certainly the material could be used for other purposes if it got left on one's hands, but no-one would voluntarily wear black lingerie. Passing Craig's I saw tins of SPAM (a ham preparation) and bought two tins, thinking it would be a change from the corn beef Mother has been stocking. They have banana butter there too, and I will buy in some tomorrow as a substitute for butter.

I visited the ARP Shop in St Vincent Street and asked for a pamphlet telling one how to protect a Glasgow flat. They gave me the four Government pamphlets that have already been sent out by the Post Office. They are useful up to a point, of course, but not full enough for my tastes.

I went up to Annette's and bought a bargain frock (red silk) at

8/11. If war comes I don't want to have to give a thought to clothes from the start to the finish.

On reaching home I found Charlie (my brother) thought the war was off, and that Mother was perfectly confident and wants to start using up her groceries straightaway. My evening was spent dissuading her.

THURSDAY, 31 AUGUST

Eileen Potter

Go to the North Hammersmith Treatment Centre, where a lady doctor is in attendance for minor ailments. Only about three children turn up, and we spend most of the morning discussing the situation, drinking tea and smoking cigarettes. The dentist arrives. He was shell-shocked and wounded in the head in the last war and has been unstable ever since. He delivers a long harangue on the subject of war in general, making many self-contradictory statements and getting into a very excitable state. The doctor, nurse and I do our best to humour him and calm him down.

One child is brought in suffering from toothache: he is sent away to a nearby centre where there is an opportunity of having the aching tooth extracted under gas today. I go to a nearby restaurant for lunch, and stay to listen to the one o'clock news bulletin. I hurry back to the office, guessing that something is in the wind. On my table I find a note to the effect that the evacuation will start tomorrow and asking me to be at East Acton Station (where I am acting as Assistant Marshal) at 7.15 a.m.

Arrive home rather late, to find (not to my surprise) that my landlady has decided to evacuate to friends in Somerset. Her son has hired a car and will drive her down tonight. She goes to the house next door but one, after consulting me, to ask if they can give me a bed there, as I do not wish to remain alone in the house, especially if there are no dark curtains, and the black-out is imminent. They agree to do so, and I am glad, as I know that the wife is very kind and the husband is an Air Raid Warden, so I feel that I shall be all right there. I go to my new quarters at about 11 p.m. and go straight to bed. At about 12 I hear voices calling under my window. It is my friends calling goodbye. They hold up the cat in his basket to say goodbye also. I stand at the window, watching them get into the car and drive away.

Pam Ashford

In general I am avoiding the newspapers as unnerving, for I want to keep my brains clear for other things. I get the 7 p.m. wireless news, and that does me for the next 24 hours. I don't listen later than that for to do so would assure my sleep being disturbed by nightmares. At the week-ends, however, I read carefully the *Sunday Times*, *Sunday Observer*, and Commander Stephen King-Hall's newsletters, also some miscellaneous matter (I like the Oxford Pamphlets on Foreign Affairs).

The department in which I work (exporting) is, of course, the one that ultimately will be most hit. Many of the trawlers that we normally bunker are at Grangemouth Dockyard being fitted as minesweepers.

Afternoon: hope of a solution is rapidly declining, and tension rises every minute. Glasgow schoolchildren are to be evacuated tomorrow.

After work I made a purchase of electric torches. Notice the gradation: on Monday I bought a 6d torch and spare battery; on Wednesday, a 1/6 torch and battery. On Thursday two 1/9 torches plus one battery and two spare globes. Yesterday Mother got a spare battery for her torch.

I then went along to Massey's and bought three tins of new potatoes and 2lb of sugar. I also bought at Craig's four 6d jars of butter substitutes (grapefruit butter, lemon curd, apricot curd, banana curd).

FRIDAY, 1 SEPTEMBER

Eileen Potter

Arrive at East Acton Station at 7.15. I am put on telephone duty. The station is a small one, with a narrow, wooden platform reached by a flight of wooden steps. At first, ordinary passengers arrive for the trains, but the station is theoretically closed to the public at about 8 o'clock. The first evacuation train is timed for 8.15. The children from the nearest school begin to arrive considerably before then. They march up in good order, accompanied by teachers and helpers and all carrying kit and gas-masks. The elder children of a family help the younger ones along. Some of the mothers and fathers come to see them off, but have to say goodbye at the station entrance as there is no spare room on the small platform. All are cheerful looking – hardly any in tears – but I feel rather a lump in my throat myself at seeing them all going off so cheerily.

Many of the children attend the treatment centre where I normally work, and I recognise a good many of our patients. The head teachers are also known to me, and several of them come and shake hands and say goodbye. There is a general feeling that they may all be coming back next week.

Christopher Tomlin
Writing paper salesman in Fulwood, Lancashire, age 28
The first thing I remember is the arrival of evacuees in Broughton. Four girls left a motor-car and what 'things' they were! Dressed in 'old clo' man coats, dirty, common, the last kiddies in the world for an 'aristocratic' spot like Broughton.

In spite of the shock the evacuees gave me, I'm afraid a lump rose in my throat when one girl asked nervously, 'Can't I stay with my sister?' She was told, 'No, you go there, and she will be across the road. You will be able to see her every day.' I was sorry for the girls because they were so forlorn. They must miss their mothers, or at least I hope they do. We must not shut our eyes to the fact that some parents are delighted to have their responsibilities carted away.

Pam Ashford
Mr Mitchell and I discussed the psychological effects of the evacuation of the children. If they are away long, the mixing of the different classes will have a marked effect on the rising generation.

10.30. Phone message that Danzig has been taken. People are not ready to accept this message till it is authenticated.

11.30. A friend phoned Mr Mitchell saying that on the wireless it is said that 'Warsaw has been bombed, Danzig taken, Gdynia vacated; Poles retaliating.' News received with consternation, but also with calm. 'We are in the war now all right,' was the general comment.

By noon the bills and newspapers proclaim the bombing of Polish towns. Intense but subdued excitement prevails everywhere. At lunchtime I bought two small bottles of *sal volatile*.

Mr Mitchell said, 'Hoarding is now illegal. This will put an end to your little game.' I said, 'After war is declared I shall buy nothing, believing the goods in the shops should go to those who are too poor to have laid stocks in already. Just at the moment I am hanging between two decisions: one, that buying is patriotic foresight, the other that it is a dirty form of hoarding.'

3 p.m. Miss Carswell (a timid nature) says if anyone offered to let her put her head in the gas oven, she would do so. It is better to die than to be tormented. Miss Crawford (far from timid) is sick of all these scares, and would not mind dying and getting out of it. I said that I shall hold on to the bitter end.

Miss Bousie on returning from lunch: 'I saw some of the children going away. They were such dear little mites. No one could object to taking them in.' There was general sympathy. This is a big improvement, as for weeks past I have been hearing from all quarters complaints, and you would really think that the prospective evacuees were the most awful individuals. Mr Mitchell and Mr Hutchinson get their children in tomorrow.

The papers make it look as if Italy is not going to support Germany. There are pronounced feelings of elation. Many humorous comparisons are being made between the present and 1914 when Italy stood out till she saw which side was going to win. Tributes are also paid to Signor Mussolini's common sense, etc. It was 4 p.m. before anyone noticed that we had all forgotten to change the calendars from August to September.

In the afternoon we heard that six children ranging from six to eleven had arrived at our Managing Director's house in Carluke. They are from Tradeston, a working class district with much slum property. Mr Ferguson, who likes children and is believed to wish he had several of his own, is delighted about it. He has bought camp beds and blankets and says that to fit the children up has cost him pounds. His own little boy (13) is delighted at the prospect of having companions. Ian is a typical, wealthy, only child; brought up by a governess and now at private school. It will be his first encounter with the raw material of humanity.

The whole town seems to be buying black paper and about every sixth person is laden with a roll. The buses and trams are running with only headlights. The balloon barrage is up. I reached home just as the wireless was beginning to report Mr Chamberlain's speech.

We listened to the news. The calmness with which I (with a long history of nervous breakdowns) am going through this crisis is a revelation. During the last twenty years there has never been a time at which fear was so quiet in my mind as it is at this moment. Yet I still have a deep-seated and long-established dread of pitch darkness. I don't know how I shall cope with that. I always sleep with the blind up to see the street lights shining throughout the night. How glad I was that there was a full moon for the first night.

SATURDAY, 2 SEPTEMBER

Tilly Rice
Mother, living in Port Isaac, North Cornwall, evacuated from Tadworth, Surrey, age 36
We arrived down here for our annual holiday on August 26th. My husband had thought it advisable to put the trip forward a week, partly on account of the international situation and partly on account of the possibility of there being a railway strike. This, in view of the fact that September 2nd, our original date, was to be taken up with the wholesale evacuation of school children from London and other danger spots, proved a very wise decision.

We arrived to find that there were little or no signs of crisis. There was a distribution of gas masks going on in the village, and people tended to congregate in groups about those cottages that possessed wireless sets.

Two parties of women-folk with their children arrived the same Saturday as I did with my two. They seemed to be more alive to the crisis than the others. Two had husbands in the Bank of England who had been evacuated and one had a husband in the reserves who had been called up. I myself felt removed from the war at first, but as things have intensified these last days, have felt an urge to be back in the thick of things.

There has been practically no sign of hysteria, excepting on the part of the maid, a village girl who, upon the calling up of her young man, was rendered prostrate with hysterics for a day.

Christopher Tomlin
The dominant thought today is: the Government knew war would come, thank goodness the children left in time.

All my customers realised things were as bad as could be. I had a dull thud in my stomach all the time. The crisis last year was bad enough, but here was another. But now everybody says Hitler must be taught a lesson.

My work day is 5 to 6 hours long (non-stop). I work every day but Sunday: no half-days at all, and canvassing is damned difficult at times. My work day would be two or three hours longer if Father wasn't here to conduct the booking, costing, mail and packing departments. There is much more to my job than filling in an order book.

Eileen Potter

On duty at East Acton Station again. The evacuation of school children continues according to plan, except that again there are fewer than expected and we get them off more quickly. We have one casualty, an elderly teacher who faints on the platform. There is a rumour that Hitler has declared war on Poland, France and Britain. I think that this does not sound like his methods, but have a vague, uneasy feeling.

Work at the office is even more hectic than before. Owing to the worsening of the situation, it has been decided to sandwich the third and fourth day's evacuation programme into one day, and this means a good deal of alteration in the train schedules, instructions to voluntary helpers, etc. We all work late at the office.

I lie awake in bed at night hoping that Chamberlain is not going to back out of his pledge at the last moment. Distant thunder can be heard, and the lightning flashes almost continuously. Presently the storm bursts right overhead with great violence and deluges of rain. I lie still in bed pretending that it is an air raid, and practicing feeling brave, but am not very successful.

Pam Ashford

At Boots' at 9 o'clock I bought two very small torches for handbags. That makes three small torches, one for each of us. Climbing the stairs at night will be a trial. I also bought two hot water bottles, for these went into short supply in the last war.

Uniforms are prominent. The policemen have on tin hats, and are much pitied by the public who think they must be most uncomfortable. The certainty of war seems to have a quieting effect, after the fever that the uncertainty of the last ten days induced. The improvement in public morale since twelve months ago is conspicuous; also the unity of purpose. This morning Mr Mitchell, with me as 'boy', set to work to darken the office.

On the floor below is a lawyer who arranges marriages and there are such a lot of couples getting married. This is considered stupid by everyone in the office, but for different reasons. Miss Carswell says, 'The girls will lose their jobs and their "pensions" will never keep them.' Miss Bousie: 'There is enough misery in the world without getting married. And they are all so young that they will change their minds quickly and then it will be too late.'

Mr Mitchell told me of the preparations he has made for the four children who are to come to him today. He says he and Mrs Mitchell will give them the same as their own two children, but it simply can't be done on 8/6 each per week. He will be out of pocket. The cessation or diminution of coal exporting will affect his income; he may lose his job, he says. I think that is super-pessimism, for Mr Ferguson's department is to bunker minesweepers and surely Mr Mitchell can help them.

After work I went to Massey's, for Mother had asked me to get three more tins of new potatoes. I had to stand half-an-hour for my turn and decided to increase the order to six tins of potatoes, three of baked beans, half a pound of coffee (vacuum packed) and half a pound of sugar. Massey's are not allowed to sell more. I went into town. The Exhibition of the Princesses' Dolls (given by the French nation last year) was closed. It opened last week.

Wireless on all the evening. If the youth of fifty years hence should ask me how I reacted to the tremendous events of today, I expect I shall 'remember' hearing the announcer's words. But the truth is I only listened with half an ear. I am desperately anxious to get our house arranged in such a way that we can best handle whatever may arise. For some time past I have been collecting big tins with tight-fitting lids and I have been begging Mother to put all the groceries at present in cardboard boxes into tins, partly as a protection against mice, partly as a protection against damp, and partly as a protection against gas. Mother, who is a Sunshine Susie, does not expect any of these troubles.

SUNDAY, 3 SEPTEMBER

Christopher Tomlin
An announcement by the Prime Minister to be broadcast at 11! I
went to 11 o'clock Mass. During Mass, as the priest went into the
pulpit, an altar boy walked from the altar to the presbytery and
returned with a note which he handed up to the pulpit. The priest
took the note and said, 'I regret to say the inevitable has happened.
We are now at war with Nazi Germany.' He delivered an excellent
address. He exhorted us to pray for the dead Poles, and the dead
Germans who were no longer our enemies. We must have charity and
try to love the German people who were betrayed by wicked men.

How glad I was when the service was over. I expected an
immediate air raid and knew we were for it if the bombs dropped on
the church. All the day I felt crushed or enveloped in an invisible
menace.

Tilly Rice
This morning everyone, barring three of the children, stayed in to
hear the ten o'clock news bulletin. And everyone seems to think war
is inevitable. This is a reverse of the feeling that was prevalent
yesterday when the BBC announcement that the Germans had *not*
invaded Poland, but were confining their activities to bombarding
certain towns from their own territory, seemed to encourage a
general feeling of optimism.

I myself have felt all along that the war would possibly be averted
at the last moment. I have felt that Herr Hitler must break soon, that
internally things are beginning to seethe uncomfortably and that if he
doesn't do something to provide his sorely tired people with
something in the way of fireworks, he's finished anyhow. I've felt too
that his hand is being forced by those surrounding him, particularly
Herr von Ribbentrop, whom I regard as a greater menace to peace
than the Fuhrer himself. But I haven't felt swayed by the alternate
waves of pessimism and optimism that affect those round me. I've
felt that we must dig our heels in and not get rattled or panicky. That
we must determine to face up to whatever is coming and that it is a
point of honour for those who are not actively involved in this
horrible struggle to carry on as usual as nearly as possible. I don't
find that point of view reciprocated by the women who have come

down here with their children for safety, but I think that with a little persuasion they will adopt it. Now I shall leave any further entry until after this fateful 11.15 news bulletin that we are all hanging about the house waiting for.

Later: We all sat round the wireless set in silence. Even the children were quiet, and after the Prime Minister had made his affectingly simple statement, no one said a word. We all sat there for some moments until the national anthem was played, then, still in silence, each got up and went up to their own rooms.

Eileen Potter

On duty at the station again. Mothers and babies are being evacuated today. At last all are safely got away, with no casualties. One of the voluntary workers has brought a portable wireless set in her car, and we sit in groups on the steps outside the office listening to Chamberlain's speech on the expiry of the ultimatum in Germany. For about the first time, I feel in agreement with the greater part of what Chamberlain says.

After the speech, instructions are given about air raid warnings, etc. Hardly have these finished than the sirens begin to sound. We wonder whether it is a practice, but decide that it must be the real thing. We scatter about the building in small groups. I go to the basement, where I have previously been working, with about four others. Some of us try on our gas masks and adjust straps. Somebody puts up the shutters. We sit there keeping perhaps rather self-consciously calm and cheerful. My predominant feeling is one of admiration for Hitler's thoroughness in timing the first raid so accurately. When I afterwards find out that it is a 'wash-out' I feel rather disappointed in him. I do not really think that the Germans will get as far as Kensington the first time.

Early in the afternoon I am sent for by the chief and told at a moment's notice to go to Guildford with an emergency party of evacuees. A voluntary helper takes me in her car to the school from which the party is starting. I find them gathering in the playground, a miscellaneous collection of mothers and babies and unattached children. I am not quite sure whether I am supposed to be the leader of the party or not, but I march them to the nearby Underground station, assisted by a boy of about 12 who says, 'We must all pull together in these times, mustn't we, Miss?' A father, seeing my LCC armlet, puts two small boys into my personal care, saying that their mother will be able to join them the next day and asking me to find a billet for her. They are aged six and four. They are very good, the only untoward incident on the journey being the dropping of a halfpenny under the seat.

Pam Ashford

I spent the morning in bed as usual, though this time very busy writing out my shorthand diary for yesterday. What I have been doing during the week has been to keep a notebook [for Mass-Observation] in Mr Mitchell's sanctum and whenever the chance arises I have jotted down a new paragraph. Then I type out the notes as occasion offers.

I got up at 11.40, so as to hear the 12 news. Charlie and I heard the announcer tell us that we were at war. We sat there with our attention riveted. Mother would not listen to the wireless, but just stayed in the kitchen getting dinner ready. She has a wonderful spirit but I think she has really been shaken up badly. In my own case Commander King-Hall has been preparing me for months past, whereas it is barely ten days since Mother realised that such a thing was really a possibility. Charlie is splendid. This crisis has made us all realise how much we mean to one another. I am thankful that today is a Sunday. We have been let down more lightly than if we had had our work to think of.

We have had our meals at the same time. Then there has been the usual Sunday ironing and mending for tomorrow. It has been just like an ordinary Sunday, but all the time there is the thought, 'This is the last of the ordinary Sundays.' It is now 7 o'clock. I am just going out for a walk, and unless something quite unexpected happens there will be nothing more to put down for today. This has seemed such a long, long, long day.

Chapter Two

TENSION ON THE CARPET

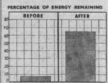
Very difficult to break down the nervousness of people: 58 per cent more energy may help.

'Don't be too rigid in your lighting economy. Don't use high-wattage blue lamps, they are wasteful. A five-watt clear glass bulb will give an equivalent effect at a fraction of the cost.

Don't open the door to your refrigerator more than is absolutely necessary, and cut down your ice consumption. Now, about baths: do you like yours very hot and brimming over? Well I'm afraid you've got to do something about that you know. My suggestion is half the quantity of water and a few degrees cooler. Find out this morning if your hot water tank is lagged, and by "lagged" I mean covered with heat-retaining material such as asbestos, which, in effect, converts your tank into a sort of big vacuum flask. If it isn't, see your plumber or electrical people about it.'

W.H. Barrington Dalby on the Home Service, Wednesday, 4 October 1939

* * *

4 September Royal Air Force attacks the German Navy. **5 September** United States proclaims neutrality. **9 September** British troops leave for France to be deployed on Belgian border. **10 September** Canada declares war on Germany; Battle of the Atlantic begins. **15 September** German armies surround Warsaw. **17 September** Soviet forces invade eastern Poland. **27 September** Warsaw surrenders to Germany; British aircraft-carrier *Courageous* sunk by U-boat in first major naval loss. **29 September** Germany and Soviet forces divide up Poland.

MONDAY, 4 SEPTEMBER

Eileen Potter

We are roused by an air raid warning at 3 a.m. and go and sit on the stairs until the all-clear sounds. At the office I am sent almost immediately to the country with an emergency party consisting of one large family, a mother and six children. As another baby is expected very shortly, a trained nurse is also sent with us.

We are taken by car to Ealing Broadway, where we join an evacuation train which has been waiting to start for about two hours. Formalities as to tickets, return vouchers, etc. are waived aside, and very soon the train starts. My family are outwardly respectable and as well-dressed as I am, but apparently they have not enough night-clothes to go round. I never quite succeed in discovering whether this is because the packing was done in half-an-hour by the fourteen-year-old daughter (who wears her hair in the latest style of curls) or because they do not possess the clothes. The father is a pastry-cook at Cadby Hall, but apparently a very large proportion of his wages goes in rent.

They have bought no food for the journey, so I have to share my packet of sandwiches with the whole family. There is just one each. I also divide an apple into eight portions, and a 2d block of chocolate. Mrs X has just a halfpenny in her bag, and borrows half a crown from me.

Ultimately we arrive at Dorchester and a lady with a big house, who is very charming, ultimately agrees to accommodate Mrs X and family, and another very charming lady offers me a bed for the night in a garden hut at her cottage. I am offered a bath at once, and then sent straight to bed, an offer which I gratefully accept, as I am feeling more tired than ever in my life. Some tea, with honey and home-made cake, is brought to me in bed, and the wireless is switched on. A record of Noel Coward's waltzes is being played, and I feel a vague inclination to lapse into sentimental tears.

Christopher Tomlin

I felt quite a hero canvassing from door to door. Nobody knew what would occur; there might be an air raid and I felt unprotected in spite of a gas mask.

Contrary to expectations, trade was nearly normal. It was very difficult to break through the nervousness of people, but I persevered and won. I think I cheered them up a little.

There was much talk about evacuees. I heard that the children were filthy, bug-ridden, wore dirty clothes, would not eat proper food for they wanted toast and fish and chips. Some of the kids had to wear fresh clothes. Many housewives buying their guests a complete rig-out from pyjamas to coats.

Pam Ashford

Today seems less removed from peace than any day in the last eighteen months. Ever since the seizure of Austria we have been undergoing a 'war of nerves', each new phase more trying than the previous one. What tension we have suffered in the last fortnight. Now that we know at least where we stand, it feels as if we have come out of a black tunnel.

We are very slack at business and I have spent the day tidying the desks, cabinets, cleaning and oiling the typewriter and duplicator, etc, 'so that they will be ready for use when the war is over.'

A Glasgow ship, the *Athenia*, has been torpedoed, but we don't know the details. Mr Mitchell is expressing indignation at the act, 'for it is not a ship of war'. There are Americans on board.

Charlie suffered so much from the gloom of the house yesterday that he begged mother to get curtain rings so that we can get the curtains back easily by day. Mother had a wearisome search this morning before she could find a shop that had any left. By what I hear I was extraordinarily lucky to get those two electric torches on Saturday.

Mr Mitchell is well pleased with his evacuees: a Glasgow lady (the wife of an engineer on board ship) with two little boys aged 3 and 4. At 2.30 he came back from the Exchange saying:

(1) that a German submarine had been sunk off Dunoon this morning,

(2) that there was an air raid on London this morning and 1,400 killed,

(3) the *Statesman* was sunk on passage from Glasgow to Liverpool.

I advised him not to put much trust in rumours.

Mr Mitchell thinks it will be a long war. 'All the frocks you've bought won't see you through.' I detailed the frocks I have bought

31

this year and not used yet – a wool suit, a wool frock, a stuff frock, a cotton frock, two blouses.

Charlie came home at 9, which seemed extraordinarily early. He had a new book with him, an autobiography of James Bridie (i.e. Dr Mavor, who is a close friend of Charlie). 'What rotten luck for Dr Mavor,' Charlie said, 'to have his book brought out today.'

TUESDAY, 5 SEPTEMBER

Eileen Potter
Morning tea is brought to my garden hut, and I awake to find the country looking very beautiful. A mist lies over the kitchen garden in the foreground, but the downs rise green and clear behind in the morning sun. I feel that I do not want to go away. The admiral takes me to Dorchester in his car, but I have a little time to wait for the train, so stroll round the town, looking at Thomas Hardy's statue and laying in a good stock of provisions for the journey. I find the train mainly filled with returning escorts, mostly from West Ham, and join a party of them. I share my provisions with a girl who has been travelling from Wales.

Christopher Tomlin
No cinemas. No decent wireless programmes. No lights. No raids. BOREDOM!

Today evacuated mothers arrived in Fulwood to the consternation of the residents. One customer said, 'You can bath the children but you can't tackle the mothers!' A neighbour took a mother and baby but was deeply thankful to get rid three days later. The mother was filthy; she switched on the lights in the middle of the night, ate food with her hands, and let the baby tension on the carpet. My neighbour is a house-proud woman. She was in tears most of the time.

The first week I funked going out for long journeys in the black-out. I am very short sighted: it is time I was tested for new glasses. On the first day of the war special police combed Fulwood Road to see if there was a perfect black-out. A friend called and I absent-mindedly turned on the table lamp in the 'lounge' – Fulwood term for front room – and a voice yelled 'Put that light out please!'

But Preston has blacked out too well; there have been many accidents. I heard an ex-serviceman say to another on the bus: 'It's nonsense blacking-out like this here. Why, we are 600 miles from the nearest point in Germany. A bomber would drop its load and return, it couldn't reach here. We'd only get a stray one.' The other man murmured: 'There are more damned sand bags around the Town Hall than were in the trenches in France.'

Umpteen rumours go around:

1) Hull was bombed two weeks ago.

2) A soldier from Brook Street and a father and son from Maudland Bank were killed on active service.

3) Two of Hitler's food-tasters are dead.

It is amusing to hear what my customers would do to Hitler. Everything from rat-pills to ground glass in his food. They all agree on a long, lingering death.

My aunts, who are teachers of dancing, complain they haven't booked a pupil since hostilities began. But mother says they will be busy before long.

Here in Fulwood we are ready. Going up Garstang Road, I saw an Evacuated Enquiries Bureau, an Evacuated Children's Clinic, a Food Control Committee Room, two Auxiliary Fire Stations, a Decontamination Centre, an Air Raid Warden's Post and two First Aid Posts. Yet Fulwood is supposed to be a safe area.

Thank goodness the local cinema opened. How strange it was and how funny I felt on my first visit in war time. This notice appeared on the screen: 'A qualified fireman is present during every performance to give warning of any air raid alarm. In case of emergency the film will be stopped, and a notice flashed on the screen. You will be asked to leave quietly and orderly by the nearest exit.' And I remember how annoyed I was at the idea of walking out into the open when the nearest air raid shelter was a mile away. You were only allowed in if you wore a gas mask.

My sister, the mother of three children – youngest is 2 – is a blood donor. A week ago Preston Royal Infirmary rang up the police station nearest my sister's at 12 p.m. 'Would Mrs Mills come at once?' 'Bob', my sister, got out of bed and phoned for a taxi. She paid black-out fare, gave her blood and had to walk home. The Infirmary people didn't offer to pay her expenses, or get a motor to take her back.

I now buy boxes of branded notepaper, then have them printed locally. But since war I have found it impossible to get certain lines.

My Preston wholesaler has a £400 order for notepaper out, but has been unable to get delivery. Nothing has come through from Manchester for 6 weeks. I am glad to say my out-of-town suppliers have no such difficulty. But they have reduced quantities and put up prices a penny in the shilling. What I will do if the war lasts a year or two I don't know.

Why should I now pay 1/- for tobacco which cost 9d three months ago? Why can't I have bacon for breakfast (none came from Denmark this week)? Mother sent me for saccharines that are usually 1/3, but I had to pay 1/8. Jam is 9d, instead of 5d a jar. Fish are unobtainable.

Last Saturday I attended a special meeting of the Workers' Educational Association and joined a three-year course on Literature. Also a year-long course, 'The Problem of Central Europe'. I am optimistic! At this meeting the speaker, an MA, said, 'It is funny, the BBC has mislaid the German word for "Mr". It is now Hitler, Goering and Ribbentrop; while there was a chance of Peace it was "Herr".' He told us that soon German operations would be called 'atrocities' and our own 'stern but necessary measures'. The WEA, he mentioned, 'will show you how to think, not what to think, for yourselves.'

Pam Ashford

Mr Mitchell had a lot to say on the subject of evacuees, who seem already to be wearing out their welcome. A poorer class woman of 30 with eight children ranging from 1 year to 9 was received at Gryffe Castle where she had two rooms and a bathroom, and servants to cook her food. She decided she liked her Glasgow tenement better and has returned leaving the eight children behind. In one case a husband came out to Bridge-of-Weir to fetch his wife home, as there was no one to cook his meals for him.

There is a surprising degree of humour about today. Incendiary bombs, gas attacks and the rest have not happened yet, and the Sunshine Susies have put in a splendid innings. The excitement is not unpleasant. The ship of state is passing over slightly choppy waters, and we are enjoying the shaking up and down. Of course, it will be a short-lived phase, but there it is for the moment.

Mr Mitchell came back with a story 'straight from the lips' of the Editor of the *Glasgow Herald*: The black-out has given rise to a big increase in crime – brawling, attacks on women, burglaries, etc. The newspapers are keeping it out or there would be a 'riot' in the country. I regarded the story with scepticism. On telling Mother in the evening she expressed belief in it, and said she was not going out at night.

Miss Carswell has developed a story of the spying activities of her former German neighbour. Yesterday Mr Mitchell asked her why, since she had known what was going on for twelve months, she had not communicated with the police. She maintained that it was the police's job to track down spies, not hers.

WEDNESDAY, 6 SEPTEMBER

Pam Ashford

I put away the folders containing our correspondence with Germany. It made me very sad. They are all such nice people. Ice cream shops in the East End have been raided.

After work I bought at Cooper's tins of C&B's soup, raspberries, strawberries and galantine of ham. We did not include soup in our previous lists, Mother being under the impression that she had plenty in the house. On further investigation she found she is completely out.

Last week I said that when war was declared I should stop buying, but I have decided to go on. Today the grocers have tinned goods rising like mountain ranges. Surely when nobody wants to buy it cannot be unpatriotic for me to do so.

THURSDAY, 7 SEPTEMBER

Pam Ashford

Miss Bousie commented upon the discontinuance of the 2 o'clock news bulletin (she has a late lunch hour) and the BBC came in for a lot of criticism from the office staff for their 'funereal' programmes. 'I don't want another day like Sunday!' she said. So far as I can gather everyone had sat about all day simply listening to the BBC repeating the same items of news over and over again.

Practically everyone thinks the war will be over in three months, but the justifications advanced are many and various. Some people mystically 'feel' it will not last; others think Hitler will soon be licked. Another friend on economic grounds pointed out the impossibility of the war continuing. Yet another friend expects both sides to be glad to arrange a truce in three months and Hitler will remain in power. Many hold that when Poland is smashed up there won't be much point in continuing the war.

Mother met Mrs Wallace, who told her that an ice cream shop has been found to be the headquarters of an elaborate spy system.

FRIDAY, 8 SEPTEMBER

Pam Ashford
Mr Mitchell says Herr Ditscher, tutor in German, has written to the *Citizen* pointing out that he and his wife are Swiss. I have been going to his classes off and on for seven years and know what good people they are. Last winter they were sorely hit, and I am afraid their position must be precarious now. I am deeply sorry. A day or two ago I read in the papers that the 'Link' had closed down. I have been a member for a year and again and again have been puzzled. On the whole I believe it was a genuine attempt to promote Anglo-Germany friendship, though some of the Nazi sentiments in their organ, the *Anglo-German Review*, shocked me.

I walked through Cooper's after work and discovered that Atora suet and Trex are the same price in air-tight tins as in cardboard.

This evening by way of a change I wrote up in shorthand my MO diary for yesterday and today. I tremble to think what my co-workers would say if they discovered that 'there is a chief among them taking notes, and faith, he'll print them.'

SATURDAY, 9 SEPTEMBER

Eileen Potter
After lunch I go to a friend at Golders Green, with whom I often play tennis on summer evenings. It is a lovely, summery afternoon, and Golders Green has rather a peaceful appearance. Being in a 'neutral' area, the cinemas are open as usual. We are shortly joined by two other friends and have a foursome. It seems strange to see girls going about in very scanty shorts, with gas-masks slung over their shoulders. It is almost too hot to play vigorously in the middle of the day, and our play is rather feeble (never very brilliant, at the best of times). After two sets, we return to the flat for tea.

My friend is a strong pacifist but even she now agrees that 'Hitler must be stopped'. She has so far refused to try a gas-mask on, however, and the air-raid warden refuses to give her one unless she will try it. The other two guests are respectively the secretary of an international hostel and a refugee lady of Czecho-Slovak nationality but mixed racial origin. The pacifist thinks that things will only be the same at the end of this war as they were last time, but the refugee and I insist on taking a more hopeful view. She and her friends are in sympathy with the idea of 'federal union'. She is also rather an expert in black-outs, having lived through it all before in Prague last year.

Pam Ashford

This morning they were allowing ten straphangers on the bus. I have no lack of work now. Everyone in Eire wants to buy cargo immediately and we cannot get boats willing to go. We have an order for 3,000 tons for the Bayonne and it is even harder to get a boat for that. Neutral boats for Scandinavia are loading and sailing without much hitch.

Two friends had written announcing a visit this afternoon, viz. Miss Janet Paterson of Stirling and Dr Elsie Cadman of Kilmarnock. Both are schoolteachers in receiving areas. The evacuees at Kilmarnock come from St Rollox, Glasgow, and those at Stirling from Bridgetown, Glasgow; the districts from which the children come are adjoining and represent the very worst of Glasgow's slums. What these two receiving areas have to put up with: vermin and filth on one hand and destruction on the other! Many kind-hearted people had been looking forward to the children who they had thought of as innocent helpless little mites, but what they got was far removed from what they expected.

The receiving authorities at Kilmarnock had the children examined before sending them to their new homes and 40 were found to be verminous. Anybody who knew how to cut hair was requisitioned. At Stirling the children were sent straight off to their billets. The hostesses had the dreadful job of deverminising them. People who lent motor cars have had to have them fumigated.

Many of the evacuees arrived in rags and with no soles to their shoes. The parents had sent them thus so that they would get new clothes in the receiving areas. A Stirling lady asked to have a little girl, and when the child arrived the hostess had to burn all her clothes, shave her head and bathe her in disinfectant. Nevertheless, the child was a nice, obliging little soul, and after three or four days it seemed as if she would fit into the household easily. Then her mother and grandmother, an indescribably disreputable pair, arrived from Glasgow to take her home again, and away she went, clothed in garments belonging to the hostess's little girls.

A boy told his hostess about his appearances in the Police Court. The woman returned him to the billeting authorities at once. It transpired that he had once been interviewed by the police in regard to a ball that had gone through a window.

What will be the outcome of this mixing of the classes? There is a popular view that it will open the door to Communism. Both of my friends think that giving the children homes, food, etc. for nothing will encourage them to be paupers. Or it may instil a higher level of cleanliness in the lower classes. It is said that one evacuated woman in Stirling is a prostitute who has begun to ply her profession there. *(This is Pam Ashford's last entry for a month.)*

SUNDAY, 10 SEPTEMBER

Eileen Potter

I proceed to Belsize Park to see my sister-in-law, who has just been moving to new quarters there, as she finds her flatlet in Sussex Gardens too lonely now. She is just settling in. She was a Belgian refugee in the last War, married my eldest brother and settled down here, taking up corsetry on being left a widow, and is now a corset buyer in a West End store. She was just about to spend a holiday with her parents in Belgium when the War broke out. She enquired about getting a passage on a plane, but was told that Belgium was not now admitting any 'foreigners'. I have quite a long journey home – my first after dark since the black-out began. The tube station at Belsize Park looks rather sepulchral. I am the only occupant of the lift, and feel rather creepy. Down below, however, all looks more or less normal, except for the large proportion of passengers wearing uniform of various kinds. On emerging from the tunnel at Barons Court, all the lights are switched off, and I change to the District Railway at Hammersmith in total darkness. The District train is completely dark, and I nearly sit on somebody's knee by mistake. On returning home, I am surprised to meet my former landlady's son and his fiancée. They have returned from the country by car to fetch some more bedclothes. They have discovered a number of animal fleas, which have bred in the room last occupied by the cat whilst the house has been shut up, and are just off to buy some 'Flit'. They show me where their car has been damaged on the journey in the black-out – having run into something in front and also been run into in the rear.

WEDNESDAY, 13 SEPTEMBER

Eileen Potter
Registration in the schools is now finished, and the unattached teachers have to return to the Divisional Offices each day to report. They occupy the room in which we have hitherto been working, and we are moved into the stock-room and the basement which is furnished mainly with mattresses and pillows used by staff who slept at the office during the rush period of evacuation. We encamp upon the mattresses and pass our time mainly in knitting for the evacuees and in talking, and all get to know each other much better than heretofore.

Mr R, the member of the staff who is inclined to be overexcited in the presence of female colleagues, now describes us as his 'harem', regardless of who may be listening. He also tells us his past. He seems to have been a bit of everything, from a boiler-maker's apprentice to a chef on the *Queen Mary*, before joining the temporary staff of the LCC. He explains that he cannot be dismissed after two years' service, like most of the temporary employees, as he is on the 'King's Roll' as a result of being wounded in the last War. The permanent employees in the office are rather inclined to despise him, however.

SUNDAY, 17 SEPTEMBER

Tilly Rice
During the period that has elapsed since my last entry here I have made a trip up to London and Tadworth and back again. For some days we went on as usual with our holiday, my mind not quite being made up as to whether I should stay down here or return to Tadworth. At length, however, as my husband was likely to be evacuated and furnished houses seemed to be letting rather readily at home, I thought that it would be better to stay on down here, and try

to let the children carry on their lives with as little interruption as possible. So on Tuesday 5th September I sent a wire to my husband telling him that I should be returning home without the children on the next day.

The journey up was so comfortable and the train in good time but as we approached London so did the signs of war increase. There was a young couple in the same carriage as ours, and the wife was obviously very nervous about returning to London. She said to me: '*You* don't seem to mind coming back into the danger of air raids!' And I replied that I wasn't in the least bit nervous, though I added that the place where I lived was supposed to be in the neutral zone.

Of course when we emerged at Waterloo we got a full realisation of the effect of the war. I was struck by the maleness of the crowd hurrying about, and amused by the sight of sober, respectable businessmen walking about solemnly with cardboard boxes strung round their necks.

When I arrived in Surrey I found that the war had created even greater differences. To begin with the place was flooded with strange people, business firms having evacuated with their staffs to big houses that happened to be vacant in the district, and war nerves were even more apparent. The Tadworth population consists largely of people who are retired and I suppose the feeling of irritability and annoyance that I could sense immediately was due to the upset of lives which had thought to be set until the end. Whatever the cause, I was acutely conscious of the fact that nearly everywhere the selfish side seemed to be at the front. Everyone seemed to be cross, and interest in international affairs had given way to interest in personal inconveniences.

There followed a very depressing week, packing up the house, arranging about 'ARPing' the windows and clearing up generally, so that I was very glad when the time came for my return to Cornwall. I hated leaving my home and had I not been expecting a baby in November should not have gone back, but would have taken a job of some sort leaving the children in Cornwall for the duration.

Back in Cornwall I was struck by the disappearance of what signs of war there had been when I left. People had given up congregating about the cottage doors to hear the news and the young men had gone away to barracks in Plymouth and other more distant places.

As soon as I returned I set about getting my eldest boy started at

Camelford Grammar School. After arranging for my youngest boy to go to a small kindergarten next door I am trying to settle myself down as philosophically as possible to a totally strange existence, consoled entirely by my writing and MO activities.

SATURDAY, 23 SEPTEMBER

Eileen Potter

Am given a morning off for shopping, before the wartime rise in prices begins. I go to Kensington High Street, and buy a warm woolly frock and a macintosh at Barkers. I also buy a small gas-mask holder, which will take the mask without the box. In the afternoon I go to my hairdresser in Soho for a shampoo and set. Though now a naturalised Englishman, he is a native of Alsace-Lorraine, and spent his early days under German rule. He still has relatives living behind the Maginot Line, but he says they are keeping calm and confident. I then go on to spend the evening with a young married couple who live in a flat on the Duchy of Cornwall Estate, Kennington. The husband is a civil engineer, and has been doing a good deal of business in providing air-raid shelters, etc. The wife is a part-time almoner, and has been dealing with the evacuation (and in many cases the subsequent return) of expectant mothers. They are anti-Fascist intellectuals, but the intervention of Russia has rather puzzled them, like everybody else. We all agree that this is the 'world's weirdest war'. They see me to the tram – a dim, ghostly shape rattling along the Kennington Road. We stop it at the request stop by waving my torch at it. I finally succeed in groping my way into the Underground at Westminster.

TUESDAY, 26 SEPTEMBER

Eileen Potter

Miss H and I go, in a car driven by a teacher, to collect twin girls of three years old from their home and take them to Bedford College. Their father is a chauffeur and they live in a mews, pretty little things with long curls and teddy-bear coats. It is pathetic to see the look in the mother's eyes as she says goodbye, and again I feel a slight inclination to weep myself. The children sit on our knees and chat happily on the way, however. It is a lovely morning and most of the crèche children are happily playing in the College gardens when we arrive. A young nurse receives us and rather surprisingly discovers a nit in one of the children's heads.

WEDNESDAY, 27 SEPTEMBER

Eileen Potter

Plans are in the air for the re-opening of schools on a small scale. Groups of children are to be collected from the streets and set to play, or to occupy themselves in some educational way. Suggestion is made that we might like to join in. The idea does not appeal to me at all as I have no gift for amusing children *en masse* (even in small numbers) or for keeping them in order. In fact, the idea depresses me more than anything else which has happened since the war started, but presently it occurs to me that it will probably fall through. (In the upshot, the working of the scheme is left to trained teachers only, and it finally has to be abandoned in favour of house-to-house visiting, as the government refuses to countenance the assembling together of more than six children at once in the evacuated areas.)

SATURDAY, 30 SEPTEMBER

Eileen Potter

My folk dance club at Morley College re-opens this afternoon. There is a large crowd there, and they seem to be bubbling over with high spirits as they dance. Evidently the re-opening fulfils a real need. One old man, alleged to be nearly 80, is capering about like a two-year-old, in spite of the fact that he has been left alone by his three daughters, all evacuated teachers. I have some difficulty in getting a bus coming home, as the people are coming out of the Chelsea Palace of Varieties, which has just re-opened with a programme advertising 'pretty girls, strip-tease, etc.' Large crowds of rather noisy people are walking along the King's Road. Two youths walk in front, singing noisily. Ultimately I catch a bus to Hammersmith, and sit in front of a woman who is assuring her husband that she will not stand in his way if he wants to 'join up', but he in turn assures her that he does not want to do so.

MONDAY, 2 OCTOBER

Christopher Tomlin
Today canvassing was hard work. In the first hour I earned 6d, in three hours, 2/-, and in six hours, 8/9. It was my fault for I canvassed council houses in ignorance. Council property is no use to me.

Sometimes canvassing almost breaks my heart; but thank goodness in most districts I am welcome. The war has improved my business; I thought it would kick my job in the head, but thankfully it hasn't.

I canvassed with a new line: notepaper in four colours watermarked 'Victory Bond: Made in Canada'. I noticed people are tired of war.

THURSDAY, 5 OCTOBER

Christopher Tomlin
As the wind had not dropped I decided to work nearer home. And met success. Three interesting chats today. A Post Office clerk said: 'When do you think the war will end?'

I replied, 'It depends on Russia. But I think it will stop quicker than we expect. In the last war people said hostilities would cease at Christmas and war went on for three years; this time they say it will last three years, so I think it will end in six months.'

The clerk said, 'It will end on October 25th. There have been many bets on it in the office.'

Chapter Three

THE *ROYAL OAK*

And now my name has gone to the bottom of the deep blue sea: relatives read a list of surivors from the *Royal Oak*.

'Once again the German Richthofen-Goering Squadron has been in action on the Western Front, but this time the red-and-white chessboard emblem of Germany's crack fighter unit was not on Fokkers nor on Albatrosses, but on Messerschmitts. Their entry into this war has not been marked with success, because although they attacked only half their number of French machines they failed to get any of them and lost a couple of their own planes which were shot down over France.

This fight – which lasted for a quarter of an hour – was remarkable for one other thing. It provided the first wireless running commentary on an air battle which has ever been given: it was done from the air and from the middle of the fight. What happened was that the French fighter pilot who led the planes to the attack had, by accident, left his communication microphone on, and back at headquarters French officers heard the pilot talking to himself as he manoeuvred and fought. They heard him swear as the Messerschmitt twisted away just as he was going to fire; they heard him shout when one of the enemy was shot down. I can't imagine any wireless commentary which can compare with the drama which that small group of people at headquarters heard in their headphones as their pilot twisted and fought his way back home.'

Charles Gardner on the Home Service, 20 October 1939

* * *

6 October Last Polish resistance ceases. **9 October** Hitler issues orders for attack on the West. **14 October** U-boat penetrates British Fleet anchorage at Scapa Flow and sinks battleship *Royal Oak*. **18 October** Winston Churchill, First Lord of the Admiralty, claims that one in three of the German submarine force has been sunk. **28 October** A German plane engaged in attacks on shipping off the north and eastern Scottish coasts is shot down by the RAF, the first over the British Isles.

FRIDAY, 6 OCTOBER

Christopher Tomlin

Delivering today until 8 o'clock. I came home in the black-out and couldn't see my hand in front of my face. I called at my aunt's who showed me her identity card and asked, 'What's it for?'

Bought the *Berlin Liar* this morning, and was very amused by this skit (repeated to a few of my customers):

An elderly retired English farming couple were sound asleep when the air raid warning was given on the approach of enemy planes. The old farmer awoke first, and, leaning out of the bed, began groping for his trousers.

His wife, disturbed by his movements, got up and remarked, 'What's to do, Joe?'

'Jerry's over,' was the reply.

'Never mind' answered his wife, 'you can mop it up in the morning.'

SATURDAY, 7 OCTOBER

Tilly Rice

During the fortnight that has elapsed since I last made an entry in this diary, many things have happened – and many things still haven't happened. Poland has fallen and Russia has made her dramatic stepping in to share (or perhaps it would be more fitting to say to appropriate) a portion of the spoils. At the present moment a line of demarcation splits the centre of Poland marking the division of the country between Germany and Russia. From the passive way that Germany has accepted this situation one can do nothing else but suppose that it was all arranged beforehand.

In the household in which I live the whole thing has been received in bewildered silence. People taking the conventional anti-Hitler point of view are inclined to extend the same antagonism to Stalin and I find it difficult to get them to see my point of view that Stalin is a much cleverer man than Hitler, for his scruples have not yet been proved to be lacking, and in the end he may be the dominating factor for a genuine peace. But that can't be seen: Russia has always been 'Red' and a menace, and now has proved it.

The feeling of anti-climax, which I think is fairly prevalent in big towns, is more or less absent down here in this tiny village. War is still going on, but as something distant with just occasional repercussions on the general lives of the community, a condition very similar to that which existed down here in the last war as far as I can remember. Also, as in the last war, 'spy fever' rages in the village. One man, a local, said to me darkly, 'If you're out here late o'nights ye'll see lights flashin'!' and when one person took it into her head to burn her autumn rubbish, there were wild reports going round that the smoke had been observed to ascend at regularly directed intervals, obviously as a signal of some kind.

The village has of course been affected by the loss of men, as most of the male population down here have already gone. There is a lack of men to take out the boats.

SUNDAY, 8 OCTOBER

Eileen Potter
The Business and Professional Women's Club to which I belong holds a 'brunch' today, i.e. a meal at 11.30 a.m., in a residential club in Bloomsbury. This is our first meeting since the outbreak of war, and the subject for discussion is the question of peace terms. I have been rather distressed to see the suggestion made in the Club Bulletin by one of our leading officials that the Munich Agreement was largely due to the organised power of the women's peace movement. I feel that if this is so it is a disgrace to the women's movement, and I go to the meeting resolved to say something about it, though the lady in question fills me with awe, being large, masculine-looking and rather overpowering. She is also a financier and I suspect that this is the real reason she is so keen on appeasement. Fortune favours me, as she is not present at the meeting, and I am able to make my protest in her absence.

There is quite an outbreak of appeasement, however, in the shape of support for the idea of a peace conference with Hitler now. The suggestion is made by a thorough-going pacifist, who is a very able speaker. There is a lively discussion, but in the end her motion is lost by a large majority and we confine ourselves to sending a resolution to the Prime Minister urging him to state our peace terms in his reply to Hitler.

Christopher Tomlin

Went to 11.30 Mass then SVP. Today the Saint Vincent de Paul Conference I attended decided to accept responsibility for three young children. The kiddies, aged 3, 5 and 7, are in excellent Catholic homes. The Conference, by request of the father whose wife has just gone to the Lunatic Asylum, has undertaken to pay 30/- a week to the Sisters who conduct the homes, until the children support themselves.

Dick, my brother, a wireless operator with the RAF, was home for the day. I forgot to say in previous reports that he comes home every Sunday, as long as he can. On the first two Sundays Dick's actual leave was four hours. The railway was chaotic: Dick's train halted at each tin-pot station and it was three hours before he finished the journey from Padgate to Preston.

Dick is delighted with new life. He's put on weight, is sunburnt, smarter and he-man.

Tilly Rice

Yesterday afternoon I went down onto the beach to join the children. It is of course nearly deserted at this time of the year, though there were about a dozen people down there, also self-evacuees, including a party of three doctor's children sent from Plymouth. Mention was made of the new RAF aerodrome a few miles away, and I wondered if this place was as 'war-safe' as any other, though in my own case it is not immunity from air raids that is the attraction so much as immunity from war 'atmosphere'.

Yesterday evening was spent, as usual on Saturday, listening to *Bandwagon*. The news was listened to attentively but gave rise to very little comment. Possibly there would be more discussion here with some provocative remarks thrown out, but I refrain more than I should do ordinarily because when a household of strange people are thrown together for an indefinite period, relations should be kept as uncontroversial as possible. I think there is some tendency to anti-German feeling, which I seemed to notice when I mentioned making a German dish this morning. It was rather inclined to be dismissed as 'too rich', and the comment was 'they won't be able to make it nowadays anyway', but otherwise there is very little said excepting for murmurs of 'too dreadful' and 'too marvellous' as various exploits of the enemy and our own men are described on the wireless.

My own reactions to the whole situation are growing more and more indifferent every day. I have felt all along that somehow I must get my children out of the way, but were I not expecting another child I would not care where I was. Children will take the place of all those who have been and will be destroyed in the current struggle, though when I observe the same old prejudices and inhibitions cropping up in the generation that has arisen since the last war I wonder how much hope there is for anything better in the future.

MONDAY, 9 OCTOBER

Christopher Tomlin
Changed three books at the County Library. Took *The London Book of English Prose, A Dramatic History of England* by L du Garde Peach and *The Common People* by Cole and Postgate.

I took some notepaper to be printed, then caught the bus to town where I attended my first WEA lecture in wartime. The subject was the Peace Treaties, the lecturer a doctor of law who is, incidentally, a Jew from Austria. (He is modest, clean, free from the oiliness of most Jews, neatly dressed and a charming fellow: my opinion on his race rises to par. What I most admire is his courage; he has started life again three times. Driven from Austria by Peter the Painter he sought refuge in Czecho-Slovakia, until Peter turned up again, now he is here.) He was late for his first lecture because he was delayed at the Aliens' Tribunal; his name was last on the list and he had to wait for four weary hours. While we waited a *Lancashire Daily Post* cameraman took a group photo. It's queer how the *Post* goes dotty over such a photo. In every issue you will see one with the caption 'Reading from Left to Right . . . '

Taking this course are 60 students, 75% women! The first lecture was very interesting. The tutor opened with: 'I must be very careful, you know I am an Austrian, but I will give the true facts. It is not for the present rulers of Germany to condemn the peace terms, but you and I are entitled to criticise them . . . '

Coming from the room I walked down two flights of stairs and groped my way into the blackest black-out I've ever seen.

TUESDAY, 10 OCTOBER

Christopher Tomlin

I saw two open haulage vans outside a house in Cadley Causeway. They were full of furniture but nothing of value. Thinking somebody was doing a moonlight flit in the daytime I asked who was moving. And was very sad to hear, 'She lost her husband a year ago and her two boys are in the army.'

A customer told me the following experiences her friends had with evacuees: One lady took a mother and baby. The mother said, 'You needn't bother about me, I'm here for a week or two. I want a holiday.'

Another woman was horrified to find her mattress, sheets and blankets ruined because a child of seven 'evacuated' in bed.

The crowning experience was that of a former lodging-house keeper in Blackpool who received five mothers and babies. These mothers intended to go out every night and leave their kids to the landlady. But she wasn't having any. 'Where do you think you're going?' she asked. 'We are going out.' 'Supposing your babies cry, who's going to see to them?' 'You are. The Government pays you to.' They got quite angry; a free-for-all would have ensued but the landlady went to the local evacuation office. An official came round and told the mothers that one of them at least must stay in, that the landlady was not paid to look after them and that she was not paid to cook their food. If they did not like the arrangement, they could go home. There has been no trouble since then.

WEDNESDAY, 11 OCTOBER

Christopher Tomlin

This evening I attended another WEA class – this time Literature. Mr Warburton, our tutor, showed how the English language grew. The egg out of which came most European tongues was Aryan. Don't misunderstand, Germans have no more right to be called Aryan than any other European nation. Their original home is quite unknown, authorities differing so widely as between a locality enclosed by the river Oxus and the Hindu Kush mountains, and the shores of the Baltic or Central Europe . . . The Aryan family of languages include the Persian and Hindu, with all the European except Basque,

Turkish, Hungarian and Finnic. Sometimes called the Indo-European, sometimes the Indo-Germanic, and sometimes the Japhetic (Sanskrit, Zend, Latin, Greek and Celtic are, of course, included).

Our tongue was developed by invasion. The conquering nation would impose its language, the conquered would tend to use their own, but as the needs of commerce grew the two tongues would fuse. Our tongue was developed by trade – foreigners would come to buy and sell or we would go to them. Many words came into the English language that way. It was largely influenced by seamen – new words would be used in town on the coast and then spread inland.

But the earliest work in our language was a poem, *Beowulf*. Anglo-Saxon. Telling how a half-human monster Grendel stole into a banqueting hall to devour humans. This is an extract from a translated version:

> BEOWULF AND GRENDEL
> Then came from the moor, from the misty hill-slopes
> Grendel, fell spoiler – God's anger he bore.
> He was minded a man in his house to entrap.
> He stole through the mists till now he saw gleaming
> The hall of the feasting and of gifts of fine gold . . .

Coming back by bus I heard a woman say, 'Those (car) lamps don't look very dim . . . ' And, passing a brightly lit butcher's, 'Ooh, that's not blacked out! He'll be for it . . . Ooh, look at those red lights!'

THURSDAY, 12 OCTOBER

Tilly Rice

While overhearing the conversation of some locals this morning I noticed the BBC coming in for a little criticism. One said, 'What I like is the way they pat themselves on the back. They say what jolly good programmes they are keeping up when you can turn on France or Germany any day and hear better.'

The children down here seem to have settled in fairly happily to their new lives, though I know my own two are homesick, particularly the eldest who is secretly longing to get back home. But he seems determined to get on with the job in hand, not so bad a job considering the lovely surroundings and the comfortable home we have at our disposal. What chiefly influences my husband and I is that down here Dick can have a proper schooling, and there's no question of it being a half-and-half affair as it would way back at home in Reigate.

My husband is up in London on a pilgrimage from one private hotel to another and seems to be finding it difficult to settle. In some letters he appears to be enjoying his new freedom and in others he is missing his family, though on the whole he is more missed, I believe, than missing. He elects to live right up in London, thinking it the safest place considering the lengths they have gone to protect it.

Eileen Potter

Two of us call for some more under-fives and take them by car to the nursery at Bedford College, preparatory for being sent away to homes in the country. Two of them are sisters, living in a rather slummy street in Fulham, but beautifully prepared for the journey by their rather attractive young mother. We go on to a new block of flats in North Hammersmith to call for another child. Her preparations are perfect. Both she and her luggage are fully labelled with name, address and registration number. She leaves her parents without a murmur, and goes to sleep on my knee in the car. On arrival at Bedford College, I put her on her feet. She wakes up, but does not cry or say a word, but takes my hand and walks quietly in.

Christopher Tomlin

Customer: 'Oh, I think Hitler's done for. Look how he swanked about his aeroplanes – "fastest in the world". Why, we make rings round them.'

Nine bombers passed over about 4 p.m. There were two formations of three (V-shaped and upside-down) and three in a single line. They were flying from south to north on Watling St Road. Too high to see if they are friend or enemy.

I asked a bus conductor, 'What will you chaps do in an air raid?'

'We've been told to leave the bus and make for the nearest shelter. We should have lists of the shelters but we haven't got them yet.'

FRIDAY, 13 OCTOBER

Eileen Potter

After being in the office all day interviewing, I go to the folk-dancing class at Morley College. Our class is held in the gym, which is also the official air-raid shelter. After we have been there about half an hour, an air raid practice takes place. All the students come streaming down from the other classrooms, and presently the chief warden rattles a miniature rattle, and we all have to put our gas-masks on and keep them on until he rings a bell. Everything goes off satisfactorily, except that one man hangs his hat and coat on the fire extinguisher.

Christopher Tomlin

Father: 'Don't you listen to anybody who says the war must go on, that we are fighting to defeat Hitlerism. Those writers are right (in *Catholic Herald*) who say the war will mean victory for Russian Communism. This evacuation is a ghastly failure, more and more people are coming to that view.'

I heard [the radio broadcast from] Hamburg, whose announcer was praising Hitler's regime: 'Lying British newspapers . . . British tourists delighted with German scenery, people and culture . . . bewildered to find Germany so different from reports in their newspapers . . . '

I was working in the country and had to walk a mile and a quarter to the nearest urinal.

SATURDAY, 14 OCTOBER

Christopher Tomlin

At 4 p.m. I went for some fruit tarts, Father's *John O'London*, a *Lancashire Daily Post* and I delivered two boxes of notepaper. Then settled down to *Bandwagon*, a darned good show.

Mother: 'What damn rot this ARP is becoming. I see the authorities are stopping ARP workers smoking! There's a new rule that wardens may be dismissed if they don't look spick and span. There've been some resignations!'

We heard Leslie Hore-Belisha [Secretary of State for War] speak after the 9 o'clock news. I thought he was damn good, but Mother said, 'That sort of talk cuts no ice. He didn't say what the war was about.'

Mother reading *Daily Mail*: 'This controlling's coming to absurd limits. There's even going to be a controller of shirts!'

Pam Ashford

The papers came at 7.30. Mother hurried in to tell me that three U-boats had been sunk and then Mother and Charlie both congratulated each other on the news. There has been a bad railway accident, such a one as would have excited horror everywhere once, but I have not heard a single comment on it today.

On reaching work I said to Mr Mitchell, 'Three U-boats have been sunk.' He said, 'No, four, one was sunk on Thursday.' Although everyone is jubilant about this German defeat, I feel so sorry for the crews. Whatever may be my mental characteristics, I don't think they include sadism.

About 11.30 Miss Bousie returned from the bank, her face a picture of horror. 'The *Royal Oak* has been sunk.'

Nothing yet has come so near to throwing me off my balance. The shocks caused by the invasion of Poland, the declaration of war, and the alleged bombing of Chatham were slight compared with this.

For one thing, I know how little we can spare so formidable a ship. For another, Devonport is my calf country, and the dreadful suffering caused last time by comparable disasters is too deep a wound for it not to bleed again today. For me, the Battle of Jutland is the memory of memories, and it takes little to call back the harrowing scenes, as home after home found this one or that was gone.

There is a personal emotion too of such a blend that I cannot analyse it – sorrow, pathos, helplessness, disappointment and I know not what. The *Royal Oak* was the bit of the navy with which I have always identified myself. My father was a constructor at Devonport Dockyard; he built the *Royal Oak*. It was his last ship. She was on the stocks in August 1914, and her construction was rushed forward at such a desperate speed that his health was undermined and he died later from pernicious anaemia.

When the keel plate of a new battleship is laid in a naval port there is a ceremony which includes the putting in of the first rivets by the 'ladies' (wives and daughters of Admiralty officials). Their names are afterwards cut into the plate. I was only a little girl then, but I put my rivet in, and ever since have thrilled with pleasure to think I had my place in the fleet. And now my name has gone to the bottom of the deep blue sea.

I remember the launch, and the May morning in 1916 when she put out to sea. That was a few days before the Battle of Jutland, and she got there in time. Afterwards the Captain of the *Royal Oak* wrote to tell my father how well she had acquitted herself and to thank him for the good job he had made of her building. There is no need now to tell you why I feel so sad.

The news did not affect the office so much, of course. Here one battleship is much the same as another battleship. 'This happened a fortnight ago, and has only been let out now.' Mr Mitchell says, 'It is to be expected. We cannot attack their ships because they are in port. The *Royal Oak* was, however, a sitting target for them.'

That explains the queer way the 9 p.m. news was given last night. The announcer began with a sorrowful voice thus: 'It has been an unfortunate day,' then he went on to say, 'for the Germans.' He knew about this *Royal Oak* disaster.

SUNDAY, 15 OCTOBER

Christopher Tomlin

Mass at 11. Dick was home when I came back. He was in RAF uniform for the first time, and he looked very smart too. He loves the life. This may be the last leave he has for some time as he expects very soon to be posted. He may go to Salisbury Plain or to Cranwell; I hope his luck continues for Dick doesn't want to go to Salisbury and be miles from any town.

Mother read a paragraph in a Sunday paper about girls making service uniforms. The lasses are timed to do one operation (for instance sewing on a button) in 60 seconds.

Pam Ashford

Spent the morning reading the *Sunday Times* in bed. After lunch did kitchen work, and then went to Yeoland's. For nearly three hours we talked.

Yeoland had just been reading Lloyd George in the *Sunday Express* and said, 'Lloyd George says you enter a war because you think you will win. But the other nation is also entering the war because it thinks it will win.'

I said, 'No. In the face of aggression, one might prefer to fight rather than yield. One may choose death rather than the destruction of principle. Surely Poland proves that she would rather die fighting; you can't say she is fighting because she is sure of winning.'

Yeoland and her mother did not know that only five foods are to be rationed at the outset, but oddly enough I could only remember four: meat, butter (margarine), cooking fats and sugar. I have since remembered bacon (which is a commodity I don't touch). They were incredulous when I said that tea was not included yet. She did not see the war coming, despite years devoted to the study of astrology. It is extraordinary what a cult this rubbish has.

Yeoland has a friend who visited Germany. When in a café who should enter but Hitler and his bodyguard, and they took a table not more than five yards away. The doors of the café were locked to prevent anyone else entering. Yeoland's friend said Hitler had the palest of eyes with a fishy gaze. I described how Janet Patterson had been present at one of Hitler's speeches at Frankfurt and what a magnetic influence he had had over her. Yeoland's friend did not seem to have experienced such an effect.

I expressed the belief that a United States of Europe would come one day and that the League of Nations or some similar body was an essential part thereof. I thought that this present war had better possibilities than the last of being the war to end wars, so far as Europe is concerned. Yeoland and her mother think America will come into the war as a belligerent.

MONDAY, 16 OCTOBER

Eileen Potter

In the evening I go with one of my colleagues to the Westminster Theatre to see Priestley's new play, *Music at Night*. I find the first two acts quite enthralling, and am glad to see a note in the programme to the effect that the show will go on even if there is an air raid, as I think the latter would be an annoying interruption. The last act is not so pleasing, however. The death of the cabinet minister, with its attendant circumstances, seems to me a bit 'creepy' for a wartime play.

On struggling home in the dark, I feel rather annoyed to find a leaflet in the letter-box from the ARP post stating that a light was visible in my window last night. I decide that it is too wet to go into the garden to investigate tonight, and go to bed as quickly as possible.

Christopher Tomlin

First air raid on Britain. Fine, sunny and cold.

Yesterday I met a boy who is usually smartly dressed. He is now in the militia, and what a slovenly appearance! To me the militiamen are 'poured into sacks' and I hate their dress. If I am called up I will try for the RAF (ground duties).

I was in the bus about 3 p.m. when a woman rushed out of a house towards us, with a gas-mask in her hand. 'Aroo! Hey! Oo! You've forgotten your gas-mask . . . they won't let you in the pictures without it!' A poor fellow came downstairs, blushing violently, to collect his precious toy.

I had a pretty good day and came home for tea. I leave home after breakfast and don't have another meal until 6 to 7. I usually take two or three biscuits out with me, in case. The wireless was on low, I heard, 'There were civilian casualties . . . ' and said to Dad, 'Sounds like an air-raid report.' He murmured, 'Yes. There has been one on Edinburgh.' This air-raid news made me feel as if I'd been kicked in the stomach. But I went to the cinema and saw *Fast and Loose* with Robert Montgomery. A packed house, and I had to stand for half an hour.

Mother says: 'The Germans weren't after Edinburgh but wanted to bomb the bridge across the Firth of Forth.' The raid was this afternoon.

Mother: 'Hitler says he's now going to treat us like Poland.' The swine will pray for death and will wish he'd never been born.

Pam Ashford

This *Royal Oak* disaster has made me very sad. Mother is collecting the cuttings, pictures of the ship, the captain's photo etc. from the newspapers. It really seems as if my father is dead now. During the long years since he died there was always the thought that while the *Royal Oak* was there, something of him lived on, and now it is no more.

I reached home at 6.15 p.m. and found Mother much excited by the announcements at 6 p.m. that bombers had reached the Forth. Soon after, the announcement was made that there were no civilian lives lost or civilian property damaged. This is getting near home.

TUESDAY, 17 OCTOBER

Eileen Potter
Evacuation queries are decreasing a little, so I decide to look up some of my cases who were attending the Special Ear Clinic in North Hammersmith before the war broke out. I pass a road which has the reputation of being one of the slummiest roads in Hammersmith and seems to be swarming with dirty, neglected-looking children playing about aimlessly. It occurs to me that the neglect of education may prove a greater danger to our civilisation than the falling of a few bombs, if it is continued too long. One basement window is ornamented with a sheet cut from the *Daily Mirror* giving a portrait of Hitler as 'Wanted – for Murder, etc, etc.'

Christopher Tomlin
Daily Mail: 'Seven German Bombers destroyed in the Forth Raid.' And 7 out of 12 is jolly good! There were approximately 33 casualties in yesterday's raids through shrapnel, but no direct hits.

Hitler admits 40,000 casualties in the Polish War, so Dad says we know there were more. There were two air raids on Scapa Flow today; some damage to the Iron Duke 'not serious'. One witness states: 'Our planes sped like cricket balls bowled in the sky!' And two Nazi prisoners from a bomber said, 'We were just too slow!'

Mother went to the Co-op and they were short of butter. In fact, each regular customer was allowed 3 ounces. When my brother was here we consumed 4 or 5 pounds a week; since he's away we consume 2 pounds. How the devil can we make 3 ounces last a week?

The ATS girls are very smart; their uniforms are just right and neat, except the fat girls whose skirts bulge behind.

Pam Ashford
The talk of the need of getting official permission from London before air-raid warnings can be sounded in Scotland has raised all the Scottish Nationalist fervour.

Miss Smith expresses the hope that the planes won't come tonight, as it is too cold to get out of a warm bed. Miss Bousie would want a cup of tea, and has been advised to keep it in a flask ready, for both water and gas might be cut off.

Strong undercurrent of excitement everywhere. It is very much as if the curtain is now going to raise on a play, for which the house has been sitting waiting.

WEDNESDAY, 18 OCTOBER

Christopher Tomlin

Mrs P, who boards dogs during the holidays, says, 'People are coming to see if I'll take their dogs in if there's a gas-attack.'

Rather disgusting: for the past three weeks I've noticed a young couple spooning at the corner of my street. Tonight they were closer than usual; black-outs have their uses.

We listen-in to Hamburg because we are curious to know what Hitler thinks of us. A few nights ago I am informed Hamburg broadcast, 'Hello proud Preston, you won't be proud very long.'

Pam Ashford

Conversation revealed that Miss Bousie and Mr Mitchell listen to the German wireless stations. Miss Bousie appreciates the 'truth' given us by the German stations.

The case is reported in the papers of cruelty to an evacuee of five in Preston.

Betty, the office girl, has had many raggings in the past because of her attachment to her gas-mask, with the result that she has been ridiculed into leaving it behind in the office when she goes out for a message. She asked me (a confirmed gas-mask carrier) whether or not she should take it, and I said I would in her place.

THURSDAY, 19 OCTOBER

Christopher Tomlin

Coming back by bus I heard this duet:

Man of 60: 'I read from tonight's *Post* that they're cutting out the cross-town service, and only half a service to the cemetery on Sundays.'

Man of 45: 'Yes, it's through the shortage of petrol.'

Man of 60: 'Well, I don't know. There are three boats in the docks, been there a week, and they can't unload their cargoes of petrol.'

Man of 45: 'It's this blooming control; but I say these controllers know what's best. If a man's paid to do a job he should know what he's doing.'

Man of 60: (Pause) 'There will be no boiled mutton for Christmas and no boiled pork, and we will be short of butter. My wife loves some good butter, it's one of the cheapest things you can buy and it's full of vitamins.'

Man of 45: 'Yes, it's a b*** shame it's pooled. Look at the firms who've wasted thousands improving and advertising their products. I've promised my wife to get her as much as I can.'

Man of 60: 'It's b*** awful the way we're made to go short; why, in the last war it was a year before food was rationed. It strikes me a lot of fellows have good fat jobs! I'll tell you what is a crying disgrace. There are thousands of crates of fish landed at Fleetwood and they can't sell it. First the Government controlled it, then it was left alone. Now it's in a b*** muddle!'

Man of 45: 'Yes. I believe some of it had to be sent to Blackburn before it could come to Preston.'

Man of 60: 'Yes, it's interesting to hear other people's ideas . . . '

Man of 45: 'Well, we have to criticise and speak our mind. Everybody has a different idea; it's what makes life worth living.'

Pam Ashford

A foggy day again, and Mr Mitchell apprehensive about the safety of Glasgow. He went to Ayr, however, and refused to take his gas-mask, though I pleaded hard with him to do so.

Mr Roxburgh called this morning, and he and Miss Bousie set to work to denounce the British Government. It would seem that everything is for the worst in this worst of all possible worlds. Both expressed contempt for the way the Allies were boasting of their successes.

'All around you hear people saying that there will be a revolution in Germany,' says Mr Roxburgh, 'but it is my belief that it is this country that will have the revolution. Greed, greed, greed everywhere.'

Then they set to work on the loss of the *Royal Oak*. 'The great Mr Churchill said that the defences at Scapa Flow had proved adequate in the last war. Fancy saying that in the face of German advance. That was twenty-five years ago. Twenty-five years behind the time. What inefficiency!'

The soap for the office has been rationed. We can no longer buy six cakes at a time and are limited to one cake. In other words, six people must each buy one cake.

The evening papers had photos of the three German airmen lying in Edinburgh hospitals who were shot down on Monday. Mother and I were so sorry for them. Then the news said two others had been found at Whitby. After being in the North Sea for two days in a collapsible boat, they reached the Yorkshire coast and, having climbed the cliffs, hid in a railway tunnel. One feels that they are no more responsible for the situation than our RAF. Of course, I have brought this point into my diary before, and I still reason that one cannot drive a wedge between the individual and the State.

We are worried about wages.

FRIDAY, 20 OCTOBER

Christopher Tomlin

Father poking the fire: 'This coal is awful. It's nothing but stone.'

Mum: 'The coal-man tells me the best is being exported; the Government doesn't care what coal we have so long as they can get money.'

Father looking up from his paper: 'I'd like to know what the Germans are doing massing all those troops and planes on their coast.'

Me: 'I can tell you . . . they will attack Britain with 3,000 bombers and at the same time try to land troops in England.'

Dad: 'Don't talk nonsense! You come out with idiotic statements. What do you think we'd be doing to let them? I might have expected a mass air attack a week or two since, but in their raid on our convoy on Monday they lost 7 bombers out of 12. No power can afford such losses. Why, those planes cost thousands.'

Pam Ashford

Intense excitement in Glasgow office and strange to say, much humour. The following sentiments were recorded in shorthand while the speakers were uttering them.

Miss Smith: 'They are determined to get to the Forth Bridge.'

I said, 'London is reported to be so well protected that they don't intend to waste their planes there. Still, I think we have plenty of guns on our East Coast too.'

Margaret: 'I want them to come at night when I am at home. I want four of us and Dandy to die together.' (Mother, father, sister, self and dog.)

I said, 'If I had such a temperamental dog as Dandy, I would take good precautions right now against him going mad. Have you got that muzzle for him yet?'

Margaret: 'Well, we kept on talking about it, but it would break the poor soul's heart.'

Miss Carswell: 'I went to see *Professor Mamlock* (a film, German with English subtitles) last night.'

I said: 'I would not trust the cinema to give a true picture of Germany.'

Miss Carswell: 'This film was true. You saw them torturing the Jews.'

I said: 'The Nazis' treatment of the Jews is disgraceful but nevertheless there is another side. I have heard the testimony of several Jews now in this country that though they suffered so badly from the Storm Troopers, they received kindness from many German neighbours, surreptitiously of course.'

Miss Carswell: 'Oh, you saw that too. What a conflict there is between the Nazis and the German people.'

SATURDAY, 21 OCTOBER

Pam Ashford

To college. I met Mr John Bourowski (British despite his curious name), the lecturer in transport. The transport classes have been very successful for several years. 'It would be a pity if this work were lost,' he said pathetically. The students are largely drivers of Corporation buses and trams, and the men seem unwilling to pay fees as they may be called up before the course is over. They think the Government should pay their fees.

He spoke of the revolting cruelty to people in concentration camps (his attitude was one of despair and pity, not anger). He mentioned (with many details of the persons concerned) the case of a British person who had sent a keg of 7lbs of butter to German friends; in consequence of which the Germans were put in a concentration camp for having suggested to the British person that there was a food shortage in their country.

Thereafter I enrolled for the German class on Wednesday at six to seven. I was half an hour late getting into the Cosmo. The chief film was *La Grande Illusion*.

Out into the black-out, my first experience of the darkness. It was not such a very dark night and I was astonished to see how much light there was in Sauchiehall Street. Buses, trams and motor vehicles with lights. The King's Cinema lit up inside. Fruit shops, stationers, sweet shops, tobacconists, open with many lights visible. The bus had blue lights on, of course; gloomy but not so dark as I had expected. Nor was it difficult to get on and off. A lady dropped a box of cakes and the conductor, not being able to see the floor, kicked them all over the bus.

MONDAY, 23 OCTOBER

Pam Ashford
Miss Bousie returned from the bank today through the front door. She usually goes in by the back door so I knew at once there was news of some sort. Last time it was the *Royal Oak* disaster, and I looked up with apprehension. Her beaming face, however, was most reassuring. The bills were announcing that 'Stalin has said No to Hitler. Russia won't give Germany military aid.'

I remarked that Stalin was only out to feather his own nest, with which sentiment Miss Bousie did not agree. 'He was out for justice,' she said. 'Justice!' I reiterated, half stunned. 'What he wanted was the return of the territory stolen from Russia at Versailles.'

Conversation turned to the cartoon in today's *Bulletin* (Hitler and Stalin). A young lady friend of Miss Bousie said, 'I admire Stalin's face. He appeals to me.' Miss Smith said, 'Stalin has a cruel face. That girl must like cavemen. Is Stalin married?' It was generally agreed that Stalin would make a very bad husband.

WEDNESDAY, 25 OCTOBER

Pam Ashford
After work I went to the class in Advanced German Correspondence about which I spoke previously. There was only one other student tonight but still the class will run. Hitherto Wednesday has always been the most crowded night and it seemed extraordinary to find the number of students so greatly reduced. Property Management, Advertising and Journalism are running. Last year I went to Shipping Law which has been discontinued. I feel so glad I got it in in time.

SATURDAY, 28 OCTOBER

Eileen Potter

After lunch, I go to Morley College again. First we have the Annual Meeting for the Folk Dance Club. Then there is a party, Mr C being the MC. He has such a stimulating personality that even the sight of him about the place seems to make the event go with more of a swing.

People arrive from all parts of London in large numbers. Everybody seems in hilarious spirits. We finish at about six and I go home for high tea. An elderly, rather poor and distinctly drunk couple are sitting in the bus singing loudly. Presently they start on 'Rule, Britannia'. A semi-sober man sitting in front of them joins in, and the drunken man begins talking to him. 'We want our freedom,' he says, 'and we want everybody else to have theirs, too!' He then asks the other man if he is English. The other man, who in the dusk has a rather Jewish appearance, replies that he is Scotch. They then all start singing 'Sing me a Song of Bonnie Scotland'. The drunken couple get out, with some difficulty, at Lambeth Bridge, and the other man continues talking to the bus conductor. He remarks upon the 'lovely spirit' of the drunken man and says, 'What good company he would make in the parlour.' He goes on to say that he thinks Hitler is bluffing and will end up by giving in.

Pam Ashford

From work I went to Queen Mary Union. There were two speakers, Dr Story and Miss Barbara Macfarlane, who mentioned evacuation. Slum children in the Highlands were tremendously excited about the 'wee bears' on the mountainsides. These turned out to be rabbits, which they had never seen before with their skins on.

I sat next to a Viennese lady who was introduced as Miss Noble. I asked her what she was doing. She said, 'I read. I have always wanted to read, but never had the time. Now I am reading all the books I always wanted to read. And I knit squares for the soldiers.' She would not agree that Vienna was in any way more beautiful (i.e. less ugly) than Glasgow. Someone said, 'We grumble a lot here about the dirt and the weather.' The Viennese said she 'felt so grateful to be here that she could never grumble about anything in Glasgow'. It seemed odd to be on such easy terms with a national of a state with which we are at war.

Mrs Tebb (President) in her remarks welcomed 'three German refugees who are with us today'. She mentioned their names but did not mention Miss Noble. I looked around and saw two Jewesses in very shabby clothes, apparently foreigners. They were with a smartly dressed girl who might or might not have been a Jewess. She seemed familiar and I have since remembered that in August she sat behind me on a bus and was talking to two German companions. Mrs Tebb said she wished 'to assure them how much we abhor the cruelty of the Nazi regime'. I mentioned them to Charlie subsequently and he expressed dislike for the Association's practice of welcoming Jews.

The newspapers have pictures of Nazi prisoners (seamen) being landed at a Scottish port.

MONDAY, 30 OCTOBER

Christopher Tomlin
No mention of war; my people and I await some devilish attack by Hitler. We know it's coming. I took three books to the Country Library – 3d to pay. I took three more. Enquired if they had any books on Mass Observation.

Pam Ashford
Mr Hutchison knows a nurse in the Edinburgh Infirmary who is attending one of the injured German airmen. He is 16 years of age and had only 40 hours' flying experience. He was crying for his mother during his illness. Now he is getting better and is glad to be here. It would seem that Goering is keeping his best pilots in reserve for difficult feats and that he is sending people who because of their meagre capacities can be spared on these expeditions to Scotland.

Suddenly the conversation turned to Scottish Nationalism. Miss Bousie indignantly declaimed: 'If we had Home Rule this would never have happened! We should have had a seat on the League of Nations and have seen that things were done properly. They are all pigheaded at Westminster.' Everyone fumed at the superior air defences of London.

I said, 'Only a fortnight ago wherever you went you heard the same comment: "The Germans won't come as far as Scotland." How on earth can you blame the Government for not anticipating what you did not anticipate yourselves?'

At lunchtime I made my debut at the Soroptimist Club (a national professional women's organisation). Conversation consisted, for me, in introductions and explanations. The subject of the speaker was 'Simple Needlework' (Miss Baird). Next week an Austrian lady is to speak on 20 years of social work in Austria.

Chapter Four

THE PAIL!

Utterly unsuited for the responsibilities of premiership: Neville Chamberlain and Alec Douglas Home at Number 10.

'You have heard perhaps of the Oslo breakfast. This is a cold meal, full of vitamins. In Norway it consists of milk, a kind of wholemeal bread, margarine or butter, goats' cheese and half an apple, half an orange or a raw carrot. They found that the children who started the day with this breakfast flourished. The London County Council has been trying it, not as a breakfast, but as a dinner. This was given to a number of children and their progress compared with that of others on the good old-fashioned hot dinner.

For every inch that a "hot dinner child" grew, the "Oslo child" grew one-and-three-quarter inches, and two inches in the case of a girl. In weight, the "Oslo boy" put on twice as much as the "hot-dinner boy". "Oslo children" were healthier, with fewer ailments and much better complexions.'

A doctor justifies the lack of cooking equipment in evacuee reception areas on the Home Service, 22 November 1939

* * *

8 November Assassination attempt on Hitler fails. **13 November** Two German supply ships scuttled when cornered by Royal Navy. **17 November** Supreme War Council agrees on co-ordination of British and French war production. **21 November** Chamberlain imposes embargo on all German trade in retaliation for sinking neutral ships. **23 November** RAF shoot down seven German aircraft over France; British merchant-cruiser *Rawalpindi* sunk by battle-cruisers. **30 November** Soviet forces attack Finland; the Admiralty announces completion of 300-square-mile minefield from Thames Estuary to the Netherlands.

TUESDAY, 31 OCTOBER

Christopher Tomlin
It has been showery all day, a blooming nuisance. You can't keep samples dry and they lose their freshness. Customers are attracted by crisp, clean samples.

Pam Ashford
Miss Bousie returned from the bank with news that the head of the German army had resigned. Mr Mitchell returned from the Exchange with the same story. It transpires that General Von Brauchitsch [Commander-in-Chief of the Army] had quarrelled with Ribbentrop, and that Hitler had backed up Ribbentrop with the result that the General had resigned. The following dialogue ensued:

Me: Fancy Hitler preferring Ribbentrop to Brauchitsch!

Mr Mitchell: Hitler is a good man, but he has bad lieutenants.

Me: (Incredulously) Hitler is a good man!?

Mr Mitchell: Oh yes, he is. Look at the good he has done his country. He has raised them out of the slough of despair.

Me: He came to power just when the world's economic situation took a turn for the better and he cashed in on it. Ribbentrop is the worst of the bunch. Ages ago I read about his character in the King-Hall news letters. King-Hall spoke of his sinister influence. He is (in my opinion) a fiend that has slunk out of the shades.

Mr Mitchell: A Mephistopholes.

Me: No, Mephistopholes was good looking and attractive. Ribbentrop is not attractive. He is just like a sewer rat. Do you know that bit in *The Maid of the Mountains* that goes 'I have seen a sewer rat, and if he only had a hat, he would be very much indeed like you'? If I ever meet Ribbentrop that's what I shall say to him.

WEDNESDAY, 1 NOVEMBER

Eileen Potter
I and my colleague, Miss F, take a party of children by ambulance to a village not far from Guildford. We assemble at a school in Fulham. A nurse is there, examining the children before they go, to see that their heads are clean. All is well in this respect. One mother asks if

her three boys can be billeted separately, as they fight so much when together. Another mother warns me that her little boy is liable to be sick when travelling by road. The ambulance is supplied with a pail and swabs, and we keep a careful eye on the boy in question. When he begins to complain of feeling sick, the pail is placed near him, but he is not actually sick until some time afterwards. When we reach the village of our destination, the children recognise some of their friends and teachers, who have already been evacuated to the same village, looking out for them in the road. We have to unload at the village hall. The driver has to reverse. As he does so, he cries out, 'The pail!' He has observed another child beginning to be sick. The pail is rushed up to her, but it is too late – the seat and floor have been soiled. After we have got out, the driver cleans up the seat and covers the floor with newspaper. We return to town in the ambulance.

Christopher Tomlin

For the past week newspapers led me to think Hell was loose and that 1,000 bombers and goodness knows how many troops would come here. Then the papers told me Hitler was 'putting his shirt' on Stalin. This morning Stalin, blaming Britain and France, tells us he is Neutral. What the blazes is Hitler waiting for? He swanked such a hell of a lot about his Air Force and Army. Is it a bluff?

Pam Ashford

9 a.m. Miss Bousie: 'So there does not seem to be anything in the story of the General's resignation. Just propaganda. The papers have to keep us going. It is always "they are falling to pieces, but we are all right".'

Mr Morrison's speech last night has turned my thoughts to food stores. It was always my recommendation to keep our store intact until the rationing started. We would then supplement the rations from the cupboard and replace with fresh purchases of non-rationed (tinned) goods as far as possible. The news that rationing is to be on so limited a scale raises problems:

a) If we keep our store intact until the rationing situation develops seriously (as it will if the war lasts three years), our tins will go bad.

b) Mr Morrison's optimistic view of the nation's food stocks encourages Mother to dip into the reserve without making any replacements.

c) There is Mother's psychology too. She does not believe the war will be either a long or a serious business. 'I have not the slightest anxiety.'

The solution I offered Mother was that she should draw on the store cupboard freely until Christmas. I will then make an inventory and buy fresh purchases to bring our stock up to the same point of strength as it stands at the present moment. Over lunch I tried to sum up the position and nearly shocked Mother out of her wits. My words were: 'Mr Morrison's optimism is most reassuring. Nevertheless, while we think we are going to win the war, that does not mean to say that we shall.' Mother unfortunately thought this was a quotation from Mr Morrison. Whatever Mother thinks about the future it has always included the utter destruction of Nazism. Of course I believe we shall win the war, but I don't exclude other possibilities.

I have never known such darkness. I wore the white cape which I purchased about five weeks ago in anticipation of this danger in the winter months. I felt so much safer in it.

THURSDAY, 2 NOVEMBER

Christopher Tomlin
I saw swastikas chalked on the walls. There are nine poster spaces to let in Addison Road. I've never seen them vacant before.

FRIDAY, 3 NOVEMBER

Tilly Rice
I believe a number of the self-evacuees have returned to their own homes, as I hope to do myself once the 'coming event' is over. One lady staying at the local hotel is reported as having been overheard telephoning her husband in London, apparently suggesting that she should return and wailing when he disapproved of the idea. 'Yes, but what is the use of being safe if you aren't *happy*!'

The Hamburg news in English has produced some smiles and some indignation. And the speculation that the announcer is Baillie-Stewart has given rise to some indignant contempt [Norman Baillie-Stewart, previously imprisoned in the Tower of London for treason]. Mrs X was wondering 'whether these Englishmen who are announcers in Germany really believe Germany's rightness or are just mercenary . . . ' My own view of the Hamburg propaganda is that at times it is very clever, being partially truthful and very difficult to refute, but at other times it is positively school-girlish.

The maid who had hysterics when her young man was called up is to have a war wedding in a week's time, that is if he is available for the wedding. Her young man, while supposed to be guarding a bridge, was found off his beat and smoking a cigarette with several others.

Christopher Tomlin

It is beautiful and calm. No mention of war beyond my advising customers to choose a light-weight paper as it would cost less to write to overseas troops.

When I came home I was overjoyed to find Dick there. He was bound for 'somewhere unknown' and had four days' leave. As he had just been inoculated against typhoid at Padgate he wasn't too well. Mother, Dad and I were glad to see Dick, but damnably sorry he was going away; we all thought he would be posted in England. And now he was off we all thought he was going to Egypt or Canada; it was wishful thinking I know, but we are a united family and try to put a brave face on partings.

Pam Ashford

Miss Bousie thinks the soldiers are safer in the trenches than we are in the cities. I said that soldiers don't give way to panic, as I dread would happen here in time of air raid. Judging by conversations I don't think that any great degree of resilience can be placed on civilian morale. It is not bad, but it is not strikingly high. People who express fear beforehand, of course, often face up to things heroically when the time comes. Miss Bousie has great faith in her countrymen's morale in time of peril. I said I certainly wanted to see the children out of the way, and we both deplored the return of so many evacuees. Of course, in the suburbs where people live in villas the children's position is not so bad. But I dread what may happen in congested areas like Anderson, Bridgeton, etc. Miss Bousie said that a teacher told her that 80% of them had returned to Parkhead. The ones who stay in the country are the children from the villas and the ones who return are the children from the congested areas.

SATURDAY, 4 NOVEMBER

Christopher Tomlin

I went on my usual Saturday errands: at the paper shop two women asked for indoor fireworks and were disappointed to hear the man reply: 'I'm sorry we are sold out. We have some Joy Bombs – full of kiddies' toys.'

SUNDAY, 5 NOVEMBER

Eileen Potter

Rise at about 6.15, as I have to be at a school in Hammersmith at 7.30 to assemble a party of children to be evacuated to Somerset. It is just getting light as I arrive. We stow ourselves in the coach as best we can and finally set out at about 9 o'clock. There are 24 children, a voluntary escort and myself, and also the driver's grown-up daughter, who is travelling with us as far as Wiltshire. I make room for myself amongst the luggage on the back seat. We have about 140 miles' journey ahead of us. Most of the children are rather big, but there is a sprinkling of smaller ones, including an unaccompanied three-year-old, who turns out to be the great success of the party, chatting and laughing all the way, except when asleep.

One boy embarks upon a vivid description of the film *The Spy in Black*, but becomes involved in an argument with another boy regarding some of the details of the plot. Another boy keeps asking questions about rabbits, pheasants, etc. in the various parts of the country. It transpires that he has been given an air-gun as a present before leaving and wants to know what he may shoot with it. Going along the Great West Road, we are stopped for a few minutes by a 'speed cop', as we have been slightly exceeding 30 miles an hour.

When we get about as far as Slough, the first complaints of sickness are heard. There is a family party, two brothers and a sister, sitting near the front of the coach together. One of the boys sets the ball rolling, and he and his sister keep on being sick in turn at intervals throughout the journey. The younger sister of one of the technical school girls boasts that she is never sick, but that her elder sister always feels sick when travelling by coach. The big girl says that she thinks that she will be all right, but ultimately succumbs, and is sick two or three times. Fairly frequent stops have to be made to empty the receptacles provided.

At last we reach our destination, a small watering-place on the Bristol Channel. By now it has begun to rain, and a chilly wind is blowing. The place looks rather desolate, and I feel that I could not blame the children if they wanted to go straight home again. It appears that the three-year-old has lost her gas-mask on the journey. A search is made under the seats of the coach but it is nowhere to be found. The children are gradually taken to their billets. I have arranged to spend the night with some friends in Glastonbury, and prevail upon the driver to drop me there on the way back. I find a good tea awaiting me. My former landlady, Mrs F, is staying at the farm with her cat 'Moses', whom I have not seen since he was 'evacuated' at the beginning of the war. He ignores me, however.

Christopher Tomlin
Today is the Feast of Christ the Kind. Mother to Dick and me: 'Whatever you do don't tell your father, he'd fly up in the air, but the ham I bought cost 4/-! I've only got as much as I buy normally for 2/3!'

Pam Ashford
Coming home I saw chalked on a side-street off Jamaica Street an invitation to a meeting to be addressed by Harry Pollitt (Communist). It ran, 'War is a grand thing for the fireside patriot, who sells guns, gas-masks, torch lights, bombs . . . '

Arising from an article in the *Express*, Mother and I had an argument about the restricted hospital services. She cannot see any sense in keeping beds free for air raid casualties when it is clear there won't be any air raids.

MONDAY, 6 NOVEMBER

Christopher Tomlin
Dick's gone. He phoned for a taxi and left at 11. I miss him! Mother told me to buy an ounce of Four Square Yellow Label tobacco before Dick went away: she slipped it into his kit bag secretly, so it will be a pleasant surprise when he's overseas. One lady remarked: 'It won't be a very happy Christmas for a lot of people!' It won't for us.

Just had a brainwave. I will advise parents and wives of men on active service to send gifts of writing paper, printed with regimental numbers.

Pam Ashford

During the morning the subject of air raids was brought up. Miss Smith said Hitler would not raid our towns because he did not want his bombed in return. I said I could not agree; he had not raided us yet because it had not suited. I thought the risk was grave. I said that his peculiar mentality might find pleasure in the thought of humiliating us on the day when his nation was humiliated (Armistice Day). This remark produced a degree of horror for which I was quite unprepared. It was quite apparent that people who go about saying there will be no raids, don't in their hearts believe it.

Miss Bousie enjoyed a talk on a German station last night on 'British Hypocrisy'. I said, 'I would not waste my time on listening to propaganda from the deputy of the father of lies.' I meant Goebbels, but she thought I meant Hitler. She said she liked to see a man getting his due. He had done wonders for his country.

TUESDAY, 7 NOVEMBER

Pam Ashford

About 10 o'clock there was a noisy hooter on the river that blared away for about ten minutes. It distressed practically everyone in the place. Is it an air-raid warning? No. Yes, it is. No, it isn't. At tea it got discussed again. The old question arose, 'Where to go in an air raid?' A fortnight ago I decided that I would stay in the office and screen myself from falling glass by getting under a table. Miss Crawford and Miss Carswell think that the concussion would bring the building down, but I cannot believe that thick stone walls would fall as easily as that.

The butter scarcity is a subject of conversation everywhere. This morning I said, 'To eat margarine would not cause me distress.'

Miss Smith said: 'Middle-class people, if forced to eat margarine, would not mind but they would want Stork at 8d, and that cannot be had. There is only one brand at 6d.' There was general consent that what was wrong with the Food Control was that it was in the hands of men.

Mr Roxburgh says, 'I have a note here for the salaries of those employed on Censoring duties. Since the war I have been doing nothing but cutting bits out of the papers.'

While he goes through his pockets Miss Bousie says, 'It must make you a very entertaining member of your household.'

He says, 'No. I am a big man here, but I am a very small man in the house.'

He proceeds to read the salaries out: 'One, £1,200. Imagine that! Two, £950. Nine Hundred and Fifty Pounds!' So on through about 20 appointments. 'But the best bit is still to come. £3.10/- a week for examining clerks. The men who do the work get £3.10/-. All those others with their hundreds and doing nothing! That makes me boil. And the Ministry of Information. The salaries! It's a scandal. Young men doing office boys' work for £500 a year.'

Firework display by Miss Bousie. Miss Bousie: 'This war is run to swell dividends.'

Privately, I am beginning to think that patriotism in Glasgow is as cheap as stinking mackerel.

I told Mr Mitchell about Mr Roxburgh's sentiments. He thinks he is right. 'The war is run by financiers,' says Mr Mitchell. 'Do you want the war? No. Does the working man want the war? No. It is the moneyed boys who want the war. It is the same in Germany. Do you think Harry Jacob wants the war? Or Fraulein Deutschmann?'

There is a story going about that all the plate glass in many Jewish shops has been scratched with insulting remarks.

WEDNESDAY, 8 NOVEMBER

Pam Ashford

Mr Mitchell and I got talking of Healthy Life biscuits. I said I have two large tins so that when the bread supply breaks down we can draw on our biscuits.

Mr Mitchell said, 'The bread supply won't break down. Not while we have the British Navy.'

I said how moved I am to see so many sailors in Glasgow. A sailor in uniform was something that did not happen here until recently. It is just like being in Devonport or Portsmouth. They look so miserable all hanging about the dimly-lit streets in the rain, not knowing what to do with themselves. I long to say to some of them,

'I'm from Devonshire too.' One day I saw one of them with HMS *Victory* on his hat and I wanted to tell him, 'I am from Portsmouth too.' (Portsmouth father, Devonshire mother; born in Portsmouth, brought up in Plymouth.)

THURSDAY, 9 NOVEMBER

Tilly Rice
Great interest in the rumour that is going round this morning that Hitler has narrowly escaped assassination by means of a time-bomb. So far the report is unauthenticated, but the one o'clock news bulletin is awaited with interest. Great hope about that Hitler will get bumped off eventually born of the conviction that his death would mean the instant cessation of the war.

Christopher Tomlin
Never be a canvasser Tom Harrisson and Charles Madge, it's the rottenest job in the world! I know!

I canvassed Powis Road and reaped 2/-. As I am the main bread-winner – Dad's on the dole, my brother's abroad and keeping what bit he earns – I told myself, 'I've blasted well got to succeed!' So I walked a mile into my next district and canvassed like a black; I went home with 14/6 in my book.

Letter from Dick to say he is going with five more RAF Wireless Operators to France. He told mum, 'Don't worry!'

There was a violent argument between Mother and Dad. We are expecting a bill for notepaper from my local wholesaler. Dad thought Mum was putting something on one side each week; Mother thought Dad was keeping something out. The bill will be for £3.10.0. It will be paid as soon as it comes, but as we have no capital I wonder how? Our total weekly income is £3.15.0 now.

Hitler escaped a violent end by 30 minutes. He had just finished spouting in a beer-house when there was a terrific explosion. My insurance agent smiled and agreed with me when I said: 'What a pity it didn't explode sooner!' There is widespread regret that Hitler wasn't bumped off.

I was thinking over this queer escape when a sixth sense murmured, 'It's a frame up!' And when I read the newspaper account again (none of the Old Guard were injured) it struck me it was another Reichstag Fire: Hitler planned it to get rid of some unpleasant folk.

Pam Ashford

An attack was made on Hitler's life at Munich last night! Everyone expressed pleasure, coupled with the regret that Hitler was not killed. Miss Bousie showed concern for the six Nazis killed and the sixty injured.

Mr Mitchell said, 'I still think Hitler won't be in power by the end of the war. In other words, he is on the downhill.' Later in the morning I heard him say to a friend over the phone, 'Germany is cracking up. I always said she would. On the day the war broke out I made a bet with a fellow at the Exchange that the war will be over by the end of this year, and I think I shall win.'

In so far as I have had time for reflection the following thoughts have been drifting through my mind:

1) Can this Munich crime be the Reichstag business again, i.e. the Nazis did it themselves to make propaganda out of it?

2) In any case someone will be blamed. The Jews? The Monarchists? The British?

3) If the Jews, there will, I suppose, be another pogrom. If the British, then I suppose all the long-foretold horrors are to break.

4) Is Hess [reported killed by the bomb] so important as to put the theory of the Nazis being behind the crime out of the question? I have heard of Hess as the Fuhrer's 'echo'. Well, an 'echo' can be spared.

5) Can it be that Armistice Day is a day of special danger? Could they say, 'You murdered Hess on our big day, we will retaliate on your big day?' No, I don't think there's any cause of anxiety on that point.

FRIDAY, 10 NOVEMBER

Christopher Tomlin

Last night my throat troubled me so I gargled with Permanganate of Potash this morning. But all day my throat was stiff and hot.

My orders came in yesterday and two-thirds were delivered this morning, late afternoon and evening. My customers were delighted; two or three 'same again'.

I came home and met my ration card, it arrived while I was away.

It was amusing to hear the criticisms of Mother and Father.

Dad: 'What idiotic rot! It's a jigsaw, they want something better to do . . .'

Mum: 'Meat's not rationed, lards and cooking fats aren't, margarine isn't. Only sugar, butter, bacon and ham.'

Their further remarks were scathing. The names of shop-keepers are all together and it means your shopping isn't private for the shopman can see where you go and could be nasty. For instance, we buy butter at Masons and margarine at the Maypole.

Mother read about our troops in France having their own printed Christmas cards. Father: 'I don't think the troops will be coming home on Christmas leave, or sending Christmas cards. It looks as if they will be in the thick of it by then.' He's right: Holland has mobilised.

Pam Ashford

Miss Bousie began the day with the remark: 'Never in my life have I read a poorer speech than Mr Chamberlain's. Not an inspired word in it! Gutless!'

I said, 'The ability to speak is an asset, but still a premier's job is to run the country not to make speeches. I myself think he's a fine man.' Miss Bousie: 'He is a man of good character, I agree, but utterly unsuited for the responsibilities of premiership.'

Miss Carswell hates Germans. I said those I had met were very nice, though they all belonged to the intellectual class and might therefore not be representative. Miss Carswell said, 'Mr Eckermann was representative. Just the lowest of the low.' Miss Crawford began to sneer at me for fraternising with the Germans.

SATURDAY, 11 NOVEMBER

Eileen Potter

Celebrate Armistice Day rather appropriately by going to see the film of *Goodbye Mr Chips*, which is excellent, but makes me feel very weepy, especially in the parts about the last war.

Christopher Tomlin

Armistice Day. Most laughable. In past years I relied on the sirens to know the two minutes' silence; I had forgotten that now we are at war all sirens must be quiet unless there's a raid, so I missed keeping the silence through a lapse of memory. Never mind, I can say a prayer.

I heard the Queen broadcasting, she was very good indeed. Mum: 'You wouldn't think she was Scotch.'

I listened to Hamburg at 11.20. They gave accounts of social injustice in Britain from accounts in the *Daily Mail* and *Sunday Express*. The accounts are true, worse luck. Both Father and I think such events are a disgrace. Dad said: 'Chamberlain has always been against increased old age pensions.' Present old age pensions are a damned disgrace! Mr Chamberlain should try to live on them.

Pam Ashford

Mr Mitchell opened the conversation this morning with 'Germany will invade Holland today. They have not observed their neutrality properly. It is just the old German game over again. They will bomb us today too.'

I had expected the silence to be observed and called attention to the clock at 10.58. Miss Smith said there was no official silence and it was left to the individual. Miss Bousie stood beside me at the window and Miss Smith, Margaret and Betty joined us. There was no observance of the silence in the street. It would appear that the silence was not observed in any other room in the office.

I visited the Cosmo (*Zauber der Boheme*). The darkness was intense, and the bus journey was difficult. Only occasionally did it become possible to see anything. I felt so frightened at one point. Had I gone too far? Then people began to say, 'We are going uphill. It must be University Avenue.' I got out on the platform and said to a man there, 'Is this North Gardner Street?' He said, 'It feels like the gusset' (you would need to see the land to understand his meaning). At last the bus stopped outside my home (188 is a corner and is called North Gardner Street by the bus men). With my torch I recognised the kerbstones and got out confidently. The bus conductor said, 'Where are we?' and I said, 'North Gardner Street,' and the man began to shout it all through the bus.

The Queen spoke on the wireless. She has a beautiful voice, yet she sounds nervous too.

SUNDAY, 12 NOVEMBER

Pam Ashford

I have decided to get a pixie hat. Yesterday afternoon I purposely went without an umbrella because I cannot but believe that an umbrella would be inconvenient in a black-out and capes don't lend themselves to umbrella-carrying when you already have both hands full with attaché case and handbag. I wore an ancient hat yesterday resigned to its ruin.

Later in the day I commented upon Mother's unwillingness to carry her mask. She said, 'The time I carried it when getting on the tram a fat woman pushed against it and it twisted round the post on the platform and then twirled round the fat woman and me; it was a dangerous position, and so I said, "Never again".'

MONDAY, 13 NOVEMBER

Christopher Tomlin

Mass at St Austin's, 11.30 a.m. In devotional mood. Canon Prescott of this church has arranged, by request of the Catholics in Preston, to give each Preston Catholic soldier a spiritual kit. It will be a rosary, prayer book, Sacred Heart badge and medals. He is of course seeing to bodily comforts as well. Now at the back of St Austin's is a collecting-box marked 'For Spiritual Kit' and we are asked to be as generous as possible.

I dusted the living room, my bedroom, the stairs and hall as I always do on Sundays. Wrote a letter to a friend in France (as my letters pleased friends in the past it might be a good thing to write to Tommies overseas. I can try to cheer them up with notes and views from the Home Front). The boy I wrote to writes: 'To meet a respectable girl here you must be properly introduced . . . there are many juicy pieces but I have no desire to make friends with them.' I commend his Christian attitude. It is so easy to go astray.

Pam Ashford

Me: 'So the invasion of Holland has not happened yet, Miss Bousie.'

Miss Bousie: 'You have been all wrong in your calculations.'

Me: 'I hope we have been wrong in our calculations, but it may be that we are only wrong in the date. Did you listen to Mr Churchill last night?'

Miss Bousie: 'No, I will not listen to him. Revenge hurts me as an individual, and I don't wish to listen to Mr Churchill.'

Me: 'He is not going to give way, but that is not revenge.'

Miss Bousie: 'I don't like the hard things he says.'

Me: 'It is the only way to handle the Nazis. It's the language they understand.'

Miss Crawford does not approve of Mr Churchill. She thinks it was like a backyard quarrel. It has lowered British prestige.

Mr Mitchell: 'I liked Churchill's speech. I wonder how the Germans will react. He was very tantalising. It was hot stuff. Goering will be wild. There will be a crack-up in Germany. They are on the wrong lines.'

Miss Smith: 'I was disappointed and I felt that we were coming down. Probably they do understand that language better, but it is a pity to descend to their level.'

Mr Hutchison says (I think in the belief that he was conforming to the prevailing opinion): 'A most unfortunate speech. It smelt too much like their own methods. He should have kept his dignity. (Noting my astonishment). Oh. I myself enjoyed it thoroughly!'

After work I bought the pixie oilskin hat. I spent the evening doing German homework.

TUESDAY, 14 NOVEMBER

Eileen Potter

Arrive at the office to find a whole family in possession of our room. The vicar of a country town in Somerset has requested to have particularly difficult cases for evacuation sent to him. Here is a woman who has been ill-treated by her husband and has just obtained a separation from him. The vicar has brought his car to take her and her three small children to Somerset. He has also to collect one or two specially naughty boys whom he has also agreed to take. We boil a kettle and help Mrs X to mix food for her baby, and generally try to keep the children amused and tolerably quiet until the vicar is ready to take them away. At last they and all their luggage, including babies' gas-masks, etc. are stowed away in his overloaded car, and we wave goodbye to them from the steps.

Christopher Tomlin

Yesterday there was an air raid on the Shetlands; 12 bombs fell. Most of them dropped into the sea. Those that fell on land made craters 9 to 10 feet deep. The announcer said the only real casualty was a rabbit, which by some strange feat of Nazi magic was changed into 'two flying boats'.

Pam Ashford

A duplicated letter arrived from the Coal Exporters' Association pointing out that we must be careful what we say about the movements of boats. The Government naturally does not want U-Boats to know when convoys will be emerging from their respective ports. It's so obvious and yet it never struck me before.

In August I stunned Mother by buying two hot water bottles for our store cupboard. Since then I have seen the price rise from 2/6 to 2/11. Today Mother's burst.

WEDNESDAY, 15 NOVEMBER

Christopher Tomlin

I was upset by this incident: a customer whom I served in the past was very curt when I called today to show her Christmas presents. She pettishly remarked: 'No, I haven't the time to look at them, I'm busy!'

Me: 'But I've one thing you must see, printed Christmas cards at 2/- a dozen.'

'I'm not sending anything this year, my boy's in the Army. I've spent pounds on educating him to be a teacher, and just as he's passed he's called up. The war hasn't done any good to me!' I told her there were others hit as badly as she was and that we had to grin and bear it. She then ejaculated: 'It won't help me to a living!'

Me to another customer: 'I've a brother in the Royal Air Force. He's in France.'

'How funny. I'm just knitting socks for them.'

Pam Ashford

Mr Mitchell says: 'There is a quietness in the air. I mean politically.' Later (with gusto): 'Do you listen to Tommy Handley?'

Me: 'Tommy Handley, Good Lord, No! I turn the set off as quickly as possible. Of all rotten comedians, Tommy Handley is the rottenest.'

Mr Mitchell: 'What about Big Hearted Arthur?'

Me: 'Who is he?'

Mr Mitchell: 'You know, in *Bandwagon.*'

Me: '*Bandwagon!* I have heard bits from it a significant number of times to know that I never wish to hear it again. BBC comedians are terrible.'

Mr Mitchell (with delight): 'Oh, they lift you out of yourself.'

Me: 'I must say I like Davy Burnaby. Gillie Potter is amusing. But Mother cannot understand Gillie Potter's jokes in the slightest. I explain them to her afterwards and she says they don't sound funny to her.'

Yesterday evening Mother told me in shocked tones that on a school facing the Infirmary is a notice that says 'Female Cleansing', which she took to be a reference to our notoriously verminous children. Quite a lot of buildings have this outside (all the baths have) and I explained to Mother about mustard gas and the need for decontamination. The whole subject was completely new to her.

In a shop near the College I bought a 3/6 gas mask carrier, with a zip-fastener. I have stuck faithfully to the haversack till now, becoming increasingly conscious that haversacks are 7 or 8 weeks out of fashion. I still think a haversack is best because in it I can carry first aid equipment, a flasher, matches, pixie oilskin hat . . . and also MO diary. However, the white cape (which will soon be in use every night) on top of the haversack is just a bit too clumsy.

THURSDAY, 16 NOVEMBER

Eileen Potter

I still have a few days' holiday due to me, left over from the summer, so I arrange to take two days now. I go to my West End hairdresser in the morning, and then go to John Lewis' and buy some rubbery black-out material, black on one side and green on the other, to match the paint in my sitting-room. It hangs quite nicely, but has a strong, rubbery smell.

I make one or two more small purchases, and then take a bus to Vauxhall Park, where I have arranged to meet Mrs F at a small whist-drive got up by some friends of hers in aid of their local church. The players pay a shilling each and the prizes are packets of groceries, with a small box of chocolates for the 'booby'. Nearly all the players are elderly women (one of whom brings her Pekingese), with a sprinkling of elderly men, and I feel about the youngest person in the room. We have a short interval for refreshments, and the conversation runs mainly on the heavy taxes which the middle-classes have to pay. The vicar comes to present the prizes. We do not win anything.

Pam Ashford
Went to the German class again tonight. There are six day-school pupils who have a very slight knowledge of German, a man of about 28, who is quite proficient already, and Mrs Murr, the German refugee who is learning English.

Afterwards I went into the Common Room with Mrs Murr. She waits there for her husband. I have been through the classes in shipping and shipping law and have the lectures typewritten; I offered to bring the papers in for her husband. It must be difficult for a foreigner who is learning English to take decent notes in a class like that. She feels too that her husband would benefit from the notes.

She told me something of their experiences in unemotional, dispassionate, restrained tones with tremors that showed how deeply they had suffered. She had a business of her own that was in the family for 150 years and the Nazis just took it away from her. Her husband was a forwarding agent and he was thrown out too. Every piece of furniture in their home was smashed to pieces so that you could not tell one piece from another. They had thought at first they would stick things out as they might improve, but after November (1938) it was hopeless. Things were horrible. About half a dozen times she used the words 'After November' with deep feelings. They did not want to go away because they had their parents, her mother and his father. Now her mother is away, but her father-in-law is still in Germany. They have relatives in America and are waiting here until they are allowed to go there; in America they will be allowed to earn their livings. Her husband wants to be a forwarding agent there. They don't want much, just enough to live. They don't know when they will be able to go, perhaps in a fortnight, perhaps in a month. I said that the Americans are kind people. She said, 'You don't get kindness in business anywhere. It will be so difficult. We only want enough to live on.'

She is going to classes in English and commercial practice. Her husband is taking many classes both by day and night – shorthand, typewriting, bookkeeping, cost accounts, business methods, shipping, transport, English (and perhaps some others). He works so hard studying that she gets quite worried. They lived in Nuremberg, but her husband is a Hamburger. She is obviously fond of Germany. Of course I told her about my German friends. Privately I shall be glad when she's gone to America for I feel that the resentment that used to be limited to the Nazis is now spreading to all Germans.

In the west was the crescent moon. How I have missed her in the last fortnight.

FRIDAY, 17 NOVEMBER

Eileen Potter

I do a little local shopping in the morning, and find a local chiropodist to come and cut my corns. I usually have this done by a friend, but she is also a nurse and is now away in the country with a patient. In the afternoon, Mrs F and I take Mrs H to the first house of *Me and My Gal* at the Victoria Palace. It is the third time I have seen it, but it is one of the few light shows that I could bear the idea of seeing at the time of the crisis last year, and I thought I would like to see how it was wearing now, and also to hear the new parts about the Siegfried Line, etc. The first part seems to hang fire a bit now, but by the end of the play I decide that it is still wearing as well as ever. The circle is not by any means full, but there are large numbers of men in khaki down below, and one of the boxes is occupied by a group of officers. After the show, I go straight to the folk dancing. Mrs C, the wife of the instructor, appears tonight.

Christopher Tomlin

We are very anxious because we haven't heard from Dick since he went to France; he promised to send a letter the moment he got there.

Pam Ashford

I told Miss Bousie about Mrs Murr's experiences. Miss Bousie said, 'When *will* they rise against it!' I said, 'So far as the Jews are concerned, there is no rising against it, the only thing to do is to get out.' Continuing I said, 'Mrs Murr said all their furniture was smashed up.' Miss Bousie: 'Oh there is that hooligan element everywhere. You would get the same thing here.'

Seeing me jotting down Miss Gibson's remarks, Mr Mitchell said he thought MO was no use. It is not representative. 'You just go on reporting what a few intellectuals think and never hear a word on the working-class point of view.' I said the sentiments found in my diary were not representative of the country but of a very small, narrow group, but I thought that many such diaries would form a really representative composite picture; also that analysis issued from time to time suggested that there were quite a number of working-class people in the movement. I expressed the view that a 'certain danger sometimes occurs to me. Diary writing appeals to introverts rather than extroverts. The composite picture may show an excessive degree of introspection.'

Long talk on margarine. 'I cannot take margarine at all – it would upset my stomach completely.' 'It is said that by melting it and mixing it with butter, it is possible to eat it.' 'Well, there's a war on, and if you aren't asked to do anything more than reduce butter, you aren't asked to do much.'

Mr Mitchell suggested that I should send Christmas cards to my German friends via our Danish agent. I pointed out that this is illegal, and in any case Christmas cards to neutrals have to be sent direct from the printers, as the War Office fears the ordinary routine can be used to send secret messages. I said that if the opportunity came I should be sorely tempted to ask Mrs Murr to send the messages from New York. Mr Mitchell wondered what Fraulein Deutschman is doing. I said, 'Poor soul. But of course, it is possible that she is saying, "Poor Pam, living in that decadent democracy . . ."'

SATURDAY, 18 NOVEMBER

Christopher Tomlin

A pass-round came from the Secretary of the British Amateur Press Association. (The BAPA is a body of enthusiastic scribblers who write for joy. The 'pass-round' is a collection of articles, stories, poems and drawings which passes round through the post from member to member. For more information apply to Clifford Russell – Hon. Sec. 'Sark', 17 Baston Road, Hayes, Kent.)

I came home and thank God a letter arrived from Dick while I was away. He is comfortable and happy, wine costs 2d a bottle, tobacco is half our prices. The French are very cheerful and polite, they cannot do enough for the RAF and the Tommies. Dick has been supplied with thigh boots, for he says, 'The rainy season has begun and the mud is 10 inches deep!'

Aunty Ivy came for tea. I went for the tarts and papers and returned hoping to listen-in, but Ivy was busy with the *People* crossword puzzle. 'What do you think this word will be, Chris?!!!' I hate and detest her crosswords; for the past ten years she has done them without success. Whenever I've gone down it's been, 'What do you think this will be?' Tonight she bought Dick 3/6 worth of sweets and got a tin to pack 'em in, so I can forgive her.

Pam Ashford

I came up the stairs with Mr Fuller, who lives overhead and happens to be the Coal Export Officer. He said, 'I see you carry your mask.' (And so does he.) I said, 'I *always* do, no matter how short a time I am to be out.' Mr Fuller said, 'I said I should sack anyone in the office who did not carry his, so I have *got* to carry mine. I have never seen it out since I got it from the school (i.e. the distribution in October 1938). I should not know what to do with it.' I said, 'It is as well to find out how it fits and wear it long enough to discover that you really can't breathe in it.'

MONDAY, 20 NOVEMBER

Christopher Tomlin

Fine and frosty. I took our first parcel for Dick to the Post Office. A customer: 'I wouldn't mind how long the war lasted if I knew all the boys would come home.'

Me: 'I don't think there will be the bloodshed of the last war.'

Customer: 'I've been told that before.'

A bomber circled overhead for about two hours from 2 to 4. From what I hear the planes seen since the war began are merely practising.

The buggers are laying mines: 10 vessels destroyed this weekend. U-Boats lay the eggs. Father: 'This may be Hitler's secret weapon . . . you remember he said it was something that couldn't be used against him? If this mine-laying goes on it may destroy our fleet . . . in our own sea too.'

TUESDAY, 21 NOVEMBER

Christopher Tomlin
Just seen STOP THE WAR chalked on a wall; it gives me a feeling of disgust. I would have rubbed it off but passers-by would think I was a crank or responsible for chalking it on.

Three Nazi bombers flew, or tried to, over England today. THEY DIDN'T GET FAR.

Pam Ashford
Dinner of tea and bread and butter was being discussed. I said, 'We cannot have that for 3 or 5 years. We should become inefficient through malnutrition.' Everyone said, 'What has 3 or 5 years to do with it?' I said, 'The Government are preparing for 3 years and the Nazis for 5 years.' It turns out that everyone in the premises thinks the war will be over within 2 or 3 months.

WEDNESDAY, 22 NOVEMBER

Eileen Potter
The treatment centre at Hammersmith is about to re-open for minor ailment cases, so I spend most of the morning looking up some of the children who used to attend my Special Ear Clinic and telling them that treatment for discharging ears can be obtained there. I am received with open arms by one mother, who seems really pleased to see a familiar face at the Centre once again, and proceeds to show me all the spots both she and her child have developed.

In the evening I go to the Strand Corner House to meet the Secretary of the Business and Professional Women's Club, who wants to discuss our future programme with me. This is my first visit to one of the big Corner Houses since the beginning of the war, and I notice very little difference in the menu, price or clientele, except that a large proportion of the latter are now in uniform. Perhaps the orchestra has now a smaller repertoire, as they play 'Franklin D. Roosevelt Jones' twice during the time we are sitting there talking.

Christopher Tomlin
Quite a row between Dad and me. He said, 'The Navy is going to seize German exports. Why should we interfere with neutrals who

have nothing to do with the war? The whole world will condemn the seizure of German exports as they did in the Great War.'

I spiritedly replied, 'What the hell do neutrals expect? To make money like America did in the last War? This is a just war we're fighting, and neutrals must not grumble at what we do!'

'Don't talk rot, the neutrals have to live!' And so on.

Father angers me; when I give my opinion it's, 'Be a little more correct,' or 'You want to think before you speak,' or 'Your judgement is shallow.'

My local printer, who supplies me with printed notepapers as well as printing papers I supply, put his prices up 25 per cent on Monday. Today my out-of-town printers inform me their prices are up 2d in the 1/-. I cannot stand these increases so am obliged to pass them on. As my present sample-book has old prices in, father made up another this morning.

A lady on the bus, whom I knew, said the service was disgraceful; it wasn't the same in other towns. I was interested to hear her opinion of the ATS. 'Those girls are having a very good time; they throw themselves in the way of any man.'

Me: 'Yes, but I must say the ATS look very smart, except the fat ones.'

Pam Ashford

Office conversation today seems to have been balanced between the horror of the mining of ships and Mr Mitchell's scoop. From 1912/1914 Mr Mitchell knew a German called Herr Dietze, who had married a Scotswoman and had a youngster, Roderich (born 1909). Mr M visited their house at Randolph Gardens, Broomhill, Glasgow. In July 1914 the family went to Germany. Herr D joined the German Army, was wounded at Galicia; Frau D has lived in Hamburg since July 1914. She and Roderich had a rough time in the First German War. Three or four years ago Mr M heard that the boy was an announcer in Germany. Recently when listening to Lord Haw Haw, Mr Mitchell was surprised to hear him pronounce the name 'Menzies' not in the BBC manner (i.e. as spelt) but in the Scottish manner (i.e. rhymes with 'thing is'). Putting two and two together, it dawned on Mr M that Roderich Dietze and Lord Haw Haw are one and the same individual.

Yesterday he called at the *News* office and they are developing the story. They have found the record of Roderich's birth; the police have supplied their records of his father; people have been traced in Broomhill who knew the child. A woman there could point to the very stones on which the child had once grazed his knees. The *News* are to publish the story tomorrow. I was always under the impression that Lord Haw Haw was Baillie-Stewart.

Today having been very wet, I wore my black-out equipment all day, i.e. white waterproof cape and pixie hat. These seem to cause astonishment to the staff.

THURSDAY, 23 NOVEMBER

Christopher Tomlin

Somebody is emptying his chamber; it is sheeting down. Another letter from Dick, amazingly well written for a mechanical mind. Dick is cheerful and contented; he waited for this war for eighteen months so is ready to get the most from it. From his mention of climate and scenery I surmise he is somewhere by the Mediterranean. It is 'sunny and warm as an English summer's day'. Wish I was there.

What Dad was certain would occur, has. Holland made a violent protest against the British Contraband Control, concluding that if they are no longer able to supply Germany with foodstuffs and raw materials as before they refuse to supply Britain and France! Wuff, Wuff! But it is deadly serious for the small countries which must export and import or perish. Part of the fouled train of war.

The *Daily Mail* wants to know why lone Nazi planes fly over here and thinks it may be the prelude to mass air attacks, but the BBC observer with the RAF said yesterday, 'Mass air attacks are not an economic possibility for this country . . . too many losses.' All I know is air raids are more and more frequent.

Yesterday a woman asked me to call with Christmas cards at lunchtime today for she wanted her husband to see. I called today in the downpour – a 10 minute walk – and was greeted with, 'I've changed my mind, I won't bother with them.' It is mortifying. What does she think I am?

Pam Ashford

The *Record* (morning paper belonging to the *News*' proprietors) has a paragraph about Roderich Dietze (with reproduction of his birth

94

certificate). It is a much smaller feature than we expected. I told Mr Mitchell that I thought they were holding up the rest of his story for Friday and Saturday.

The *News* contains no reference at all to Roderich Dietze.

All last week I was looking forward to this week when there would be a full moon early in the evening. Tonight is the first time it has been clear and I have had my wish. A walk between 6.30 and 7 p.m., down Turnberry Avenue and up Clarence Drive! How light it was with the full moon above and how I loved to stretch my legs. If I live into post-war days this paragraph will make me smile. In previous years walks on winter evenings were always along busy shopping areas, but now there's a war on and I choose just about the dullest road in the neighbourhood because there I won't be harassed by the fear of being run over.

FRIDAY, 24 NOVEMBER

Eileen Potter

I go to the folk-dancing class in the evening as usual. The atmosphere is less stuffy than usual, and less suggestive of an air-raid shelter. There is also an unusually large proportion of men in the class tonight, and it occurs to me how sometimes this war seems like a queer sort of dream, so much like ordinary life sometimes. It is a moonlit night, and I take the tram over Westminster Bridge, admiring the appearance of the blacked-out Houses of Parliament.

Christopher Tomlin

Just read – I knew it would happen – a song dedicated to the Prime Minister and called 'God Bless You, Mr Chamberlain'. The author is Harry Roy and he says he has even received the Premier's consent, despite the lines which go:

> You'll look swell
> Holding an umbrella
> All the world loves
> A wonderful fella.

It makes me spew – what blasted rot!

A man sitting beside me in the bus carried a gas-mask. Another fellow entered and addressed the first: 'You won't get gassed today!'

First man: 'Do you wear your mask, Bob?'

'Only when I'm going down to town or out of it.'

First: 'What are you doing in the black-out?'

'Well, I go to the pictures and to a lecture once a week. And see all-in wrestling.'

First: 'Don't they get badly hurt?'

'No, it's acrobatics really. I've never seen any real violence.'

During the past two weeks I haven't carried my gas-mask. I don't think it's necessary. But tonight after listening to Lord Basil of Zeesen (Lord Haw Haw] I think it may be wanted, for the Nazis will hit back for our seizure of German exports.

Pam Ashford

On returning from the Exchange, Mr Mitchell told me that a U-boat had been sunk off Gourock, also that they had been dropping depth charges galore in the Firth of Clyde. I could not but say, 'It is horrible killing people like that. We are treating them like insects.' Mr Mitchell then told the story to the general office which began to buzz with exultation. I said, 'You will probably be expecting me to say that I don't accept the story until I have heard it officially from the BBC.' This seems to be the light in which I am generally regarded. On going back to our Department I said to Mr Mitchell, 'How is it that the Exchange knows so much more than the BBC does?' He said, 'It is because the BBC are so inefficient that they don't get to know things as quickly as men who are engaged in shipping.'

Miss Bousie bought a battery in a tailor's shop. 'It is the only thing they are doing. No one wants clothes.'

Mr Mitchell very despondent about future business. I said, 'But when the war gets properly underway, there will be plenty of work for good men.' He said, 'Don't you believe it. Look at the morning's paper. Minister of Pensions' daughter getting a job when more deserving people are out of work. All the boneheads of the world are put into the Controls just because of influence.'

Nothing in today's *News* about Roderich Dietze. Charlie says the newspaper offices have had about twenty people submitted to them as Lord Haw Haw, all complete with irrefutable testimonies.

The BBC did not have a talk after their 9 o'clock news and I idly turned the handle round, which is a thing I seldom do as I much prefer the BBC to the foreign stations. However, I idly turned the handle round and was startled to hear the famous Lord Haw Haw giving a news bulletin from Hamburg. I listened to the end, but I doubt if I shall bother about him again. He refers to the British cruiser (*Belfast*) which he alleged had been struck by a mine.

SATURDAY, 25 NOVEMBER

Tilly Rice
Tonight I overheard a fisherman say with great forcefulness, 'If I got 'old of a German spy I'd cut his bloody 'ead off!' And at that particular moment he really meant it, and would have been capable of such bloodthirsty action as any young Nazi sadist.

Since my last entry here (owing to exceptional circumstances – that is, a wife in a supposedly delicate state of health) my husband has been allowed a few days' leave to visit us. The two boys, not having seen their Daddy for three months, were in a wild state of excitement and went up in a car to Launceston to meet him. The eldest started talking the moment he met my husband on the platform and was still going strong an hour later when they arrived at home. One of the first things that struck me was my husband's preoccupation with his gas mask (mine lies more or less forgotten in the bottom of my wardrobe). It was carefully removed from his suitcase, placed on the dressing table, then, like its fellow, forgotten.

At first I thought I could detect signs of the stress and strain of these times in my husband (he seemed very strung up and inclined to talk rapidly and excitedly) but after a day or so the tranquil calm of this little place had its effect and he subsided into normality again. One thing I could not help noticing was that although he was usually a man of very definite opinion, he now seems to have no opinion at all, and when I, thirsting for a little enlightened discussion, tried to lead him on to tell me what he thought about things, I found he had very little thought for anything at all but the way his work was going at the Ministry.

Armistice Day down here was recognised with a service round the village war memorial and the depositing thereon of a wreath of poppies.

Christopher Tomlin

I read of two soldiers' wives sued for non-payment of rent. Judge: 'The landlord has no right to sue these women, he should sue the husbands.' The landlord asked how he could get satisfaction when the soldiers are in France. Judge: 'It's up to you!' While sympathising with soldiers' wives and mothers, I consider little landlords are treated abominably. If a man depends entirely on house rents to live and his tenants cannot pay because of war, it is the obvious duty of the Government to recompense him. We are in danger of forgetting that landlords – not all – are also human beings.

My local printing firm is happy-go-lucky. They haven't sent their statement through, and it should have arrived two months ago. Their bill will be £4.15.0. How it will be settled I don't know; but you can take it for granted it will be paid even if we go on starvation rations for a week or two. We always have met accounts immediately they were due and have no intention of escaping our obligations.

Really though it's the fault of the firm. Mum had the money ready in September and October, but when Dick joined up there were extra accounts of his to pay. His £3 isn't coming in and we feel the difference. Fortunately if the worst occurred and Dick or I died, Mum and Dad get £100; both of us have endowment policies payable even if either is killed in action or in an air raid. All furniture is our own and we are buying our home. We are a darned sight better off than many more. I have a splendid father who has had a raw deal; he still draws the 'dole' and has done for two years now. My mother is sweet, a damned good manager and a dear.

This morning in spite of the rain, vile to me but badly wanted by farmers and water boards, I walked two miles to deliver a few orders. I got 9 repeats and one cancellation. When I got back I was soaking although I'd worn macintosh legs. No sooner did I enter than Dad took out my sample books from the wet case and thundered: 'What the devil do you mean by taking these out on a day like this?' I was in no tender mood and there was a violent row. I am sorry for it now because I hate to feel sore with anyone. I try hard to practice my religion.

Pam Ashford

The 8 o'clock news contained a statement from the Admiralty that HMS *Belfast* had struck a mine.

Mr Ferguson learnt from an unimpeachable source that the keeper of the lighthouse in the Firth of Forth was arrested on Tuesday. He has been tapping naval messages and passing them on to the Germans. That is why there has been so much action in the Firth of Forth.

On mentioning this at home at lunchtime I was received with roars of derision from Charlie (and Mother also). This must be just about the most sceptical house in the kingdom. (About a year ago an inhabitant of Arbroath reported Charlie to the local police because he had seen him looking at a map of the town. Detectives followed Charlie about wherever he went that day and subsequently asked him for an explanation.)

Mother went to a military whist drive with her friend and neighbour Mrs Stewart. I felt that the bright moon made it fairly safe and I pointed out that from the Grand Hotel there is a way of reaching a bus stopping place which does not necessitate crossing the road. I am anything but desirous that Mother goes out alone at night. However, it was a joyous party, for their table was top and each came back with a prize.

SUNDAY, 26 NOVEMBER

Tilly Rice

A wet, windy day, confined to the house, and one curses from the bottom of one's heart the war and its makers for exiling one far from one's friends and interests. The only effect of the war that can be noticed today is the absence of the maid, whose marriage *did* come off a fortnight ago, in spite of the bridegroom's delinquencies. She has gone over to Saltash for the day to see her husband and incidentally to discuss the getting together of a small home. All the early war hysterics have now vanished and she appears able to discuss quite equably whether her husband is to be sent to the front or not.

Our ration books have arrived without a hitch and all registration with tradesmen completed. Up to now there has been no shortage of any kind of food.

MONDAY, 27 NOVEMBER

Christopher Tomlin

Eight poster spaces are bland in Strand Road. A giant one used to advertise Ethyl Petrol; it is strange to see nothing there. The posters that are on advertise cigarettes, cocoa, Sanatogen Tonic Wine, Nestlé Milk and stout.

The Germans intend to drop disease germs; they don't care what they do so long as Britain's wiped out. They will do it if their mines are a flop.

A wireless comedian: 'I'll give you my four most precious possessions in the world – a fountain pen and three torch batteries.' It seems impossible to buy batteries here. I bought two small home-made ones (made with cells from high-tension batteries), and when I tried to put them in my torch they were too small.

Mum: 'I wonder what we will do when the disease bombs are dropped; probably go about in oilskins.'

Dad: 'They will drop them in reservoirs.'

Pam Ashford

Miss Bousie came to work hot with indignation over Mr Chamberlain's speech. I asked what was wrong.

Miss Bousie: 'I will not approve of mothers' hearts being broken to satisfy a few greedy individuals.'

Me: 'But if the Hitler system is allowed to go on every woman in Europe will have their heart broken in the end. Under their teaching a woman is just a maternity machine. You don't want that idea to spread, surely?'

Miss Smith: 'Mr Chamberlain's speech amounted to this: Come on and do your damnedest. If you say to a bully, "Come on and hit me," he will hit you.'

Me: 'Nothing of the sort. If you face up to a bully, he takes to his heels and bolts.' (Office completely of the opposite opinion.)

Miss Bousie: 'The Conservative Party have let every opportunity slip for twenty years. No attempt has ever been made to settle Europe. If I felt like you I should join the Forces.'

Me: 'I filled up the National Service form in the way in which the booklet advised, and I have been told what my name has been put down for (War Office, Censorship Dept).'

Miss Bousie: 'But you have never done anything!'

Me: 'I have done what I was told to do, I can do no more. I am not conscious of the deflection of duty which you impute to me.'

Subsequently in the cloakroom I said to Miss Bousie that I did not think it fair to taunt me publicly with not joining the Forces, knowing as she does that I could not pass a medical examination.

Later: The Soroptimist Club. Mrs Allan, optician, has just begun to black out her house (she lives alone). She says, 'In our village there is a club, and the "members" go around late at night looking for chinks, and if they find one, the person concerned has to pay a forfeit by serving the whole party with tea.'

Conversation then turned on the knight who had committed suicide after murdering his wife 'because he was worried over the evacuees'. Someone said, 'In the last war a butcher in Bearsden committed suicide over the Government control forms. Dear knows how many people will commit suicide over this war. There are so many more forms.'

TUESDAY, 28 NOVEMBER

Christopher Tomlin

A row with Sidney who prints notepaper for me. He has been lax, and we parted friendly as a raven and a worm. I feel ready to finish with him; I didn't pick the quarrel, he was waiting for me. He is paid the moment he brings the goods; but as he is 27 (18 in intelligence) and has a friend who urges him to 'get as much out of them as you can', he is impossible.

Saw *Lambeth Walk* at Empress. A very funny show. I was disgusted at the clowning with ermine robes and coronet because I hold tradition and its trappings 'sacred'; but I quickly saw the humorous side.

Tilly Rice

The news of the sinking of the *Rawalpindi* has been received with some anxiety down here as the ship was manned entirely from Devonport, where all the Port Isaac men have to report. At the moment there is no news of any local losses.

The three month letting lease on our house in Tadworth expires at the end of the coming month and there is some discussion as to whether the tenants are going to renew or not. Personally, I haven't been able to resist a secret desire that they won't, for without another let we should return home after Christmas.

The village today is bathed in lovely winter sunshine. The air is soft down here and even when it is cold there is no edge to it. The landscape is daily becoming browner as the farmers obey the national injunction to 'plough up', and one can see miles over a stretch of agricultural patchwork right to the foot of Brown Willy. Farms on the whole round here appear prosperous, though all the farmers are complaining about the wartime difficulties of getting enough petrol to deliver their milk in the mornings and the trials of getting the cattle in during the black-out.

Pam Ashford

Mr Mitchell and I discussed magnetic mines. He has made it his business to master their mechanism. I said that since magnets neutralise magnets, surely we could put magnets on the bottom of our ships. He said this would be very expensive. He has an idea which he illustrated with diagrams and which seemed very good.

The subject of Christmas presents has arisen again. I for one don't intend to refrain from giving. It would seem that the staff holds the view that you must spend all your money on wool and knit things for the soldiers. I pointed out that to ruin the trade in the Christmas present line was anything but patriotic. Miss Smith alleged that Sir John Simon [Chancellor of the Exchequer] has said we must save and not spend money on Christmas presents. I have pointed out that the President of the Board of Trade advised us to buy Christmas presents and further that the Queen wants us to go on buying dresses.

Mr Mitchell and I again indulged in the conversation which runs thus: 'What is Harry Jacob doing?' 'What is Fraulein Deutschmann doing?' 'Perhaps he is in the Army, perhaps a concentration camp (we always suspected from his name that he must have a Jewish streak somewhere).' 'Perhaps they are very busy with the export trade.' Perhaps, perhaps, perhaps, and never to know.

WEDNESDAY, 29 NOVEMBER

Christopher Tomlin

A customer: 'My husband says, "Why don't we attack, what are we waiting for?" but I tell him to leave them alone, for so long as they are like this, Bob my nephew is safe. In the last war by this time there had been millions killed; but this time it's different. We have Poland to thank for giving us the chance to get our men across to the Western Front, for if Poland hadn't fought back, Hitler would have pounced on us. I say Bravo Poland!'

My nephew, age 5, examining a toy bomber: 'Mummy, it was made in Germany – are they going to win the war?' His mother: 'No dear, God wouldn't let wicked people win.' 'Well, isn't their God fighting our God?' 'No. There's only one God.' 'Well, isn't there God and Jesus Christ?'

There are four torches in the house and only one is usable.

Pam Ashford

Miss Carswell speaks of someone who is in the balloon barrage. It is just driving him crazy. They have nothing to do but just look at the balloons, and he feels like putting a pin in one some day. He is hardly ever off duty. His home is near the balloon but he is not allowed away. What he wants more than anything is a hot bath.

I have used the morning translating some letters into French. When war was declared I listened carefully to the broadcast directions. One said that you should not write in a foreign language unless it was impossible for the recipient to understand English. Everybody we know in France can read English, so throughout September and October we were always careful to write in English. I have had visions of getting so rusty after the war I should have a deuce of a job to write in French again. However, Mr Mitchell and I have taken the view that if the Censor cannot read French he must be a sausage, and we are accordingly using French again.

THURSDAY, 30 NOVEMBER

Eileen Potter

In the evening, four of us from the office go to the Palace and see Jack Hulbert and Cicely Courtneidge in *Under Your Hat*. We have supper in a vegetarian restaurant near Leicester Square, on the advice of Miss H, and get a very good *table d'hôte* meal for 2s 3d, including some delicious soup containing asparagus, mushrooms and peas. We decide to take a taxi to the Palace, which costs us 6d each, and have just time to settle comfortably in our seats before the show begins. I have seen it before, but it well bears seeing again. No important modifications have been made in it, and no references to the war have been introduced, which is rather a relief I find. We have comfortable seats in the back row of the upper circle for 2s 6d each. We thoroughly enjoy the show and Miss McF and I share a glass of orangeade, with two straws, and an ice, with two spoons, in the interval.

Tilly Rice

There is a definite feeling now that perhaps the need to get away from London wasn't so great. Mrs X said to me the other day, 'I never felt so sure of anything as I do now – that there *will* be air raids!' Her tone almost implied that she hoped that her evacuation from London would be *justified* by air raids.

The maid has been making a great fuss of getting her name changed on her identification card. 'I can't do it until I've got me marriage lines back from the Army people,' she said. 'Such a nuisance it all is. I'd have never got married had I known what a bother it was.'

Have decided that my Christmas presents this year cannot be better than to take the form of local kippers, very juicy and fat.

Last night a concert was given to raise funds to send gifts to all Port Isaac men serving with the forces. All the local talent was rallied, but some criticisms were levelled at the performances. The vicar sang 'Take a Pair of Sparkling Eyes' with much effort and little success. Various other turns were presented, but the audience was reported to have been a little unruly in the back seats.

Later: The news of Russia's aggression on Finland has just been received over the radio. My own reaction is one of utter disgust that I ever allowed myself to believe for one moment that the Communist Party was any more intelligent than any other. The time was when I held quite an admiration for Russia. That has of late, I will admit, faded a little as it was forced on me more and more how alike Nazism, Fascism and Communism were. I've been criticised very strongly in the past by my Left Book Club friends for this point of view, but I think that in the events of the last few months it has been very strongly borne out.

Christopher Tomlin

Sir John Simon says, 'We must be prepared for fearful sacrifices, it is impossible to lead a normal life in war, most people haven't felt the difference yet between this and peace.'

Perhaps I misjudged Sir John but he talks like a blindfolded man. 'People haven't felt the difference . . . ' – haven't they by Harry! *We* have: now Dick is away we have £3 less a week coming in. Other families are just the same. Sir John must squeeze the 4% of the population who control 90% of the country's wealth until the pips rattle. At the moment Sir John is a self-opinionated ass!

Ladies this afternoon wanted to know what I thought of the war. Two said: 'It hasn't started yet.' Another said: 'You should ask sailors' widows and wives what they think about it.' And airmen too. I think some people would like to see wounded soldiers walking about.

Pam Ashford

Two evacuee stories. A hostess on receiving her evacuee said, 'I will give you a nice hot bath and then we will have supper,' to which the boy replied, 'Eh, Missus, cut out the washing and let's get down to the eats.' One little girl was terrified of having a bath lest she drown.

FRIDAY, 1 DECEMBER

Christopher Tomlin

A poster outside the Town Hall asks citizens to co-operate in making a mile of pennies in the market place on December 10th. The proceeds will go towards a free buffet for the services on Preston Station. There was one in the last war; naturally it was very popular with soldiers and sailors going through or coming to Preston. I am proud of my town; perhaps you don't know that although there are other Prestons in England, our citizens do not need to write 'Lancs' when addressing. All other Prestonians must put the county on notepaper. You see, there is only one Preston which matters.

In the *Catholic Herald* I read proposals of Mr J.M. Keynes: all workers' incomes be deducted at the source to pay for taxes and be invested in blocked bonds, bonds which are redeemable gradually after the war. I am disturbed because at the moment we and thousands of others find it hard to carry on. What it will be like if his proposals are acted upon I shudder to contemplate. I'm afraid my job will go west, for men and women won't be able to afford printed writing papers.

Pam Ashford
Mr Roxburgh comes in with a photograph of the Cabinet. 'Our defenders! If you do a day's work you are entitled to your money. But *these* people!'

Miss Smith has been much shocked by the invasion of Finland by Russia. 'It is just dreadful, the way these big brutal nations are trampling down the small nations, and we cannot do anything and America cannot do anything. Perhaps Scandinavia might do something.'

I said, 'I doubt if they can give anything but sympathy.'

Miss Carswell: 'I could murder the Russians. It is just as if the old cannibal instinct has come back.'

Me: 'It is obvious that if Europe is to be saved there is only one thing that can save her: a United States of Europe, achieved by one way or another. The nations, neither big nor small, cannot go their separate ways. They are all units of one body, Europe.' My point was not understood, I felt.

SATURDAY, 2 DECEMBER

Christopher Tomlin
The pillar boxes are covered with bills advertising the new Defence Bonds.

A lecture, 'How to Care for Allotments', will be given in Fulwood. It strikes me allotments will be necessary for everyone if a slump comes.

We have a letter from Dick saying he has written many letters and has yet to get his first one. But we have written six altogether. Four have gone to his old address in France (he is now with Royal Air Force Signals in another part of France), two went to his old address in England. Evidently they have not been forwarded to him. It's vexing, for we went to a lot of trouble to send toffee and handkerchiefs.

I will just quote from his letter: 'We are living in an outbuilding attached to a large house, clean and dry and free from rats or vermin.

I have at last got my hands on some first class radio gear; believe me, it's a treat to get back into it again. Nineteen of us are here and we have made the place into a 'home from home'. At the present time everybody is busy making arrangements for a really good Christmas party. Each man is paying 50 Francs towards a kitty and the officer in charge of our section has started it with 200 Francs. (He is a fine man and does everything he can for us.) We are going to decorate the billet and fob up one end with a bar; the other end will be filled with beds ready-made for those men who can no longer stand on their feet – rather a good idea I think. We aim to have a party which will make us forget we are having a Christmas in a strange country.'

Tilly Rice

It really seems as if America is being awakened to some real concern at last at the way the war is taking its course. President Roosevelt, in guarded terms certainly, has suggested an embargo on Russia and no doubt his suggestion will be taken notice of. The Russians treated the Finns to a horrible air raid on Friday during which 200 people were killed, though one must bear in mind when looking with horror on this death toll that in all probability a like number would be killed in England during one day owing to our black-out.

Chapter Five

FUNF

Adapting ourselves to the inconveniences: a motorist gives himself a chance in the black-out.

'The records at Kew Observatory show that the first wave travelling through the earth from Asia Minor arrived at 3 minutes 26 seconds after midnight, and, as we know how fast such a wave travels, we can say that the earthquake occurred two minutes before midnight on the 26th by our time.

Of course, the great majority of the inhabitants were indoors, and this accounts in part for the heavy death toll, whole families being killed as the houses fell on them. The people of Asia Minor are by no means unfamiliar with earthquakes. The worst on record occurred as long ago as AD 17, when 12 cities, including Sardis, one of the places now affected by the floods, were destroyed.

No doubt the lesson has been learned now. The Government will see to it that the rebuilding of the towns is according to the stringent rules which have been adopted after severe earthquakes in Japan, India and California.'

Seismologist F.J.W. Whiffle analyses the Erzincan earthquake and Black Sea tsunami shortly before Boxing Day 1939, which claimed between 30,000 and 40,000 lives. The BBC Home Service, 3 January 1940

* * *

4 December German pocket battleship *Admiral Graf Spee* sinks liner *Doric Star* in South Atlantic. **7 December** Denmark, Norway and Sweden declare their neutrality. **13 December** Battle of the River Plate: *Admiral Graf Spee* engaged by *Exeter*, *Ajax* and *Achilles*; following heavy damage, the German ship takes refuge in Uruguayan capital, Montevideo. **17 December** *Graf Spee* sinks in the River Plate after being scuttled. **18 December** First Canadian troops arrive in Britain, followed a week later by Australian airmen. **30 December** Finns inflict humiliating defeat on Soviet forces at Suommusalmi.

SUNDAY, 3 DECEMBER

Maggie Joy Blunt
Freelance writer living in Burnham Beeches, near Slough, age 30
I have a friend in the Women's Land Army who is keeping a diary of her experiences for the duration. She suggested that I should do the same, but I hesitated. Like Russia, I pursue a policy of cold self-interest, but I do not think it will attract the same attention.

Since October 1938 I have written some articles on the architecture of Malta, six short stories, and I have moved from a flat in Hampstead to a cottage in Burnham Beeches. One of the articles has been published. Two others may be. None of the short stories has so far shown the slightest sign of stirring an editor. But the cottage is a gem of its kind, and as I sit this Sunday afternoon by a coal fire with my little cat on my knee and chew toffees I reflect that, before this war is over, my comfortable, exclusive existence may be rudely disturbed, for it depends on certain inherited securities which are threatened by a rising overdraft, and as I have done nothing yet to justify the sum spent on my education, a weekly account of the war from this sector of the home front might, after all, be a practical investment.

We have been at war with Germany for fourteen weeks. I was staying with relations when the news of Germany's pact with Soviet Russia burst upon us. 'These Dictators!' snorted my uncle. 'All of them unreliable.' By the end of the week he was measuring windows.

I returned to my cottage, believing wishfully that threatening clouds would pass. I began to prune ramblers. All that week I seemed to be perched on the top wobbly steps in the late summer sun wrestling with dead rosewood and wavering crimson-tipped new shoots, waiting for news, waiting for news. Cabinets met. Dictators conferred. Troops were massing. Danzig Nazis had seized two Polish trains. I received a despairing letter from a friend in London, the man-servant next door was summoned to Plymouth, two women with children came looking for a cottage.

I sat and wept through a nine o'clock news bulletin. My little cat climbed on my lap and licked my chin. The next morning there were rumours that Germany had invaded Poland which were confirmed officially by mid-day, Hitler having been obliged, so he said, 'to meet force with force'.

I began to search for rugs and old thick curtains, and at nine o'clock my friend N arrived with two friends of hers on their way to Bridport. It was a dreadful week. We none of us knew what the next day or hour might bring. By next week, bombs might be dropping on England's docks and cities and important centres; posts, telephone, transport would be all disorganised; the country flooded with town refugees; hospitals and first-aid posts working overtime. Horror piled upon horror in one's imagination.

We listened without comment to the Prime Minister's broadcast on September 3rd. N had lost her job, but we expected a great demand for women in all the professions and trades to replace men called to the front. N has a London science degree, and good teaching and journalistic experience at home and abroad. She was confident that she would soon find work.

We began to line curtains, paste the windows, and tack felt along the door cracks. We discussed where the safest place might be in the cottage during an air raid – in the kitchen near the stove as that was the strongest flue, or one of the garden sheds? The cottage, I knew, would probably collapse if a bomb fell within 100 yards of it. I had no gas-proof room. Did I know how to deal with an incendiary bomb? I did not. We must have a bucket, shovel and sand, and hadn't I better remove all valuable papers from the room under the roof? I think that, after the first two, we slept through the air-raid warnings of the first week.

The weather was perfect. We took our lunch and our gas masks each day into the Beeches. We listened to every news bulletin. We devoured two newspapers daily and studied the *New Statesman* each week. There was a stimulating feeling everywhere of unity, adventure, new comradeships. Propaganda leaflets dropped on Germany instead of bombs – an exciting start to hostilities. We were duly impressed by the Government's evacuation scheme and other emergency measures. We were uplifted by the expression of sympathy and the offers of assistance from all parts of the empire.

All the news was heavily censored in those first weeks. We grew tired of reading the day's radio bulletins in the next morning's papers. The Ministry of Information became known as the Ministry of Little or No Information, the Ministry of Misinformation, and later, the Ministry of Malformation. 'We are under a polite dictatorship,' said someone.

Week followed week: no air raids, no activity on the Western Front, no jobs vacant on the Home Front. What were we waiting for? A revolution in Germany? We heard that Nazi leaders had invested their fortunes abroad. The *Courageous* had been sunk. That the Duke of Windsor had visited England. That summer-time was to be continued. That the Russians had entered Poland. Friends came, and stories of unemployment, confusion and distress were tragically universal.

We went once or twice to London. Our old college was deserted and sandbagged, the basements were converted into public ARP shelters and an auxiliary fire engine was in possession of one of the quadrangles. I marvelled at the patience of bus conductors during the after-dark rush hour. Many people must get away without paying their fare.

The uniforms everywhere, the general tension in the air, gave me a queer sensation of being back in the last war, and made me think that the interval in which I had grown up had been a dream and that I should go home and eat potato cakes and see my mother's tired face blanch again at the sound of air-raid warnings.

Troops, planes, battleships, heavy taxation, rationing plans, and all the Government's preparations for a three years' war – could it be that they will be unnecessary, after all? Is this to be a 'Table' war and won without a wholesale massacre? I dared not believe it. But, said N, it was a struggle, really, between Vested Interests and Socialism, and this was a division that cut through each country and each class and was not drawn at the Western Front. We were possibly on the brink of a World Revolution.

I began to knit a sweater. N knitted socks and worked at her novel and applied diligently for jobs while I applied myself diligently to the garden. A willow tree that had been blocking out the light and air behind the cottage was cut down. A rose arch was removed. N began to saw the green willow timber into logs for me. We read Arnold Bennett, Emily Brontë, Conrad. We listened each week with joy to *Bandwagon*.

Now I am alone again and the hostilities between Russia and Finland which N prophesied have begun. What have I done since she went away? I have put a patent polish on the bedroom floor. I have altered some curtains. I have altered a short story. I have planted pheasant-eye narcissi beneath the rosemary hedge and stolen moss from the beeches for the flagged paths. I have picked violets and thought of a story centred around my little cat who should have a whole book devoted to her. I have cut down my cigarettes from 25 to 10 a day by not smoking until after black-out time. I have read with great interest of the formation of an Arts Bureau in Oxford at the instigation of Paul Nash 'to open up new possibilities for the legitimate use of talent during the war'.

The RAF is said to have dropped the famous Shetland rabbit on the Reich for Goering. Do the Germans ever think of doing things like this? What is their sense of humour? Have they one? A collection of war cartoons from all possible sources would be interesting. Shall I begin one? I collect architectural photographs as it is, and newspapers and journals, and used stamps for the Girl Guides and waste paper for the Boy Scouts and silver paper for the hospitals. I have read of a man who collects the papers that oranges are wrapped in.

Hitler wants to keep his army stationary 'until the morale of the Allies wilts'. Then, when he has conquered France and Britain, which, the *New Statesman* has heard, German military authorities calculate he will have done by mid-July, he intends to drive Russia back beyond the Urals and build a German Reich finer and greater than it has ever been.

But before that happens I should like to visit London again. In fact I should like to visit London again now. I should like to go to the zoo. I should like to see the 'Art for the People' exhibition in Stukely Street. I should like to hear one of the lunch-hour concerts at the National Gallery. I should like to see Priestley's new play at the Westminster, and Farjeon's *Little Revue* and some ballet. I have not seen even a film for two months.

MONDAY, 4 DECEMBER

Christopher Tomlin

A lady: 'I don't think the war will last. It's been terrible, nothing but murder from beginning to end!'

Coming home I read 'Insist on a Doctor of like Sex' on a poster. It is very funny; I've just read an account of those posters in the *Daily Mail*. Whoever is responsible has a sex obsession.

Pam Ashford

Last night Miss Bousie paid a visit to Jordanhill and was shocked by the negligence shown regarding chinks. It is quite different in Pollockshields. Two people who sat on the tram in the front of her were pointing the chinks out thus, 'There's another, there's another.' Miss Bousie felt like phoning the police. On the other hand, when the tram was passing through Bridge Street (which I should have called a commercial area, but which Miss Bousie regards as lower-class), there were no chinks at all. 'It is always the same; the lower-classes do their duty by the nation, but the professional classes will not.'

TUESDAY, 5 DECEMBER

Christopher Tomlin

I am weary and fed up so I took some Kruschen.

Large number of coconuts on sale at fruiterers which is unusual at this time of year: they are just 2d each.

A letter from Dick who writes: 'Hurray! Hurray! Hurray! At last word from home and a topping parcel containing four letters!'

Tilly Rice

From everywhere I get news of people returning to their homes. And with it a gradual resumption of as near as possible normal conditions. Our own fate is not decided yet. One friend tells me that London looks much the same as usual, with the exception of the sandbags. Apparently the Corner Houses are full of people. I was interested to learn, however, that she feels the atmosphere to be completely different to that held in the last war. She reports no anti-German feeling such as is common down here. Hitler is the only person who apparently comes in for any brickbats, she says, 'and even that you seldom hear, except from the less enlightened man or women given to laying down the law in trams and buses to the accompaniment of "What I always say is . . ." and "If you see what I mean . . ." and, thank goodness, none of that hysterical "Your King and country need you . . ." tripe, with silly women chucking white feathers about and feeling noble.'

It seems to me that much more reflection should have been given to the evacuation business. I'm not absolutely sure of its being a good thing, for it seems to me that the psychological disruption of evacuation may well be equal to the evils of living under war conditions. All the money that was spent on evacuation could quite well have been devoted to making schools safe and the building of adequate air-raid shelters.

THURSDAY, 7 DECEMBER

Eileen Potter

A party of children from Special Schools is to be evacuated today. I have to be at Deptford by 8.45 a.m. to meet the ambulance at a small boy's home. It is a small, cottage-like house opposite a factory, whence an unpleasant smell emanates. I knock at the door and am shown into a room on the ground floor, containing an unmade bed and other signs of recent getting-up. The mother explains that there is no fire in the other room. It is at least warm in there, and a retreat from the fog outside. The little boy is from a Physically Defective School, and looks pale and rather delicate. The mother warns me that he will probably be sick.

We next got to Vauxhall Park to collect another girl from another school for physically defective children. She is also ready and waiting for the ambulance. She has a nice warm-looking pair of red gloves, but neither of the others has any, and we have rather a chilly drive through the fog to the school in Fulham where the main party is assembling. A family of German refugees arrives to enquire about having the children evacuated to join the school which they had already begun to attend before the summer holidays. The parents rather proudly display their certificate from the Aliens' Tribunal, marked 'Fugitives from Nazi Oppression'. The father cannot speak English at all but the mother speaks fairly well, and I am struck by the superiority of her manners as compared with those of many of our English parents. The Divisional Dispersals Officer promises to write to the billeting officer about the children, but we explain that nothing can be done for the parents.

Christopher Tomlin

The manager of a big Preston cycle store: 'The only firm in England who is making batteries is the Ever Ready people. They are making 2,000,000 a day: the demand is for 4,000,000 a day but the Government takes 6,000,000 a week. The Ever Ready firm has control of all the battery manufacturers in England.'

Later: Three blasted cheers! I've got a new Ever Ready battery through a customer.

FRIDAY, 8 DECEMBER

Pam Ashford

Miss Smith broke up the conversation with a story of a first aid practice. Miss Smith's story was that when carrying a stretcher case up the stairs, they let the 'patient' fall out and dislocate his shoulder. The warden bent over the injured man to express his sympathy and his steel helmet fell off and knocked the victim unconscious.

Miss Bousie had heard of a stretcher case that was dropped and the man required three stitches in his head.

At Kilbarchan the heaviest man in the village was chosen as the 'patient' to be carried along the main street. The six stretcher-bearers had to put the stretcher down twice so as to rest their arms.

Miss Carswell comments upon the cartoon in yesterday's *Bulletin*. Some blacks switch off the wireless programmes from Europe saying, 'Cut off that civilisation.'

SATURDAY, 9 DECEMBER

Eileen Potter

Spend the first part of the morning putting the finishing touches to my toilette. The wedding of my landlady's son Jack F is at 12 noon, and Mrs F, Jack and I share a taxi to the West End, as the ceremony is to be held at St James', Piccadilly. After leaving Jack's bag at the Criterion, where the reception will be, we proceed to Lyons' Corner House, where Mrs F has a spray of orchids made up at the flower department. The two men then leave us, and we have a cup of coffee with plenty of whipped cream. The guests and friends are already beginning to assemble when we arrive at the church. The altar is sandbagged, and a piece of Chinese embroidery has been draped across the front of the sandbags, but it is not nearly big enough to hide them. An elderly clergyman from Gloucester has come to officiate. The bride wears a smart two-piece in air-force blue, and a spray of mauve orchids. There are no bridesmaids, but she is attended by a cousin. The bride's family and friends mostly have rather a Jewish appearance; I always suspect that they are Jews, though they do not admit it and are not of the Jewish religion.

The clergyman takes liberties with the marriage service in places, but includes the word 'obey' in his exhortation to the bride. We then proceed to the Criterion for the wedding breakfast, for which a suite of rooms has been engaged. First we have cocktails in an ante-room, and then proceed to the dining room, where an excellent spread awaits us, with red and white wine, followed by champagne in which to drink the health of the bride and bridegroom. There are about 24 guests at the wedding breakfast. It has rather an international atmosphere, as the bridegroom is a teacher of English to foreigners, and first became friendly with the bride through belonging to an international club. I sit next to a naval commander who is employed in censoring messages for the Ministry of Information. He has to be back on duty by four o'clock. He attends the ceremony in full uniform, but, like the rest of the bride's friends, he has a distinctly Jewish appearance.

The wedding breakfast goes off very satisfactorily, with only two short speeches, and no tears or rows between the respective mothers-in-law. Two taxi-loads of guests go to see the bride and bridegroom off from Waterloo. They are going to Bournemouth for the weekend.

MONDAY, 11 DECEMBER

Christopher Tomlin
Why are we now told we 'are fighting the German people'? Mr Chamberlain and others were more emphatic that we were struggling against *Nazism*. Why the 'about turn'? Is it to prepare us for bombing raids on German towns? I'm convinced there's something the War Office is about to do.

TUESDAY, 12 DECEMBER

Christopher Tomlin
Father is in a bloodthirsty mood. He would chop Germany into little bits, he condemns all Germans. 'A nation has the leaders it chooses. The Germans are never content unless they're at war. It's the same nation which caused the war last time!' Father can't see why God doesn't stop Germany and Russia and won't listen when I say, 'God

gives all peoples free will, the power to choose between good and evil, and it's by loving, serving and obeying God we reach Heaven. Earth is a school of preparation.'

Father and I are mad that the British submarine didn't fire a torpedo at the *Bremen*.

Pam Ashford

The air-raid practice proved a damp squib. Perhaps if we had opened the windows we should have heard it better, but Miss Crawford (Air Raid Warden) was firm. 'When the real warning comes, the windows may not be open.' Miss Bousie and Agnes who were in the street at the time heard the sirens distinctly. Agnes said there was a man gesticulating wildly and evidently unaware that it was only a test.

According to the newspapers we were to have 2 minutes of 'raiders approaching', then 30 seconds of silence. The whole thing was to wind up with 2 minutes of 'raiders passed'. When it was all over Miss Smith came out of Mr Ferguson's room to ask if that was the air-raid signal.

Miss Carswell had heard someone at lunchtime say, 'Supposing the Germans came when we were making the test,' and she seemed unable to divert herself of this idea.

At 9.15 the BBC gave us the first of a new series. Mr Sinclair of Edinburgh University will expose Hitler's speeches. It promises to be good.

WEDNESDAY, 13 DECEMBER

Eileen Potter

I have to be at Whitechapel by 8.30 to pick up a party of children. One mother comes up to me and asks me to keep an eye on her boy, as he is a refugee from Vienna, and cannot speak much English. Another elderly mother with a strong German accent comes to me and says how grateful she feels towards England. 'It is the best country for children.'

Nearly all the children to be taken in the party today are from a Jewish school. Ultimately we get into the ambulances and set off.

My party are very quiet, about the best-behaved party I have had, except for one boy who keeps up an almost incessant conversation. He tells me his mother keeps a hat shop and a wool shop in the Mile

End Road. He has been away to the same district before, and liked his first billet (a country pub) very much, but his mother took him away after he was moved to a smaller house. He is rather a Jewish looking type, but his younger brother must be a reversion to a 'Nordic' ancestor, as he has sandy hair, blue eyes, and a round, rosy face. The elder brother gives the lie to the idea that Jews cannot settle happily on the land, for he seems to have thoroughly enjoyed dealing with the farm animals, as well as helping to serve at the bar. He says, 'I don't want to be billeted in a posh house: I want to go on some old farm where I needn't bother to wash.' At the same time, he has a tendency to brag about his possessions – his puppy, his bicycle, his pocket money and also his various exploits, particularly in connection with his bicycle. One big girl is rather badly sick, and another one slightly so. Several others sit with their heads down on one another's knees, looking rather sorry for themselves. In general they seem to have slightly less stamina than the ordinary English child.

Pam Ashford
Mr and Mrs Murr, the German refugees, are leaving on Saturday week from Liverpool. The name of the boat is not known beforehand. A subject that would seem to have been much discussed between them and their friends was whether to go on a British or a Dutch boat. They have chosen a British boat because it will be convoyed. They used to think a neutral boat would be safer but now they see that neutrals are being attacked indiscriminately.

She wishes she could stay in this country which she likes very much. The bustle of America does not attract her. I pointed out what I have always been silent about: 'This country has some hard knocks coming to it. You are able to get out of the way, and you are wise to do so.' That this country should suffer seemed more painful to her than it is to me.

THURSDAY, 14 DECEMBER

Christopher Tomlin
An order came through the post. I tramped three miles to Penwortham with a load of depression; I don't know what I would have done if today was a flop. But thank God it wasn't! I'm not one

to shove religion down anybody's throat, but I must say prayer has never let me down. I sold 26/- worth of stationery – hurray!

I went to my WEA class hoping Dr Vodak would choose my paper to read to the class (he promised to read the best received). I was disappointed because he neither read it nor returned it. On New Year's Eve the WEA hosts a hot-pot supper and social (1/-) and in two weeks Dr Olaf Stapledon will speak on 'Federal Union' at Booths' Café.

FRIDAY, 15 DECEMBER

Eileen Potter
Go to see some children off by ambulance from one of the Hammersmith schools. We first go to North Kensington to pick up two small boys. The elder one at first says he will not come, and begins to cry, but is pacified when his mother gives him a toy policeman filled with sweets.

We go on to another house near Shepherds Bush – a much cleaner and more prosperous type of home – to pick up two more children, a boy and a girl. They both declare that they will not leave mummy and daddy, and kick and struggle and scream when put in the car. All three children are put into the back seat and locked safely in, whilst Miss X and I sit in front. We drive off, the children still screaming in the rear, and several of the neighbours looking on. Gradually the sounds of sobbing subside, and I look round to find them beginning to sit up and look around them. When we come to Clapham Common, they murmur, 'We're in the country, in a car!' Presently they begin to sing 'Run, Adolf, Run', and something is said about rabbits, from which I conclude that they think 'Adolf' is some kind of rabbit.

I do not feel much like dancing tonight, but I decide to go as usual, and am soon asked to join in a set for the sword dance.

Christopher Tomlin
I am absolutely fed up with black-outs, cold weather, having to finish about 3.30 because it's dark and waiting in a queue for motor buses. I'm strong as an ox but these irritations get me down.

I called at the CWS [Co-op] tobacco department for 2 ounces of Tom Long. How the blazes women manage to carry baskets in a black-out like tonight's gets me guessing. I had only a torch in my hand, yet I'd difficulty in avoiding passers-by. Three times I saw a mild collision: there was no cussing. It was accepted as part of the price of war.

It is pleasant to read the *Graf Spee* is cornered. But it's only a pocket battleship and was shelled by four cruisers. Britons are supposed to play the game: 4 to 1 isn't cricket.

Pam Ashford
Ethel [recently married office assistant] has not turned up this morning, and everyone presumes her husband has leave. The malice is terrible: why should she get extra holidays? Why should she get extra money (separation allowance)?

Mr Mitchell has heard that an aeroplane works requires a secretary for a director at a very attractive salary. I am going to apply. This subject has dominated our conversation together today, and bids fair to hold my thoughts for some days to come.

In the afternoon Ethel came up to the office. Her husband *is* home on leave, and she says she is not coming to work while he is here. Mr Ferguson said to her, 'Your husband may be the boss in France, but he is not the boss here.' Everyone thinks Ethel has a cheek. I seem to be her only defender. I say, 'He may never come back, you would not want Ethel's memories to be clouded by the thought that she had neglected him when he had his last leave.' Mr Ferguson will decide over the weekend whether or not she is to be sacked.

SATURDAY, 16 DECEMBER

Eileen Potter
I proceed to the school in Hammersmith where my party is to assemble, to be taken by ambulance to Paddington to catch the train to Frome.

I and my six children occupy one compartment comfortably. All is well so long as they are eating their lunch, but when they have all finished they begin to stand up on the seats and run out into the corridor. One small boy suddenly lets out a howl, just as the District Transport Officer is coming into the carriage. He has been standing on the seat, leaning through the window, and his cap has blown off onto the line. We explain that we cannot stop the train to look for it,

123

and that it was his own fault for hanging out of the window. He calms down, but presently begins to howl again. This time he has swallowed a sweet, and thinks that it is stuck in his throat. We look down his throat, and nothing can be seen, but he still continues to whimper and presently he is sick on the floor. Then he brightens up again, and goes out into the corridor. Yet again he lets out a howl – this time he has pinched his finger slightly in the sliding door of the compartment. I begin to feel that I do not envy the household on whom he is to be billeted.

Christopher Tomlin

'Bob', my sister, called. She had a bath here, there isn't one in her home, and afterwards I walked back with her. She says I'm wrong to think it unfair for three British boats to attack the *Graf Spee*, for the cruisers are smaller than the German vessel.

Bob showed mother a letter from Dick in which he writes: 'We have been filling up bomb holes here at the Aerodrome . . . ' Mother: 'He never told us that!' Father is very much annoyed: 'Dick's a wireless operator, they can get hundreds of men for the other job.' Father also grumbled, 'This leave business amuses me. Dick is coming home on leave for ten days (in February), and he's only just gone out to France. No wonder the war's costing £6,000,000 a day!'

Maggie Joy Blunt

Life at Wee Cottage goes on as usual. There have been numerous articles and comments in the press recently on How Our Lives Have Changed. But I protest that, for the majority, this is just what they haven't done, yet. We have had to suffer a terrible uncertainty that they might. We have had to suffer certain inconveniences – the black-out, petrol rations, altered bus and train services, a lack of theatrical entertainment, rising cost of food, scarcity of certain commodities such as electric light batteries, sugar, butter. Large numbers of children are experiencing country life for the first time. A number of adults are doing jobs that they have never done before and never expected to do. But there has been no essential change in our way of living, in our system of employment or education, in our ideas and ambitions.

At the beginning of last week I went to London to do some belated Christmas shopping. Christmas stocks were in full display. Christmas shoppers from suburb and province crowded pavements. There might be no war. In Berlin, it is reported, they are saying too, 'There might be no war.'

While I was there I met and mixed with a little group of people who before the war had strong pro-Nazi tendencies. They know and love Germany and the German people. They admired Hitler and all that his National Socialism had done to improve social conditions in Germany. They closed their ears to concentration camp rumours and found excuses for the treatment of Jews. They still admire Hitler, but blame his advisers. They still believe in National Socialism. Nothing will shake their faith in the German people. Stella, of whom I saw most, still chatters heatedly: why, she said, should we expect the German people to remove Hitler at our dictation? She did not approve at all of Mr Churchill. She hoped that we should eventually unite with Germany against Russia – we had so much in common with the Germans, more even than with Americans, as the American idea of morality was so different from ours. She hated all Communists and the idea of Communism, she hated Left Wing ways, the Left Book Club, for instance. And the Mosley faction – had I heard? – Mosley supporters were increasing at the rate of 20 a day! If you wanted to get through the traffic in a certain part of London you had only to give the Fascist salute.

Yet Stella and her brother Paul are among the kindest people I know. Paul is an architect who has been very busy indeed since the war building ARP shelters, and stood four of us lunch the day I was in town.

We are adapting ourselves to the inconveniences. It is as though we were trying to play one more set of tennis before an approaching storm descends. The storm does not descend and we go on playing tennis. Nothing happens. A local MP, addressing members of a Comforts Fund Working Party recently, remarked that he was not in favour of this 'half-asleep war. Scattering pamphlets is no more use than scattering confetti. I am sorry to have to say it, but we shall have to make the Germans suffer before we can make peace possible.'

But what, I wonder, does he suppose is happening at sea? We forget, seated comfortably at home, this war at sea which the Germans may have substituted for the Blitzkrieg we all expected. Mr Churchill has stated that two to four U-boats are destroyed each week. The *Doric Star* on her way home from New Zealand and

Australia has been attacked by the *Admiral Scheer* and reported missing. The destroyer *Jersey* has been attacked and damaged. We have attacked and damaged the *Admiral Graf Spee* (O glorious feat! Thirty-six Germans dead and sixty seriously wounded). Magnetic mines cause losses daily; the week before last our merchant losses totalled over 33 thousand tons. Daily men drown and die of exhaustion in a winter sea while we sit at home wondering why nothing happens.

Sunday next will be Christmas Day. 'Peace and good will towards men,' said my neighbour bitterly.

SUNDAY, 17 DECEMBER

Christopher Tomlin

Father says the *Graf Spee* victory is one of the most important happenings in this or in the last war and 'if it had escaped, Churchill would have had to go: the British people would have forced him to.'

I watched an ARP practice. I saw the decontamination squad arrive in a 'Cleansing Department' lorry. Six men clambered out, put on gas-masks and capes, and waited for the lorry to turn round. They then took out picks, shovels, sand, chlorate of lime, lanterns, wood blocks, iron stakes, ropes and a hosepipe. A square was roped off and notice boards saying 'Gas – take care' were propped up at each corner. In this square splashes of oil represented liquid gas. These splashes were covered with lime and then with sand. The crowd – civilians, Special Police and wardens – laughed when the rope barrier collapsed.

MONDAY, 18 DECEMBER

Pam Ashford

Mr Ferguson is ill with pleurisy. This news has produced the same reaction in everyone: 'This will save Ethel's bacon,' meaning that she will be back at work before he is well enough to sack her.

The 8 a.m. told how the *Graf Spee* has been scuttled. This seems a good way out of her pickle. Miss Bousie is more than delighted at the saving of life. Mr Mitchell says, 'What a humiliation for the German navy.'

Miss Bousie: 'I listened to Lord Haw Haw last night. He was very humble pie. He thanked people for listening to him. He was on about the evacuated children being verminous. Also about the miserable pittance that our soldiers get, also how little the unemployed are paid.'

Miss Bousie, leaving for the bank and looking at the fog: 'Mr Hitler will not come today.'

Miss Carswell: 'You say that, yet you carry your mask.' Miss Bousie: 'I always carry my mask. I hate it. That is why I carry it. It is a punishment. It is my cross. I did not work hard enough to prevent the war.'

This sentiment produced profound astonishment, everyone pointing out how much she had done for the League of Nations Union. 'No,' she said, 'I did not do enough. When the peace comes I shall work harder.'

TUESDAY, 19 DECEMBER

Christopher Tomlin

A woman in a newsagent's: 'I want you to cancel my newspaper delivery for a little while.'

Newsagent: 'I'm sorry, we can't.'

'Well, I'm going away for ten days!'

'Sorry, but that's the rule.'

'Is it because of the war?'

'Yes, anyhow you'll be able to use them for covering shelves.'

Pam Ashford

Mr Roxburgh: 'Would you like to join the mine sweepers? By God, those are brave men! They, sweeping the seas, and we, sitting in our offices drawing in the money at the cost of those men's lives. It is they who should be getting the plenty.'

The postman delivered a Christmas card from America to Miss Bousie in mistake for someone up the street. Miss Bousie looked at it closely before finding out it was not for her. It was printed in the conventional style – 'Merry Christmas to you' – but the sender had crossed this 'Merry Christmas' out and written 'Peace'. Miss Bousie thought that the sender must have been a person with a lovely mind.

Christopher Tomlin

BBC 6 o'clock news: 'Captain Langsdorf, Commander of the *Graf Spee*, committed suicide'!

Today I was handing notepaper to Mrs W in Penwortham when a woman passed by with a pram. 'Oh, Mr Tomlin!' she called, 'are you taking cards to 22, Priory Road?'

'No, I'm sorry they haven't come in yet. I'm expecting them any moment.'

She: 'Well it's too late now, I'll have to cancel them!'

I told her it was only Thursday tomorrow and there were four days yet until Christmas. She was off-hand about it and I then said, 'I'll try to get them here tonight.'

She snapped, 'I'll wait until tomorrow afternoon and if they come later I won't accept them!' with which parting shot she sailed away.

Mrs W overheard the conversation and expressed surprise. 'I don't know how you put up with it, Mr Tomlin. I feel like giving her a piece of my mind. There are some rotten people!'

Me: 'Yes, the beauty of it is she ordered my cheapest Christmas cards – printed ones at 2/- per dozen.'

Mrs W: 'Good Lord, 2/- a dozen. No wonder she can walk about in a fur coat.'

Father thinks, 'If we go on sinking Nazi ships like we are doing, the war will be over very soon.' During the week Father cursed and condemned the Germans with 'Kill them! Kill! Kill! There's only one good German and that's a dead one. This war and all the wars of the past came from Germany. They are a hateful wicked lot and better off below ground.'

Pam Ashford

A mean theft! My flasher was stolen from the pocket of my coat while I was in the cloakroom (during German class). Mr Brought (head janitor) said the stealing was worse than ever this year.

THURSDAY, 21 DECEMBER

Christopher Tomlin

6.30 p.m. broadcast: A camp entertainment by troops in England. It was jolly good and put us all in a good humour. It put many so-called variety turns to shame.

Mother: 'Damn good voices! The best I've heard for a long time. They are so fresh.'

Gunner Smith sang and father couldn't stop exclaiming, 'He had a grand voice. He gets those high notes beautifully.'

Mother chimed, 'He has a beautiful delivery.'

I agreed and father spoke with a wistful sigh: 'He has a cultured voice, and it's men like that who get killed!'

At 8.30 I went to the Empress Cinema to see *The Little Princess*. Before the feature there was a short in which a dozen stars wished us a happy Christmas. Unfortunately I saw this short at the Empress last year; and it is a pity Santa Claus pointed to 1938.

Pam Ashford
Mr Mitchell continues to show great appreciation of *It's That Man Again*. He frequently speaks 'ITMA', and now someone called 'Funf' is entering the conversation. Today he sent off a gift token with this on it: 'With this token, Funf has spoken.' I hope the recipient understands.

Mr Mitchell has won a parcel of tinned goods in the Kilbarchan Red Cross raffle!

FRIDAY, 22 DECEMBER

Eileen Potter
Begin my holidays. Do my packing and hurry to Euston Station, where I am to catch the 10.40 to Lancaster. There is only a blue light in our compartment, so it is impossible to read. We ultimately arrive, and I am met by my youngest niece, aged 16, and her puppy.

The rest of the family are awaiting me at the house. I am spending Christmas with my eldest sister and her family. Her husband is Modern Languages master at the local grammar school, and her eldest daughter is married and living in Dartmouth expecting her third baby. My second niece, aged 21, has had two shots at nursing, but threw it up on both occasions. She has made several attempts to join up with various things since the war, but is handicapped by her shortness, being only 4 foot 11 inches.

Christopher Tomlin

A Christmas card from Aunt Ivy: 'I can't afford to send cards or presents this year.' With her card was a PO for 5 bob.

A friend who is in the Army Service Corps writes, 'I'm just about broke . . . 2 Francs!' Well, I will send him this 5/- postal order from Ivy. My friend also writes, 'put my name down for all the comfort funds. What would I give for a bottle of "Lion"!'

I took a tin of CWS peas from the pantry. I eat them with bread and butter on Abstinence days. Mother said, 'Go slow with those. You won't be able to eat them as often as before; I think they are all being brought for the soldiers.'

Pam Ashford

Business is very slack. If the war goes on, dear knows where we shall end up. There is little Christmas spirit. Miss Gibson baked and gave us a cake with icing and marzipan that will last us about a week for the 11 o'clock tea. Miss Smith gave us tea this afternoon with an iced cake and shortbread. I have given her, Miss Gibson and Miss Bousie presents and received presents too, also presents to the two office girls. The others are determined to ignore Christmas altogether so as to save the costs. As Agnes puts it, 'People who give Christmas presents are damned pests.' As usual I have given Mr Mitchell a cigar and sweets for his kiddies.

At 5.30 I went to Grants to choose a book with the token he gave me yesterday. There were many I liked. First a new book by Joad on the Philosophy of Politics. I felt I should like to read it, but then I foresaw it would go the same way as many other serious books of mine; year after year I go on yearning to read them, but no matter which evening I sit down to do so, I am always too tired to give them my mind. There was a book by Mr Voigt, *Unto Caesar*, but I reckoned that would fall into the same class as the Oxford Pamphlets, which I never fail to buy, though I only turn the pages over on the bus going to and fro, and say how tip-top they are. There was a remainder copy of a book by Eric Newton, full of lovely reproductions, the difficulty in that case being the number of nudes, which I thought might prove an embarrassing feature if I showed the book to Mr Mitchell tomorrow. Then *The Testament of Youth* – I have heard so much about this book, but did not realise it was good until I had it in my hands. What made me hesitate was the cost (4/-)

for I should have had to choose something else for the remaining 3/6 of the token. When my eye lighted on *I Married a German* by Madeleine Kent (7/6) I knew at once that it was the right choice.

SATURDAY, 23 DECEMBER

Christopher Tomlin

Delivered seven Christmas orders: all were pleased. I've had a good 'reception' this year: 5/- from Ivy, 2/6 from Aunt Bee, 2/- from father, a box of cheroots from mother, and 25 packets of cigarettes from my sister and her husband and good wishes from all.

Though there's no midnight mass this year, I am determined not to be done out of communion. So I went to confession this afternoon. I haven't been well recently, I'm not yet free from 'piles'. There is no bleeding but I itch like hell.

SUNDAY, 24 DECEMBER

Eileen Potter

Go for a walk with my young niece and her puppy. We soon get away from the town, past the County Mental Hospital, which occupies a prominent position on the top of the hill, and strike out into the open, moorland country. It is a beautiful morning, sunny and not too cold, and everything seems peaceful here. In the afternoon we go to a carol service in the nearest church. My niece has recently been confirmed and has a soft spot for the vicar, so I go partly out of curiosity, to have a look at him. He looks as though he would be rather nice in private life, but has an affected manner of taking the service, and I do not think much of his or his organist's choice of carols – Victorian and dull, with unintelligible words.

CHRISTMAS DAY

Eileen Potter

After some hesitation, I decide to go to 8 o'clock communion with my middle niece. We go to the Priory, and the service is taken by the Suffragan bishop, a great improvement on the local vicar. We go home to breakfast and then comes the family ritual of opening Christmas parcels, which are all put in a heap in the drawing room.

My brother-in-law picks them up one by one, reading out the name of the donor and the recipient, who then comes forward and opens his or her parcel. The pup creates a good deal of amusement by getting quite excited over a squeaking rubber doll which has been wrapped in a parcel and labelled for him.

We all change into our best clothes for the Christmas dinner, which is just as usual. Afterwards we listen in to Gracie Fields, and do a little singing and dancing ourselves, but in rather a desultory way as compared with former years. This is the first year that the family has not had a Christmas tree.

Christopher Tomlin

The King's Speech: It was pitiful to hear him at first, but after making one or two false starts he warmed up and ran successfully.

For dinner we had roast duck with apple sauce, sage and onion and mashed potatoes, followed by plum pudding with brandy, and glasses of red wine. I enjoyed the meal immensely, for I knew I'd earned it.

£195 is subscribed by Prestonians towards the comfort fund. A letter from Dick arrived in a 'blue' non-censored envelope.

Pam Ashford

I spent the morning at the Exhibition of Pictures at the Institute of Fine Arts. Christmas did not seem any different this year from previous years so far as the Partick streets are concerned through which I passed on the way to the galleries: all the shops were open; all the children were living on the streets; all the housewives were engaged in their usual Monday washday duties.

I passed the RC Church. An old man stood outside begging and I felt I must give him something. He said, 'God bless you,' which I felt quite touching. I could not resist the temptation of running up the steps and peeping in, and coming down the steps afterwards I found an usher shooing away crowds of children who were reviling the Catholics.

Christmas dinner – chicken, pudding, mince pies. I washed up as quickly as possible so as to hear the Empire Broadcast and the King's Speech. Mother and I enjoyed both immensely. Then I set to work to complete the application form for the aeroplane factory.

The wireless was ghastly tonight. Tommy Handley! I ask you, if you had not heard him, would you have believed that anyone could be so terrible?

BOXING DAY

Pam Ashford

Miss Bousie did not think it was like other Christmases. Miss Gibson said – and I don't believe her – that she got drunk. Ethel is back again.

Mr Mitchell and Miss Crawford had a long conversation on the subject of spies. Both believe every word of the following stories:

Mr Mitchell: 'A porter at Paisley Station saw a nun. She dropped something and when picking it up he noticed it was a man's hand. He warned the police. The nun was a spy. The porter has received a letter from the War Office thanking him. That proves it is true.'

Miss Crawford: 'No, you have the story wrong. The facts are these: my friend's friend went from Glasgow to Greenock late one night. She got into a carriage in which there were nuns. During the journey a nun dropped something and the girl noticed that it was a man's hand that picked the article up. She warned the police. She has a letter from the War Office thanking her.'

Several people drew a comparison between our two office girls. Betty (14) notices every bill in the street and can always tell you what the latest is; Margaret (18) never notices anything at all. Several people wondered if she knew there was a war on. I commented upon the fact that Margaret often says, 'Daddy says the only thing that matters is if I am happy.'

A curious piece of natural history. For the seven years from 1932 to September 1939, Dick, our canary, fell into a somnolent position at tea-time and the family did not get much pleasure from his company thereafter. On the day that war was declared he changed completely, and now spends the evenings singing and hopping and being as sociable as he can.

Christopher Tomlin

I am very lonely. Mother went to my sister's where there was a party. Father had a fit of depression – sulks is a better name – and sat alone in another room. (Yesterday I cried a little, unknown to anybody. Mother was sad too and quietly went out of the room once or twice.

It is the first Christmas Dick was absent.) Perhaps today's gloom is a reflection of our secret sadness. Yesterday I lit a candle for Dick in church and made special prayers for him.

WEDNESDAY, 27 DECEMBER

Eileen Potter

I do a little shopping (New Year cards etc.) in the morning, and have a drink at the Milk Bar with my young niece. In the evening, my nephew and the middle niece go to the pictures. They invite me to accompany them, but in the meantime I have picked up *I Married a German* by Madeleine Kent, which somebody had borrowed from the library, and I prefer to spend the evening finishing that.

Christopher Tomlin

Letters take three days to come from Liverpool to Preston. Seventeen extra trains were used to cope with parcels this Christmas.

Our next door neighbours the Theobalds are gone. Mr Theobald was a volunteer reserve and immediately war was declared he left for France. Mrs Theobald works for the Army Pay Corps and earns only 35/- a week in spite of starting at 8 a.m. and finishing at 9 p.m. six days a week. They were buying a house through a building society. They have a motor-car which they want to sell and can't because there's no demand. Mrs Theobald is paying for a washing machine and other gadgets on HP and she paid 10/- a week to a neighbour who looked after the baby boy. The Theobalds are a young couple – he's 35 she's 30. It is now impossible for them to keep their home. Poor Mrs Theobald is living with a sister. Mr Theobald came home on leave a week ago and what a rotten homecoming his must have been when he knew he'd lose his bit of liberty.

THURSDAY, 28 DECEMBER

Eileen Potter

Snow has fallen in the night. I go on to Warrington to spend a few days with my brother and his wife. The train is extremely crowded, but I manage to worm my way into a corner seat. Warrington is the seat of our family timber business, in which my two surviving brothers are employed. I am rather surprised when the one I am staying with tells me that the older one, who had a stroke soon after the beginning of the war, turns out to be rather badly in debt, and that the managing director of the firm wants to see me tomorrow to discuss the position of our affairs in general.

Christopher Tomlin

My bad habit conquered last night: mortal sin.

A notice in front of an air raid shelter in Leyland Road close to Euxton: 'This shelter is private and is limited to a certain number of people who are already arranged for. The owner will be reluctant at refusing admittance but it will be compulsory. By order.'

Snow covers the ground to a depth of three inches in places. Father still persists that all Germans are evil and we should 'Kill! Kill! Kill!' He suggests one thousand Royal Air Force machines should bomb Germany and we should simultaneously strike at the Siegfried Line. 'We seem to be impotent. Nothing's happening unless Germany is doing it!'

BBC News: Turkey lost eight thousand souls in a violent earthquake. Twelve towns are ruined. Sugar is rationed three quarters of a pound each week. Meat will be rationed in February.

Australians and Canadians are here. I would like to meet those boys. I'm curious to know how they talk.

FRIDAY, 29 DECEMBER

Eileen Potter

Go to see the managing director of the family business, now a private company. We talk a little about general business affairs, and he says that trade was good in the early part of this year, but that since the Government took over the control of timber there has been very little doing. What with the control, the war, and the bad weather, hardly any timber is coming into the country, and so much English timber was cut down during the last war that there has hardly been any time to replenish the stock. We then pass to a discussion of my elder brother's affairs, and Mr C produces a large sheaf of unpaid bills, dating mainly from the time of my brother's second marriage in the early part of last year. It appears that he has been getting into debt for some years, and it seems as though he paid off his old debts about the time of his second marriage, only to begin piling up new ones. Mr C points out that he has suspected something of the sort all along. This does increase my confidence in him, as hitherto he has always urged me to take my brother's advice in business matters.

SATURDAY, 30 DECEMBER

Christopher Tomlin

Thirty thousand dead in the Turkish earthquake. Thousands more are believed to be underneath the debris.

I went to the Workers' Educational Association Hot-Pot Supper and Social. I never enjoyed myself more; I hadn't danced for ten years but was complimented by the ladies. We didn't pay at the door, a member came round with a tray. I was sorry to see many throw nothing on – most of the delinquents were women. I consider the do was worth 5/-. We danced the military two-step.

I came out into a dense fog, no moon nor stars. I groped along: Thursday's snow thawed this afternoon and froze tonight so I had to be careful. My battery was almost exhausted when I left the social but I know Preston very well. I got in, looked at the clock and – voila! – midnight. I thought it was 11.

SUNDAY, 31 DECEMBER

Eileen Potter

Spend a quiet day, reading, writing letters, listening in. We sit up to 'let the New Year in', but do not have any visitors. We all kiss each other, and drink a glass of wine. The next-door neighbours are Scots, and sounds of revelry are heard from their house. They are, however, very disappointed as one of their sons has been called up for the Army, and has to begin on New Year's Day.

Christopher Tomlin

Mother knows I asked Brother President for a £5 loan but father doesn't know yet. When he does the fur will fly: we are a proud family, proud we didn't owe a sou. Dick went away and we thought we'd be okay. The £5 had to go to settle his insurance and another bill or two. It was two months or more until his voluntary allotment passed through the red tape. We were about to sell the typewriter I use. I hope circumstances will never compel us to.

The Booths, a Catholic couple next door, have a party on. For two hours they sang carols, hymns and 'profane' melodies, then musical chairs, and now they are shouting 'snap!' It's a pity the wall is so thin.

12 midnight. Next door's party is still going on.

New Year. Quo vadis?

Chapter Six

THE GOVERNMENT
TAKES YOUR SON

Thank goodness I have at least a year left: conscription beckons for the young.

'We work in a huge Victorian prison on the outskirts of London which has rows of cells arranged on skeleton iron balconies. It isn't particularly cheerful, but it is very well suited to the job, as the cells make the multitude of small private offices that are needed, and for the big rooms required there are the gym and the library. The concert hall serves as our canteen, and has such a draught that we are nearly blown through the roof. I have Cell 86 with a heavy iron door that doesn't open from inside, and a little window too high up to see out of, with bars.

The organisation of our department is pretty thorough. There are the postal, the telegraph, the codes and cyphers, and cryptics departments; and a large staff of translators, financial experts, trade experts, specialists in metals and chemicals, card indexers, recorders and so on.

It isn't glamorous or romantic work by any means.'

Eve Farson describes her work as a military censor, BBC Overseas Service, 12 January 1940

* * *

1 January 1940 Conscription extended to 20-27 year-olds. **5 January** Hore-Belisha resigns as Secretary for War, to be replaced by Oliver Stanley. **8 January** Rationing of butter, sugar and bacon begins in Britain. **12 January** The height of the freezing weather conditions in Europe. **15 January** Belgium refuses Allied request to advance through its territory; an announcement that almost twice as many Britons have been killed on the roads in the black-out than by enemy action. **22 January** Destroyer *Exmouth* torpedoed off Wick by U-boat, with all hands killed.

NEW YEAR'S DAY

Christopher Tomlin

Inside Nazi Germany, published by the German freedom people, is on sale at a newsagent's in town. The poster advertising it says 'published in spite of the Gestapo'. It is 3d a copy.

40,000 dead in Turkish earthquake!

'Porridge and milk are far better for you than bacon and butter,' says Sir John Orr speaking on the BBC. 'Potatoes are good . . . We should grow some vegetables even if it's only in a flower pot.' His propaganda point is to avoid imported foods and to grow as much as we can. Me to Mother and Father: 'I don't like to suggest it, but it looks as if the Government's scared.'

'How do you mean?'

'They think we won't be able to get enough food across with all these boats sunk.'

Eileen Potter

I go to Liverpool to see my eldest surviving brother, who is still in a nursing home. I have been warned not to say anything to him about his financial difficulties, as it might bring on a relapse. I find him looking remarkably cheerful, and I wonder whether he remembers anything about his money troubles or not. His brain seems quite clear on other subjects, though he cannot speak very distinctly. He even begins discussing politics, and I regret to say that he suggests that we cannot afford to weaken Germany too much as we need her as a buffer against Russia. In the main, however, he seems mostly interested in comparatively trivial matters such as the Christmas cards which he has received, and which are all arrayed upon the mantelpiece in his room.

I stay at the nursing home for about an hour, and then leave to have lunch in a big department store near the station and return to Warrington. My sister-in-law meets the train and we go to the pictures together and see *Captain Fury*, with Brian Aherne, my favourite film star. It is not really a very good film, but I cannot help falling for his Irish charm, and my sister-in-law says he has a face like an angel.

TUESDAY, 2 JANUARY

Christopher Tomlin

I doubt if it could be colder than it is today. For a week it has been impossible for me to make diary notes outdoors. Thanks to my insurance agent who advised me to buy quinine and phosphorus pills I can stick it better this year.

I got another torch battery from a customer who manages a big cycle store in town. I asked for him and was invited into the office, as he doesn't want his assistants to know. He tells me I need never be without a battery if I will ask for him. Returning home by bus I was greeted by a St Vincent de Paul brother who is a traveller for Matthew Brown's. I showed him my battery.

I chatted to a customer about the new age groups, 20 to 27, to be called up this year and said, 'Thank goodness I have at least a year left in civil life!' I want to be anything other than an infantryman (cannon fodder) but don't know what to join. I'm not a tradesman. I know much about printing but I can't print. So what the deuce will they pop me in? I'm very short-sighted and have that distressing complaint – itching piles. My brother laughs at his friends who laughed because he joined up in September. Now they are pathetically eager to choose a position instead of being shoved into an unpleasant one.

I asked Mr Evans, the local firm to which I paid the £5, how stationers did in the last war. 'They did well, but one of my customers who ordered a large consignment of pads to retail at 2/6 was left with them on his hands, for the war ended three months after the pads came in. And the peace-time selling price was 1/-.' The moral is don't obtain big stocks. Mr Evans has helio and blue 'penman parchment' in, but no envelopes to match. He said, 'Your customers haven't got to the point of putting blue or helio paper into white envelopes as people did in the last war. They were glad to get hold of anything.' I told Mother what he said, and she remarked: 'Printed writing paper wasn't heard of then. Today it is so cheap it's no longer a luxury. Why shouldn't ordinary folk have their addresses on?'

WEDNESDAY, 3 JANUARY

Christopher Tomlin
Water left in the washbowl in the bathroom is frozen. The lavatory cistern had to be thawed. My shaving brush bristles are like iron. The sponge is a brick. I'm just about to wash myself from the stomach up and believe me it needs every gramme of courage and resolution I've got.

Tommy Farr leaves the Royal Air Force! Excuse: eye and ear trouble. Mother and I think it queer for there are chaps in the Royal Air Force with worse ailments than Tommy's. An assistant in Evans thinks he was chucked out. I wrote to Dick, 'Has he got cold feet?' Boxers are supposed to be in A1 condition.

THURSDAY, 4 JANUARY

Christopher Tomlin
We are disgusted at the evacuation of civil servants from London to Blackpool: how the devil can a chap run two homes on £4 a week? The Government does blasted blundering things. We are annoyed that the minimum rate for a parcel to France is 9d. As father only too truly says, 'The Government takes your son and then when you want to send a parcel to him you must make a profit for the Post Office.'

A young man and a maiden sat tête-à-tête on top of the bus. He murmured, 'It's all right,' and handed her a cigarette, 'you aren't in uniform.'

She smiled. 'I'm in the mood for breaking rules. I've been tied so lately. I'm only allowed out until 10 on weekdays and get a late pass until 11 on Saturdays and Sundays.'

He: 'What happens in the ATS if you break the rules?'

'Oh, CB and your pay is stopped. I'm all right though, I get £2 a week and allowances for wear and tear.'

'Oh that's why you had a New Year's party?'

'I was miserable on New Year's Eve. I was on my own.'

'I wish I'd known. I was odd-man-out that night as my drinking pals had all gone to private parties.'

'Why didn't you give me a ring?'

It's a damned good job I am not spying for the enemy, for the young things chatted about the movements of troops from Preston.

The ATS girl said the local searchlight battalion were off to Scapa Flow on ***, a batch of Loyal North Lancs was due for France on ***. She mentioned the movements of six lots of troops. She was a damned little fool.

Eileen Potter

I go to Chester to spend the day with an old school friend. She tells me about her latest love affair. She is music lecturer at a training college, and has been having an affair with a cathedral organist who was unhappily married. He has now divorced his wife, but my friend has discovered that he has also been making love to another younger girl. They are now at the stage of writing to each other giving long explanations of what has happened.

FRIDAY, 5 JANUARY

Christopher Tomlin

I went for a 2d Aero but was told, 'No milk blocks at all after the Christmas rush. I can't get hold of stuff. My normal order is fifty boxes a month, but I can only get fourteen and if I sold those I would have to wait three weeks before I can get any more.'

I told a customer to tune in to London Regional as the BBC is giving special broadcasts to the troops and there's another 24 hours of variety a week. Customer: 'They want to get some fresh artists. They are all the same.' 'Yes, Tommy Handley was all right at first . . .'

'Now he's a pain! They have the same old names like Barbara Cooper in the plays.'

To the cinema, where I saw *Hound of the Baskervilles* with Basil Rathbone as Sherlock Holmes. It was an exciting gripping drama.

Pam Ashford

Jock's Box was brought into the conversation this morning. This is a fund that a Glasgow paper is raising to send Scottish soldiers boxes of goodies. According to Miss Crawford's information, a soldier got a box in which the cake was stale and the other articles most unpalatable. I mentioned the village of New Deer where my friend, Mrs Angus, is a leading light of the Women's Rural Institutes. The members cooked plum puddings which they gave to be put in with the socks, which were sent by the village to their local lads in the services. The men have been describing these puddings as one of the horrors of war.

On the way back from lunch Miss Bousie saw a bus full of people in their uniforms.

'They looked serious,' she said.

Miss Smith: 'They would not be much good if they were not serious.'

Miss Bousie: 'And in fur coats!'

Miss Smith: 'They are advised to keep warm.'

Miss Bousie: 'What about anything falling on them? Fire? They would just go up!'

Miss Smith: 'They would just singe.'

SATURDAY, 6 JANUARY

Christopher Tomlin

Hore-Belisha resigns [as Secretary of War], Oliver 'Silver' Stanley takes over. Mother said, 'HB is too theatrical, too much in the limelight.'

Father: 'He wanted to boss the Generals, I never cared for him. But I don't think much of Stanley.'

Mother: 'Is it because he's a Jew? He said he never wants to be in another cabinet under Mr Chamberlain. I think Chamberlain should resign, he's too weak.'

Nosmo King: 'I'm going over to the States for three months.'

Hubert: 'Why?'

Nosmo King: 'To buy a new battery for my torch.'

SUNDAY, 7 JANUARY

Maggie Joy Blunt

The war in Burnham Beeches remains a distant unreality. All news of it we receive in caution for at the back of our minds is the knowledge that there are individuals in authority who, as H.G. Wells puts it, 'love to twist and censor facts . . . and do their best to divert the limited gifts and energies of . . . writers, lecturers and talkers to the production of disingenuous muck that will muddle the public mind and mislead the enquiring foreigner.'

So my friend Julia and I forgot the war and decorated the sitting room with holly and Xmas cards and red Woolworth candles. We were enticed by a full moon to walk through the frosted woods at night. We celebrated Xmas Day with pheasant and plum pudding and cherry brandy. We patronised the local cinema on Boxing Day. And one morning it began to snow. Flake upon soundless flake fell into the notches of trees, between blades of grass, onto the flat surfaces of evergreen leaves until the garden and roof tops and roads were thickly covered. And there it stayed for more than a week, transforming the woods and the village into a pantomime set of fantastic loveliness. My little cat was wildly excited. She had never seen snow before and seemed to think that it was there for her especial pleasure. She raced round the garden, over the rockery, underneath bushes, up her favourite tree, not minding at all that the snow collected on the long hair round her tummy and froze into lumps.

The thermometer fell. Water pipes and wastes froze and road surfaces became the delight and terror of children. Julia began to clear the garden path. Our coal supply ran out before the new order had arrived and I had to saw frozen timber for the fires. We visited Windsor and High Wycombe. We surrounded ourselves with Sunday papers on Dec. 31st and studied the New Year predictions. We saw the New Year in playing rummy and drank to each other's absent friends in port. There was no more snow but the first fall did not thaw until today.

Julia designs Xmas cards. She receives a small allowance from an old, eccentric family friend, both her parents are dead, and she knows none of her relatives. She was educated at an expensive South Coast convent until she was 15 when she was removed on account of her delicate health. Her mother was descended from the old French aristocracy. Her father was a well-known actor but came of an Old English county family and refused to believe that his daughter might ever have to earn her own living. Quarrels and misunderstandings in her family left Julia penniless at her mother's death – penniless, fastidious, delicate and proud with artistic ability and scout training. She has nothing now but contempt for the privileged classes. She regards Mr Chamberlain and his government with loathing. She reads the *News Chronicle* with ardour, is interested in communism, music, films (the only form of entertainment she has been able to afford for years) and dietetics. She also follows the astrologers eagerly, and through her I have been introduced to Mr Edward Lyndoe's predictions in the *People*. Someone else has mentioned them to me as being astonishingly accurate months ago but I had forgotten this. Now I have made a note of his forecasts for 1940. We shall see. January, he says, will bring about the death of a Soviet leader which will be a forerunner of events that will eventually mould the union. He predicts a short war, ending possibly in September, but not before we have passed through a very tough struggle. I wrote to him for my horoscope. It is mercifully vague but gives the impression of a year of complete gloom.

Christopher Tomlin

Lord Milne always writes good, sound, sensible stuff for the *Sunday Chronicle*. Today's leader says the air raids we expected in September will occur in a few weeks when the days lengthen. My God, I hope not. I now understand men from 20 to 28 will be called up soon. I thought it was only to 27.

MONDAY, 8 JANUARY

Pam Ashford

The Soroptimist Club again. The fog is, of course, the big subject of conversation today. However, this gave way to comments upon the excellence of the address today: Miss Frances Stevenson on a Trip Up the Yangtze Kiang.

Eileen Potter

The last day of my holidays. Return to London. My brother-in-law drives me down to the station in a little van in which he takes his produce to market. Although it is a small country station, there is a good train service because a director of the BMS Railway formerly lived in the neighbourhood, to say nothing of a good sprinkling of aristocracy.

(This is Eileen Potter's last entry until May.)

TUESDAY, 9 JANUARY

Christopher Tomlin

Mussolini signs a pact with Hungary against Russia. Stalin appeals for help to Hitler. And Hitler refuses to allow arms to pass from Mussolini to Finland. Hitler and Mussolini will soon drift apart.

WEDNESDAY, 10 JANUARY

Christopher Tomlin

A customer: 'I'm very worried at the moment. There was a big merchant ship that went down yesterday and a friend was on it. I only said goodbye to her last Thursday; she needn't have gone yet to South Africa.'

Me: 'The *Daily Mail* "Stop Press" says all passengers were saved.'

Customer: 'Well, they would lose all their belongings. My friend had £100 with her, they wouldn't let her land in South Africa without it and the passage money was £70 . . .'

They are very public spirited in Penwortham: most women are in ARP, many in the Civil Nursing Reserve. It's a pity such enthusiasm is latent in peace-time. It needs a war to solve unemployment. It needs a war to unite all classes.

Germany admits holding up supplies from Italy to Finland and Il Duce protests. German airmen are found in shot-down Soviet planes. Big names and newspapers warn us dreadful things are about to happen.

I tuned in 'The Trial of Captain Kidd' and mother expostulated, 'Good lord are you going to listen to that damned thing again?'

'Again!'

'It's nothing but a blasted row!'

Ten minutes later I switched off. Mother was right as usual.

THURSDAY, 11 JANUARY

Christopher Tomlin

I think victory propaganda is overdone. Surely editors don't expect readers to believe everything the Allies do is a success? Yet our planes are 'unbeatable', our Navy is 'supreme', our soldiers win important victories *behind* the Maginot line. If the Navy is so good why are there any sinkings of merchantmen? If our Air Force can't be challenged why the devil do we allow Nazi planes to escape our shores?

FRIDAY, 12 JANUARY

Christopher Tomlin
Father was in fiery mood at breakfast: 'These mealy-mouthed preachers . . . How can God allow the war to go on? I don't think much of him, he's on the side of Hitler . . . Why, Turkey has more people killed in that earthquake than all who were killed in the Great War. Not content with sending an earthquake God sends floods to finish them off . . . The mealy-mouthed buggers of preachers and people who say the Versailles Treaty is the cause of this war! It's not the Treaty – it wasn't severe enough. We should have crushed the Germans and not left them alone to breed again! The Royal Air Force want to go over there, bomb all the German towns and give them hell. There'll never be peace until they are wiped from the face of the Earth!'

I made £2.15.0 this week, which is excellent for the first full week after the Christmas holidays. It is better than January 1939. Most people now write at least one letter a week to a soldier in France. When more servicemen are called for I should do better still.

Pam Ashford
Miss Bousie: 'I had a Christmas letter from a friend in Edinburgh who watched the air raid there and she said, "I would not have missed it for world." She belongs to Jehovah's Witnesses and quoted scriptural texts to prove that everything was coming as prophesied. What was so funny was that she was so doleful, and yet it was just as God had always willed it! There are to be 144,000 souls saved and she hopes to be one.'

MONDAY, 15 JANUARY

Christopher Tomlin
The sirens blew at 12 o'clock. I thought for a minute that Fritz was here but realised it was just a practice.

I have been in business for nine years but today is the first time I received a 5/- piece. Mother summed up: 'I wonder how long somebody's kept that, it shows they are hard up or they would never had given it away.' I hope to keep it, for it may be valuable one day.

I don't feel too comfortable with 'Save, don't spend' propaganda. Granted it is wise to buy necessities and eschew luxuries in war, but I am worried over the possible effect on my business. My lines are cheaper than plain papers sold at exclusive stores in town. I don't think they are luxuries in wartime but will others think as I do? The shopkeepers aren't skilled workers, they cannot take an active part in making munitions. What can they do? What will happen to them? What about me? How the blazes can I or my people save when we haven't enough for necessities? Father and I would love to buy overcoats, our present ones are years old. But we cannot see our way to. We must rest in peace and pay as you go.

TUESDAY, 16 JANUARY

Christopher Tomlin

Father told me to hurry out to work and not waste such a lovely day. His words were just spoken when it began to snow, and then he said, 'I wouldn't canvass if I were you . . . ' I walked to Sydney's in the swirling snow (to take the orders) and made up my mind to succeed even if flakes covered me to the eyebrows. I arrived in town as the snowstorm ceased and set out with grim determination. I expected the worst because I believed Government advice to save would make women tie their purse strings. My first ten calls were duds but I carried on. I needn't have fretted for I sold 25/- worth of stuff and made 14/-. From my bicycle shop manager I was lucky enough to buy an Ever Ready flat battery.

Pam Ashford

Sleep was the subject of discussion this morning. It would seem that almost everyone has broken nights. The war has not had this effect on me. After 12 months of broken sleep (when I knew that the die was cast) my sleep returned. Someone said she had heard that we ought to sleep more during the war to make up for the strain on the nerves. Miss Bousie said, 'Who could sleep more?'

Continued to read *I Married a German*, and at every page I have asked myself, 'Can I too have a false romantic idea about Germany

151

that would rapidly expire were my knowledge and experience better?'

THURSDAY, 18 JANUARY

Christopher Tomlin

So Hitler has his first gift from the Pandora's Box he's opened: an influenza epidemic in Germany. Because he drove Jewish doctors from Germany he hasn't enough to cure those who are ill.

Cold as ever, my throat is tender and I have a bad chest cough.

Pam Ashford

Miss Bousie considers that the only way to cope with the situation is to decide never to allow another war to arise. I said, 'Only religion can induce that point of view.' Miss Bousie replied, 'No, not all religion. There are hundreds of people going about calling themselves religious. It is Christianity that is required." I said, 'I used the word "religious" because I do not wish to exclude Parsees and Buddhists and various other Eastern religions.' So far as this country goes, it is Christianity that is wanted . . . with a small number of Jews perhaps, some of whom I know to be quite desirable people.

SUNDAY, 21 JANUARY

Maggie Joy Blunt

It was with difficulty that I remembered the war while I was in London. The humming of the air through the wires of barrage balloons near Hampstead Heath, stories of unemployment, news of acquaintances of both sexes in the Services, limited butter and sugar portions in restaurants and cafés – all served to remind me now and then that we are fighting Against Aggression, *For* Peace, Liberty and Freedom, but they slid easily into the background and could have been ignored and forgotten in an unhindered round of social activities seeing people and plays and shops.

For a few days I stayed with June and her husband Kassim. They own a house of four flats in Hampstead where before the war they lived together on the ground floor and I once rented the top. Kassim is an architect, employed at the moment by a Borough Council to inspect air-raid shelters in which he says he has little faith. His

152

employment is only temporary and he may find himself without work any week. His view of the future is tinged a little with his own bitterness. It is the professional classes, he says, that are suffering.

Less than 50% of the population seem to be carrying gas-masks now. June and I decided to take ours when we went out, on principle, but it was an effort and an irritation. The black-out has slackened considerably. I noticed streaks of light from doors and windows which would never have been allowed at the beginning of the war, but I hear that regulations are still strictly enforced in all coastal towns. Tube trains are plunged into darkness when they emerge above ground, which is disconcerting at first, but one gets used to it. Returning late one evening to relations in the suburbs even the glimmer lights in my carriage failed and a group of people near me began to sing. They were not drunk. I do not know that they were even happy. Old Songs. Popular songs. 'On Ilkley Moor', 'Annie Laurie', 'Wish Me Luck', 'Auld Lang Syne'. A girl's fine soprano sprang into a descant above the leading tenor. I think that in the darkness the sense of what it might one night mean drew them to express their courage in the only medium they knew.

June grumbled at the use people make of torches in the streets at night. It is true that one can get used to the darkness if lights are not being flashed on and off continually, but stumbling up and down kerbs can be very unnerving, as I know to my cost. I stayed for a little while with my darling aunts Ella and Aggie who live some seven miles from Piccadilly, and one night I just missed the last train to their town but caught one which landed me at a station two-and-a-half miles from their house. It was after midnight and all buses had stopped. There were no taxis and my torch battery had given out. I know the district well but it was some years since I have walked from that station to my aunt's home. I nearly sat on the kerb and wept. All the stories I had heard of violence to lonely females in the black-out rushed through my mind. There was, however, nothing else to do but stumble through the lifting fog for two-and-a-half dreary miles. I called at a police station on the way in the hope that a friendly constable had a torch to spare, but the sergeant in charge looked only astonished and suspicious.

I went to a new comedy in which a childhood friend of mine is playing a lead. Miranda and I used to gambol together in one or other of our adjoining gardens during the last war. I am four years older than she is, but when I saw her after the show, she reduced this difference – rather graciously I thought – to six months. She makes no secret of her age, is a clever little actress and deserves her success. She and her film actor husband do not lack engagements. Musical comedy and revues seem to be the major demand at present.

I do not remember such a long, hard winter. I returned to the cottage in trepidation to find my worst fears realised – all pipes and tanks frozen nearly solid, which, when thawing under the influence of cautiously applied heat, began to drip ominously at various joints until one near the sink came violently asunder and flooded the kitchen while I rushed out to my neighbours for help.

Now I must set to work in earnest while I await developments of this curious war. I have ideas for several new short stories, but even if I can get them written, what chance of recognition does an unknown writer stand today? 'Give New Authors A Chance' pleaded Sir Hugh Walpole in a recent *Daily Sketch*, at the same time pointing out that publishers are not likely to venture on a new, unknown writer when his book will cost 10s and Sir John Simon has told us not to spend money on luxuries.

MONDAY, 22 JANUARY

Christopher Tomlin

During my Saturday delivery many clients said they were either frozen-up or had bursts. We were frozen-up until 5.15 when the hot water taps came on. At Mrs Booth's a few houses away the hot water pipe burst yesterday and 15 gallons of water flooded her house. The plumber popped in to take a look, and says we are in no danger. He couldn't see to us at once for he has 150 people to attend who are worse off than us. He heard water pouring down the stairs of houses whose occupiers work all day.

Announcer: 'German newspapers mention an influenza epidemic in England. There is no truth in the story.' Isn't there? It's true for Preston. German prisoners of war don't like our bread and complain they haven't enough work to do (*Daily Mail*). I think they should be used to sweep away the snow.

Pam Ashford

Today the cold touches depths of the kind described as 'the worst in living memory'. In the *Observer* yesterday there was a comment upon the lack of weather reports nowadays. It seems funny to be passing through such a severe period and to read only about its effects abroad. Again and again I say to myself, 'If it is true that the cold spell benefits Finland at the expense of Russia, then may the cold spell continue till Midsummer.' There is a shortage of coal coming, or already come. We have no coal in our Govan depot and today people have been going along with prams to take coal home, but in vain.

The Soroptimist Club. The lecturer was Mr Claythorpe who said they were manufacturing gas at the present moment in Germany, and that the plant had been made in Scotland by Scottish inventors. When I told Mr Mitchell this later he said, 'We are making poison gas in Swansea, and the man in charge is a German who learned his job in Germany.'

Miss Bousie: 'I cannot understand why we make so much fuss about Finland, and yet we did nothing for Spain or for Abyssinia. We allowed the Germans and the Russians to spray the people of Spain with machine gun fire and our Government stood by complacently. I cannot understand this change of attitude.'

I said, 'You want the British to be the policemen of the world.'

Miss Bousie: 'I do. We are a great, powerful nation and we could be the policemen of the world if we had men with courage.'

TUESDAY, 23 JANUARY

Pam Ashford

The dense fog came down again at sundown and as I made my way to Jamaica Street, I reflected in these terms: 'If only I could convey in that MO diary how detestable conditions are tonight.' Snow, trodden down for five days; pea soup fog; the densest cold 'within living memory'; black-out; and the traffic. What a hazard it is to cross the roads, what a struggle to get on a bus or tram, what an interminable time the journeys seem to take. The newspapers, of course, aren't allowed to reveal the state of the weather and the historian of the future, if he goes by the papers, will think that we have been concentrating our thoughts on this or that aspect of the war. But we have not. All the time it has been the cold, the cold, the cold.

WEDNESDAY, 24 JANUARY

Pam Ashford

The *Exmouth* has been lost with all hands. It is a shock, but we are getting used to war now and we receive such news with a measure of – I don't know what to call it – a sort of 'it's all in a day's work' feeling. It stands in marked contrast to the feeling that the loss of the *Courageous* produced in the first month of war.

The German class again tonight. Mr Amour has promised to lend me some books about German systems of shorthand. He said, 'Unfortunately the books are out of date for the Nazis have introduced a new system of their own.'

The Zoo faces our office windows and I thought of a photo in the *Bulletin* of a keeper saying goodbye to his lions 'ere going to the war. Mr Mitchell says that if there is a raid the lions will be shot straightaway. My mind is torn in two. It is hard lines on the lions, but I am sure I don't want them loose in this area.

SATURDAY, 27 JANUARY

Christopher Tomlin

My brother writes, 'Don't worry about the weather in England, mother. It's summer to what we are having in France. It's ten degrees below zero and I wake up in the middle of the night to find the top blanket frozen stiff. I woke up two or three times one day this week it was so cold.'

I heard Winston Churchill talking and sat up with a jerk at the fierce interruption. I could hear some fanatic call repeatedly 'I want ***!' But what he wanted I don't know. I heard the announcer say to Winston, 'Shall I call for ***?' and Mr Churchill replied in a very low tone, 'No. I've had forty years' experience of this kind of thing!' His speech was grand.

SUNDAY, 28 JANUARY

Maggie Joy Blunt

I spent an hour clearing the paths. The *Observer* states, 'It can now be revealed that the Thames was frozen over at Kingston and for eight miles between Teddington and Sunbury. Temperatures in

London were well below freezing point for a whole week and twelve inches of ice covered London reservoirs. The snap was the coldest since 1894.'

Salisbury Plain manoeuvres have brought the army into much evidence in this district. Houses in the forest have been commandeered for the military, and disused saw mills, stables, vicarages, are being used as billets. There are soldiers in our village too. A large new garage was commandeered at the beginning of the war and khaki-coloured lorries and officers' cars being driven in and out of it are a familiar sight. No doubt spy rumours abound. When I was in London I was told of enemy transmitting stations discovered in an old church tower and the petrol tank of a woman's car. One might do worse than cash in on spy stories now. I could imagine myself as a suspect. Or the bachelor who used to live in a neighbouring cottage and has now bought an enormous house on the edge of the Common where he is living alone and unattended except for my Fanny who 'does' for him 2 days a week . . .

Strange war. When will it begin, if it is going to begin? I look at the deep snow which covers the garden and think of the thaw that must come, the bulbs that I planted in October, the promise I have had of lupins and dahlias to add to the summer pageant, and I want the time to pass quickly. But the thought of spring this year is shadowed with dread.

Chapter Seven

MISS BOUSIE WISHES TO KNOW

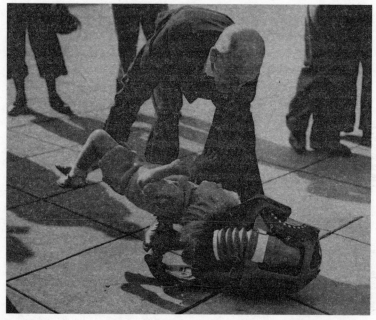

Faithfully carrying out those ARP duties: an unusually pliant child enters a gas bag.

'When I arrived at the deserted empty-looking house, the captain in charge took me to the large old-fashioned kitchen, and introduced me to the staff, saying his batman, Gunner Shields, would show me the stores and tell me what there was to cook for dinner. I think you housewives would have felt for me if you had seen those stores. No neat jars of sugar, tea, rice, which are our pride at home. Just a few paper bags filled with odd amounts of tea, sugar, prunes, custard and so on. The bags didn't even say whether the flour was plain or self-raising.

Have you ever tried to cook a roly-poly pudding with no pudding cloth, no rolling pin, no pastry board and no flour dredger? I had to.'

Honor Daplyn, a member of the Women's Voluntary Services, finds it tough-going at the barracks, the Home Service, 31 January 1940

* * *

5 February The Supreme War Council sends belated and insubstantial assistance to Finland, and decides to intervene in Norway. **6 February** The 'Careless Talk Costs Lives' anti-gossip campaign is launched. **12 February** First Australian and New Zealand troops arrive in Suez; Germany and Russia agree new trade pact. **16 February** 300 British prisoners rescued from the German supply ship *Altmark* in Norwegian waters. **22 February** Two IRA bombs explode in London, injuring 12. **23 February** The crews of *Exeter* and *Ajax* cheered through London after returning from South America.

THURSDAY, 1 FEBRUARY

Christopher Tomlin

I'm making this entry four days after the above date. The after effects of last week's flu left me as weak as a filleted herring. I get no sick benefit. It's the first time in my life I was in bed for a few days.

Pam Ashford

Orders are coming in from Switzerland, Sweden, Belgium and elsewhere which, if we could fulfil them, would make our fortunes for life, but we cannot fulfil them. We are working our hardest on a most tantalising situation.

In the evening General Swinton gave his weekly war commentary. Tonight he had some words to say about Lord Haw Haw. Mention of Lord Haw Haw to me is like putting a match to a barrel of gunpowder, and the people with whom I work seem to avoid the subject in my presence. I always say, 'If you don't approve of Lord Haw Haw, why do you listen?' and yet they go on listening and then have long talks on the way the BBC should counteract his influence on the British public. Mr Sinclair's talks on the other hand don't seem to be listened to much. He is a highbrow.

When the General had finished his talk, Mother nearly exploded with indignation. She has read in the newspapers about the way Lord Haw Haw is giving the names of men who have been saved from the submarines, always one or two at a time. It was the way he got people to listen in again and again. Mother was aflame with the cruelty of it. 'Think of the state of mind of the relatives waiting to hear day after day.'

FRIDAY, 2 FEBRUARY

Christopher Tomlin

Mother came into my bedroom with very bad news: 'Your father's dole was stopped yesterday.' This means that all we now have to live on is what I can earn, about £2.10.0 a week. I dread failure; so much depends on me now. I sold 33/6 worth of stuff.

SUNDAY, 4 FEBRUARY

Maggie Joy Blunt

A glassy thaw began on Wednesday when I had an appointment with my bank manager in London. I hesitated at Slough station, and dithered on the bridge, thinking how foolish it would be to continue my journey and find myself stranded because frost or fog had delayed trains and stopped all buses. But quite suddenly and, as it were, out of the grey heaven, I heard an elderly man who had been wheezing up the stairs after me, say, 'It's unlucky to go back.'

My bank manager was grave and kind. He advised me to accept the cash offer for my smallholding and reinvest in the old 3% War Loan, the government stock being not only a patriotic investment, but as safe a one as any, since if the government crashes everything else crashes too. 'But it will not come to that,' he said, 'though we have hard times to face. Government stock may drop still further. Taxes are heavy. We shall all suffer. I am receiving less now than I was two years ago although I am earning more.' He can grant no more private credit: all available credit is being reserved for the Government. Money for bombs at all costs.

Fanny has heard that Hitler is to be in London on April 21st. She said with a twinkle, 'Don't you arrange to go up *that* day, Ma'am!' It is reported that he intends to be king of England. An odd ambition.

TUESDAY, 6 FEBRUARY

Tilly Rice

Quite a long gap since I last wrote, accounted for partly by the business of having a baby, and of getting over same and returning home to Surrey.

Christmas in Port Isaac was quite a pleasant interlude save for the fact that the cold and uncomfortable journey down on 23rd December sent my husband to bed for several days with a very bad cold. After Christmas I spent the time remaining to me, for the first time, really enjoying being down there. It was almost like a deferred summer holiday, and, except when it was mentioned in conversation, war was very remote indeed. But now it threatens to come nearer to the little village as I believe it is planned that this lovely Port Isaac Bay is to be utilised as a bombing practice range and a large tract of ground has been purchased to make a landing ground for aeroplanes. All fishermen sailing out from the Padstow district received notification that fishing was to be prohibited and there was quite a loud outcry against it.

I spent several days taking long walks about the countryside. A young man, a native of the village and a bachelor, accompanied me on several of these walks, which considerably heightened their interest as he was a nature lover. The village of course noticed this and I was highly amused to have it reported to me a day or two before I returned that it was being said 'that my husband had sent for me as he could not have such carryings-on'.

And so it came to this Saturday when I, together with one small child, one baby (Janet) and one typewriter, had to make my journey back to London. It is a long journey at most times, but under winter and war conditions with a change in the middle, I was definitely not looking forward to it. But the train was only ten minutes late and everything went off well. There were just three other women in the carriage (smoking). The baby was praised as being good, and we all settled down to gossip. One was a WRAF just returning from a fortnight's course at Plymouth, the other an army officer's wife travelling to Aldershot and the third, a nervous lady with a shoulder that twitched and who appeared to be apprehensive about something, so much so that the WRAF took her under her wing when they had to change at Salisbury for the south coast. The WRAF talked the most at first, and I was struck by the freedom of her speech and for the first time thought of the blue posters enjoining one not to talk of official things. I was interested to notice that the officer's wife was tolerant to the Germans while the WRAF was all fire and blood, and I tried to keep the balance between the two.

I felt quite fresh when we steamed into Waterloo. Here again I was agreeably surprised at the amount of light in the station and the streets outside. Perhaps due to a light sprinkling of snow, I could even see where I was from the windows of the taxi which took us to a small hotel at Charing Cross for the night.

After the children were safely in bed under the watch of an obliging maid, my husband and I ventured forth into the streets. This was the first time I had been in a town for over five months, never having once been away from Port Isaac while I was down there. I was able to lead my husband without a mistake to a little pub in a side-street that I myself had only visited once before. Sitting by a nice fire with a glass of beer I felt my heart warm at being back in London again. I think it was more the feeling of returning to normality that was such a relief.

That Saturday was 27th January and on the next day the great snowfall began. We just got down to Tadworth in time before the trains were held up and arrived to find the house without water, the main having frozen in the cold snap. I have been wondering how the successful censoring of the weather is going to affect people: will they realise that if one piece of news can be so firmly squashed so can another, and in view of that, how can we tell which way the war is really going? Isn't it just the same thing as they do in Germany?

Once settled in, I turned to look at what changes the war had wrought in Tadworth. Everyone (a little to my surprise I must confess) is still faithfully carrying out those ARP duties, and I think it really gallant the way they are doing this despite the fact that there is nothing doing and it must be a very boring routine. The whole thing seems to be run in a businesslike manner, and I must say that since the war, Tadworth has 'snapped to it' admirably.

There are still many strangers about, all the firms that came down here at the beginning of the war have remained, barring one – Foyles – who have returned to Charing Cross Road. I find that it is difficult to get women to do housework as they are all making money out of taking boarders. The old ladies who rented my house have settled down here permanently, as have several other people who came here five months ago. So apparently we shall never be quite the same again, even if nothing else happens.

Christopher Tomlin

The snow which was five feet deep has now melted into porridge: it was vile to walk about in but I was bound to make money. I have a rotten cold in the head and am suffering from 'flu depression. Again and again I said, 'I wish I was dead . . . I wish it was all over.'

Pam Ashford

Bad news this morning. The son (23 years old) of Mr Peat, a leading coal exporter, was lost on the *Sphinx* on Saturday. It was the first time he had been out to sea. Mr Mitchell is very much cut up about it. 'That is the price of an empire. Fathers, brothers, sweethearts, lost . . . ' Further bad news: the woollies given by Mrs Campbell's work party were given to another minesweeper which went down.

The date and the amount of the meat ration has been announced today. It was a pleasant surprise to have confirmed that meals in restaurants will not be included. Charlie has at least five lunches a week out and I have one. In brief, the ration gives four lunches. We have never taken up our bacon ration. That will come in useful now. The suggestion that we should regard the Sunday joint critically, however, produced a strong negative reaction. Nothing would persuade Mother to make any change there.

Mr Ferguson is getting the wind up about stationery.

WEDNESDAY, 7 FEBRUARY

Christopher Tomlin

I coughed and sneezed last night and Father wanted me to stay in bed all day but I knew it was impossible. I got up and thank God sold 26/- worth of writing paper in three hours. Coming in I saw a telegram on the table: 'Will be home tonight. Love, Dick'! I danced with joy, it was so unexpected. Three times his leave was postponed and yet he was coming!

Pam Ashford

This afternoon produced an unusual amount of war commentary. Mr Mitchell returned at 2.50 saying that Mr Moffat had told him that he had been told by the porter at Dunblane station this morning that the officials at Fife had told him to beware of what appear to be children's balloons. It was suspected that the Germans had set a lot free in our atmosphere. These balloons are full of poison gas. Anyone seeing one should refrain from touching it, but should call a policeman instead.

I said I thought the Germans would hesitate to use such a method, because the direction of the wind is west to east and we could so easily retaliate, and there was a risk that their own balloons would blow back on them. Mr Mitchell did not agree.

At 3 p.m. Miss Bousie returned from lunch saying that there were bills about saying 'Small balloons, don't touch'. Miss Bousie wishes to know why the Government have not told us how to handle such a balloon. Should one put water on it? Mr Mitchell's advice was to call a policeman. She rejected this as there may be no policemen in the vicinity. Mr Mitchell said, 'Then just go on and forget about the balloon.'

Miss Bousie: 'There may be people in the vicinity who could not know that it was dangerous. No. I would stand beside the balloon – no matter how long I had to stand – until a policeman happened to come that way. Go on and forget that it was there? Good gracious no! There was too much of that sort of thing in this world. People just thought of themselves.'

I began to tell Mother that there was a wild rumour going about on the subject of balloons. She said she knew of it already for the BBC had issued an official denial at six. Mother's words were: 'This fool put a lighted cigarette against the balloon.'

'What fool?' I said.

She said, 'In the factory where they were making the poison gas. There were a lot of balloons with gas in them and this fool went in with a cigarette which he had no business to be smoking and puts one up alongside a balloon, and it exploded. No damage was done.'

SATURDAY, 10 FEBRUARY

Christopher Tomlin
£1.14.0 sales, not bad eh?

Boiled rabbits for dinner. Meat is scarce. Dick advises me to join the RAF as an assistant or clerk. But on no account as an aircraft-hand (general duties) the lowest paid and rottenest job of all. They empty slop buckets!

MONDAY, 12 FEBRUARY

Christopher Tomlin
Aunts Bee and Ivy, the teachers of dancing, gave a dinner to Dick and me tonight. There was roast pork, sage and onion, apple sauce, mashed potatoes and greens. Fruit and Devonshire cream. Sherry. And a bottle of LB pale ale each. It was excellent. My aunt gave me a copy of September 1939's *Prediction* magazine which contains big banner headlines: 'There will be no war!' It's damned ironical to read now.

Pam Ashford

The Soroptimists' Monthly Business Meeting today. The American Soroptimists have been sending messages of sympathy to our governors. One lady in America saw the Queen last year and picked up a rose petal from her bouquet. She sent this as a token of sympathy.

The Soroptimists' movement throughout the country has now more than £700 collected for their ambulance fund; £500 is the amount for one, and they are well on their way to the second. They would like the ambulances staffed by Soroptimists, but it is doubtful if this is practical. The Dundee club gave £100. It was thought that if Dundee could do that Glasgow could do better.

Miss Dewar (artist) set the whole table laughing. She had been reading an English newspaper on the subject of economical cooking in wartime. One recipe described Scotch Haggis. Never has one heard such a collection of misdirections and misstatements.

TUESDAY, 13 FEBRUARY

Pam Ashford

This morning at breakfast Mother produced the label off a tin of her favourite brand of corn beef (Fray Bentos) with the request that I buy in a large supply before the meat rationing starts. I promised to do so, though inwardly I laughed at the thought that in these days one could stipulate which brand one wished. I went into Cooper's at 8.50 and was not prepared to find their stocks of tinned meats so terribly low, nor the prices so exalted. So as to please Mother I bought the lowest priced tin there, quite a small one, at 2/2.

Tilly Rice

More frost and more snow. It really seems as if the elements were conspiring to make the pursuing of the war as difficult as possible, and I find myself wishing that the weather would behave itself as intensely as possible. Let it freeze its hardest in winter, and broil its hottest in the summer, so that man may find the struggle against nature's great strength something beyond his puny, pettifogging powers.

I notice that the confident talk of Germany's 'cracking' that was so prevalent four months ago now has given place to 'there will be no revolution in Germany yet . . . ' Surely the evils of going on with the war and the evils of the chaos of revolution must appear to be almost equal in the eyes of a people who have already suffered so much. I think people are still waiting for air raids, though feel braver about the idea now than they did formerly.

The new Fougasse posters are very good ['Walls Have Ears'], and will do a great service to mankind if they can teach them to keep a curb on their tongues. What a thing to have achieved, to have taught people not to gossip! The WRAF coming up in the train from Cornwall was very free with her speech, telling us about the courses she had been taking, the new arrangements for the WRAF in her home town, and the discrepancy between the RAF casualties given out in the paper and their actual number. Some of that information might have been useful; I didn't know and neither did she.

WEDNESDAY, 14 FEBRUARY

Christopher Tomlin

I curse two items in the *Daily Mail*: what the hell is Altrincham council doing to sack two boys because they are conscientious objectors? What has conscience and soul to do with a public body? The people of England must stamp heavily on such bloody bureaucracy. A man's conscience is an affair between himself and God. The second item is: the Government refuses to pay compensation to victims of the IRA outrages. What blasted incompetence it shows. Evidently the Government is afraid to pay because it can't check terrorism.

Pam Ashford

Today is St Valentine's Day. For some obscure reason last year the City workers went Valentine-daft. That is, however, all over now. No-one seems much inclined to repeat the fun.

The preceding page was written at noon and as I read it over on the bus going home to lunch I thought, 'That page would do to set beside Jeremiah. The world is full of brightness. It is just like spring. The lovely blue sky and sunshine bucks you up enormously. The Nazis cannot do us out of the joys of nature.'

On reaching home I found a Valentine awaiting me! Feeling sure it had come from business sources, I took it back with me after lunch and we have had the 'mostest fun'.

THURSDAY, 15 FEBRUARY

Tilly Rice

The other day I got an interesting insight into the wheels-within-wheels in the running of a war. I was talking to a young man, an employee of a Council Library.

He said: 'We send all our old books to the troops, those that are fit for them. We mustn't send anything to destroy their morale!'

'Such as pacifist literature.'

'Yes. There were two in the last lot that had to be put out.'

The war seems to be taking a grimmer turn. I think much hinges on the resistance of the Finns. To allow Russia a victory there will be, in my opinion, disastrous, for I think that Germany is only waiting for Russia to settle that before the Alliance becomes a more real thing, before the two powers link together in an attempt to crush the democracies. Admittedly, we are making some show now of sending assistance, but what a feeble show and how tardy. A licence for the British to join a force to help the Finns: how long is it going to take them to be recruited, trained, and sent to Finland? Much longer than it can take Stalin, with his stupendous manpower, to drive his victory home. More muddle and mismanagement, more political myopia.

Pam Ashford

Mr Mitchell's spirits touched their nadir today. It is his temperament to find relief in words. I like Mr Mitchell very much, and in his serious view of the situation I follow him, but the excessiveness of his feelings certainly makes me smile sometimes.

In the course of the afternoon Mr Mitchell learned that two U-Boats were sunk in the Firth of Clyde yesterday. He heard it from a man who knew a man who saw the bodies of the Germans being brought in.

At 5.15 I said to him, 'What you want is a bit of fun tonight.'

Mr Mitchell: 'There is no fun in this world.'

I said, 'There is. Go and have some fun with the children.'

He said, 'What fun is possible?'

I said, 'There must be something. There is probably snow at Bridge of Weir, why not go out with the toboggan?'

He: 'What a simple view! Having fun at night and coming to work next morning to find all the business gone.'

Mr Mitchell then put on his hat to go home. After which he confided in me that it was he who had sent the Valentine.

FRIDAY, 16 FEBRUARY

Tilly Rice

Last night Janet's protective helmet arrived. A huge affair in a large cardboard box which it would have been absolutely out of the question to carry about with you. I've not inspected the contrivance yet. I don't like the look of it, and I'm sure that Janet will object lustily when I come to try it on her. It was brought to me by Mr B, one of our local wardens. Mr B I remember chiefly because during an early morning alarm last September he came rushing out to go on duty and, when part of the way down the road, he suddenly said to his companion warden, 'I must go back – I've come out without my teeth.' 'Good Lord, man,' said the other, 'what does that matter? Do you think you're going to bite 'em?' And when another alarm was sounded, some elderly ladies who had had an elaborate shelter constructed in their garden failed to hear the warning, but took cover when the all-clear went a little while afterwards. They stayed there two hours before they were rescued by the gardener.

This morning for the first time since I returned I went out for my morning walk. I made my way to my usual little pub and was accorded a cordial welcome by the proprietor. He told me that his trade had fallen off sadly, owing to the black-out. He went on to say that now that trade was dropping off they had raised his assessment an extra thirty-four pounds, so that he would need to sell at least 10,000 extra glasses of beer to pay for it.

It was good to drink a beer there again after the thin synthetic stuff one got in Cornwall. Neither in Cornwall nor Wales can one get good beer, and there aren't so many pubs in England where one can get as good a beer as this little place. There was another man in there that I knew and he too had comments to make on the cost of the war. 'The best thing the Government could do,' he said, 'would be to take all we've got and then just allow us two or three pounds a week. We should know where we were then.'

Several more people greeted me today with the words, 'Are you back?' I thought it rather obvious, myself.

Christopher Tomlin

Dick went back tonight and left depression behind him; we miss him so. He is the life and soul of the house. He left me 7/- worth of cigarettes from France which were presents to him. He also bought Benedictine, Cointreau, Cognac, eau de Cologne and a beautiful silk scarf for mum. Though Dick is away and out of work, I am determined to make a staunch fight to keep us going. But this vile weather! It's snowing now.

Pam Ashford

This morning the Mines Department are sending someone to investigate the coal shortage in Glasgow. Mr Mitchell says he won't do any good. He is a bonehead. He would not be in Government service unless he was a bonehead.

Mr Roxburgh called this morning. Everyone seems to dread these visits. There is no doubt he comes to talk, and there is no getting away from him. He spent a lot of time in Mr Mitchell's room. Mr Churchill was the member of the Government who came in for much of the vituperation this morning. Mr Roxburgh traced his career showing that at every stage he had failed. In his last broadcast you could hear that he was drunk. He always was a drunkard. He has never once expressed admiration for the bravery of our sailors, never once sympathy with the widows and orphans of naval men. (Mr Mitchell said he had done so many times, and there was much arguing about this.) Mr Roxburgh's point was that Lord Halifax was the only good man in the Cabinet.

Mr Mitchell has learned all about the two submarines destroyed in the Clyde two days ago. I said, 'If submarines are knocking about the Clyde like that I think I will wipe Rothesay and Dunoon off my holiday list.' Mr Mitchell thought this was excessive caution. I said, 'I don't fancy Scarborough again. I should not like the East Coast in the Blitzkrieg.' Mr Mitchell thinks that during the summer months the Germans will concentrate on East Coast holiday resorts so as to undermine the morale.

MONDAY, 19 FEBRUARY

Pam Ashford

Today the Soroptimist Club entertained a party from Erskine Hospital. This is a hospital for men wounded in the last war. I sat down beside a patient who turned out to be a most delightful man. His arm was in a large sling. The second man at the table was a very perky, amusing individual, who had a wound in the leg. The third man was a pitiable creature. His arms were shaking all the time, and he did not join in the conversation at all.

It was 1.10 when proceedings started, with community singing ('Pack Up Your Troubles in Your Old Kit Bag' and 'Tipperary'). The thing I noticed most on entering the room was the men's age, and nearly all of them grey or greying. I have not seen wounded soldiers since the last war, and they were mostly young fellows then. Somehow I expected to see young fellows again today. Seldom has the passage of time been brought home so forcibly to me as today.

Conversation began with two topics – how much better the songs in the last war were, and how well the men at Erskine were fed. I asked how many men there were in the hospital, and he reckoned about 180, on the medical ward, the surgical ward, the 'Ralston Boys' (paralysed men from the old Ralston Hospital), and the boarders. Men are going back. They have been all right for 20 years, and then their wound opens up again.

WEDNESDAY, 21 FEBRUARY

Tilly Rice

The weather has now turned very warm and wet, the sort of weather I love really, soft-grey days that show the earth up in its full wealth of subtle colour. Waking life brings a thrill to the air and the earth is on tiptoe with excitement for the new season. I would be so happy and content – with the new baby, my boys growing up to be interesting beings, with my head full of ideas for my writing and with a painting urge upon me – if it weren't for the horrible pass into which life has fallen. One can't believe in the rightness of anything save of purely intellectual thought, and what an impotent thing that is these days.

Aeroplanes over us this afternoon flying very low. I hate the things with their disturbing and distracting hum, and yet I have always hankered after flying one. Man's most mistaken invention: how much better off we should have been without them.

Various countries are still arguing over the *Altmark* incident. The re-capture of over 300 prisoners by a band of twenty-five men was certainly something to talk about. Norway is trying to justify itself, Germany still burbling about piracy, while this afternoon Russian bombers raided a Swedish town 'by accident'. The tangle grows more ravelled and the light darker.

Pam Ashford

Recently Miss Crawford saw a notice in a fish shop: 'Fish cheap today.' On looking closer she found the stock consisted of a few pieces of sole at 3s 4d. Since the war broke out I have stopped looking at the fish shops for I know the prices would be too high. It transpires that practically everyone has ceased to eat fish, but the price is not the sole cause. Miss Carswell said she could not bear to eat fish because she remembered what perils the fisherman had been through to get it. Then she continued that she could not bear to eat fish in case they had been feeding on all the dead bodies. Her mother had offered her tinned salmon, 'for that had been canned before the war began'.

(This is the last entry from Pam Ashford until early April.)

THURSDAY, 22 FEBRUARY

Tilly Rice

I've been very nervy these last two nights, having waking dreams and a recurrence of my old nightmare of the ceiling falling down on top of me. Nowadays, with the possibility of air raids, it has gained in realism and the other night it seemed as if it really had happened at last. The beams on the roof were pressing down upon me, and there was an added terror in water trickling down too. Then I woke and the beams of wood melted away into darkness. The sound of trickling water was explained by the fact that I was clutching the hot water bottle agitatedly. I found the electric light switch and when I put the light on found that in my attempt to get out of bed in a panic I had put one foot into the baby's cot which I had drawn alongside my own bed. She has now been removed to the foot of the bed for safety.

FRIDAY, 23 FEBRUARY

Christopher Tomlin

Mother coughed badly and kept us awake all night. She has bronchitis and influenza and we can't afford a doctor. I've never known her to be in bed for a week before. Now Father is going down with it too and I'm not well. On top of our sickness is the spine-freezing knowledge that the £5 I owe must be paid at the end of the month. I wonder how?

Coming from town on the bus with two workmen behind me, I heard one ejaculate, 'Just look at that, it's a rum shop!' I saw a new shop with a notice on the window: 'Dog and cat meat 3d a pound' and saw meat hanging from hooks at the back. A workman tapped me on the shoulder: 'Meat for cats and dogs and we've a hard job to get it ourselves.' I pulled his leg: 'We may be glad of meat like that before long.' His companion replied in horror, 'I hope you're wrong.' He went on to complain of frozen meat which 'chills my guts'.

To the Empress, the first evening out for a month. A packed house which is unusual for Friday. I saw *Andy Hardy Gets Spring Fever* and enjoyed it. I like Judge Hardy pictures for they are entertaining and have the trite-but-true moral that 'the darkest hour is before the dawn'.

SUNDAY, 25 FEBRUARY

Christopher Tomlin

The clock went forward an hour at 2 a.m. So there was an hour less to revel in bed. I walked to town for the 11.30 mass at St Austin's. The priest exhorted the congregation to attend the sacraments regularly and he deplored the slackness of his parish.

It looks as if I will be called up this year and not next as I'd hoped. All the age groups up to 28 will be registered by July.

Chapter Eight

WE ARE AT WAR

I could get no steel needles: mass production of Anderson shelters in Wales.

'My Missus entered one of the largest drapery establishments in the city but seemed to have some difficulty in getting served. The young ladies appeared to be all crowded together in the centre of the showroom indulging in some mild form of football scrum. Presently mother caught a passing assistant and asked what was the matter. 'Oh,' she replied, 'there's a sailor in the middle of that lot.' It was one of the *Exeter*'s crew who had been caught, and was diligently signing autograph albums, notebooks, old envelopes and any odd scrap of paper. In the street I saw another Jack Tar signing papers against a shop window. He had a waiting queue halfway across the street.'

A.J. Coles on the return of HMS Exeter *to home port after the victory of the River Plate. Forces Service, 1 March 1940*

* * *

6 March Hitler adopts 'Plan Sickle' for invasion of West through Ardennes; German aircraft mine the Suez Canal, blocking traffic for three weeks. **12 March** Treaty of Moscow signed with Soviet forces to end the war in Finland. **16 March** Germans again bomb Scapa Flow naval base in the Orkneys. **19 March** RAF attacks German air base at Sylt in retaliation for Scapa Flow raid. **21 March** Reynaud becomes Prime Minister of France, with Daladier appointed Minister of Defence and War. **3 April** A Cabinet shuffle in Chamberlain's government appoints Churchill to head the Ministerial Defence Committee. One of his first acts is to obtain final consent for the mining of Norwegian waters.

Maggie Joy Blunt

I was working in the kitchen this afternoon – knitting and books and newspapers, letters and cigarettes, face flannels and a table cloth on a clothes-horse, coke crackling in the range, kettle humming, Dinah on my knee – when I saw a sprightly lady in a costume the colour of Parma violets pass this window. She was scented and made-up discreetly, wore a brown felt hat, a fox fur, brogues and dark thick stockings. She was small and bony and I recognised her at once as the owner of a dachshund I have met in the Beeches. I have heard her talking to the dachshund as I talk to Dinah and ordering him about as I would never dare my little cat.

She asked if I had heard of the National Salvage Campaign, looking at me doubtfully as though a young woman in grubby grey slacks with untidy hair and a dirty face might very well be ignorant of it. I had heard of it. I have spoken to Fanny about it frequently, bemoaning the fact the Scouts had grown faint of heart at the sight of my waste paper and wondering why the local council couldn't arrange for the dustmen to collect usable refuse separately. I asked the Lady in Violet into the kitchen with due apologies, while Dinah sat on the hearth rug looking very annoyed.

The Campaign was explained, and a list of salvage items (waste paper, metals, textiles, bottles, glass, rubber, even electric batteries and bulbs) and the address in the village where they were being received was handed to me. Were there collectors? I asked. 'No,' said the Lady in Violet, 'collecting I *cannot* undertake.'

Coal shortage has been acute everywhere. Windsor had none at all for over three weeks. But I have been lucky. Every week I have been able to get at least one cwt. of something combustible. What large households have done I cannot imagine.

Summer Time began again yesterday. 'One will now be able to go to the pictures or a matinée or to see friends and get home by daylight,' writes Aunt Ella. I have nearly finished the socks I promised for her godson. I could get no steel needles. The new stock of Woolworth eau-de-Cologne is in bottles of very reduced size for the same price. 'I think it's wicked,' said the girl who served me. 'You have a big bottle while there's still some left.'

The weather since I last wrote my diary has repeated itself in a series of frosts, thick snowfalls, thaw and fogs, until last week when every fraction of snow disappeared in the breath of an hour, the thermometer rose, the sun shone, birds burst into a torrent of song, and one went round the garden with greedy eyes and filled one's lungs with the scent of moist earth and last-year's decaying leaves. Snowdrops have been in flower for weeks. They came into bud beneath the burden of snow and blossomed bravely above it. Green shoots of Madonna lily bulbs have burst through the soil. Violets are still waiting to bloom. Broad beans are showing their heads perkily. But the cabbages suffered. Out of the 30 I planted I can see only three or four. Two orange trees, grown from the pips of an orange I ate in a garden long ago, were housed in an unheated shed and have died with a striped aloe. The winter has taken a toll of all delicate things.

Dinah's love affairs are reaching a conclusion. Ginger Tom, by a really awe-inspiring determination, is established as the accepted suitor. I had great difficulty in keeping him out of the cottage if Dinah was in it. The moon grew full. Dinah stayed out night after night while my sleep and probably my neighbours' was disturbed by Ginger Tom's piercing love songs and Dinah's replies in tones of terror and excitement.

But I forget. We are at war. Kassim is out of work again. An architect of my acquaintance, who has had no other employment since war began save that of waiting in a London Auxiliary Fire station, is planning to join a contingent for Finland. His wife is in the Censor's office, translating Hungarian. My friend Paul has testily given up reading or listening to war news, distrusting all information given to the public. Some friends of his discount 95 per cent of all they read and hear. The boys in the village are leaving one by one. 'Soon,' said the butcher, 'there'll only be us old ones left.'

Christopher Tomlin

A strange dream. I was in a graveyard looking at a curious tombstone. The figure of a cavalier was carved on the lid. I dreamt that I saw how he died: two other cavaliers murdered him. I got a feeling of horror and felt as if I was shut in a tomb.

Before going to bed, I worried very much about repaying the £5 I borrowed and about earning a living for myself, Father and Mother. I felt trapped with no way out. A 10/- order by mail and also 35/- sales today.

To the New Victoria where I saw *Nurse Cavell*. I cried when I watched the Belgian boys saying farewell to their parents, wives and sweethearts at the beginning of the film. It reminded me of Dick and my own goodbye to come this year: for all age groups up to 28 will serve by autumn. My turn will come just after. Dick says hundreds of young fellows are taking a full course at the local wireless school to escape military duty. They are exempted as long as the course lasts. Rain tonight.

WEDNESDAY, 28 FEBRUARY

Christopher Tomlin
Don't know why, maybe it was a sudden inspiration hatched by desperation; anyway, I went to a typewriter dealer in town and told him I wanted to sell my machine. He promised to call this afternoon. He didn't. I hope to get £9.

THURSDAY, 29 FEBRUARY

Christopher Tomlin
Leap Year Day. 29/- sales. I am in despair through my inability to pay, in a lump sum, the £5 I borrowed. The mechanic from the typewriter shop called this morning. He told Father the buyer would call between 1 and 2, and I wasted two precious hours waiting for a chap who never came. Mother says they aren't interested in the machine, a Royal in grand condition.

Tilly Rice
A tree in the front of my house has burst forth into a positive cascade of golden dangling catkins, while at the back, down the row of gardens belonging to the small houses, I can see the inhabitants industriously digging deep holes in their gardens for the erection of their Anderson air-raid shelters. SPRING IS ICUMEN IN.

FRIDAY, 1 MARCH

Christopher Tomlin
23/- delivery and 24/- sales. I am desperate to find some way to repay the money borrowed. If only I had never got into this awful mess. Unfortunately there will be another bill from my local firm soon.

SATURDAY, 2 MARCH

Christopher Tomlin
A heavy day delivering £5 of notepaper. I phoned the typewriter depot and was told the buyer has been unable to call: 'We've been so busy.' But he will come first thing on Monday morning.

SUNDAY, 3 MARCH

Christopher Tomlin
Mass at my own church. I went to my SVP (St Vincent de Paul Catholic Brothers) meeting. At the end, Bro President smiled and patted me on the arm, as he walked out. 'Bro Treasurer wants to see you now.' I waited until there was just Brother Treasurer and myself in the room. He said, 'I wondered if we could come to some arrangement about the loan. We don't want to lose you, you are too valuable a brother as Bro President may have told you.' I explained that through sickness and bad weather I was unable to pay the £5 at once, that I was very worried, but I would certainly see the loan was repaid as quickly as possible. He then said, 'You are foolish to worry. You can pay a pound or two anytime you are able. It is purely a matter between us and Bro President, nobody outside the three of us knows anything about the loan.' I should say in explanation of 'we don't want to lose you', I had foolishly stayed away from SVP meetings and unwittingly given a false impression. The truth is I was damnably nervous.

Maggie Joy Blunt
I divide my visitors into two groups: those who like to be treated as guests, and those who won't be treated as guests. The guests like their breakfast in bed and the whole morning in which to perform their getting-up in the privacy of the bedroom. They like a little walk before lunch and a long hour after lunch over the fire with coffee; a walk before tea; and to go to bed early with hot drink and Health Tea or whatever they take for the good of their insides.

The Won't-Bes clean their teeth over the kitchen sink, breakfast downstairs in their pyjamas and wander half-dressed all over the cottage. They play patience when the spirit moves them, knit at meal times, torment Dinah and don't mind an audience when having a bath. The truth is that they all behave exactly as they like. There are no restrictions at Wee Cottage other than those my visitors chose to impose on themselves, and menus are arranged as nearly as possible to suit individual tastes.

One intellectual 'highbrow', who has 'feelings' which are never wrong, 'feels' now that peace will be made in May. If it is a just peace I hope she is right. But the Government is advertising widely for helpers in the ration issue stores and canteens. Women are to receive from 15/- to 30/-, and men from 30/- to 55/- a week with board, lodging and uniform.

I have a mounting pile of war and political literature waiting to be read. I don't think I shall ever get through it. *Case for Federal Union* by W.B. Curry; *Unser Kampf* by Sir Richard Acland; collected pages of Wells' 'Declaration of Rights Debate' from the *Herald*; the monthly pamphlets of the National Council for Civil Liberties; recent broadcast talks by John Middleton Murray printed in the *Listener*; and this week I shall probably have *The Politics of Democratic Socialism* by E.F.M. Durbin from the Labour Book Service.

MONDAY, 4 MARCH

Christopher Tomlin
26/- sales. It poured most of the day and cleared at 4 p.m. when I began to canvass. The typewriter man called and offered £4. The price of scrap iron. My Royal is in grand fettle, it isn't a very modern model but it has every up-to-date gadget. I hope and intend to get £9 for it. I am disgusted with the dealer who hasn't acted in a business-like way. If I wanted to buy a machine I would come immediately!

Father holds it a crying disgrace to the Allies that Finland is allowed to fight alone. 'If she's beaten the whole world will mock us, for didn't we go to war to save little nations? What have we done? Look at Poland and look at Finland now! The whole war's a complete farce!'

TUESDAY, 5 MARCH

Christopher Tomlin

According to Father, Sydney would like my typewriter and has no money to pay for it so I suggested Father tells him he can buy it with stock. He went to Sydney's to pay for the week's orders but said nothing when he returned. It strikes me Sydney can't even afford to take it in the way I propose.

Seven days ago I wrote to Dick to say I was worried about the future and lacked confidence. I told him I now made about £3 a week. The reason why I'm nervous is because this is the first time my folks depended on me. I love freedom and loathe responsibility but I've made up my mind to keep the home going. Today in his very cheerful letter Dick writes: 'You ought to be proud you are the main man in a splendid business you built up from nothing. You are doing very necessary war work at home.'

SUNDAY, 10 MARCH

Christopher Tomlin

Communion at 10 o'clock. I went home for breakfast and at 11.45 I walked into the SVP room where Bro Treasurer was alone. I handed him a £1 towards the £5, and he said, 'Thank you. Splendid!' I feel much better. It gives me new spirit and will show I am trying.

TUESDAY, 12 MARCH

Christopher Tomlin

The Finnish war ends at noon! My reaction to this news is a mixture of contempt and anger. Why the blazes didn't the government send troops, planes and so on, immediately they were necessary? I'm disgusted with our do-nothing-but-wait-for-Sweden-to-move attitude. I am convinced we will pay to our last farthing for our laziness to do what should be done. The Government must take its head out of the sand to face Germany and Russia too. No sane man believes Stalin will be content to 'stay put'; he's tasted blood and will howl for more.

I wonder why we are still at war? We set out to save weak nations, but both Poland and Finland are gone, and we call England 'Mother of the free'! My father said, 'If only those weak-kneed yellow-livered buggers in Parliament had half the spirit of little Finland! Chamberlain and Co. knew Finland was at her last gasp, drained of blood, but they didn't do a thing, and now on the eve of this forced peace they calmly, casually inform the world that for three months 50,000 men and ships were waiting to go to Finland when the Finns asked us for help! Finnish spokesmen have done nothing else for the past month. Whatever comes or goes in this war, this is the biggest defeat ever suffered by the Allies in this or any other war!'

6 p.m. News: Chamberlain's speech makes us sick, it's a slop bucket full of soft soap and crocodile tears. It's a good job there's no general election for the Government would lose every seat they hold!

The firm will buy my typewriter for £5.

THURSDAY, 14 MARCH

Christopher Tomlin

After 7 days' rain it is exceedingly pleasant to feel the warmth of the sun.

Chamberlain is not wanted. One woman customer thinks, 'Chamberlain has money invested abroad. He is in the banking business and there are things going on we don't know about . . . too much underhand! Anthony Eden should be Prime Minister.' Three other women, who were not asked who they would choose, also said Eden should be PM. The government, except Churchill, are unpopular. No wonder!

SATURDAY, 16 MARCH

Christopher Tomlin

The typewriter firm took the machine on Tuesday and promised to bring the money 'right away'. We are still waiting. Father went to the shop this afternoon and was told by the man who took the machine: 'I told Mr Davis (manager) that Mr Tomlin wanted cash right away. All our accounts are paid by cheque and we carry very little cash in the shop. A cheque should have arrived from Blackpool (the headquarters). It's strange it hasn't come . . . ' Father told him in a very direct way what he thought about their 'businesslike ways'. I don't trust the word of anyone in that firm.

SUNDAY, 17 MARCH

Christopher Tomlin

The elusive £5, the end of Finland and incompetence of the government put us in a rotten humour. Churchill is the one man: Eden is misunderstood but there is much good in the boy. Note: I do not listen to Lord Haw Haw. My thoughts are my own.

WEDNESDAY, 20 MARCH

Christopher Tomlin

They paid £5 cash after all! I was able to pay £3.15.0 to my wholesale stationers and salt the rest. I hope to pay another £1 to the SVP this weekend.

A golden letter day. A letter from Dick says he is now a 1st class wireless operator having passed a very stiff examination. It is almost unknown in the RAF for an aircraftman to jump from AC2 to AC1 in 7 months: it takes most aircraftmen two years. We are delighted with the news. A few days ago Nazi airmen killed a civilian and wounded others in Scapa Flow, so now we pop across to Sylt to give Hitler hell. An 8 hour raid in which we made a damned mess of the island. About time we moved! Perhaps the war will not now be a let's pretend one.

FRIDAY, 22 MARCH

Christopher Tomlin

Good Friday. After breakfast I called on 12 'after care' cases. (After care: all Catholic boys who leave school are periodically visited to see they are OK and if they need advice and assistance. The after-care committee of each parish is composed of St Vincent de Paul brothers who visit their boys until they turn 18.) I handed another £1 to Bro. Treasurer.

MONDAY, 25 MARCH

Christopher Tomlin

Easter Monday. I set out at 7 p.m. to see *Thunder Afloat* at the Empress cinema. There was not a seat in the place and all seats but two at the front were booked for the second house. I wasn't in the mood for another night indoors so I took a bus to town where I studied the titles of films showing at the cinemas. It was a lovely collection for Easter! I chose the only one possible, *First Love* with Mickey Rooney and Deanna Durbin at Preston's premier theatre, the New Victoria, thousands stood in the queues. Many soldiers and Air Force chaps were there too. It was a weary, time-wasting, foot-aching vigil and I got in at 8.45 after standing for 85 minutes.

The show was passable. Women enjoyed it, for I heard their remarks when the show was done. But it wasn't worth the trouble I'd gone through. There were enough people in the bus queue afterwards to fill six. I caught the 2nd one but the conductor had to throw a man out. He wouldn't budge: 'Who's going to put me off?' The conductor quickly showed him who. There's a nasty, narky attitude among a few passengers.

TUESDAY, 26 MARCH

Maggie Joy Blunt

Fighting in the air and at sea continues. Tension over the Balkan situation increases. I am anxious for the possible fate of Suez, as my brother is stationed there with his wife and small daughter. We do not seem to be dealing with the unrest in India very successfully. Changes in our Government are mooted.

Though these events determine our future we have no control over them. We live from day to day in a kind of resigned doubtfulness, unable to make plans for more than a month ahead. My brother and I are joint owners of a house on the outskirts of London which tenants have recently vacated and we are faced with the problem of finding new ones. We might try to sell but have been advised to wait. A fortnight ago one man had all but decided to take out a three-year agreement when the war news scared him off the venture. 'A forest of notice boards' was our agent's description of one street. Kassim told me when I last saw him that empty houses are being burgled for lead and brass: he had recently surveyed some property where damage to pipe and drainage would cost hundreds of pounds to repair.

We are on meat rations now. The price of unrationed meat is exorbitant. Calves' liver, for instance, is anything from 2/- to 2/8d a lb. Even the humble heart of a sheep once bought for 6d is now 9d.

One night after 11 p.m. I was experimenting with foreign wavelengths on the radio when I heard a cockney voice speaking from a German station. A German announcer said in English, 'Now give your name and address. Come, speak to your mother in Englant.'

'I am a prisoner in Germany,' said the English voice. 'I am not wounded. I am in the best of health. I send my love and kisses to all at home.'

More prisoners were brought to the microphone. Each gave his name and address. The address of one was near Bath, one near London, one in Berkshire. Said the announcer to one of them, 'You are keen on football, I understand? You took part in a match against the German team, did you not? State in your own words the result of this match.'

'The Germans won,' came the reply without enthusiasm. 'By 3 goals to one.'

To another prisoner the announcer remarked, 'You have not shaved this morning?'

'No,' answered the Englishman, 'I have no kit.'

'Why is that?'

'I left it in the trenches.'

'You did not bring it with you?'

The Englishman began to stammer and was faded out. 'No . . . I . . . it was all too quick . . .'

Christopher Tomlin
War Cabinet changes. Father on Churchill: 'If they move him from Admiralty we are bound to lose the war. But they'll never get anything done until they get rid of Chamberlain.'

THURSDAY, 4 APRIL

Christopher Tomlin
It is the second time in a week I am asked, 'What are you selling mister?' by police. Why this official nosey parkerism?

It strikes me people are hoarding writing paper. They fear it will be impossible to buy it before long.

Sydney, my printer, owes money all over and doesn't seem to care. He takes life as it comes. As he is 28 and will be called up soon, he knows creditors can't put him in court if he's in the army. He could easily pay all he owes if he smartened up and went canvassing. But he's content to stay at home and look after the baby, while his wife goes to work at the Empress where she is an attendant.

A Sunderland flying boat shoots down one Junker and frightens five more. According to the *Daily Mail*, the RAF rear-gunner held his fire until the Junkers were 100 yards away, then he let 'em have hell. But what Father can't understand is, if the rear-gunner didn't fire until the machines were near, how is it he wasn't killed by the Nazis? Surely they didn't hold their fire too? Father says that both English and German news must be divided by three to find the truth.

Overheard: 'If Mr Chamberlain is 10 times more confident of victory, what must he have been when we declared war?' Hear hear! Customers say, 'The war will be over before you are called up.' I reply, 'I don't think so.' Why am I nervous and blush whenever I pass a policeman?

Chapter Nine

THE MILKMAN'S REPORT

The shadow of the future is creeping over everything: business as usual in the London shops.

'Of one thing I feel sure: the United States will not be tripped or tricked into war by the machinations of its government, or by the subtle pressure of British propaganda. We shall hold tenaciously, too long perhaps, to our neutral safeguards, and give them up only if we're convinced that the defeat of the Allies is probable and imminent. We shall give them up if we have to, one by one, hoping that each extra fragment of aid will turn the necessary trick. And if we finally become involved in the war we shall probably send free material and ships, and withhold troops until the need for men becomes overwhelming.'

Seven months before Roosevelt is re-elected for the third time, the influential commentator Raymond Gram Swing puts the case for the wait-and-see. Home Service, 20 April 1940

* * *

9 April Germany invades Denmark and Norway, and Copenhagen is occupied within 12 hours. **13 April** Seven German destroyers sunk in Narvik Fjord. **14 April** British and French forces land at Narvik. **2 May** Allies withdraw from central Norway after fierce fighting around Trondheim. **10 May** Germany invades France, Belgium, Luxembourg and the Netherlands; Chamberlain resigns, and Winston Churchill becomes Prime Minister in coalition government. **13 May** Churchill proclaims he has nothing to offer but 'blood, toil, tears and sweat'. **14 May** Anthony Eden appeals for the formation of Local Defence Volunteers, to be renamed the Home Guard at the end of July. **15 May** Holland surrenders to Germany.

Pam Ashford

I must preface 'Volume II' of my MO diary with an explanation of the long interval of silence. I stopped writing the diary about the beginning of March because it had become quite obvious that I must concentrate my attention on the preparation for the bookkeeping examination, and the diary was competing too strongly for the little leisure time I have. The examination was held last week.

The terrific jolt that Europe has received today cannot pass unrecorded. For seven months or more I have expected Germany to walk into Denmark, and for as many weeks I have feared the invasion of Norway. Expected and feared these happenings . . . yet the news of their fulfilment on the 8 a.m. news was quite a shake up.

I met Margaret, office girl, 19, backward and immature. I said, 'You know the news. Denmark is invaded. The war will take a move on now,' and her eyes were shining, cheeks glowing, absolutely thrilled at the prospect. (She has been born and brought up on films and regards war in a 'film-going' manner.) So far as I can judge, the 'masses' have divided into two distinct groups, those who are filled with horror and those who are elated.

Miss Bousie has been most uncommunicative today, and I know well that this is a sign that her sensitive nature has been cruelly hurt, a frame of mind that is described as 'thoughts too deep for words'. She said, 'It is shocking! There is something far wrong with statesmanship.' I said, 'There is something wrong with human nature.' She said, 'No, statesmanship. It is all greed.'

Mr Roxburgh came in, saying, 'We must exterminate them. If you have a lot of rats you tramp on them and kill them. You have got to give them about ten times what they give you.' (Miss Bousie clearly looked shocked by these sentiments.)

5.30 p.m. The man who sat next to me on the bus spread his paper out very wide, and said to me, 'The battle has begun.' He beamed. In all my 22 years in Scotland, never has a stranger spoken to me on a vehicle (here people don't talk to strangers as they do in the South of England). Not knowing what to do, I said, 'The situation is very grave.' I have never seen anyone enjoy a newspaper like it. He was a supreme case of a person who was pleased the active phase had come. I am another!!

My evening was filled with a task that I little enjoyed, mending Mr Roxburgh's gloves. The old gentleman, of course, does not know that the interest I take in his war commentaries is part of my MO routine, and I have suddenly become a favourite.

Christopher Tomlin

Midnight news: Hooray, the war begins at last! We will not allow Germany to use Norway's waters. Father: 'I am glad the rats are out of the hole. There'll some naval battles now, you just see!' I feel light-hearted, but I am sorry my brother won't be home in May. He wrote, 'I will get leave if the balloon doesn't go up,' and it has done.

At last I am notified that *War Begins At Home* is waiting for me at the county library.

WEDNESDAY, 10 APRIL

Pam Ashford

Mr Roxburgh arrived. He believes Hitler is the greatest brain Europe has seen for centuries. 'He brings a fresh outlook to bear on everything. He gets things done. Of course he commands the respect of all these small nations. I always said what this country needed was three or four years of Hitler. Did you ever see a country like this one? 7 months of war. Everyone trying to manoeuvre himself into a highly paid job and nothing being done to resist the enemy. I went along to the Food Control and told them what I thought. The Food Controller is Mr ***, a local baker. He is getting £950 a year.'

At 5.30 I went along to the German class, and was surprised to find that the bookkeeping results are known, and delighted that I have passed. It is difficult to concentrate on study in time of crisis, as I learnt last year when Munich, Barcelona and Albania played havoc with my work.

Harry Lauder was on the wireless tonight, and Mother thought he sounded as if he were deeply affected, having lost a son in the last war.

Christopher Tomlin

I am on tenterhooks to know how the fleet has done. People are delighted the lion is trampling on the swastika but are sorry to think blood will be shed. I've prayed earnestly since the invasion began.

9 p.m. News: The Allies – Britain, France and Norway – retake Bergen and Trondheim. This made us shout with joy. Father believes Hitler will wish he never was born before this week is out. I say it is just about time to squash the bloody swine.

THURSDAY, 11 APRIL

Pam Ashford
I opened up this morning's conversation with the words, 'We are living in stirring times.'

Miss Bousie seemed more like her old self this morning. She said, 'On the tram home last night I was talking to a gentleman who kept exclaiming, "We have the Germans bottled up, bottled up!!!" He was most enthusiastic, and I said I wished I thought as he did.'

Confidence in the British Navy is constantly expressed, and it is a sincere sentiment, not words to buoy us up. Pride, elation, excitement, pity, horror, apprehension are all present.

I feel extremely sorry for Mother, who has taken it badly. 'It is the terrible loss of life that I am thinking of,' she says. For myself, the strongest feelings are pride in the Navy and satisfaction that we have emerged from that detestable calm we called the War of Nerves.

FRIDAY, 12 APRIL

Pam Ashford
In the *Herald* was a notice of a creditors' meeting of Burns & Crosbie, a Glasgow beautician. Mother said, 'Who would want beauty in these days?' I said, 'The war has not affected the craze for beauty. Hairdressing is more elaborate than ever.'

Miss Crawford and Miss Carswell want the entire German nation destroyed. We should bomb Berlin immediately. I pointed out that we may not have air supremacy. We did not in September. We have progressed since, but have we air supremacy? However, the cry was, 'On to Berlin with our bombers.'

SATURDAY, 13 APRIL

Christopher Tomlin
My sister who has just whitewashed her yard is tickled to death,

because her neighbours say the Nazis will see the white walls and drop bombs. She lives close to Preston Dock.

I heard the wonderful news at 10.15. It is splendid! Seven Nazi ships and 1,000 men gone to hell! Or should I hope the men will go to heaven for dead Germans are no longer our enemies. We mined the Baltic early this morning: it is wonderful news which will cheer Sweden, for now Germany cannot invade her. I anticipate action from Stalin.

SUNDAY, 14 APRIL

Maggie Joy Blunt
I knew that something must happen soon but had given up trying to figure out where. The news came as a terrible shock. It is terrible to think that Norway must suffer. Yet the Nazis could hardly be in a better position from our point of view. Did they really imagine we would not interfere with only the North Sea between our forces and theirs? They claim that they are protecting Norway from our intended aggression because we were busy laying mines in Norwegian territorial waters at the beginning of the week. Who but the staunchest Nazi supporter could possibly believe that? Why should we want to attack Norway?

I heard Harold Nicholson on the radio the other night describing a visit which a neutral friend of his paid Hitler. Hitler spoke with eloquence for two hours on his plans and ambitions and then expressed a desire that he might meet an Englishman of his own calibre with whom he might talk as he and the neutral had just talked. Hitler said, 'I would say to him, "Give me Europe and I will give you the rest of the world!"'

The invasion of Norway must have required months of careful preparation, and though our successes are broadcast and splashed in headlines, it is evident, from the comments of certain non-belligerent sources, that Nazi determination and guile is in no way yet defeated. This is only the beginning of the stupendous events we have awaited so long.

I sit alone, grinding out short stories which no editor wants, and wonder whether I should not be playing a more active, a more obviously useful part in this war. Voluntary ARP work for instance or a full Red Cross training. Yet something (it may be laziness) says, WAIT.

It is difficult to understand why the German people tolerate and even approve, as they seem to do, the actions of their rulers. There are two opinions current in England at the moment. One is that we are fighting the Nazis, not the German people, and that if we destroy the Nazis everything will be all right. The other is that Nazism is the natural expression of the German character and therefore the whole German nation must be punished. I don't see what right we have to punish the nation for Nazism. I think it is more important to find out where its roots lie and to see if its energy can be diverted into saner channels.

Here and there – in a book, an article, a broadcast discussion, a casual conversation – one can find fragments of illuminating information on the German character. Articles and broadcast talks on the German people are popular at the moment. A little while ago the diplomat Sir Joseph Anderson, who has spent thirty years in Germany, was broadcasting his impressions of the German people. He said they have a normal tendency to make war. They believe it to be proof of their courage and honour, which they consider the finest qualities in a human being. They are willing and eager to use force on all occasions, believing that war is not only right but a natural condition of mankind and good in itself.

This military spirit has influenced the ruling classes for generations. Hitler himself is so stirred by it that he says in *Mein Kampf*, 'The principle which once made the Prussian Army the most wonderful instrument of the German nation must form . . . the basis of our State conception.'

Yet I do not believe this to be true of the mass of the German people. I believe the middle- and working-classes to be simple and hospitable, as I have found them in Bavaria. But they are stolid. They lack spontaneity. They have too, Sir Joseph Anderson pointed out, a great respect for efficiency and for 'expert'. The aim and goal of every good German is to become an 'expert'. They believe that all 'experts' are infallible, that those in authority are necessarily 'experts' and cannot therefore be wrong; they are content to leave everything in their hands and do as they say. Also, the middle-classes suffer – as do ours – from suspicion that any change in the social order means Bolshevism.

Now they are trapped. They may not criticise their government or question its movements. Their acquiescence is maintained by the threat of the concentration camp. Labour representatives were speaking tonight on the radio: P.G. Walker, candidate for Oxford City, Herbert Bullock of the Trades Union Congress Council and National Union of General and Municipal Workers, and two anonymous members of German trade unions. The Germans made it quite clear that the present Labour Front is not all it is made out to be. It publishes no accounts. Workers are treated solely as impersonal parts of the armament machine. The Strength Through Joy movement has more publicity than merit.

Talking of publicity, I heard this story broadcast the other night. When the Germans marched into Prague a picture in the *Illustrated Press* showed German soldiers distributing shoes to bare-footed Czech school children. It was seen everywhere. What actually happened was this. When the children arrived one morning at their school in Prague, they were told, much to their astonishment, to take off their shoes and leave them outside the classroom. Half an hour later they were led out again and photographed getting their shoes back.

Pam Ashford

I woke up at 10, and having made a pot of tea, settled down to read the *Sunday Times* (this, the *Observer* and the *Express* are left at the door at 8.30). Mother had had a good read of something already. She burst in upon me, 'Wonderful doings with the Navy!' and went off. 15 minutes later she returned, 'What do you think of it?' Mother was still bursting with pride. 'We have swept the Germans off the seas. Great battle at Narvik, lead by the *Warspite*! We have them licked. Hardly a German ship left! Charlie heard it on the wireless at midnight.'

I jotted down the above notes before going on with my newspaper reading. The mention of the *Warspite* fills me with emotion. She was built at Devonport about thirty years ago, and I constantly heard of her in my childhood. The constructor was one of my father's closest friends. She was retired once and used as a training ship for reserves. Last June in a MO report I mentioned a talk I had with Neil Bennett, a Glasgow boy who had been on her, and I have often thought since, 'If Neil is representative of the reserve, they are fine lads.'

This morning I could 'recognise' Mother again, beaming over with pride and supremely optimistic. We have swept the Germans off the seas!

Pam Ashford

Miss Bousie has a naval friend who visited them last night. The naval man said the sailors had no hardships. They just looked on it all as being part of their day's work, and in battles they just said, 'If we don't get them, they will get us.' It was more like a game of football than anything else.

This morning I received a letter from the *Anglo-German Review* asking for 2/-! I shall not reply. Mr Mitchell wants me to burn the letter, Miss Bousie wants a sharp reply sent. Miss Carswell and Miss Crawford are flaming with anger. They want every one of Germany's 80 million killed in cold blood.

During the period I was not writing this diary, preparations were made for protecting this building, and as this office is the only one that is not shut at some time during the day, we are to take in the equipment. A helmet was delivered to us today. Someone on the staff humorously labelled it for Miss Bousie's use. She saw the humour but was angry too, saying, '1940! We are going back to the days of barbarity.' Mr Ferguson said, 'I could chance a brick on top of my head with that.'

TUESDAY, 16 APRIL

Christopher Tomlin

At last there are air raid shelters in Fulwood, two in the next street to where I live. There are many noticeboards directing people to them.

An old client – an Irish woman – is suspected by her neighbours of being a member of the IRA. They follow her in town, ask the postman if she gets letters from Eire and are within hearing distance whenever there is a caller at her door. My customer is a Catholic, her husband fought in the last war. And both her father's and mother's people were British Army folk.

WEDNESDAY, 17 APRIL

Pam Ashford

I am afraid that the Germans are getting a firm grip on South Norway. I believe in the British Army, but my confidence is not so high as in the Navy, and I feel less buoyant today.

Mr Ferguson was at Granton yesterday and learnt that thousands of Canadians have sailed for Norway, complete with fur caps. Mr Mitchell and I agreed that the Canadians were more used to the cold than we and many of them were used to roughing it.

I said, 'I don't like the way Goering is speaking of our bombing open towns, which we never did. It sounds like a prelude to air attacks on this country.' Miss Smith: 'That is what he intends to do.' I said, 'Between the intention and the execution there is a gap. I have great faith in our forces.' She apparently has less faith. All round there seems a sobering process taking place.

Miss Smith is full of tales of the Gestapo rounding up all sorts of innocent people.

THURSDAY, 18 APRIL

Pam Ashford
This morning Miss Smith passed round the holiday list, and I shall have either the second fortnight of July or the first fortnight of June. Mother wants Scarborough. I feel hesitant for I am not as confident as she that air raids are an impossibility, and also I anticipate travelling difficulties and Scarborough is a long way away.

There seems a widespread dread of the East Coast, and also of all places far from home. It is plain that Largs is in for a bumper season, also the Ayrshire coast. People speak of Rothesay and Dunoon with shudders. The Firth of Clyde is mined, and they are afraid of crossing the waters, and also there won't be the pleasure steamers to provide the customary amusements.

In regard to dates, I shall earmark the second fortnight in July and if I change my mind, it won't be hard to get June. To Mother the first fortnight of June is ludicrous, but I said, 'Is it? Six weeks later the war might be hell let loose.' (Mother thinks that if it becomes hell let loose she would rather stay at home.)

FRIDAY, 19 APRIL

Pam Ashford
Mr Mitchell has read that the police are rounding up members of the Link. This amuses me intensely: I should enjoy a visit from the police.

Mr Roxburgh says that the relatives of Scottish soldiers have been warned not to expect news from them in the immediate future, which proves there are many soldiers going from here to Norway. 'If there is dirty work to be done, they will put the Scotsmen first.'

I said, 'Yes, but they will take the kilt off them first. They have tried to take the kilt from the Highlanders already.'

Miss Bousie: 'They have done so! It's disgraceful. It is a matter of principle!'

Much discussion followed about kilts in wartime.

Miss Smith: 'It is not suitable for battle.'

Miss Crawford: 'I don't like the suits they have now. The jumpers are most untidy-looking.'

Miss Bousie: 'And the trousers!'

Miss Smith: 'They say that in the last war the pleats of the kilts got infested with fleas.'

Miss Smith says someone in one of the other offices was saying to a friend coming up the stair, 'You know, Norman is in Norway.' No one knows who Norman is, but much sympathy is expressed.

SUNDAY, 21 APRIL

Christopher Tomlin
Canvassed in Penwortham: 20/- sales. What a hell of a week this has been. I am off-colour with boils; my blood is out of condition. I started the week wishing I was in another job. In short, I am blue and in need of excitement.

The Sunday papers are very thin: there's no wood pulp coming from Norway or Sweden. I see that letters may cost 3d to send and it makes me ill. Here I am battling to keep the home going, and first there is a 30 per cent restriction on the paper supply and now comes the threat of increased postage. A Penwortham customer says there are many houses in the district where two members or more work in the munitions factory. They are in reserved occupations and bring in approx. £5 each per week. And here are we – my brother is in France, Father is out of work, and I am breaking my neck for a paltry £1. I will be called up in June I expect and what will happen to Father and Mother then I don't know. The so-called 'dependants' allowance' doesn't keep a kitten.

TUESDAY, 23 APRIL

Pam Ashford

Quite the most interesting piece of news tonight is that certain former members of the Link are likely to be interned. How I laughed! I have been chivvying mother with advice as to what she should do when the police come to fetch me away.

Mother has been to a whist drive for the seamen's mission. A lady at this event who has just returned from London compared wartime there and here. 'London is so bright, and the shelters are underground and don't disfigure the place as ours do (brick buildings). People in Glasgow are so gloomy and depressed, Londoners optimistic.' I made two comments to Mother: Londoners are bright and Glasgow people dour at all times, it is the nature of the respective peoples and has nothing to do with the war; secondly, Scotland has had all the bombs or nearly all so far.

Christopher Tomlin

What a budget! My customers will dwindle. I dread canvassing tomorrow. Even a postcard will cost 2d. As for tobacco! I bought an ounce of Tom Long today. There are three prices marked on the end of the packet, 9d, 10d and 1/-, with the first and second prices marked through. After tomorrow there will be a fourth price, 1/3. In 12 months my tobacco has risen until it costs 9d more than it should. I smoke my way to victory.

WEDNESDAY, 24 APRIL

Pam Ashford

The budget was, of course, commented upon this morning, but not very vigorously. The rise in postage is considered ridiculous. 2d would have been enough.

Miss Smith: 'There will be no postcards when we are on holiday now. Who is going to pay as much as that?' I said, 'There will be no more boxes of sweets sent when we are on holiday either.'

The *Manchester Guardian* does not consider the budget sufficiently drastic; I cannot judge the limit of taxation but I should like it heavy.

Mr Mitchell is of a similar persuasion. 'I would have made it more severe. We are fighting for our freedom and our future. Look what the seamen have to bear. If the Chancellor had taken everything we had and given us only 1% interest, we should bow down and lick his hand.'

Tilly Rice
I had a friend to tea this afternoon who is an air-raid warden and I asked her what they did in the air warden's post at the end of our lane. She said, 'Oh, they rehearse plays in there sometimes.'

People seem convinced now that we shan't get raiders over London, partly because of Mr Chamberlain's veiled threat that we should retaliate. I think there is quite a lot in that. I spent time in Cologne in 1918 (when I joined my father who was with the Army of Occupation), and I can remember the lady of the house where I was billeted saying to me in an awestricken voice, 'Ah, it was terrible when the English aeroplanes came and dropped bombs.' And I was struck at the time with the little that was needed to put the wind up the Germans, for our raids were very mild indeed compared to those the Germans made on London.

My children don't seem to be taking much notice of the war. The eldest boy has come home with various songs ridiculing Hitler and making fun of the ARP, such as 'Snow White made a shirt, Hitler wore it, Chamberlain tore it, Blimey what a shirt.' Sometimes the names are reversed so I don't know which is the correct version. Another is, 'Underneath the spreading chestnut tree, Hitler dropped a bomb on me, Now I'm a blinking refugee, Underneath etc.'

A friend of mine last Sunday went for a walk across Hampstead Heath. 'I didn't hear a word of English spoken all the way across,' was her comment when she came home.

THURSDAY, 25 APRIL

Tilly Rice
My thirty-seventh birthday and, in spite of the war, I can still retain the ghost of the lightsome, delightful, birthday feeling of my childhood.

Today when my grocer called he poised his pencil over his order book and enquired, 'A dozen matches?' Everyone had been ordering them against the rise in price next Monday, and he'd booked orders for several gross. I told him that I didn't use them as I have a lighter on my stove, though come to think of it it would be prudent to lay in a few boxes in case the gas supply should fail for any reason. I feel that I am living from day to day, and it is only because I am the mother of a family that I think of any precautionary measures at all.

FRIDAY, 26 APRIL

Christopher Tomlin

What is wrong with North-Western Expedition Force? When the first batch reached Norway the newspapers told us the troops were picked men – Canadians, French alpine troops and Britons who knew how to ski and sleigh. We were informed the troops were wonderfully equipped and what a magnificent feat it was to get soldiers there rapidly. Now the papers confess our troops are far from well-equipped. There are no planes or guns to safeguard them. If this is true the government minister responsible must be kicked out.

Pam Ashford

Miss Bousie's association with pacifists is a far more serious element in her life than mine with the Link. She says that there are pacifist groups all over Glasgow. One meets at Giffnock in a private house each Sunday night. A fortnight ago a policeman called before they started and asked if there was to be a meeting held there, and took down the names of all the people who were to attend. I said, 'We (i.e. the British) believe in freedom of speech, but at the same time the police must be vigilant. The police are always welcome if they want to know anything from me.'

Miss Crawford has been repeating the old sneers at my German friends and associates. Miss Carswell, who professes to know everything that there is to be known about German spies, is glad that the Link is to be cleared up, also most relieved that I see the truth at last, and appreciates that my motives were pure friendship.

On the bus coming in I sat beside a lady who conversed with another lady, standing, over my head. Educated, professional class. They talked about people who lived on investments and are feeling the income tax badly, but 'they are frightfully patriotic and don't mind a bit'. One of the ladies knows of an old woman of 91, who, being too deaf to hear the wireless, went out in the black-out to buy a paper (in the winter of course), fell and broke her leg. The leg has, however, mended, though it is now two-and-a-half inches shorter than the other. She does not mind a bit. 'What spunk!'

SATURDAY, 27 APRIL

Christopher Tomlin

The whole world is watching our battle in Norway. The whole business is a nightmare. Mother, Father and I feel it is murder: raw recruits sent there without artillery or supporting planes. Father: 'There's only one chap tackling the job properly and unfortunately he cannot be head of the navy and army as well!'

No letter from Dick this week, the first time he's missed in 7 months. Mother fears he is moved to Norway.

Pam Ashford

Today is Charities Day, when carnival comes to town. It seemed a very subdued affair this year, but it was fine of the students to continue their efforts. I have since learnt that the sum raised was £7,000, a very big drop, but no doubt a great help to the hospitals.

In the evening, Mother and I went to the Film Festival. Charlie is one of the adjudicators along with Mr Oliver Bell, Mr Forsyth Hardy (*Scotsman*) and Mr Jeffrey (*Herald*). The proceedings began with remarks by the Chairman, Sir Thomas Moore, MP for South Ayrshire, and fell into three parts: a long tribute to John Buchan (the first Chairman of the Scottish Film Council), a plea for Sunday opening of cinemas, and remarks about the films to be shown. The plea for Sunday cinemas was associated with the black-out and the need for men in the forces to have somewhere wholesome to go. He said as things are, they are falling prey to 'harpies'. Thereafter eight films were shown. Strangely enough, one of them arrived with no title – this had been deleted by the Censor. It was shown under the name of *Round Wick Harbour*. Practically all the films were pre-war. Then came the announcements of the awards. The adjudicators were surprised and disappointed that no one had recorded the evacuation.

SUNDAY, 28 APRIL

Pam Ashford

The Sunday papers are extraordinarily thin! Hitherto there have been few Sundays when I managed to digest all three of ours from cover to cover, but I am not going to find that a difficult feat now. It seems to me that we are doing badly in Norway.

In the afternoon I went for a walk at Knightswood. Wandering along beside the canal I was thinking of a wireless talk some years ago in the *I Was There* series. The speaker had been on a boat in anchorage at an island some distance from Krakatoa when there was that famous eruption. He said that only one eyewitness survived. On an adjacent island there was an observatory, behind which rose a mountain. A scientist was high up on the mountainside when he noticed that all the little fishing boats were making for the shore in desperate haste. He wondered why, and then the waters of the sea divided. He saw a streak of fire and the waters rushed in. The bed of the sea had cracked and the water was pouring into the fiery cavity beneath. Then the island blew up.

I feel that we are like all those little boats, conscious of an impending catastrophe and trying to rush to a safe anchorage. The little boats never reached that safe anchorage.

MONDAY, 29 APRIL

Christopher Tomlin

A letter came from Dick at 5 p.m. All OK. Home on leave in the 1st week of June.

Pam Ashford

In the early pages of this diary there seem to be so many entries about shopping. Having bought large stores, this subject faded into the background. Now those stores are getting depleted and the old problems arise, with of course fresh experience and implications. One thing experience has taught me: Del Monte ground coffee in vacuum tins, supposed to last forever, is an utter failure, whereas Nestlé Café au Lait has a long life of usefulness.

TUESDAY, 30 APRIL

Pam Ashford

Yesterday Mr Mitchell went to Granton to see his customer, the British Consul at the Faroes. Consul Lutzen said that 250 marines arrived at the Faroes and are now billeted among the Faroese. The British Government lent the Faroes £25,000 when they took the island over and are going to lend a much larger sum. The Consul was also visiting representatives in this country of American oil, iron and the canning industry. Consul Lutzen cans puffins, lobsters and crayfish for the American market and wishes to introduce these lines here.

Tilly Rice

On Sunday a young friend who had just joined up visited us, looking very fit and handsome in his uniform. He seemed as happy as it was possible for a young man to be who has been plucked out of his normal life and set down in a strange place some hundreds of miles from home and friends. I think, though, that army life as such is good for the majority of young men, even if it only brings a greater appreciation of the amenities of civilian life. I shan't be sorry for my sons to serve their term.

I don't think the average young man in the army today has any illusions about the glories of war. One doesn't find them entering into the whole thing in the spirit of a glorious lark as one did in the last war. Young men who enter the army when they are called up do so, according to my observation, with a solemn resignation. I think they have a totally different viewpoint from their fathers. Maybe they are more selfish, maybe they are more thinking, but whatever it is, I have yet to meet a young man who is burning with the old patriotic zeal.

At Port Isaac, from what I hear, all the fishing has stopped and most of the men have gone to work at the aerodrome.

WEDNESDAY, 1 MAY

Tilly Rice

Rather a gloomy May Day this year in spite of warm, misty weather. Everyone I met out seemed to be depressed – but no, that's not the right word, perhaps I should say gravely doubtful about the way things are going in Norway.

This war is muddled up by old and inept minds, by men whose ideas are all pedestrian, and if they are not turned out of office soon they'll be put out by someone who would treat them with even less respect.

I find myself visualising what is happening in Norway with a far more acute sense of reality than I ever did before. I imagine all those boys being hastily packed into troopships, having uncomfortable crossings in the still wintry sea, of sea-sickness endured under crowded conditions, of the difficulties of landing and settling down subsequently on the land, when it was only possible for the men to bring what they could carry off the ship. Fancy facing up to the night in wintry Norway and then the fighting, inadequately supported by aeroplanes, the free hand to the German bombers, and above all the grappling with what must have been unfamiliar equipment. I read of troops with skis. Where could our men get experience with handling those difficult appliances? I can imagine it all, and the brief and clipped accounts we get of the fighting in Norway all fits in neatly with my mental picture. And it is all the fault of those stupid, groping old men at Westminster.

THURSDAY, 2 MAY

Tilly Rice
Things strained over the breakfast table. E working under great pressure tends to be even more unsympathetic than usual over difficulties on the home front. Rising prices make the usual economics impossible and so the only thing to do is to go without. Cigarettes can be cut out. But that doesn't amount to much anyway.

Dick and I are losing ourselves in a re-reading of *Nicholas Nickleby*, so sweet and remote from the disturbing and uncomfortable present day.

Yesterday a German bomber crashed and destroyed more than fifty houses at Clacton-on-Sea. That's just the sort of catastrophe that always haunts me, and the pictures of the wreckage recalled the details of my current dream, of the roof falling on me.

FRIDAY, 3 MAY

Tilly Rice

Well, Mr Chamberlain's statement came, to the effect that the British troops had been withdrawn from Southern Norway. It was all very skilfully and plausibly put (how it was really a sign of strength on our part that we could withdraw, how it was for the safety of our men). Yes, but what about those that will be left behind dead, in a wasted effort?

A lovely spring day today. The only thing that really absorbs me and takes my mind off the terrible events is my fiction writing. I immerse myself in my heroines, and with a wide new scale of possibilities to put them through I really enjoy myself and forget everything. Otherwise one lives from day to day and prays that one hasn't had these three nice children in vain. Even next week seems distant and unpredictable.

Have listened to Haw Haw this evening for the first time for some days and found him disappointingly boring. He was reading the details of our supposed naval losses, with a meticulous regard for detail, very, very slowly as though he had to spin his material out. We had expected snarly jubilation.

Christopher Tomlin

I am stunned, very disillusioned and afraid of our retreat from Norway. Because I understood Mr Chamberlain was '10 times more confident of victory' and he made me believe we would drive the Germans out of Scandinavia. Now the wind is out of my sails; I feel subdued and expect to hear more bad news. I am afraid because I know the wrong men are at the helm. Chamberlain must go. We want a man of fury, devilish cunning and energy. But where is he? Certainly not in politics. Can't we find more men of Churchill's breed? Considering the millions there are in Britain surely there's one man among them who can outwit Hitler?

Aunt Ivy brought me a raincoat (17/-) for my 29th birthday tomorrow.

SATURDAY, 4 MAY

Pam Ashford

Mr Mitchell told me that some French Alpinists are here.

These Alpinists wear navy blue uniforms, brown leather belts, very heavy brown boots, and on the lapels of their coats are embroidered yellow horns. The officers have gold braids too. Miss Crawford says that large sections of the French Army are in camp in Renfrewshire awaiting transportation to Norway. Someone down that way asked two in to tea and neither side knew the language of the other. The Frenchmen were 'so thankful to have a proper meal' that they kept on saying 'Merci, Merci' over and over again.

On the way home I found Glasgow full of the Alpinists; hundreds of them strolling about, not knowing what to do. (Glasgow has little to offer the sightseer.)

MONDAY, 6 MAY

Tilly Rice

A young man in the building trade came in today, and I found that his opinions had greatly clarified since this time last year. He was definitely more 'red', or perhaps one should say more definite in his views, whereas this time last year he thought that we should make greater sacrifices to re-double our efforts. He said, 'You know there's a lot in that "guns before butter" idea.'

I said that I thought that the public were waking up to the fact that our leadership wasn't everything it should be, but he said he doubted it, and that he still heard people say that they had every faith in Chamberlain and Co. I said I thought that something would happen this week, after Mr Chamberlain had made his statement in Parliament tomorrow. And I think something *must* happen, and if it doesn't we should give in at once and save as many lives as we can for it is patently useless to go on under present leadership. I think that Mr Chamberlain is sincere enough in the statements he makes (I think he speaks the truth as far as a politician ever *does* speak the truth), but he hasn't the vision, the competence or the driving power to deal with opponents like the Germans, and I maintain that if he persists in office it will be the end of the war for us, however long it may drag on. He is damaging what reputation we had the whole world over by his incompetence, his fumbling.

E reports that folk coming back from Belgium say that the people in that country are in a state of high jitters, in the expectation of invasion hourly. The W's who live nearby have, flaunting their daring, gone over to France today for a holiday, an action typical of the selfishness of this age that even now cannot understand how much their lives are to be disturbed and shaped by the war. Many would call their action unpatriotic, unnecessary, luxury in wartime, a view which would never occur to these typical and unthinking young people. I'm not patriotic by a long chalk, but somehow I felt a faint disgust . . .

Was wondering today what I should do in the event of an invasion. Gather my children round me and stay put, I suppose.

TUESDAY, 7 MAY

Christopher Tomlin

Mr Chamberlain must go. One cannot be sentimental in wartime and though he is an excellent peacemaker he is no use for war. His pitiful excuses yesterday, muddled thinking, and idiotic saying, 'The people of this country don't realise what they are up against!' Don't we? He most surely doesn't know when he is '10 times more confident of victory' and believes Hitler has 'missed the bus'. Blasted rot! What a rotten lot of bottom-warming, chair-polishing humbugs there are in the Cabinet to be sure.

Tilly Rice

Am wondering what the result of the debate in the House of Commons today will be; has Mr Chamberlain got away with it again? It's amazing, the blindness of this man – he seems completely enveloped in the fog of his own complacency, out of which he has the effrontery to say that 'the people don't realise the seriousness of the situation'. Don't realise . . . My God! The Opposition have not shown themselves in any real opposition so far. Perhaps tomorrow they will wake up.

From the comments made on the wireless, apparently my imaginative picture of the hardships and difficulties in Norway was no exaggeration. One phrase of the soldier's recorded speech stuck in my mind. He said, 'The boys were a bit shaky at first . . . ' That's what I've thought: I've thought of all the boys who have gone from Tadworth and I've been trying to visualise them as fighters, and I can't. I wonder if this generation will make an army of like fibre to that of 1914. The sergeant who gave the broadcast said that the Germans were not the Germans of the last war. Are the English?

Pam Ashford

Things don't seem to be going well. Mr Mitchell is clamouring for the removal of Mr Chamberlain, who he thinks is too old for his job. He wants Mr Churchill as Prime Minister, and a Cabinet including Mr Lloyd George and Sir Archibald Sinclair. 'This old diplomacy, this old school tie system is worn out. These are new times, and we want new men.'

The situation at Narvik is developing, of course. It seems to me it would be dreadful if we failed to hold out there; after all Narvik and iron ore had so much to do with introducing the Norwegian phase of the war, and one feels intense pity for the Norwegians who would then have their country entirely in enemy hands. Mr Mitchell, however, thinks we should clear out at Narvik, which he reckons is not worth our losing many lives. Mr Mitchell expects Belgium and Holland to be attacked soon so that Germany may get air bases nearer to the UK. He says, 'There is tension everywhere, all of us expecting air raids soon.' Personally I don't think Belgium and Holland are the next victims on the list, for the reason that they are two countries which Britain and France could most readily help.

The Alpinists are everywhere. Will they be sent back to France now, or are they to go forward to Narvik? Yesterday three Alpinist officers visited Ailean Mitchell's school. They described their training, how they climbed the mountains, tumbling over rocks till they grew proficient.

WEDNESDAY, 8 MAY

Pam Ashford

Mother having read the papers at 7.30 was sorry for Mr Chamberlain and still supported him. However, at 1 she had turned over and explained to me that he was too old. I myself don't see any of these signs of deteriorating mental power in Mr Chamberlain, though I can well believe it if he feels weary. Mr Churchill is his obvious successor, and if Mr Churchill and Mr Chamberlain can work it out together, why hasten Mr Chamberlain's resignation?

A new age group is announced, men born since 10/5/1903. The gap between those who were involved in the last war and those who are now to register is growing very narrow. Charlie and I and the 'children' we spent our childhood with belong to that one little section left, still untouched by either war, those born between the autumn of 1900 and the spring of 1903.

At the Exchange the rumour going about today is that Mr Chamberlain visited the King this morning so as to give his resignation. I call it a shame to torture such a good and wise old man like this.

THURSDAY, 9 MAY

Tilly Rice

Uproar in the House last night led by Herbert Morrison, much to my satisfaction. All the family after the paper this morning. I got it first and read it as I fed the baby. Then at 6.50 down comes husband and takes it off upstairs. At 7.10 down comes Dick. 'Where's the paper Mummy?' 'Daddy has taken it upstairs.' 'The twerp!' Dick always likes to scan the headlines before he goes off to school.

Out this morning. FA at the bank said, 'I agree with these Labour people but all that shouting in the House is no good – they should work behind the scenes.' I replied that I thought there were occasions when a little rudery was more effective in bringing things to a head than diplomacy. Things get too urgent in these times for that method. I asked him what he thought would happen next and he said either an attack on this country or Holland.

Christopher Tomlin

I asked customers if there was any fresh news of Chamberlain. 'No he hasn't resigned. He's still there.' To which I replied, 'If he doesn't move we'll blast him out.'

Age groups 19 to 36 are now called upon! And I hoped I wouldn't be wanted until the end of this year.

Eileen Potter
(after four months' absence)
I am just getting up when I hear the other occupants of the house saying: 'Holland and Belgium have been invaded! The milkman says he heard it on the 7 o'clock news!' I hurry up with my dressing so that I can listen in at 8. The milkman's report is, of course, confirmed.

I go to the Divisional Dispersals Officer's office. Everyone is busily discussing the situation, with particular reference to the new evacuation plan: will it come into force or not, and if so, how soon? I am single-handed today in our little queries department, two of my colleagues having already gone on holiday and the other being engaged at medical inspections. I feel that Hitler has caught us on the hop as usual, both nationally and locally. All members of the staff likely to be concerned with evacuation are told to 'stand by' in case of being wanted for the execution of 'Plan IV', but those already away are not to be recalled, as the Government wishes to discourage travelling.

After a hasty lunch in the office, I set out for Fulham, and by this time posters of the evening papers are appearing: 'French Towns Bombed', 'Raid on Calais'. I catch a glimpse of a headline in somebody's paper – 'Cabinet Changes Postponed' – and start wondering how the new invasion will affect Chamberlain's precarious position.

Everything seems so unsettled that I decide not to go to my usual folk-dancing class tonight.

I go in to Mrs H to listen to the 9 o'clock news. The announcer begins: 'The Right Honourable Neville Chamberlain . . . ' I mutter, 'Good Lord!' thinking that Chamberlain is going to make some sort of appeal for the support of the nation in view of the new invasion. This impression is strengthened when he begins by emphasising the need for national unity at a time like this, and I am quite taken by surprise when he announces his resignation. This is what I have desired almost more than anything ever since Munich, but now that it has come there seems something rather pathetic about it. Presently Mr H, who is an air-raid warden, comes in from duty carrying a pile of printed instructions as to what to do in case of air raids. These have to be distributed to all houses in the neighbourhood, but first the names of the nearest wardens, first aid posts, etc. have to be written on the forms. We all set to work.

Christopher Tomlin

Shades of spewing Sam! Belgium and Holland invaded. We are warned to carry gas-masks, look for nearest shelter and ARP post. The BBC announcements almost make me tremble, but pray God we fight, not muck about as we did in Norway.

Tilly Rice

This morning it was announced that Mr Chamberlain could not form another Government, but now that this news has broken it rather looks as though we are to be left with him as leader, as there won't be any time for any other adjustments. However things have happened so quickly that one can't quite see yet what is going to happen. (Hope the Ws have a good time in Biarritz – there were air raids last night over a wide spread of districts in France. Anyway, I don't suppose that they will be able to get back by air. Now they'll be wishing they'd gone to Blackpool.)

The kids will have to start carrying their gas-masks to school again. Dick was only released from the obligation last week. Have washed all husband's clothes in case he is suddenly evacuated.

My grocer was very late this morning on account of the news, everyone stopping him to talk about it, so that by the time he got round to me he was thoroughly sick of it. But nevertheless I could see that he was disturbed, and that his faith in everything being all right in the end had received a nasty knock.

My next-door neighbour, Mrs C, tells me that her husband will come under the new proclamation for the calling up of men up to 37 years. Am wondering about FA at the bank.

Have been pondering on the possibility of a return to Port Isaac. I expect Auntie will be expecting a telephone call from me. But I think I shall stay where I am. I think so. We must see.

Pam Ashford

Individual comments at the office consist almost entirely of the word 'terrible'. At 9.20 Mr Mitchell arrived and has been talking more or less all the morning. I am trying to summarise his views now at

12 when he has gone out. He began thus: 'There are our Dutch and Belgian connections gone. I told you that my Antwerp shipments would not come off. It is not what we have been expecting. German parachutists in Dutch uniforms too! They tried that game in Norway, with parachutists in British uniforms ... '

He continued: 'America will come in now, within a month. America has interests in Holland. American and Dutch export/import trades are inseparable. Roosevelt has Dutch forebears. This will open up the Western Front. Hitler's Norwegian adventure was a failure. He has not got the iron ore and he has lost one-third of his navy. He will have to evacuate Narvik soon, and he has had to turn the Germans' attention in another direction. We have got to bomb his railheads and munitions works there today. If we have not bombed Essen by noon, we are mad .... '

In September I hid away the German customers' files because it hurt to see them, and now I might as well put away Anders Holth (Fredrikstad), Imperialkoks (Gothenburg) and the Belgian and Dutch people. Hitler will have something to answer for in the next world.

Mr Mitchell 'This is part of a plan. Hitler said he would do it this way, and he has.'

I said, 'Napoleon had a plan too, but it did not work out as he thought in the end. There was always the British Navy to upset him. As he said at St Helena, "Wherever there was two feet of water he found a British ship there."

Mr Mitchell: 'But the Navy is not the same now there is air power. That is where he is strong. What does Charlie think of aeroplane production?'

'He says exactly nothing at all.' (During the time I was not writing this diary, Charlie became the head of the Air Ministry for Scotland.)

Home to lunch. Mr Fuller got off the bus and walked up the stairs with me. I've seldom seen anyone so miserable. 'This is war to the death. Isn't it beautiful weather? They've bombed a great number of French towns.'

The news was dramatic at 1 o'clock. It took up so much time that Mother and I got in little conversation. However, I made sure she knew where her gas-mask was, and I took mine back with me. I told her where the nearest shelters and first aid stations are, all ten to fifteen minutes' walk. I advised her to remain in the hall which has no outer walls, and I intend to strip the walls of pictures for we don't

217

want flying glass. She feels things badly, never having believed that they could possibly have come to pass.

I took to teasing her about the 'Kitchen Front', telling her she was generalissimo and quite the most important member of the family. She however considers that I am always afraid of our starving. In point of fact it is not the British Navy's power to defend our food supplies that I have apprehensions about, but the deplorable wastage that goes on in British kitchens. It annoys me that sailors' lives should be risked for foods to deteriorate and get thrown away because the housewife cooked them badly or forgot what was left over from yesterday.

I came back with my Soroptimist friend who represents shipping. She said there was a rumour that Switzerland had been invaded, and I explained that according to the BBC what had happened was that bombs had been dropped on the railway line to Basle. She takes the situation calmly and with humour. There's no point in getting panicky. She lives in a stone house which she reckons would stand up to anything, but she might go down to the dog's kennel, a small room beside the kitchen with no outer walls and warmth from the kitchen fire. She has a mixture in which flannel will be soaked to wrap round the dog. Her mother has an old cosy which will be placed on the dog's head to keep him quiet. Dick, our canary, is so timid that I am afraid he will get heart failure.

Mr Hutchison and Mr Mitchell had a talk about strategy. They agree that Mr Chamberlain will remain Prime Minister now, with Mr Churchill to supply the vigour.

Mr Hutchison goes off saying there is to be a terrible debacle on the Western Front. I said to Mr Mitchell, 'What's a debacle?' He said, 'Slaughter.'

SATURDAY, 11 MAY

Christopher Tomlin

200 Nazi planes down! But I must be very calm and wary over alleged successes after the Norway debacle. I've made £3 again this week.

Pam Ashford

Now that Mr Chamberlain has resigned, Miss Bousie is full of his qualities. 'He was a very fine Chancellor, a businessman. Poor old man, I could have wept over him last night. He is tired. He has always followed what he believed to be right.' Mr Churchill is also accepted as satisfactory. We shall see if that attitude continues.

The Coal Exporters' Association is anxious to help firms distressed through the dislocation of markets. Those who specialised in German and Scandinavian business are hard hit, while the specialists in France are raking in a pile. Mr Mitchell suggests a pool to operate on all shipments irrespective of destination. This war has badly hit the 'all the eggs in one basket' firms. We are very widely spread, and our losses have come in stages, and we still have something left.

The warning about parachutists has fairly tickled the imagination. I said to Mr Mitchell, 'They will be watching the Highlands closely.' He said, 'That is why the French troops are here; in case the Germans invade the Highlands. It is all round the town now.' I said, 'It's a funny situation with the British Army in France and the French Army in Britain.'

The carrying of gas masks is developing.

SUNDAY, 12 MAY

Eileen Potter

I go for a walk through Kensington Gardens and Hyde Park with Mrs H and Peggy. The latter, who is interested in the Army, suggests that we count all men in uniforms. The total number of soldiers in the Gardens and Park amounts to only 67, not including the band or the anti-aircraft gun crews. We see only seven RAF men and three sailors, all the latter taking a busman's holiday by rowing on the Serpentine. Mrs H, who did the same walk about a fortnight ago, says that the park was swarming with soldiers then, but of course today so much leave is stopped.

I go back to Mrs H's to listen to the 9 o'clock news. Further Cabinet appointments are announced, most of which I approve, but I do not like the tone of Maurice Healy's propaganda address which follows the news. It suggests that the only people who ever did anything wrong since the last war were the Germans. I like the touch about our Prime Minister being made a cat's-paw by Hitler at

Munich, however, and reflect that this would probably not have been included whilst Chamberlain was still Premier.

Pam Ashford

In the afternoon I went to Knightswood and took a circular walk across the footpaths. I felt dead tired and crawled along. I was thinking, 'If my great-grandmother had kept a diary on the Eve of Waterloo and recorded all the trivialities that I put into mine on the eve of this terrible battle that is coming, well I should think she was daft.' The present is normal; but the shadow of the future is creeping over everything, so that the 'normality' of the present seems ghoulish.

Charlie has been surprisingly communicative today, three war comments escaping from him: 1) The Italian Royal Family is set against Hitler, and if Mussolini does try to bring Italy in, the Royal Family will use all their influence against him. I read once that Prince Umberto did not get on with Mussolini and had said when he was King he could rule the country without the Fascists. 2) Charlie has suddenly become scared about our going to St Andrews, and that is ruled out by mutual consent. 3) He gave me some information about the relative strengths of the German and British Air Forces.

WHIT MONDAY, 13 MAY

Eileen Potter

Bank Holiday has been cancelled. The whole office has a 'crisis' atmosphere. Many mothers call about the possibility of getting babies away, or getting away themselves, and voluntary helpers are still offering their services and all have to be interviewed.

Pam Ashford

The turn of events has made me very nervous and is disturbing my sleep. I find it best not to go out of my way to learn the latest news (I am not at all likely to miss anything striking). My feelings are so strong – horror and pity for the Low Countries and a growing apprehension for this country's future – that I have to impose reticence on myself.

The Chasseurs Alpins continue to be the main theme of conversation among individuals, and their untidy uniforms were much commented upon. The question on everyone's lips is, 'Why on earth are they staying here so long?' One lady said, and others agreed, that 'the Frenchmen must think it strange to see so many men going about Glasgow in mufti. They must think we are not mobilised.' That seemed a general impression, but I said, 'When one looks around one's circle of friends, one soon sees that the young men are going.'

Christopher Tomlin

Since the invasion of Belgium our thoughts are on Dick who is on the Belgian frontier. It is terrible not to know how he is going on.

6 p.m. News: We are warned to avoid an optimistic outlook! Father believes there is some bad news to break soon. I told him and Mother that the BBC should say, 'You must not take a *pessimistic* view.'

TUESDAY, 14 MAY

Pam Ashford

The parachutists seem likely to evict the Chasseurs Alpins from being the chief theme of conversation. Everyone has made up his or her mind that we shall have them here, and Mr Mitchell is full of stories of policemen watching the woods at Bridge-of-Weir. I myself don't expect to encounter a parachutist, for parachutists would be fools to try to come down in such a crowded locality as this where everyone would see them. I wonder, however, what we should do?

WEDNESDAY, 15 MAY

Christopher Tomlin

Holland surrenders! It needs a gigantic effort to keep panic under control. Germany is invincible. All the articles written about Holland's wonderful defences months before this battle began . . . and she is smashed in 5 days. Britain is in terrible danger of air raids from Dutch bases, parachute troops and bombs. The war will be over if Britain is smashed to pulp. I am very much afraid we won't defeat Germany. Of course, I am determined to keep these thoughts to myself. I will try to steady people's morale.

Holland hasn't given in! Just two provinces – more than enough though.

I have a feeling of futility. I cannot do anything to help, yet Dick must be in hell. I can only work and pray. The Royal Air Force is fine.

Pam Ashford

During the seven months or so that I have been writing this MO diary I have found great interest and pleasure in observing other people's reactions to the war, the changes which it has introduced into their lives, and the respects in which it has not changed their lives. That interest has evaporated. This morning I feel I have had enough of the war, and all I want is to escape from it. I have heard the 8 a.m. and 1 p.m. news on the wireless, and read the *Bulletin*, and that is enough for me.

Mr Mitchell has some sensational news this afternoon collected from the Exchange and elsewhere: 1) Turkey has declared war on Italy and Italy has declared war on France. 2) Hitler's 'secret weapon' is known now. It is a tank with gas jets stretching out for 100 yards in front of it. 2,000 of these are in operation near Brussels. 'Something terrible is happening there.' 3) 150,000 Dutch and Belgian refugees are coming to Scotland and will be billeted upon us. 'A lot of spies will come over with them,' Mr Mitchell says.

Refugees are to go to evacuation and neutral areas, not reception areas. One of my friends, Griselda Tomory of the WVS, is busy with arrangements for their reception. I don't know whether the authorities have any compulsory powers to billet refugees on householders. We have four rooms and a kitchen and I would gladly give accommodation, but Mother is almost 'knocked out' by the suggestion. I have said, 'In any case there will be no lack of empty beds in Glasgow, left behind by the schoolchildren who will be evacuated when the trouble starts.' Nevertheless instead of trying to encourage Mother to do national service, I have come to the point of arguing that the Admiralty would not want aliens looking into their windows (the Admiralty is on the other side of our street).

Tilly Rice

Today the Dutch Army in Northern Holland laid down arms. Another trick to Hitler. And corresponding depression among the people one meets.

The accession of Mr Churchill to the premiership, however, has heartened up the country and one notices that people, though quieter about things, are now more determined in their spirit. The new government has been welcomed on all hands and I in particular was glad to see Herbert Morrison go to the Ministry of Supply. Now, if it is not too late we should pull it off, and I believe we shall, quite truly without wishful thinking. I believe we shall. I think we shall have a damn near shave, but I think we shall pull it off. That came to me suddenly today.

Mr Chamberlain on his retirement made a speech, partly pathetic, and it made me feel conscience-stricken and almost personally responsible for his deposition . . .

Mr Eden's call for volunteers for a defence corp met with much enthusiasm and I talked to one man who had volunteered this morning. 'I hope they give me a gun,' he said, 'I'm just dying to have a pot at one of them fellers comin' down!' 'What about me!' said his wife, all enthusiasm. 'Can't I have one too?' I said, 'Your job is to keep up the morale on the home front.' 'I'm doin' that all right,' she replied, 'on my knees.' By which statement I take it she meant scrubbing, not praying.

Mrs R came round this afternoon to know if I could billet a refugee, but I pointed out that the house was too cramped for us as it was and she said, 'I knew that you couldn't but I must ask everyone.' I asked her how many offers she had had and she replied that up to that moment she had none. People said they remembered the Belgian refugees from the last war. But we never know, we might all end up by being refugees ourselves, and though I shouldn't like the idea, I would take in someone if I had the space available.

The other day my young Dick said, 'We don't discuss the war at Reigate Grammar . . .' Today, however, he gave me a detailed description of the landing and equipment of parachute troops. I said, 'How do you know all that?' 'Oh, a boy at school told me!' 'I thought you said you didn't discuss the war at school.' 'Oh, we do if it becomes tense enough.' So Hitler had better look out, Reigate Grammar School is discussing him.

Last night I felt lousy, there was no other word for it. 'Come out and have a drink,' invited E. 'No, I'm too tired, but I can give you a glass of beer if you want it.' 'I don't particularly – I should like to get out for a bit.' So we went over to the Rat, where in spite of the news, the company was very cheerful, and I came home feeling a different woman.

I feel that I must write in my diary regularly these days; things are happening so quickly and one feels that one has a seat in the front row of the stalls at the making of history. Sometimes I feel that we are coming onto the very evening of civilisation, and that the noise and roar of battle are the last crashing chords of the finale. But my deeper conviction is that we shall come out in the end . . . if we can hold them now. If. I don't feel nervous that the grim drama is going to come down and include me, although sometimes I suffer some apprehensions on the behalf of my children. I can so easily conjure up the hateful possibilities of myself and the children homeless, of the feeling of utter desolation that must come upon people in those circumstances, the loss of security and stability and above all the terrible feeling of being unprotected. But that, let us hope, is only the playing of my imagination.

I have thought that for the first time I have noticed some effects of the war on the general atmosphere of my children. Dick, aged 11, is quietly excited, almost as a boy is just before a firework display. But Bobbie, aged 6, is getting rather strung up. Only Janet, the baby, remains calm and cheerfully smiling, all the time.

Chapter Ten

BOMBING WHERE MY FRIENDS LIVE

It was hell let loose . . . troops were crossing in all kinds of craft: the wounded return home from Dunkirk.

'I have had German friends in the past, and I hope that I may live to have a German friend or two again one day. I hate to have to say this to you, but I find it my duty to say it and say it I will: be careful now at this moment how you put complete trust in any person of German or Austrian connections. If you know people of this kind who are still at large, keep your eye on them; they may be perfectly all right – but they may not, and today we can't afford to take risks.

If you do what I beg and keep your eyes open, and if you find out something which seems to you sinister, don't please just tell your wife's second cousin about it because her husband retired from the Mudshire constabulary two years ago and therefore has access to Scotland Yard. The police hate secondhand stories. Go to them yourself with chapter and verse written from your personal observation, and they will be grateful to you.'

Sir Neville Bland, British Minister to the Court of the Netherlands, speaks with experience of the Fifth Column on the Home Service, 30 May 1940

* * *

17 May Germany take Brussels. **22 May** Britain cracks Luftwaffe's Enigma code; German tanks advance towards Channel ports. **26 May** Operation Dynamo: Evacuation of Allied troops from Dunkirk begins. **27 May** Calais falls. **28 May** Belgium surrenders to Germany. **3 June** Germans bomb Paris; Dunkirk evacuation ends: 220,000 British troops rescued alongside 120,000 French and Belgians.

THURSDAY, 16 MAY

Christopher Tomlin

The 'Allied Line Pierced in 3 Places' – the headline leaped at me from the *Daily Mail*. My sensation is one of fear and crawling. The fate of Britain hangs on a thread. People are full of hidden fear, fear the Government will blunder again, fear that the confident assertions of public men, generals and so on, are mere poppycock. Doesn't this Government realise the population isn't optimistic but despairs through recent experience? We *know* there's a serious shortage of aircraft. There are probably many other shortages we know nothing about. I am not such a damned fool as to mention my fears to anyone but you. 26/- sales.

Since the battle in Belgium we have a nasty anxiety over Dick who is in the advance Air Striking Force at the Belgian frontier. We haven't heard from him for a fortnight.

Pam Ashford

Mr Mitchell and I had an argument. He said, 'Why should the Belgian Royal Family get (refugee) preferences over other people? As for Queen Wilhelmina, daughter and granddaughters, it was just class distinction bringing them here first.'

I said, 'They are the heart of Holland, and it is only right that we should give them hospitality.'

He said, 'If they are the heart of Holland, they should have stayed there. What about the other Dutch people? Why did we not save them?'

I said, 'Our powers are not limitless.' He said we should save all, or none. I said, 'If things had gone badly here, probably Princess Elizabeth and Princess Margaret would go to Canada – the invitation was given to them last summer – and rightly so.'

FRIDAY, 17 MAY

Tilly Rice

Went to see Mrs G, who has now accepted the idea of invasion so seriously that when, the other day, finding four stalwart men in forces caps and overalls stalking down her garden, she was sure the parachutists had arrived. I immediately went to see (I'm sorry for *any* parachutist who comes up against Mrs G in full blast), but it appears that they were only foot soldiers, who, working near on camouflaging a lorry, came in to beg a cup of tea.

M still busy dealing with contributions for refugees. She told me of a woman who drove up to the office in a car and presented to the hall porter – much to his acute embarrassment – two unwrapped chamber pots. But the next day she presented herself again with the regretful request to have her property back. It was a different porter on duty, and when she refused to say what the crockery she was seeking actually was, didn't know what she was talking about. She grew very red and asked to be shown to the crockery section, and the porter went with her to help her. At first she couldn't find her chamber pots and the porter kept asking her what it was she was looking for. She was getting redder and redder and consistently refused to say until, just as the situation was becoming impossible, she found them.

Pam Ashford
Miss Bousie: 'I saw a board saying that we were bombing German towns.' I: 'Not German towns, but railway lines. We are bombing where my German friends live.' I took out the atlas and showed her Duisburg. 'There is Dusseldorf too, where Marthe lives, she was here as an *au pair* for a year. And Anne stays somewhere in these parts. Of course, they all went to the same school, a Roman Catholic convent school in that district.'

The evening papers mentioned that the German press is saying that Duisburg has been bombed by the RAF and three people killed there. I am sorry for my friends, but somehow my feelings have changed since the autumn. I cannot distinguish Germans and Nazis nowadays, except those Germans who are openly outside Hitlerism. My friends used to abuse the Nazis when they were here, certainly, but they accepted them when they were at home.

SATURDAY, 18 MAY

Pam Ashford
In the afternoon I went to the Cosmo. They are having a month's French repertory. It was *Un Carnet de Bal* today. Charlie says that 200 free seats are given to the Chasseurs each afternoon, but I think Saturday must be excluded. In the newsreel we saw Mr Churchill,

and there was the sound of clapping from half-a-dozen parts of the house. Never have I heard this at the Cosmo before, nor so far as my memory goes in any city cinema.

After the show I walked along to the Mitchell Library. Scores of French sailors with the names of their ships on their hats, and you begin to wonder if this is Glasgow or Marseilles. French sailors conform to the established custom of having a girl in every port, and the Chasseurs seem good pupils. Goodness knows how many pairs there were, and often trios (girl with two Frenchmen, one on either arm). Of course they cannot converse, but that does not seem to matter.

Christopher Tomlin

We laugh at America's protests to Germany. Presumably Roosevelt thinks Hitler is afraid of him. It is high time America pulled up its sleeves and decided to come in.

Tilly Rice

Down to Reigate to a parents' meeting at Dick's school. The head, a young man for his position, seemed a different person from the man I saw last June. He is one of those who have been knocked sideways by the war and he seemed frightfully oppressed. Of course, he has a great responsibility, but I was sorry to see it, for it must be reflected in the school and it is definitely not conducive to the spirit of resilient courage that I would like to see in people. There was some discussion of the advisability of sex teaching being introduced in the school and I was amazed to find that there are still some parents who allow their children to grow to thirteen in (supposed) ignorance. A drab lot the parents looked, most of the mothers appearing to be middle-aged and 'upholstered'.

Eileen Potter

After listening to the 6 o'clock news, I go to the Cecil Sharp House for the Saturday night 'Popular Hop'. I have been meaning to go to one for some time, especially as the MC is usually our own instructor, Mr C. I decide to go tonight, in case there is not another opportunity. About a dozen turn up for the party. Mr C has to dance himself nearly all the time, to make up the numbers for the sets. There are almost equal numbers of men and women, so that this means if nobody else asks one member to dance, Mr C will. This suits me well, as I would rather dance with him than anyone else, and I get three dances with him during the evening. It hardly seems worth his while coming for such a small party, to say nothing of the two accompanists, but he throws himself into it heartily and we spend a very enjoyable evening. There is a huge man there who charges about like one of the new German tanks, but anyhow he seems to be thoroughly enjoying himself, and is a source of general amusement.

It is such a beautiful evening that I decide to go home by bus. The parks and trees are looking lovely in the moonlight, and it seems terrible to think that such a gory war can be going on in such glorious spring weather. I notice that the woman sitting next to me in the bus is muttering to herself. 'It's insanity,' she keeps repeating, 'that's what it is.'

SUNDAY, 19 MAY

Tilly Rice
Great excitement this morning over a drifting barrage balloon. An aeroplane was after it, and I expected to see it go down in flames, though I've learnt since that this doesn't happen. I remarked on my surprise that it apparently wasn't hit. Old H, who was working in the garden in which I was standing, straightened up his back and said 'Perhaps 'e don't want to 'it it! Perhaps 'e don't want to be too good if he has a nice safe job over here.'

There was a great load of wounded brought into a local station last night. French, Belgians, Germans and English. We've had no tally of casualties but I expect they are pretty terrific.

Eileen Potter
Spend the morning turning out my clothes, and putting aside some old things for the Dutch and Belgian refugees, who are supposed to be arriving in Chiswick today. I discover that I have about 24 pairs of stockings, in various stages of decrepitude.

After dinner I go for a walk with the H family. Motor-boats, scullers and canoes are about on the river, which is at full-tide, and several crowded pleasure steamers pass us. We are amused to watch two girls sitting on the grass nearby, who 'get off ' first with two soldiers, and then, almost immediately the soldiers have gone, with two AFS men in uniform. We return home by bus, having bought some Walls' ices by the bus stop.

Christopher Tomlin

Mass. The rector who served the mass left the altar after unrobing to give an exhortation from the pulpit. He told us to pray hard, and attend the services more wholeheartedly. For 'you know what would happen if the enemy won. I would be the first to go and then you!'

We were profoundly disappointed by Churchill's speech. 'If . . . If . . . Might'! What is wrong with the Allied leaders? The Nazis will win the war if we aren't terrible and strong. [Churchill: 'The long night of barbarism will descend, unbroken, even by a star of hope, unless we conquer – as conquer we must – as conquer we shall.']

TUESDAY, 21 MAY

Christopher Tomlin

6 p.m. News: The Nazis take two more French towns. I don't want to be pessimistic but I am afraid we've lost the war. Unless a miracle happens, the French are sunk. Have we no 'brains' to smash Germany?

Mother: 'You see, the fools didn't blow up a bridge they should have done and they've let the Germans through.'

The men seem to be responding enthusiastically to the request for parashooters. I believe it is so as they can have a gun to play with. At least that's what most of those I've known to be joining up seem to be keen on.

WEDNESDAY, 22 MAY

Pam Ashford

There was a meeting of tenants today to discuss ARP for the building. Immediately thereafter the war clouds became more ominous than I have ever known them. I think people let their imaginations run away with them. Agnes is almost hysterical by now. 'Nothing can avert the total destruction of the UK and everyone in it.' Mr Hutchison and Mr Mitchell with grim faces got down to First Aid, about which neither knows anything at all. They want First Aid boxes on every landing. I said (with humour that was not perceived),

'There is enough *sal volatile* in my drawer to bring round everyone in the building if they are going into hysterics.' (*Sal volatile* is a good cure for flatulence, which is a trouble of mine.) Mr Hutchison is very angry with Mr Chamberlain and says pointedly to me: 'Now you can see he has let us down. He should be put up against a wall and shot.' Then carrying identity cards came up, and the need to always have one's name and address on one's person. 'Ghastly,' says first one and then another.

THURSDAY, 23 MAY

Christopher Tomlin

A sunburst of golden glory: a letter from Dick, whom we secretly thought would never come home again. He is stationed since Tuesday 21st May in England: 100 miles away. He is safe and well. He left Belgium on Sunday with his pals. During the day they hid in woods and marched at night. They lost all their equipment. Oh, God for your mercy we thank you: grant us victory!

Mother said at breakfast, 'I knew something uncanny was going on with him. I could feel he was in great danger.'

I am delighted the Government is moving like hell . . . But alas it seems too late, for the enemy are on the coast of France.

The Germans are on the coast. The end is near.

Tilly Rice

The evening of May the 21st brought the bad news that Amiens and Arras had fallen (how the repetition of these town names as battlegrounds takes me back to my childhood). Lord Haw Haw triumphantly announced that the Germans were on the coast, and M. Reynaud made a solemn speech to his colleagues making no attempt to conceal the extreme gravity of the situation, telling them that incredibly foolish mistakes had been made and one assumed that the dismissal of Gamelin had its cause in this defeat.

E came home and thought things were bad. We discussed taking the children back to Port Isaac. E was rather inclined to think that I ought to take them straight away, but I said no. The next day I had got an appointment with an editress whom I had been trying to see for nearly ten years and I wasn't going to let Lord Haw Haw panic me into not keeping it.

So yesterday I went up to town. By then the news had come through of the re-capture of Arras and by the time I got into Fleet Street the feeling of that part of the world, which I have always regarded as being almost feminine in the degree of its variability and fickleness, was running high again. One man I spoke to said, 'Yesterday we reached rock bottom, but now the tide will turn,' which may have been wishful, but was a good indication of how folks were feeling, and the news of the assumption by the government of what is practically Socialism was increasing this heartening-up.

It occurred to me that the people of England would welcome a dictator, and that perhaps all this time unconsciously they had been wishing they could copy the continental idea, adapted to our own characteristics, of course. On the other hand, such a measure relieves the private individual of responsibility, and the distaste for taking personal responsibility has been the bane of this age, in my opinion. All very well for people to bleat of the disappearance of democracy, but if the Chamberlain government with its dismal lists of muddles and failures is the best that can come of democracy, the sooner it goes the better.

It may be in the end that this war has been a good thing after all. It bears out my long view which regarded all this horror as just a step in the process of evolution; we must look upon our present fears and trials as the labour pains of a new birth. There was much that was good in the Nazi regime – that must be admitted. Nothing in the world is entirely bad, or is entirely good. But Hitler was impatient to grab all he could, and could not stop to build his state on firm and true foundations. He resorted to evil, the evil of destroying trust between human beings, and of course like resorting to drugs, he has gone on and on. He has built on a rotten foundation and through that must, I believe, come destruction in the end. This bloody business will settle it, and one must adjust one's ideas to every hour that passes.

Pam Ashford
Miss Bousie is buying her spring wardrobe as usual. I said, 'The civil population should not call on production for one article more than it needs.'

She said, 'But I did not buy last year as you did.'

234

I said, 'My mind was torn then; on the whole I think the Government did not mind us buying last summer, for it helped to ease the unemployment during the early days of the war. In any case, practically all the clothes I have were bought between December 1938 and August 1939, actually before the declaration. A gamble that war was coming.'

Miss Bousie: 'If you don't buy now it affects the shops, and causes unemployment.'

FRIDAY, 24 MAY

Christopher Tomlin
I am afraid to read a newspaper.

Pam Ashford
Mr Mitchell was full of grave news this morning. 'The Germans mean to seize Calais, Dieppe, and all that line of towns . . . at any rate they are going to destroy them so that we cannot use them. They mean to encircle the Northern Army and say to us – BEF, French and Dutch – "Surrender!"'

I said, 'Our forces surrender!!!'

Mr Mitchell: 'No, we won't. We shall re-embark, but we shall be peppered in doing so.'

I: 'If the Germans had full control of those Channel Ports our Navy would bombard them. We are not beaten yet.'

Mr Mitchell: 'Why don't we bomb Essen? They have bombed Aachen. Two months ago I wrote to the Air Ministry and said, "If and when you bomb German towns, start with Aachen. They make there the Electrode Coke which is essential for aluminium production for airplanes." I think they must have acknowledged my letter.'

I: 'Perhaps they will give you an OBE when the war is over.'

He: 'I don't want an OBE. All I want is to do my duty. The Germans mean to direct waves of airplanes against us, and drop parachutists in thousands.'

I: 'I should have thought you would have been able to become a parashot. Probably, however, they won't have you – being a member of a decontamination squad.'

He: 'That's it. We would like to join the parashots. There is a squad of 100 at Bridge-of-Weir.'

Miss Bousie entered the room looking most distressed and started, 'Lord Haw Haw . . . .' But Mr Mitchell cut her off sharply and kindly, saying, 'You should not listen.' She said, 'I don't. But the last two nights he has come on by accident.'

Tilly Rice
Another lovely day, if one really noticed the weather. There were a lot of aeroplanes about last night, and I woke up every time one came over which seemed about three times an hour. Yesterday and the day before I heard or rather felt the impact of very distant gunfire. As I was bathing Janet I suddenly noticed the windows move and creak twice and then again a few moments later, although there was no wind to account for it. I believe that in the last war gunfire was heard on top of these hills from many miles away.

News fairly good. Apparently we are holding them again and also cutting in on the spearhead of their attack, a daring plan which would be a wonderful move if it succeeded but a mad waste of life if it doesn't.

(The news still going on, and then, inserted casually among the other items, the announcer said: 'It has been learned in London that the Germans took possession of Boulogne last night.')

Sir Oswald Mosley and various other Fascists including Joan Beckett were arrested yesterday. What about Unity Mitford? The only drawback to that sort of thing is that it immediately converts the people concerned into political martyrs.

SATURDAY, 25 MAY

Christopher Tomlin
My brother and his squadron are just in England after terrible experiences. He lost much equipment. My sister lost a new frock she brought and luckily recovered it. And I lose 15/-. Perhaps next week we will all gain something unexpected.

MONDAY, 27 MAY

Eileen Potter
I leave the office at about 6 and hasten to Golders Green, where I am going to play tennis with some friends. I am only in time to play one

set before supper, as the journey is so long, and there is a slight delay on the way owing to a breakdown of the 28 bus. Miss B, our hostess, is a keen pacifist and internationalist, but by now she seems to be getting more or less reconciled to this war. Among the guests is a young Hungarian, who took refuge in Czecho-Slovakia owing to his political views, and then had to flee from that country after Munich. He plays tennis extremely well, considering that he began only last season. Miss B also has a middle-aged German Jewess spending a few days at her flat, in between jobs. While we are there, she hears by telephone that her daughter has actually been interned today. We all try to pacify her, including the Hungarian, who states that several of his friends have already been interned, and that the only thing they really minded about it was that in some cases they were included in the same parties as real Nazis, who were most unpleasant to them.

Tilly Rice
Last Saturday the local ARP organisation staged a procession for the purpose of recruiting more volunteers. They all togged up in their rompers and steel hats and enlisted the services of a band and a loudspeaker. Our local post stood at the bottom of the road all ready and looking very spruce, then along came the procession and swept by at such a rate that the post had no time to join on to it.

My eldest son was wondering this morning if the next war would come just when he was about to go to university. He was sitting working it out.

TUESDAY, 28 MAY

Pam Ashford
9.30. Mr Mitchell reports that the Belgian Army has capitulated. I said, 'What of our men?' He said, 'I suppose we shall evacuate them.' Gravity, anxiety, apprehension and determination is on every face. Mr Mitchell said, 'The Germans have a line from Norway to the Channel now. They mean to launch air raids on this country.'

Miss Smith: 'All the little buffer states are gone now. They stood between us and the Germans. It remains to be seen now if France makes a separate peace.'

Miss Carswell: 'It is the obvious thing to do. If France makes a separate peace, our number is up.'

Agnes: 'Of course, we should make a separate peace. We are not going to have Germans here murdering old people and children.'

Personally I would rather fight to the death and I believe that the British Empire can fight alone.

This is the loveliest week of the year too, so far as the West End is concerned. All the trees in the University grounds are species that flower now. Lovely red hawthorns, some white hawthorns, many laburnums, a few cherry trees, rhododendrons. What a vista of colour one gets going back and forward on the bus.

Eileen Potter

By the time I reach the office, several of the men are sitting about with very long faces muttering about the bad news. We are very busy, however, and it is not until about midday that I actually learn about the Belgian surrender. Not knowing yet that King Leopold had given in without warning anybody, I point out that they can hardly be blamed and that it is not for us, who have not as yet been invaded, to pass judgement on them. Later in the day, when more facts are available, I revise my judgement.

WEDNESDAY, 29 MAY

Christopher Tomlin

The *Daily Mail* tells how and why the BEF is hemmed in. I want to do something – I am ready to face the bloody hun. I register on the 15th of June and now await it with cold fury, sadness and determination. We will beat back the bloody swine or die. We will never surrender. Maybe the incompetent leaders in France have gone.

Later: Mother says, 'Our men are fighting wonderfully.' How thankful we are Dick is in England, not there.

The Empress cinema was quarter-full. At 'God Save The King' we all stood still. Not a movement until the last bar.

Pam Ashford

I asked Mr Mitchell if he thought we would be invaded, and he said emphatically, 'Yes, I do.'

I said, 'I wonder where they will strike. Not the Highlands?'

He said, 'No, they won't waste time there; they will try and get the aluminium works at Kinlochleven.'

Miss Crawford: 'A spy was caught at Elderslie on Saturday. He was looking at a map, and a local inhabitant, knowing he was not a native, called for the police. He was a German on his way to Greenock.'

Miss Carswell knows someone who knows someone who knows someone etc . . . who had an Austrian maid. On reaching this country the girl was very bitter against Hitler. Then one day the mistress had occasion to reprimand her, and the maid said, 'Wait till Hitler is here. You will need to be careful what you say then.' This excited the mistress's suspicions. She called in the police. The girl was a spy.

Miss Carswell: 'It is Mr Chamberlain's fault. He had not the guts to resign.'

I said, 'Mr Chamberlain was the last bulwark of democracy in this country. When he went we became a totalitarian state holus bolus.'

I was out twice this afternoon. Mr Mitchell said, 'Any news?' I said, 'Our men must be having a terrible time in Belgium.'

He said, 'They must. The tanks are mowing down women and children in the streets.'

I said, 'They would do the same here if they could, and worse. My Mother refuses to regard the situation as serious.'

He: 'She will wake up one day and find this country is invaded.'

Certainly we are getting used to the idea of an invasion, but it is not here yet. What I cannot understand is the mentality of the women in this office. Practically all of them want to surrender right away. They won't hear of fighting on British soil. They seem to think it is far better to be ruled by Germans. It seems to me that they think it would be just another change in Government. Hitler would just become Prime Minister and everything would go on as before.

THURSDAY, 30 MAY

Eileen Potter

I am aroused in the early hours of the morning by the sound of what I take to be anti-aircraft guns. I look out of the window, and see a red glow in the sky. I decide to wake Mrs F, who has not heard the noise. She comes up to my bedroom to look out of the window, and then decides to go to her room and get dressed. Presently there is a crash on the stairs: Mrs H has fallen down and has cut her chin. I decide to wake up Jack F and his wife, whose bedroom is on the ground floor. We all gather in their room, and Mrs F lies on the bed, and presently is sick. We go out into the back garden, but all is quiet and peaceful in the summer dawn.

I have arranged to go into one of the schools first thing, to make arrangements for a dental inspection. On the way, I see women picking up fragments of something out of a gutter, and saying, 'If you get a large enough piece you can see the name of the firm on it.'

I arrive at the school and rather apologetically explain my business (which seems rather futile in times like these). I ask the head teacher if she had heard the noise, but she says it was not an air raid at all, but an explosion in a light bulb factory. The fragments in the streets were pieces of charred paper wrappings, apparently.

Pam Ashford

Mr Mitchell and I did not do much talking this morning, chiefly because we were too busy. Also the sheer awfulness of the situation seems to freeze words on the lips. I said, 'The roads are blocked with refugees.' We both think the German air losses are such that Germany must rapidly be losing her superiority in planes. It is certain that a terrible struggle lies ahead, but we are confident that the British Empire cannot be downed. If the very worst happened in this country, then Canada, Australia and New Zealand, and South Africa too, would still hold the fort.

Miss Crawford is saying that in the *Herald* there are terrible casualty lists.

FRIDAY, 31 MAY

Christopher Tomlin

The American, like the skunk, has a nasty smell. The dollar jingles round his neck, and what the hell does he care for France and ourselves. All he's after is money!

It is an absolute miracle our boys are evacuating Belgium – I'd given them up for lost. Lord Gort is to thank for it.

They are overdoing this 'girding' up your loins for the struggle business.

After I returned from the cinema, Mother said two plain clothes policemen had been to see if I could 'help them with a little incident'.

SATURDAY, 1 JUNE

Pam Ashford
The success that is attending the evacuation of the BEF towers above all other items of news today. Mother was able to announce at 8.30 that all was well. I said, astounded, 'What about Italy?' and she said that they have not done anything. They are playing a waiting game. I met Mr Hutchison coming to work and he said he hoped it would be a wet weekend. I said, 'Oh, you fishers always want it wet,' and he said, 'It would help the troops avoid air attack.'

MONDAY, 3 JUNE

Maggie Joy Blunt
Fanny tells me that a local man, one of the BEF, just returned from Flanders saying that the papers do not exaggerate. Germans bomb the wounded; he saw them. It was hell let loose. They had to run – how they had to run! – and he a man of 50 who had served in the last war. Troops were crossing in all kinds of craft – little fishing boats, motor boats, anything. The Admiralty has issued a statement describing how these were summoned and how they responded. What a magnificent achievement.

We hear the sound of guns on still days. I thought it was practice somewhere near but I am told it is the guns of Flanders. This is no longer considered a 'safe' area. They fear for the trading estate and are taking all precautions. All signposts are down and there are no indications of Police Stations, etc. The LDV [Local Defence Volunteers, later the Home Guard] is on duty in shifts the whole time.

A story is going round the village of a caretaker cleaning in a church one evening. A clergyman came in, said he was tired and wanted to rest. The caretaker went on with her work and left, but for some reason returned and heard a lot of noise in the belfry. She went for assistance and they discovered the 'clergyman' with wireless set transmitting messages to the enemy.

Pam Ashford

I met Miss Whittan on the bus at 5.30, and she said that one of their ships brought 1,000 men home from Dunkirk. She had said to the captain this morning, 'How did you get them on? They must have been like sardines in a barrel.' The captain said, 'Worse than that.' They were harassed by machine gun fire and brought a German plane down with their ship's guns. Seven soldiers were killed on deck. The captain brought the boat from Dunkirk without any instruments whatever, and then wanted to be given another ship to go back for more. Miss Whittan and I think our men are wonderful, and she, like me, thinks this war is a case of do or die. We both feel contemptuous of those weak-spirited people who go about saying that if there were an invasion they would rather surrender to the Germans than risk losing their lives.

Today has been lovely again. How much I enjoyed my evening walk around Kelvinside. Red and white hawthorn, laburnum, rhododendrons, and green trees, combined with clear visibility so that the hills that lie all around Glasgow showed up very distinctly. Let us hope that this fine weather that civilians love does not encourage those diabolical Nazis to make air attacks still more.

Eileen Potter

One of the busiest days we have had at the office since the outbreak of war. It is officially the closing day for registration for evacuation in the schools, and the parents seem to think it is also the last day for making arrangements for the under-fives, and for making the private arrangements which they all seem to prefer to the Government scheme. They arrive in large numbers all day.

I go up to Golders Green for my weekly tennis and supper. The Hungarian does not turn up tonight. He has sent a message and we wonder vaguely if he has been interned himself. The German Jewess has left, but we are told that she heard from her daughter, who is quite happily settled in the Isle of Man.

TUESDAY, 4 JUNE

Christopher Tomlin

Dick came home absolutely unexpectedly on four days' leave. We were delighted to see him! I dare not write his views on the situation for if this diary got into the wrong hands we would both be in trouble.

The two detectives called me at half-past-ten: 'What was I doing asking questions: did I advise anyone to tune in to 26 metres?' I explained about the BBC survey [an opinion poll about public opinion and morale]. I told them I had not told anybody to listen to 26 metres. They were apparently satisfied. A woman living in a council flat had reported me, with 'trimmings' added of her own.

Pam Ashford

Miss Bousie is working in the YWCA canteen at the Lyric on Monday nights from 6 to 10. She serves at the tables, fries ham, eggs, chips, etc., washes dishes and dish-cloths. Many of the volunteers are unreliable; if it does not suit them to come they don't, nor do they advise the supervisor beforehand, or send a deputy. Unless you are regular, you are no use, Miss Bousie says. She does not like serving for she feels shy. I wish I could do something like that, but I've not got the strength to do four hours on my feet after a day's work.

In the afternoon the painter (whom I have observed to be a blood-thirsty kind of a fellow when Germans are mentioned, though very pleasant to deal with) learnt that Munich had been bombed by the French and hundreds killed, and that was the reply to the bombing of Paris. This news gave him and Mr Mitchell great satisfaction.

I nearly collapsed to read that one of our customers, Mrs McMillan, had been charged with murder. Many times I have talked to her on the phone, and cannot believe that anyone with so nice a way of going about things could possibly be guilty. I hope she is acquitted. I cannot believe she poisoned her husband.

Chapter Eleven

JOAN AND ROBERT

The time will produce the man: Churchill arrives at the Admiralty.

'At this time of cancelled holidays and long working hours, it is particularly important that we should avoid over-straining ourselves . . .

I think we tend to exaggerate the importance of sleep. People vary enormously in their needs, and no rules can be laid down. The traditional seven or eight hours has little but tradition to support it. The value of sleep is that it rests all parts of the body simultaneously. The same thing can be achieved if we learn to relax. Try it. Lie down quite flat with just a pillow. Don't cross your legs or fold your arms. Now close your eyes and proceed deliberately to think of relaxing all parts of your body. It's perhaps easiest to achieve by concentrating your attention on your own breathing, and counting to yourself like this – in, out, in, out. Then deliberately try to make your mind a blank. It can be done, but it requires practice, and I know from personal experience that in 15 or 20 minutes you're a new person.'

New ways to cope with the war, Home Service, 17 June 1940

* * *

8 June Allied forces and the King of Norway are evacuated from Narvik as armistice is signed. **10 June** Italy declares war on Britain and France. **14 June** The Germans enter Paris. **16 June** Marshal Pétain becomes French Prime Minister and seeks immediate armistice. **18 June** Hitler and Mussolini meet in Munich; Soviet forces begin occupation of the Baltic States; de Gaulle makes broadcast from London establishing a 'Free France'.

WEDNESDAY, 5 JUNE

Pam Ashford

Miss Bousie: 'Did you hear Mr Churchill's speech? They expected 30,000 lost. It is beyond understanding.'

I: 'And after France, our turn will come!'

Mr Mitchell: 'If the Germans came here and took control you would have to surrender.'

I: 'I never would. You never know what opportunity might present itself. The person who assassinated Hitler would be doing a glorious deed. Not that I expect to do that.'

The wonderful weather goes on. I could have had the first fortnight of June for my holiday. Now I wish I had gone. The point is, one feels one ought to be working and not enjoying oneself at all. Still, I am already feeling run down and I know I need a fortnight in the fresh air if I am to keep up at my best in the coming winter. What will the world be like then?

The *Eroica Symphony* on the wireless tonight. That is better than war news. Also, at 9.25, a talk on what to do in an invasion.

THURSDAY, 6 JUNE

Tilly Rice

Since I made an entry here last, exciting things have been happening. When I last wrote it seemed hopeless to even think of evacuating those men from Flanders, and now, by a marvellous operation, they are mostly home. What pleases me more than anything else was the display of pure genius in utilising a great fleet of tiny boats for the evacuation instead of several large troop ships.

There seems to be a great heartening-up going on. Everyone wants to get down to something and even I am feeling restive at having to stay at home and continue with my ordinary life. Dick tells me that the boys at his school have been having a great time watching the BEF come home and several of them have acquired some interesting souvenirs. One boy has a Belgian forage cap, another a sailor's hat and so on. Apparently the men threw them through the windows of the trains as they passed though Reigate.

The weather continues beautiful and one cannot help thinking what a lovely Derby Day we should have had this year. I wonder what we shall have next year, if there is indeed a next year for us. I was thinking the other day on the possibility of good arising out of all this beastliness and horror. It may be that Liberty will sharpen its teeth and wits at the clashing steel of these hideous battles. It may well be a badly needed purge (as I thought that I remembered a saying of H.G. Wells' that until you made the experience of peace as exciting as that of war, peace would never get a chance). These days *are* exciting, and every minute may bring a new development. I thank my lucky stars that I am living in 1940, and I pray to my gods that I may live to see the end of it all, not so much because I wish to preserve my own life but because I want to see how it all turns out.

We have all had our gas-masks fitted with the new additions to the canisters. Bob was very good trying on his mask, so much so that Mr S (at the ARP post) remarked on it. He said, 'You *are* a fine little fellow! I wish all the little boys who came here were like you. You don't mind having your gas-mask on, do you?' 'No,' said Bob stoutly. 'You're not afraid, are you?' 'No,' said Bob, even more stoutly than before. 'It's silly to be afraid, isn't it?' 'Yes.' As we were going up the hill afterwards Bob said to me with light inconsequence, 'I like going to see Mr S, the gas-mask man!'

The Premier's speech – which I thought was the finest bit of rhetoric I had ever heard, and the like of which I thought was never produced nowadays – seems to have been received everywhere with enthusiasm. It's what the country has been wanting for years, and I am reminded of Auntie's remark of some months back, while inveighing against the hopelessness of the Chamberlain administration. She said, 'The time will produce the man . . . ' and by George it has in Churchill.

My hunch over our ultimate victory has grown from a hunch to a conviction. Now that everyone is wakened up we shall do it. It is going to be a bloody business, but worthwhile, my God how worthwhile.

FRIDAY, 7 JUNE

Tilly Rice
The Germans have started the big offensive: Hitler appears now to be making for Paris. I listened to Haw Haw last night for the first time for quite a while and thought that the propaganda had deteriorated

considerably. There was a long rambling tale of a hospital being bombed in the Rhineland and I was amused to observe the German attempt at mental acrobatics. On one hand saying that the raid was ineffective, and on the other that it had ghastly effects. The whole thing was too puerile to even be comic.

As I was passing the butcher's this morning I heard an emphatic voice proceeding from within saying, 'A new world will rise after this war. Mr Bevan will see to that!'

More raids along the coast last night, up as far as Hampshire. We heard nothing up here, though Dick reported a conversation he overheard from a woman down at the shops saying that she heard an explosion during the night and that there had been tanks passing through here and a soldier's voice saying, 'Have a drink mate!' all about 1 a.m. All of which excited Dick much more than it should have done.

Mussolini continues to wobble on the fence. I don't think that much notice should be taken of him; if he's coming in against us he's coming in, and it's absurd to be frightened by his 'bogey bogey' any further.

Pam Ashford

Mother has been reading that glass is to be restricted, and not having bought any tumblers since 1925 and having broken nearly all the ones she bought then, she has come to me in an excited state to see what I can do.

Mrs McMillan has been found not proven. I am so glad, so is Miss Bousie.

Mother bought her tumblers at Boots', which she described as having the largest glassware department in Glasgow, and instructed me to get 4 or 6 (according to price) of the formerly 1/- tumblers, to match what we have left from the 1925 purchase. Boots', however, had no tumblers whatsoever, and as they got theirs from Holland, they will have none till the war is over (they seem quite sure that Holland will be producing again then).

Eileen Potter

Go to my folk-dancing class. As I am waiting for my refreshments in the refectory, a khaki-clad figure approaches – a man who used to come to the class a year or two ago. 'Hello,' I say, 'are you in the Army?'

'I feel as though I were in the Navy as well,' is his reply, and then I guess that he has just returned from Dunkirk, which proves to be the case. I always considered him rather insignificant and uninteresting, and both he and his wife were rather pasty-faced and unhealthy looking, but now he is broad and smiling and has the air of having been through a great experience, and altogether seems very much improved. He comes to the class and does one or two dances, but evidently he finds dancing in battle dress is rather too hot, and sits beside the accompanist and reads the paper and tells war stories.

SATURDAY, 8 JUNE

Pam Ashford
During the morning Miss Crawford was saying that last night the parashots were out practising in Kilbarchan. I said, 'I should think that the parachutists were better shots than most of the parashots are likely to be,' but she differed. 'In the country many men are used to firearms and should be able to wing a parachutist.' It seems a ghastly business. There was also talk about the use of rifles. Miss Carswell would shoot anyone in the ankle, but only in the ankle. Miss Bousie would strike a parachutist, but only with her hand, never would she use a rifle.

Elsie spent today in Glasgow, and phoned to ask me to meet her at the picture house at 2.30. She mentioned the film *For Freedom*. Mr Mitchell warned me against this, and so did Charlie. On seeing her I said at once, 'This is the worst show in town.' She would not hear of going anywhere else, however. And what a rotten film it was too. Oddly enough, she liked it, and when they came to the battle of the River Plate, she began to strain forward in her seat, giving ejaculations – 'Good . . . Splendid . . . That was a fine point,' etc. In fact, the boredom that the film induced in me was relieved by watching Elsie's reactions to it. Before the film was screened, a Glasgow man called Macmillan came on the platform and related his experiences on the *Altmark* – terribly boring too. I have mentioned him to Mother who says he went to a whist drive she attended last night and made a speech there too.

Maggie Joy Blunt
Germans have launched a furious attack on the Somme but we are

251

holding them back. On the outcome of this battle, says the *New Statesman*, the future depends. If we can hold out until October says Harold Nicholson, Hitler will not last the pace, the nerves of the German people will crack.

These are days of most appalling tension. One lives from hour to hour. Raiders are over the South and East coasts nightly but no serious damage or casualties have been reported. When I was in London I heard of people in Deal who say the town is barricaded and wound with barbed wire like nothing in their knowledge. Their house shakes nightly. All townsmen who can have left. Troops are in possession.

London was calm. There are more sandbags and shelters. The sky was sprinkled with barrage balloons. But the daily life of the city continued on the surface quite normally. I lay in bed in the morning listening to the footsteps of early workers, and the leisurely progress of a milk cart. In the West End women shopped as usual. June sunshine had brought out a crop of light frocks, white hats, sunglasses. Strawberries were on sale.

Ella and Aunt Aggie have Belgian refugees. I met them – a master plumber and his wife, homely, pleasant folk. Ella said that when they arrived they were in a terrible state. He burst into tears. They left two sons in Belgium, one recently married, a gendarme, but they have no news of them. They think their home and business are gone. They help in the house. They speak very little English but he speaks French. He told someone he was so glad that this house was clean, a point we overlook: while we fear 'dirty' refugees (I remember stories from the last war), we forget there are decent folk among them who may fall into bad billets. The couple were refugees in the last war (think of it – twice in a lifetime!). They were then billeted at Letchworth and were free to move about the country as they liked. But not this time: they even have to get a permit to go to London.

The older generation are very depressed and seem to think we are already beaten, with no hope for young folk at all. June says that the atmosphere in her parents' house in Bournemouth is intolerable.

I returned to a sun-baked garden. Kittens are scampering now all over the place, and I hope I find a home for them. I cannot believe that the possibilities which threaten us are true, that the Germans may conquer France and attack us without mercy, or that we may submit to humiliating defeat.

Eileen Potter

I go to the Divisional Treatment Organiser's office to complete my medical work, and find the staff in a state of excitement because a message has come through from County Hall to say that we all have to have our photographs and particulars about our date and place of birth and appearance attached to our identity cards as soon as possible, in case we are required to go into places where ordinary members of the public are not admitted. I think this sounds rather exciting, and decide to go and have my photo taken at a place near Victoria Station, where I had my last passport photo taken, as it was rather good. I wonder whether there will be any enquiries as to why I want a passport photo taken just now, but there are not, and the whole thing is done within five minutes.

Tonight is 'visitors' night at the Cecil Sharp House, and there is to be a demonstration of country, Morris and sword dancing by the headquarters team, for the first time since the War. The director of the Folk Dance Society is absent, and rumour has it that he has a temporary job working amongst the aliens in the Isle of Man. The Secretary, a woman, acts as MC, and our instructor, Mr C, takes the lead in the dances. He is now a middle-aged man, and I have been watching him take part in such demonstrations at intervals during the past ten years or so, but I think I have never seen him dance better than tonight. It gives one a feeling of confidence to think there are men of such a fine type about in this country, especially as he now belongs to the parashots.

SUNDAY, 9 JUNE

Maggie Joy Blunt

The heat seeps down. It is as hot as it ever was in Malta. I was up before 7 a.m. and gardened for three hours in the coolness of early morning. The rest of the day I have done nothing. The *Listener*, the *Sunday Times* and a Pelican edition of George Moore's *Confessions of a Young Man* curl in the sun. I wonder if I shall have any visitors, hoping yet not hoping because of the effort it involves.

My championship of Chamberlain is short lived. I have not studied politics long enough to realise the extent and enormity of his crimes . . . Scarcely anyone but Fascists have a good word for him now, in fact one is suspected of Fascist tendencies if one says anything for him.

Tilly Rice

The weather has been continuing hot and blazing again and I long to hear the refreshing sound of pouring rain. I have constantly thought of the added hellishness the heat must bring to the men fighting in France. Perfect weather for Hitler and his tanks; if only it would pour and pour with rain and bog the lot.

Things on the domestic front proceed quietly. With extreme care I manage to make the sugar ration go round. Meat and butter present no difficulties at all. Vegetables are the chief difficulty now. Salad comes out at a great price. I had to pay 1/3 for a scrappy little bit that only did for Dick, Bob and me.

Later: On the six o'clock news bulletin we heard that Mussolini had declared war on France and Britain. I don't think I feel any increase of apprehension, but I do think that things will now happen very quickly and I feel very glad that Sir Stafford Cripps is on his way to Russia. I may be wrong, but I believe that a good deal will now rest with Stalin, that man whose mind works in an Asiatic dispassionate way, who has never traded on emotion, and who will plan every move with great deliberation.

M has now finished with the refugees. She says that it has been an awful business trying to keep track of them because they shift about and she hopes that the police have got their records complete for it has been impossible to do it at her headquarters. I find that the war has awakened in her a greater sense of citizenship than she ever possessed before. All her savings are invested in National Savings, and if we lose the war all that goes, all her little assurance against the future and old age. I said I thought she would be wise to keep just a little money by her, preferably in silver. She said she had thought of it, that she would like to get the whole lot out, but she went on, 'If everyone did that, we'd have no hope of winning at all.' I was glad to hear that and have decided to cut down cigarettes in the same cause.

Pam Ashford

This morning soon after nine Ethel and her soldier husband came to the office together. He has 48 hours' leave, but through fortunate train connections it is actually three days. Ethel, as on previous occasions, intends to spend these three days with him. Ethel is leaving at the end of the month, and we are advertising for a new telephone operator. The soldier husband was a very likeable young fellow, apparently quite indifferent to what he went through at Dunkirk. He said the Germans were cowards and would only attack in large formations, and singly they ran away.

At the Soroptimists Club luncheon the speaker was Mr Tweedie, on 'The British Association for International Understanding'. He began by saying that during most of our history the man in the street knew nothing much about foreign affairs and did not care. Wars were fought by the regular army and the man in the street had only a mild interest. Then came 1914 and the nation found that it was called to give 100% energy. The men who went through four years of fighting, when they came back, wanted to know what they had been fighting for. Interest in foreign affairs began to heighten. During the last six years that interest has risen considerably. Prior to that there were very few people in this country who had any international association at all; John Smith in this country did not know what John Smith in Berlin or New York was like, but during the past six years there has been an enormous expansion in the knowledge that ordinary people have of ordinary people elsewhere.

Then at Munich the 'curve' rose so sharply that it almost went off the page.

Not having heard the 1 or the 6 o'clock bulletins I was disposed to listen at 9. I was quite unprepared for the news that Italy had entered the war.

Christopher Tomlin

Customers timid – not all though. Funnily enough they perk up when I say, 'I am registering on Saturday and look forward to going. I am just ready to tackle the B's!' Don't know why but many seemed to think we (young men) weren't too keen to smash the bloody swine. They are also upset by the reported shortage of munitions. Some are afraid to listen-in to news.

[To Mass Observation:] If the worst happens – God Forbid! – and Germans conquer this country, I beg you most earnestly to burn all the data you have.

TUESDAY, 11 JUNE

Maggie Joy Blunt

These are heavy days. Italy, that land of colour and enchantment, declared war yesterday. Now my brother and his family in Suez are cut off from me. Malta is a little besieged island, a lonely fortress in the Italian sea. No Italian hostilities are yet reported, but the press lashes out in fury against Mussolini.

It is odd. Both sides in war profess confidence in their cause and that they will win. I suppose this always happens yet it is never true. Listen to Mussolini – 'We are going to war against the plutocrats who are strangling our economic life . . . ' And Hitler again – 'In September 1939, British and French politicians declared war on Germany without any reason . . . ' (are we really lunatics?) ' . . . refusing all offers of peace . . . The increasing disregard for Italy's rights had now definitely bound together our two peoples.' We are Invincible because we are a Right, Pure, Misunderstood people and God is on our side. Recently a woman was arrested in Bath who had been writing to her friends in Germany in this strain: 'You must be proud to have such a wonderful Fuhrer. I was really convinced he was definitely sent to make the world a cleaner and better place . . . and the world is crucifying him.'

Two children got off the bus with me this morning and followed me along the narrow footpath towards home. I heard them behind me: 'Look Joan, there's a cow in that field!' 'It's not a cow, it's a horse,' answered Joan.

Presently they overtook me and we began to talk. They were returning from school in the village. Did I know where they lived? No. 'Shall I tell you? In that big white new house just round the corner. You wouldn't think from the outside that it was a very big house would you?' said the boy. 'But it is. It has 13 bedrooms.'

It is a modern, reinforced concrete house, whitewashed, with flat roof and flush doors which I have noticed with interest. I had been told that it was the work of a young architect but did not know who. I find that he is the father of these children. 'But he's in the army now,' said the little boy. They chattered on. 'Do you know my mummy?' asked the girl. 'I'll tell you her name and I'll tell you ours. I'm Joan and he's Robert . . . '

Christopher Tomlin

I am a Catholic and the betrayal of Catholicism hurts me. Why does Mussolini murder innocence and purity? He is a vulture hovering over the 'dead'. But France is alive!

Pam Ashford

Copy of letter of 11th June 1940:

> Fabrique de Cellulose de Bois Attisholz SA,
> Attisholz,
> Switzerland.

> Dear Sirs,

> Many thanks for your letter of 30th May, contents of which we have read with great interest.

> In view of the present state of affairs in Europe, we regret it would be impossible to suggest any route by which we could deliver a cargo of coal to Switzerland. All we can do is await the change in the strategical position, and there *will* be a change for the simple reason that the Allies are going to win this war!

> In due course we will have pleasure in approaching you regarding fuel supplies, and in the interim we are keeping our tails up, with one thought foremost in our minds – doing all to achieve Victory for the cause of Justice and Truth.

> Yours faithfully,

> The Forth & Clyde Coal Company

WEDNESDAY, 12 JUNE

Christopher Tomlin

The two detectives call again. They are satisfied, but the superintendent is unsure. They took all papers relating to the BBC surveys. I was very much annoyed though I didn't say so to the policemen. On thinking it over, I admire their tenacity. If all police are as cautious, the fifth column will have a damned bad time. The two detectives were gentlemen – 'Sorry to make this fuss. We know it's all okay, we are satisfied. But the superintendent phoned up as we were coming off duty at 11 last night . . .'

Pam Ashford

When the painters were here five years ago a number of large maps were stood against a wall at the back. Now we have had the place painted again we have been wondering what to do with the maps. It was decided to avail ourselves of the services of a workman repairing the blinds to re-hang them. Mr Mitchell accepted the offer of a map but when Italy was brought in he changed his mind. All the maps are obsolete and it was next decided to give the glass to a glazier as a gift. So the maps were hung around the back of the premises. I have often looked at the one of England and Wales, and everyone was saying, 'There won't be any England and Wales soon, but only Scotland,' to which I replied, 'There will always be an England.'

I said to Mr Mitchell that I am sure there will be bombing in this country soon, which he thinks too. I could not but say, 'What a change has come over us. We are getting used to the idea of bombing.'

Fear for Paris is rising steadily, and in the course of the afternoon there was a 'doubles tournament' – Agnes and Miss Carswell versus Miss Bousie and myself. Miss Carswell began by saying drastically, 'If Paris falls that means we are finished!' Agnes: 'If Paris falls our number is up.' I and Miss Bousie: 'Nothing of the sort. If Paris and France falls the British Empire will fight on.'

THURSDAY, 13 JUNE

Pam Ashford

About 11.30 Mr Mitchell came in saying there was a notice, 'British troops surrounded and surrender in Normandy.' Miss Carswell: 'The Germans have defeated us at every turn. We cannot defeat them.' I said, 'That is a defeatist point of view. You should keep it quiet.' A few minutes later I looked at Mr Mitchell's paper and saw that under new Emergency Regulations people who expressed despondent views can be put in jail. Miss Bousie returned from the bank at that point very distressed: '20,000 of our men are captured!' This shocked the place. Subsequently it transpired that it was a German report, and I scoffed at it saying, 'Wait till we hear the truth.' Happening to remember the new defence regulation, I said to Miss Bousie, 'Don't be despondent, or you will be put in jail.' She said she knew this.

Immediately afterwards I went to Queen Street Station and all along the way read the chalked notices, but only one contained the figure 20,000. At one o'clock the wireless gave the figure 6,000.

I went down the stairs at 5.45, just as the caretaker's husband was coming up. We have passed scores of times but never with more than a 'Good night'. This time he held me in conversation for about five minutes, pointing to this and that item of news in his papers. What he objects to are the reserved occupations. When he was 22 he was away fighting niggers and yet now young men of 22 are 'reserved' (deep contempt).

Eileen Potter

The first day of the second evacuation. We are not being used as escorts this time, so do not have to get up especially early. The appearance of the place is reminiscent of last September – a line of LCC cars outside, helpers sitting about on the steps and a general buzz of activity within – but somehow on a milder scale. Several parents come in still wishing to register their children to go away. There are one or two spare doctors on the premises and we are able to utilise their services to examine individual cases going to the reception areas at their own expense, such as 'under fives'. They seem to have dug out some of the oldest doctors in London for this purpose. One of the pioneer woman doctors is amongst them, and a man so old he seems hardly able to walk up or down the steps.

Maggie Joy Blunt

Paris is becoming a deserted city. A great tide of humanity is fleeing towards the West.

Andre Maurois broadcast a moving appeal for arms this week. The French must have them now – NOW! Our industry is working at full pressure, America has rallied at the eleventh hour. But in the meantime Paris is all-out besieged, and the Blitzkrieg has descended upon France with terrifying effect. But should Hitler suppose he can crush the spirit of men? Does he suppose that when he has won 'according to plan' the war against him will end?

I remember my father saying sometime around 1933, 'Hitler! The man ought to be shot.'

A fury of hate rises in me. I know that if he 'conquers' Britain, parties will band in secret to overthrow him. He will engender hate no tanks or bombs will destroy. The Germans besieged Paris in 1870. One of its defenders then rose to great power and dictated terms in 1918. His name was Clemenceau.

6 p.m. News: 'The French Government will never give in. They will move to North Africa, to their possessions in America . . . ' Fresh British divisions have arrived to support the French Army.

Mr C still hard at work. Says his men won't be able to stand the strain much longer without rest. Thinks we have as good a government now as it's possible to get at any time.

All church and chapel bells are to be used now only to notify the arrival of parachute troops.

Christopher Tomlin

13 is usually an unlucky date. It wasn't today. Sales topped 40 bob. Customers think the delay in calling-up is a disgrace. Many 24s haven't gone. I expect six months will elapse between my registration and medical exam.

Sir John Anderson tries to scare us with 'Britain must be prepared for unheralded attacks . . . there may not be time for sirens!'

Evidently we are losing.

FRIDAY, 14 JUNE

Tilly Rice

All the time, with the quickly changing events each day brings forth, I feel I am watching a scene on a stage on which the lights rise and fade every minute. Each news bulletin has the possibility of completely changing the atmosphere of life. However bad they are they never give me the jitters; rather, bad news fortifies me and deepens my belief in the victory of good.

L was up from her 'south-east coast town' again yesterday and said that going back last time she ran right into the return of the BEF. She said, 'They all looked so lovely, so cheerful, hanging out of the carriage windows cheering, and if I could have got at them I would have given them all the money I'd got . . . ' She also told me of the local police sergeant's adventures in dealing with the prisoners of war brought into town. One airman arrived looking very crestfallen with all the distinguishing marks cut off his tunic, and when asked what had happened to his various badges and buttons he said all the British soldiers had been taking souvenirs off him. Of four other airmen, one wanted to go back and fight for the Fuhrer, but the others only wanted to know when they were going to be shot. Apparently it is quite true that the Germans are told that we shoot our prisoners.

Dick came home yesterday thrilled to the marrow because he had sat next to a BEF man on the bus. He seems to have recovered his equilibrium now and I don't think his tummy is likely to capitulate again. I don't mind admitting that I would like to get the children off down to Cornwall again, but that is impossible at the moment, and I have heard it said so many times that no place is so very much safer than another nowadays.

Later: The one o'clock news reports that the Germans are entering Paris.

Pam Ashford

The atmosphere is subdued today. People keep on saying, 'It is terrible,' but not much else. Mr Mitchell says that when Hitler invaded Norway he said he would have Paris by 15th June, and he has it on the 14th June. Hitler also said he would have London by 15th August. Many of them are disposed to believe that he will.

In the evening I went to a public meeting (organised by the Saltire Society) on 'The Arts and the Public in Wartime'. The Lord Provost was in the Chair, and began by saying, 'I don't know whether I should apologise for addressing you, or you should apologise for being here. On the day that Paris has fallen our thoughts lie far from the paths of peace and the peaceful arts. The nation is crying out for aeroplanes, etc. and we come here to speak of the Arts. A paradox. I cannot conceive of the world as happy when the Nazis are in our spiritual home, Paris.

'There is point in our discussion on Art, however. In my discussion with soldiers, sailors and airmen they have shown themselves interested in art, music and literature. I have a postcard from a man in the forces in Orkney. He wants Penguin novels on Art, Modern Architecture, Economics and Journalism.

'Three men from Norway came to see me yesterday. Penniless. Had no food since the day before owing to the lack of intelligence on the part of the military officials. I gave them a meal. Then they said,

'Where are the art galleries?' The soldiers would regret it if the civilians did nothing to preserve the Arts.

'Soldiers in France ask for postcards of pictures in our galleries. The originals are hidden and only the curator knows where. If he is killed, we shan't get back Rembrandt's *Man in Armour*, until some miners dig it up by accident.

'We are required to cultivate the interest of the ordinary people in art. Don't be content to attend meetings. There are 4,000 to 6,000 soldiers here every day. Why not take them to the art galleries, art clubs, etc? The French might learn from the Glasgow School, just as the Glasgow School learnt from the French.

'The Glasgow School of Art is to be closed. I hope this decision is rescinded, or that would be the greatest victory Hitler could have achieved. The Scottish Orchestra. I hope it decides to go on. Let us organise with smaller orchestras and have more concerts decentralised. Why should Gracie Fields have the monopoly to entertain soldiers and sailors? Airmen particularly would like good concerts.'

Maggie Joy Blunt
Because of the food shortage all dogs in Germany are to be killed.

SATURDAY, 15 JUNE

Christopher Tomlin
A delivery day. Hard at it until 5 p.m., when I registered for military service. I sincerely hope I'm called-up very soon. One customer wonders how the French will save Paris from destruction when the Germans are pushed back. The French beg America to send thousands of bombers immediately – 'It is not a matter of months, weeks or days, but hours!'

Pam Ashford
In the afternoon I went to see Mrs Fraser ('Lil', a widow). She lives at Ralston which is in Renfrewshire, halfway between Glasgow and Paisley. When I speak of Glasgow in this diary I mean really the West End, Sauchiehall Street and the commercial centres. I am as nearly ignorant of other parts of Glasgow as I am of China; when I visit them I feel like a tourist.

When the tram reached the Paisley Road Toll area I began to think that there were a fair number of shops boarded up. Some had written outside, 'British subject', 'British subject, born in Paris, no connection with Italy', 'Owned by British subject now in the forces', 'British owned, no Italians employed'. In fact, in that area, there was only one ice cream shop with a normal appearance, Canadian Café, with an advertisement of a polar bear serving Arctic ices.

On the return journey, in order to be sure of my facts I made a count and saw within a quarter mile of the Toll (a rough locality, of course) two shops – ice cream & fish and chips and barbers – that had definitely been smashed up (i.e. the boardings were not of a preventative character). There is an ice cream shop (still open) in Sauchiehall Street, with smashed windows, and the Continental Café in Byres Road (still open), also damaged.

Another astonishing feature of the journey was that at one point two walls were being built across the road with a space of about 20 yards between them. The tram lines are left clear and only through this break can traffic or pedestrians pass. I thought it must be to help the police check the papers of motors at night (there seems to be a lot of this going on). Mr Smith (Lil's father, lived with her since her widowhood) thinks guns are to be mounted in the space between the two walls to arrest the passage of parachutists.

The golf course opposite her house is covered with trenches for the parashots to do their practising. The golfers continue golfing and don't half fume when their balls fall into the trenches.

Mr Smith has turned the garden into a vegetable plot. Cabbages, cauliflowers and radish leaves were a mass of holes, and I said, 'Surely there must be an insect pest,' and began to look for caterpillars, but there were none about. They don't know what is the cause, but don't take the holes too seriously. Mr Smith (74), hale and fit, wishes to do something. 'They have been saying there is work for everyone, but I have been waiting for someone to tell me what to do, and no one does.'

They are a cheerful pair and attribute their cheerfulness to never listening to the BBC news bulletins.

Christopher Tomlin

I paid another £1 to SVP, and at Mass there are special prayers for France.

I am pleased to see the way people are facing up to things. There's quite a lot of laughter about, though some folk are taking the possibility of German victory in a more matter-of-fact way than I think is good. One occasionally hears remarks such as 'They won't bomb London because they will want it to have their troops march into,' and 'May as well spend your money now – you won't get many reichmarks for it,' and 'This time next year we shall only be allowed to dance German folk dances . . . '

I feel that things are not being pursued in a ruthless enough manner. The Government should fearlessly take greater advantage of its new powers; we might just as well have our own dictatorship if through not having it we shall have to bow to a foreign one. And I almost wish the air-raid siren would sound. I shall feel an anxiety about myself until I have been really proved in an emergency.

Maggie Joy Blunt

A depression of such blackness envelopes me. I hardly know how to write about it. The Germans are in Paris.

Yesterday Stella brought SS for the day. SS is a woman of between 40–50, has written and travelled extensively. She is an admirer of LH (now in prison with Mosley). She knows Germany but is not violently pro-anything. She realises the corruptness of the capitalist system, the great need for social reform, has a tendency to blame the Jews, loathes Churchill, cannot see what right we have to be smug about the Empire and sees in Fascism a remedy of despair. When the Germans arrive here she says Churchill will fly to Toronto or somewhere secure and broadcast a moving appeal for us to fight the last ditch and stone and whatnot to save our Empire and all it stands for. Stella, like a little gnat, buzzed round and after her. They sat and talked treason in loud voices on my lawn.

SS said at one point, 'The Germans should come over here and be so nice that people would change their minds about them.' I protested. They would be met with most frightful resentment. I may manage my own house badly but I'll damn well clear up my own muddles in my own way, however efficient and well-meaning my neighbours may be. She thought that that was true of the British up to a point but that we needed someone like Hitler to help clear things up. 'People are so scared by these tales of concentration camps and brutality . . . ' she said.

She complained of wasted woman-power here. She wants a job and is willing to do any sort of war work and had her name down on various registers, but can get nothing. When others are worked off their feet, sweating blood, it does seem appalling that so little is done about it. She drove an ambulance in the last war.

She was in a bad state of nerves. Her views have lost her many friends. She does not know what to do. She believes we shall have a terrible winter. There will be food shortage (every meal she looks on as the last), coal shortage and plague. I said rather feebly, 'But the war must end soon!' 'They said that last time,' she answered.

In between writing this I have been playing Patience, having tea and reading A.A. Milne's *Pooh* stories. Beloved little animals in the forest. Our foolish, childish, blundering selves – muddled, well-intentioned, happy when the sun shines, given to poetry at odd moments, lazy, silly, tender and amusing . . .

MONDAY, 17 JUNE

Christopher Tomlin
Black Monday.

A small delivery. On my return I heard the 1 o'clock news and we were horrified to hear France was suing for peace. My first reaction was, 'they won't buy printed notepaper now,' then a blanket of foreboding covered me. It seemed God had turned aside and we'd lost the war. Finally a surge of patriotism, a fierce desire to 'get' the bloody swine, mixed with fear lest I prove cowardly. I canvassed a high-class residential avenue and was surprised that everybody was in a mild panic. I soothed them and said, 'We young fellows are determined to settle Hitler. I can tell you that if I "go" I'll take 10 of the B's with me!' It cheered them immensely.

Pam Ashford
10 a.m. The war will become a deadlock in Mr Mitchell's view. We cannot defeat Germany on the continent. They will raid us no doubt

but our navy and air force will keep them at bay. Eventually our blockade will wear them out, and they will come to terms. The war will be a draw.

11.30. All shipments to France have been stopped.

I felt so sick I knew I could not enjoy the food at the Soroptimists and almost decided to save my 2/6. But it was with a sinking heart that I made my way to the Gordon, every chalked notice proclaiming the gravity of the situation. The atmosphere was charged with tension, and I was declaring my complete confidence in France, while most of the others were saying she would back out. Then at 1.15 Miss Stewart entered with the news that France was giving up.

Mr Mitchell came back about 2.30 saying, 'This is the biggest surrender in history. Hitler is going to speak from Versailles on the anniversary of the treaty.' Mr Mitchell heard also that some people are leaving London and Portsmouth. He expects there will be big battles all along the south coast of England now. He will live off Europe and bomb us.

Miss Smith: 'There will be great jubilation in Berlin tonight. The man who can do no wrong. He said he would do it, and he has. We have been expecting bombs but it is going to be an invasion instead!' Quite a half-a-dozen people have said this today, and I have always replied, 'We have not come to the end of the chapter yet!'

Tilly Rice

That 'gutsy' little man Reynaud threw in the sponge and today's list of the new ministers appears to be almost Fascist in tone.

But over here everywhere one comes across a greater determination. Over at the Rat last night people, although admitting their gravity, were more firmly cheerful than I have ever seen them before. There was some jocular talk of the LDVs, about how it had been seized on eagerly by men as a good excuse to get away from their wives. 'They need never know where you are . . . ' 'That's usually here,' said another. 'It's the headquarters of the LDV!'

Maggie Joy Blunt

We are alone in Europe, an incredible situation. The French have been outwitted in a very new kind of warfare. And as we are now I don't think that we stand any better chance. What of the BEF? What of our feeble Home Defence? What of Southern Ireland? I have a ghastly feeling that we have worse days than those of battle in front of us – when the Mosleys will be released and restored to power and little, stupid people patted on the back and awarded high positions.

I met the children Joan and Robert again today. Their father has been killed in Belgium.

TUESDAY, 18 JUNE

Tilly Rice

Yesterday the BBC said that hostilities had ceased at midnight, but this morning they say the French are still fighting. Hitler and Mussolini are meeting today. I'd love to see a little finesse used in this war; it's been all biff and bash up to now.

After the one o'clock bad news yesterday there was supposed to be some light theatre music on the programme. I thought, 'Good, I could do with a little cheerful music after that announcement.' But no. The BBC goes all ponderous and substitutes one of Elgar's longest and gloomiest symphonies as more fitting to the occasion. In desperation I searched the continent for something to cheer me up, but every programme had a German voice bellowing away about 'Francais.' Then I thought of Athlone. That should be all right. I tuned in to hear the announcer say, 'The next item in our gramophone record request programme is rather an odd one and comes from patients in the Something or Other Hospital. It is Chopin's Funeral March.' Finally, after I had given up all hope of finding a gleam of cheer anywhere in Europe I got Leningrad and found them playing English dance records. Geraldo and his Orchestra.

Have been thinking seriously of investigating this Dominions evacuation business when details are available. I shouldn't mind taking the kids to Ottawa or somewhere like that, a fine thing for the boys.

Christopher Tomlin

Easy to canvass. There is a settled, determined, calm spirit around: 'Now we know where we are . . . we will now know our true friends.' There's a great deal of thankfulness and joy that our boys are safely out of France.

Maggie Joy Blunt

We shall fight on, said Mr Churchill yesterday.

Some fighting still continues in France. Russia has been active in the Baltic States – fortifying frontiers, issuing ultimatums, changing government. Italians have bombed Malta, Corsica and Tunis. In France an old woman pushing an invalid husband . . . Families in cars, on bicycles, walking, weeping at the roadside because their petrol has given out and there is no more to be had, turned away from overcrowded villages, hungry, lost, desperate. While German broadcasts taunt them with the Versailles treaty.

Never has anything so vividly imagined by me come true. To leave the cottage, my books, Dinah and her family . . . to who knows what occupants. The weeds will grow, the flowers run to seed. It will break my heart. But I must be practical, be prepared. What should I take? I must make a list.

If I thought the Nazi form of government any better than our own I would not feel so already broken. You may suppress criticism by threats and punishment but that will not change opinions or make your form of government into a good one. Our attempts at democracy may have failed. But that doesn't mean that real democracy could never succeed. Some fighting and some pain may probe whether we are soft to the core yet or not. Oh, God help me to endure the moment when I have to leave the cottage! It is not easy to be alone just now.

Pam Ashford

Mr Mitchell is asking where I am going for my holidays. At the weekend I chose Keswick, but now it seems too far away, and my thoughts turn to Dunoon.

Mr Mitchell wrote to French friends (Nantes) and incorporated the following sentence, which we later expunged, in case the letter got into German hands and caused them trouble:

'Our earnest prayer is that France, like ourselves, will rise phoenix-like from the present difficulties and march on to victory!'

Fancy being afraid to tell a Frenchman that!

The world awaits the news of the Hitler-Mussolini terms. I said how grieved I am that France did not come into a union, though I am conscious of great constitutional difficulties. If she were part of the British Empire she should acknowledge our King as head, which probably she would not wish to do. Mr Mitchell says she may come into a union yet, but the time to do so should have been long ago. It is always 'too late, too late, too late' on everyone's lips nowadays.

WEDNESDAY, 19 JUNE

Pam Ashford

The air raid last night would seem to have been on a bigger scale than previous ones. I said to Mother at once, 'Don't you want a shelter now?' She said, 'Damn a shelter!' But 15 minutes later she changed her mind – without any pressure at all – and seemed quite disposed to do something. I must get something done this weekend. I have made many attempts to buy the Government pamphlet on protecting your home against air raids. None of the booksellers seem to have ever heard of it. The Post Offices have sold out.

Mr Mitchell learns that the *Queen Mary* and many other large ships are in the Clyde with Australian troops. This morning at 11 he pointed out of the window excitedly, and there was an Aussie walking along Oswald Street. I could have cheered.

On returning at 2 I was much shocked to hear the boys shouting Hitler's peace terms – total surrender of France. Practically everyone seems to hold that nothing else is to be expected. Charlie's view is that Hitler is making a desperate bid to finish the war before the winter, for Europe is going to have the worst famine for a very long time. One third of the cattle of Denmark have been slaughtered already to feed the German population. Charlie expects pestilence too through the destruction of drains. I don't think anyone reading this diary needs to be told that food shortage at some future date is never far from my thoughts. I do believe that the Dominions will keep us going here, but I do want us to be in the position of being able to reduce our imported foods to a minimum when peace comes so that the Scandinavians, the Low Countries and other innocent victims can be helped.

I very much enjoyed my evening walk. The early summer months are always lovely, but never have they been more lovely than in this fateful year. Just at present there are many sparrow chicks about. Two were sitting on the telephone wire beside our kitchen window, watching me solemnly for an hour or more.

Christopher Tomlin

There was a flag day in Preston on Saturday. Don't know what for. But the emblems sold were tiny Union Jacks. Mine is remaining in my button-hole. I am ready to die for my country; in simple terms it's what service for the crown amounts to. You may be fortunate for a while, yet in the end fate gets you. I've no illusions.

Eileen Potter

Announcements are made on the wireless telling parents to apply to their local education offices for particulars about evacuation to the Dominions. We have had no official instructions, and I wonder what we shall have to tell them when they come.

Somewhat to my surprise, the instructions arrive at the office by this morning's post. We have already had several queries, and have taken the names and addresses of the parents provisionally, and we are told to keep other enquirers in the waiting room while Dr T decides what is the best course of action to take. Amongst our queries this morning are two from refugees – one from a German, who points out that Allied refugees are mentioned in the paper in connection with the scheme, but that nothing is said about Germans, etc., and the other from an Austrian Jewess with a highly intelligent small son who seems very keen on getting to Canada or the USA and who offers to pay his own fare. Both these have later to be told that they are not eligible, and the Austrian family are referred to Bloomsbury House to make further enquiries.

In the evening, Mr H has a practice in his back garden for the neighbourhood stirrup-pump crew – four men from nearby houses. We watch the proceedings from the flat roof. An incendiary bomb is exploded, and also an ordinary fire is lit, and the crew are shown how to put both out with the pump. The bomb looks rather like part of a firework display, but at the same time one can realise that it would do a good deal of damage if left to rage unchecked. I have put on my old clothes, with a view to practising with the pump after the men have gone, but they stay talking so long that by that time it is too late.

Christopher Tomlin

Mrs Booth next door lent me a *Lancashire Daily Post*: two women, a mother and daughter, were killed in their sleep when a bomb fell on their house somewhere in the north-west. No town stated. Mrs Booth thinks the plane was looking for a local munitions works. It is very comforting and consoling to know the black-out is admirable. Mother thinks the black-out is useless just now, for it's never dark. Father slept in his clothes last night.

Those I speak to are cheerful and resolute, and refuse to be upset by Nazi scum. Certainly the best preventative of the blues is to do something useful, and I sincerely believe civilian morale can be raised if the government gives each of us a little war job. Voluntary duty is no good at all, we must be ordered and made to do something no matter how simple. We want to feel we are taking a share of the burden.

P.M. news: It is highly probable America will 'come in' as in 1916. Thank God! I am not banking on it, as the recent news has been too demoralising.

Pam Ashford

It is said that Portsmouth and Southampton are having frequent visits from the enemy. It makes me anxious for I have friends and relatives in both cities. I suppose that here in Glasgow the degree of abnormality introduced into our lives is as yet meagre, though there is much tension. My father had a cliché that was couched in mathematical language and which I often heard in childhood – 'What happens when an irresistible force meets an immovable body?' Well, that is what we are going to find out, and what we shall find out I'm sure is that irresistible forces are not irresistible at all.

The proposal to send children to the Dominions is much discussed. Mrs Mitchell has a sister in Canada and Mr Mitchell clearly favours sending them away (girl, 14, boy, 11). The children, however, don't want to go and are making no end of a fuss. Office snippets: 'It's going to knock family life to pieces . . . you cannot start again where you left off . . . children are impressionable, and will forget their parents.' (Chief contributor: Miss Bousie.)

Last night when Duff Cooper was announced [as Minister of

Information] I said to Mother, 'Miss Bousie will be running him down tomorrow!' She used to think the world of him, but now he is a member of the Government he has lost favour. Sure enough, we got the following: 'Did you hear Duff Cooper? What *was* the point? It was sheer propaganda. It is time we stopped that sort of thing. It was on the level of Rule Britannia. And the poem! What had it to do with the prosecution of the war?'

FRIDAY, 21 JUNE

Christopher Tomlin

The longest day. No raid last night or none reported. Wouldn't surprise me if Adolf bombed shoppers in towns – Friday is the day on which he could kill most women and children, a thing he longs to do. Just at a time when I want to be fit I'm troubled with very slight bleeding (piles) again. They are outside not inward. I'm annoyed with itching too.

Good job we don't rely on the BBC to cheer us up and build morale. The programmes are putrid! Why in the name of King Kong does the BBC give promenade music whenever there's grave news? People are upset enough and don't want to be made melancholy. Give us cheerful music, an English play, a little variety to whitewash our blues. No letter from Dick this week, we hope he wasn't hurt in Monday's or Tuesday's raid. He's posted in the south of England.

Maggie Joy Blunt

Still alone waiting for news. French plenipotentiaries have met German and been handed peace terms which have not yet been published. So far there have been no alerts near here or London. Neighbour Mrs C has just told me that if there is a raid here I may go and sit with them, which is very sweet of her.

Our turn will come. I MUST do something. The *New Statesman* this week points to the millions of men and women who if invasion comes will find themselves useless civilians. We have not been organised or called upon. I suppose it is left for us to volunteer but it should be made more constructively possible for us to do so. There should be some urgency and appeal about it.

Am reading Maugham's *Of Human Bondage*.

Tilly Rice

Discussed with Mrs P the possibilities of going into this stirrup-pump business. She was very enthusiastic so I rang up the local AFS and before I knew what had happened had been roped in to get the names of people in the lane willing to participate in the project. As the result of all this I found myself over in Banstead last night having a demonstration of working the pump and also a lesson in dealing with fires. A great lark the whole thing, crawling about on your front in a dark underground passage full of smoke made by paraffin fires. I wasn't coughing, so apparently I found the pure air near the floor. After this first test a man came out and said, quite seriously, 'Of course in a real fire there wouldn't be the smell of paraffin so it wouldn't be so bad . . . ' After that an ancient three piece suite was set on fire and put out very effectively several times with the pumps. When a rather inexpert rescuer let the victim's head crack against the concrete steps down which they were supposed to drag the body, there was a gale of laughter.

I find that trousers, or slacks as the more polite like to call them, are the only possible wear for this sort of thing and noticed what a disadvantage the women who had been foolish enough to come along in cotton frocks were at. I came home looking like a sweep, stinking of paraffin, but quite exhilarated with my evening.

Since the Germans have got so much of France I'm gradually changing my mind about Cornwall, for if they extend that twenty-mile danger zone along the coast right down to Penzance, Port Isaac will be as near to it as we are here. Then there's the invasion idea, with the lonely south-west coast the ideal and obvious place, and on top of that, if things did go wrong, there's more likely to be difficulties over food, particularly in a place where one is more or less a stranger.

Went down to the bread shop and found little Mrs B a-bubble with delight because her handsome naval officer son was home on leave. I was duly introduced. His eyes looked heavy with sleep and he said all he wanted was to get to bed and have a good long sleep without having to get out and man a gun every two hours.

Pam Ashford

News on the wireless that 800 or so British refugees from France have arrived.

Lord Beaverbrook has been writing to the Provost thanking him for the great effort Glasgow is making to build airplanes and Mother takes this to be a great compliment to Charlie. She goes on, 'And to both of us.' I said: 'Well, you feed him, you can take part of the credit, but I do nothing.' To this she said, 'You keep up the morale of the house.'

Miss Bousie was saying someone told her that Lord Haw Haw had said that the Germans don't mean to attack Scotland. They are going to land many Germans here and they will marry Gaelic women and found a healthy German stock. I should regard this as so fantastic to be funny, but it was treated as serious news by some people here. Miss Carswell (in deep gloom): 'Oh yes, when the Germans come here, we shall all have to marry Germans.' I said, 'Well, if that is not super-defeatism . . . ' Again I was in hot water. 'You don't know what may happen. The French thought they were all right. You don't know what you will have to do!'

There is a story that soon the Government won't allow one to travel more than 12 miles from one's home. That will complicate our holiday problem even more. Miss Crawford says she cannot leave her village in the evening without signing an ARP warden's book.

I have laid in a stock of acid drops in the office. Fear makes one thirsty.

Chapter Twelve

THE FIRST WARNINGS

Most shops were sold out immediately: siren suits get the model treatment.

'I suppose there doesn't really seem to be much connection between new pennies and winning the war, but the Government's action [penny production was suspended] has been taken as a measure of economy. Pennies are made from bronze, which are nearly all copper, and in time of war copper is essential for munitions making. What the Government wants us to do is to use more of the twelve-sided threepenny-bits. These threepenny-bits are much more economical to make than pennies are. It is estimated that the Government's plans will save nearly a thousand tons of copper a year.'

R.J. Martin of the Red Cross Society, Home Service, 26 June 1940

* * *

22 June France signs armistice with Germany and Hitler prepares to tour Paris. **1 July** German U-boats attack merchant ships in the Atlantic. **5 July** French Vichy government breaks off relations with Britain. **10 July** Battle of Britain begins with first major dogfight over English Channel.

SATURDAY, 22 JUNE

Christopher Tomlin

Letter from Dick arrives. Tells us to watch the Mediterranean: 'The war will be won or lost there.' Spain and Italy with Germany will try to seize Gibraltar and block the Suez Canal, thus cutting our sea communications and bottling the fleet. Egypt and Turkey who are now wavering will then go over to the axis powers.

Notification from the local council – evacuees are coming from Manchester. It wishes Fulwood to take children and threatens forcible reception if the response is not satisfactory. If they force children on us I will be roarin'. We've done more than enough for Britain with Dick and I in the forces. I refuse to have my home ruined.

Rained heavily from last night until 7 p.m. today and ruined a garden party locally.

Pam Ashford

It is very clear that a moderate degree of 'panickiness' is abroad. During the morning I decided I would get the windows strapped. On reaching home at 2 p.m. I found that Charlie had already had the same idea and he and mother were just going to start. Last August (some time before the war) I visited Woolworth's ARP counter and as people were buying rolls of paper strips I bought one, quite mystified as to its purpose. Today it has perished. The two stationers opposite the house were both sold out, but Murdoch's on the hill had rolls several inches wide, which could be used if halved. They said it was becoming difficult to get rolls. I bought two, 23 yards each. Charlie did the back of the house.

I did housework in the afternoon and when they had gone to the pictures went to Hyndland School to get the three gas-mask filters fitted. Then I set to work strapping the windows in the front.

At 8.15 Beethoven's Seventh Symphony came on the wireless! I began to learn German at 28 for apparently no motive at all, though Beethoven did have a lot to do with it. I felt that the nation that produced Beethoven must be my spiritual home.

Eileen Potter

I go up to the West End to have my hair done. I rather dread meeting my hairdresser, as he is a native of Alsace-Lorraine, and lived under the German rule there in his childhood, and he still has friends and relatives in that part of the world. He is more cheerful than I expected, however, and still thinks that we shall win the war and that a good many Frenchmen will keep on fighting. He says that they are still fighting hard in his part of the world.

We listen in in the evening, and I am glad to hear Jack Warner on the air again.

SUNDAY, 23 JUNE

Christopher Tomlin

9 p.m. News: 'There will be no peace without honour,' said the French government. The worst we anticipated has happened: French fleet and air force will be used to fight us. A great speech by Priestley who's vastly improved.

I want to be called up at once, but mother asks me to 'put in' for three months' grace. I don't wish to wait, for the war may be over before then. I feel down tonight. The calm acceptance of such vile terms from Germany. Now the French are cap-in-hand to Mussolini who only came into the fray when he knew France was beaten; the slimy cobra – or should I say 'eel' – did it to get hold of Corsica and Nice and if the French determine to be wretched beggars 'for peace', Musso will receive all he wants.

My bedroom window – the 'French window' kind – and the bathroom window were covered with strips of brown linen cloth by Mum and Dad this afternoon. We carefully collect paper, rags, metal and so on.

Pam Ashford

Mother cannot have the shelter ready quickly enough now. All the tins are out. The cupboards look like those in grocers' shops, there are so many tins. I was a bit surprised myself, though a leading contributor.

How black things look! Charlie went away this morning to Harrogate, and will sleep there tonight and possibly several more nights. I wish it was not so, and I do hope they don't have 'visitors' tonight.

In the afternoon I went to Hogganfield to see the advised demonstration of incendiary bombs. The demonstration was given in an enclosure around which people were standing 4 or 5 thick. Like many others I went to the slope overlooking it. It was too far off to see the details but one could get the hang of things. There must have been hundreds of people present, a large number being juveniles. The demonstration was given by the women fire-fighters, and one or two police inspectors assisted.

In the road there was a 'tank' (Cleansing Department vehicle with canvas sides advertising the need for collecting waste). There were a number of vehicles inside the grounds – a fire engine, water tank of a car, ARP ambulances, Church of Scotland Canteen, vehicles belonging to the rescue and decontamination squads. There were rows of buckets and six corrugated iron houses filled with straw and old furniture. While we waited, entertainment was provided by a pipe band. There was the inevitable 'lost child' found by the police, whose patrol van with loudspeaker announced his safety. From this van too the programme was announced.

Four 'houses' were set on fire and four squads of women extinguished the blazes with stirrup pumps, one to bring the water, one to pump, and one to fill the buckets. Then a lady demonstrated a snuffer, while the houses were being refilled with straw. Then a lady demonstrated a scoop, by which time the houses had been filled with straw again. The stirrup pump teams came on the field again for a third demonstration, and so did the rain. There was nothing for it but to run for the tram. However, I don't think there could be much more to learn; probably the show would have been abandoned.

Hogganfield is outside the boundary on the east of Glasgow, but the tram for the most part passes through residential parts. There was quite a lot of evidence of Italian shops having been the scene of riots.

I spent the evening strapping drawing room windows.

MONDAY, 24 JUNE

Pam Ashford

Last week the papers reported that hundreds of refugees were coming to Glasgow 'after 36 hours' journey', and we were mystified. These are the Guernsey children. They had 6 hours waiting on the beach for another boat, 6 hours in the boat, 16 hours on the train. Through this long journey they had no food (I don't believe this). On reaching

Glasgow they separated the boys and girls, and one little girl was very upset on leaving a brother. It was heart-rending. The Glasgow policemen who had to separate them at the station were officious (perhaps only one was, but you know how stories develop). People are saying, 'The Authorities must think Glasgow safe that they bring the children here,' but we are being told that they are only here temporarily and are to proceed to an unknown destination. Nine church halls have taken the children. It is thought we shall abandon the Channel Islands as not worth defending.

Maggie Joy Blunt

The stocks smell heavenly tonight. The terms to France are monstrous but nothing less than one expected. Germany is to occupy all the Channel and western coasts, the whole of northern France and territory from Tours to the Pyrenees. At cessation of hostilities all artillery, tanks and weapons to be surrendered and the armed forces to be demobilised. French fleet to return or be interned. Everything in fact is to be done to aid Germany in the war against us. Italian terms are yet to come.

The French government is now strongly pro-Fascist. It is believed that commanding officers in the fleet have been replaced by 'safe' officers or political agents. General de Gaulle's name has been struck off the military roll (he has broadcast from here to all Frenchmen to continue the fight with him. Britain had called on all Frenchmen to join her).

I cannot rid myself of the sickening fear that we may be beaten for the same reason as France has been. The Nazi technique is to exploit the differences and doubts of a nation by subtle propaganda within the country and then swoop down with their heavily mechanised, highly organised army. We are not united as people. Think of the division there is among us – all the complacent conservatives in all classes who really believe there is nothing wrong with our constitution and that we shall win in the end because we always do and because of our resources, and the Socialists (divided again, down to the Communists) who want to resist Fascism but hope that the struggle will bring about better conditions, a different system. And the millions with no political leanings at all who bitterly resent the idea of a German invasion.

The end seems near and inevitable. Hitler said, 'The Fate of

Europe (or was it Germany?) in this battle will be decided for the next 100 years.' During the last war Barbellion wrote in his journal, 'Why not let the Germans have their day? Think of the dynasties of Egypt compared with ours in Europe – there is plenty of time . . . '

Perhaps this is true, like the conclusion of Somerset Maugham's Philip Carey [in *Of Human Bondage*] that life has no meaning. Man is born, he suffers, he dies. Accept this. Incidentally, I hear that Maugham is lost in France and has not been heard of for some months.

Builders are busy with air-raid shelters and coal bins, but materials are difficult to get. I need coal storage space badly.

Christopher Tomlin

Why is Winston amazed at France? I knew and others knew it would happen, and if Mr Churchill didn't know in advance it is a dire omen for the country. As the *Catholic Herald* truly says, politicians are little use in war. I would put my heart, body and soul into the struggle if the heads of the Navy, RAF and Army dictated to the government.

I am very depressed after reading the *Catholic Herald* leader which compares us to another Finland facing overwhelming odds. It is the first time I really understood what our struggle means: victory to me is a mirage. But this mood of mine will pass. Today I cheered one or two elderly people and calmed them. Is it any wonder they've a choking feeling when there's nowt to anticipate but a high explosive bomb?

Joey, next door's tortoise, laid an egg yesterday.

TUESDAY, 25 JUNE

Eileen Potter

I am awakened at 1 a.m. by the preliminary hooting of the sirens. I am wondering whether it is a warning or not, when they begin to wail in good earnest. I at once jump out of bed, draw the curtain over the window, and begin hastily to dress. I have some old clothes all ready on a chair by the bed, as usual, but I feel that my fingers are 'all thumbs', particularly when it comes to putting on my stockings. I run upstairs for some cushions to take down to the Anderson shelter, and to let out the cat. We put on his harness, and decide to take him to the shelter with us. At last we are ready, and set out across the garden to the shelter. By this time, Mr H, who is a warden, has looked in at the back gate to see if we are all right. The cat begins to struggle, so we decide to take him back to the house and shut him up on the ground floor. We settle down in the shelter, with cushions, rugs, etc. Brenda is just sitting down when she notices a spider, and gives a little scream: 'I would much rather be bombed than have to sit on a spider!' she says. I am conscious of feeling intense thirst.

Jack F does not seem able to settle down quietly, and soon announces his intention of going into the house and making some tea, as there is no sound of bombs or gunfire to be heard. By this time Brenda has already dropped off to sleep again in the corner. I feel I could settle down quietly for a while, but both Mrs F and Jack are very restless. I begin to feel that if anything destroys my morale (short of the actual noise of the explosions) it will be the idea of being cooped up in a shelter with such fidgety people.

Brenda has brought a pack of cards down to the shelter and we attempt to have a game of 'switch' by torchlight, but it is not very satisfactory. Everything outside continues to be very quiet, and in the end even I start wandering about, paying a visit to the H's shelter to see how they are getting on. Ultimately, Mr H tells us that he thinks we might go back to bed, as nothing seems to be happening, so we do so. I am just settling down again in bed, having kept on some of my clothes in case of later warnings, when I hear the 'all-clear' sounding. Almost immediately afterwards, the birds begin to sing at dawn.

My sister-in-law is going to be married again and wants me to go to the wedding on Saturday. After breakfast I ring up the office to ask if I can have another of my days off, and go to Kensington High Street to buy a new hat. There are very few customers in Derry and Toms this morning. In the afternoon I go out with Mrs F to Richmond, where she buys herself a siren-suit ready for the next air raid warning. I decide not to buy one, as I am rather too fat to wear trousers. We go to Kew Gardens, where the roses are beautiful, though a little past their best. Two or three family parties are trying to get extra milk at the cafeteria for the children, but this is not allowed.

Maggie Joy Blunt
Last night we had our first air-raid warning since last September. I woke at 4 a.m. to the 'all clear' warden's whistle.

Tonight I am keyed up, excited, not at all depressed. Have a new filter fixed to my gas mask, have placed bucket of ashes and shovel by back door, filled the bath with water, have torch, gas-mask, patience cards at hand and my clothes all ready to dive into.

Damage and casualties are reported from east and south coasts and Midlands. Sweetshop man told me that one of the towns hit was near Cambridge. Hitler, I am told, is to be in London now by August the 18th.

Collection of salvage is to be made compulsory. Good.

Says Kingsley Martin in the *New Statesman*: 'Mr Churchill rightly assumed that the British are a stubborn people ... but he misunderstood their feeling when he talked of this as the finest moment of our history ... To talk to common people in or out of uniform is to discover that determination to defend this island is coupled with a deep and almost universal bitterness that we have been reduced to such a pass.'

N said, 'I feel far more angry with the Baldwins and Chamberlains who have played with our lives while pretending to save them than I do with Hitler.'

Events of this tragedy: the failure after the last war 1) to unify Europe on a federal basis, 2) to substitute a collectivist for a capitalist economy, 3) to prevent the perversion and destruction of the League which might have been made into an efficient instrument for tackling these problems, and 4) to realise the growing strength of Hitler and that the new Germany sought not only territorial domination but the total destruction of the ideas on which Western civilisation has been built. A 'Grand Alliance' might have saved the situation but our rulers were terrified always of the common people and the workers, and refused throughout the Spanish War and at Munich to touch the hand of Russia, seeking instead to go into partnership and appease the Axis powers, the enemies of our civilisation.

The war would have been prevented. Britain and France could have begun a new era in Europe. When we called for collective security we were told we were warmongers. Instead of an alliance with Russia to resist Hitler we instead guaranteed Poland without Russian support. Only now is it beginning to be understood how criminally incompetent the last government was and some of our ministers and civil servants still are. Also, our political education was sadly neglected. We were not expected to study or understand politics. We were allowed to be careless and indifferent. If we, the people, had properly understood the situation these men could never have been in power.

Tilly Rice

I've just had my first air-raid warning. Last night I was awakened from a nice deep Barbitone slumber to the calling of Bob and the screeching of the siren. 'What is that funny noise Mummy?' I tumbled out of bed, still half asleep, and in my drowsiness went into my husband's room instead of the children's and said, 'It's only the air-raid warning!' About five minutes later, by the time I'd got really awake and had put on a woolly coat and some slacks, my husband came in and said, 'Oh, I thought you were sleep walking again.'

The children were quite calm and not at all disposed to get out of bed. I knew that having been wakened at that time (1.10 a.m.) I should be certain to be awake for a couple of hours, so I said I'd keep guard while the rest of the family resumed their slumbers, and I would wake them if I heard anything else in the distance. I went downstairs, lit the light in the lounge and then went outside to make sure the black-out was all right. In the gardens at the back one could see little dancing lights of the people making their way to their Anderson shelters. There was a lot of chatter and laughter going on, but otherwise everything was very still. Occasionally there were footsteps, very leisurely ones outside, air-raid wardens I presume. And a motorcycle tore the silence now and then. I got out my typewriter and spent the whole three hours writing. I didn't feel frightened exactly, but rather like I felt when I was waiting for my first baby to be born. Just as dawn was breaking the 'raiders passed' came and I got back into bed. The people at the back all stayed in their shelters until the end of the raid and it was rather funny to see them trooping back into their houses in the pale light of the dawn.

Christopher Tomlin

More cheerful. Am eagerly waiting my medical exam for I want to know if I'll be in the RAF. By hook or crook I mean to be!

It is high time the authorities taught soldiers not to play with rifles. There's too high a proportion of accidental deaths for my liking. Evidence of blasted idiocy, horseplay and relaxed discipline. Since using witch-hazel ointment (first used five days ago) my little pile trouble has gone. 3o/- sales in Ashton.

WEDNESDAY, 26 JUNE

Pam Ashford

An air-raid warning at last!

At 12.45 a.m. I had not yet achieved sleep when the warning went. I shook Mother who was fast asleep. At first she refused to believe me, so I opened the window. There was no doubt, it was a warbling note. My first thought was for Charlie, who I had not heard come in yet (he often spends the evening with friends and comes back late). I ran into the dining room and his supper lay untouched. A sad feeling ran over me – 'He has been caught away from home.'

Mother was still in a sleep condition and wanting to know what I wanted her to do. I said, 'We will put on our coats and stockings, and then lie down again. If there is gun fire we will go into the press.' Then through the open door I saw a light beneath Charlie's door, and in amazement and relief I said, 'Why, he's in.' Mother thumped on his door, shouting 'Charlie, where are you?', and he said, 'Where do you think I am?' Mother (pealing with laughter and pointing at me) said, 'She thinks there is an air-raid warning on.' Charlie said, 'So there is. Can't you hear it?' Then we went back to our room, and laid down.

Darkness terrifies me, and after a few minutes I had to raise the blind and draw back the curtains. Very soon Mother divested herself of coat and stockings as too hot. At 1.45 I heard a noise and having made sure it was all on one note I said that it must be the 'raiders past' signal. So we settled down to sleep. At 2.30 there was a terrible din. At first I thought it was all on one note, but then it changed in pitch. I said, 'The darned things are back again.'

I certainly did not take things in properly at the time. The noise at 1.45 must have been the noise of airplanes. The 2.30 sirens must have been the 'all clear'. Many people clearly share my difficulty in distinguishing the warbling from the steady notes. Experience will teach us, I suppose.

Here are some reports of the way other households took things. Miss Carswell was the only member of her family to be awakened. She woke her sister who said, 'You are dreaming. In any case, that is

286

the "all clear" signal.' They have actually packed handbags so as to be able to flee to New Zealand at short notice.

Margaret also dressed at top speed and sat up. She said, 'The dog was as good as gold. He slept most of the time; now and again he opened an eye, and I said, "It's all right, Dandy," and he just went to sleep again.'

The Bousies (4 sisters) went down to the close and completed dressing down there. Today they are moving their beds into one back room which can be blocked easily at the window. It will no longer be necessary to get up then.

An air-raid warden next door to the Carswells slept through it. Miss Crawford, ARP warden, slept through it. Mr Mitchell, foreman of decontamination squad, slept through it.

In our household we agreed anyone lucky enough to sleep through the warning shall not be disturbed by anyone who has not been so lucky.

Christopher Tomlin

It is a sound idea to show why people were killed or saved in air raids (*Daily Mail*) for it shows us what to do and avoid.

I'm bucked up at our raid on the enemy coast – so much better than waiting for King Kong.

Maggie Joy Blunt

Another warning last night which I slept through until the all-clear sirens went.

On Hospital Sunday (and the day of National Prayer) Dr Graham Howe spoke in St Martin's Church. M sent me the following rough summary of what he said: It is not enough to have courage, we must have more than courage, we must learn to live *now* as well as after the war. If this war is not to end in utter waste it must be followed by a great spiritual revival. We must give all we have – not just a part but *all*, and hold nothing back. We must not depend on an external God to save us, we must save ourselves. Let each one say to himself, 'It all depends on me,' and act as though it did all depend on him.

287

FRIDAY, 28 JUNE

Christopher Tomlin

My summons to the medical examination is overdue. Every morning I eagerly look for it and am disappointed.

Aunt who lives in Lincoln hasn't been to bed for a week through fear of air raids. As father says, 'It is a pity that an old lady of 86 who has worked hard all her life can't pass her last days in peace.' I'm highly suspicious of 'the planes did slight damage (to this country)', 'our planes bombed Germany and did heavy damage'. Who defines 'slight' and 'heavy'? I cannot forget that when zeppelins bombed the east end of London in the last war it was said, 'the damage is slight', and yet it was revealed after the war that the damage had been very heavy. We want the naked truth. We don't want it draped. Am rather irritable.

Maggie Joy Blunt

Warnings are not to be given, I heard an ARP worker say in the Post Office, unless planes are overhead.

It will come. 'No one could imagine that the air raids that have come our way so far are more than reconnaissance and trial flights,' says the *New Statesman*. One NS critic writes, 'Every day I receive fresh news that the Home Office has completely lost its head. German refugees who are obviously anti-Fascist have been interned [while] "non-political" businessmen among whom is greatest likelihood of Nazi agents are still at large . . . The Home Office finds that nearly all anti-Fascists are Left Wing politicals and suspects them of anarchism and Bolshevism. It had not yet discovered that the foreign agents of Hitler's revolution are never "politicals" but respectable businessmen, society women, guileless servant girls – people without clearly defined political faith for the most part.'

Questions were asked about the activities of the LINK in Parliament yesterday. Mr Davidson (Lab) asked if the Home Secretary was aware that ex-members of this pro-Nazi organisation met in London last week and discussed the question of peace terms under a sympathetic government. Sir John Anderson replied that he had no information to confirm a statement to this effect.

Have received a cable from brother in Suez. Mails home have been stopped temporarily, but the family is all right so far. Russians have entered Bessarabia.

Pam Ashford

I spent a few minutes with the French Chartering Mission, the body which, with their associates the French Traffic Control, have been controlling exports to France. I said to Mdm Pommier, 'How sorry I am' (just the four words). She said, 'Is it not terrible? Such a beautiful country, to be overrun by the Germans. Who would have thought anyone could be so wicked?' I said, 'I am afraid I was very slow to realise how wicked Hitler is.' She said, 'We all were.' I can write down the words, but I cannot write down the sorrow in her voice and her looks.

SATURDAY, 29 JUNE

Tilly Rice

Mr S at the Post Office had a great tale of grievance to tell of his previous night's LDV duty. He was on duty with a man of rather silent habits. 'A religious chap he is, and he never spoke a word except to talk condescending. About four o'clock I get proper fed oop wi'it, so takes me armlet off and I give's him me rifle and I says, "Here, ye can get on with t'job yerself as I'm not good enough to keep guard with you." And I went straight off t'boss and told him what I done and he said, "You done quite right, that feller needs checking."'

Amid great secrecy a local garage had been taken over for aeroplane repairs. Everyone knows, of course.

I'm most anxious to know what has happened to Somerset Maugham, not so much for the man, whom I don't know, but for his gift, which I know so well. I think he is the greatest writer without exception since de Maupassant. It would be terrible if anything happened to him, for I consider that his work is still on the upward grade.

Eileen Potter

Have the morning off for my sister-in-law's wedding. At 9 a.m. I go to the local hairdresser and have my hair trimmed, shampooed and set. The frock I intended to wear has not come back in time from the cleaners, so I decide to go to a rather nice local shop and see if I can find anything which will do. I am not very easy to fit, but I find a very nice flowered silk frock which only needs a little shortening. I arrive at Brompton Oratory, where the ceremony is to be held, just on time.

My sister-in-law arrives looking very attractive in pale grey costume and hat and a wine-coloured georgette blouse. I have not met my new brother-in-law before and view him with interest. He looks a nice, pleasant-looking man, though not particularly handsome.

It is a quiet wedding, with only a few guests. We sit right in the front of the church, but the priest murmurs in such a low voice that hardly any of the service can be heard. My thoughts go back to her first wedding, to my eldest brother, in 1917, when she was a young refugee from Belgium and I was still at school. It occurs to me that I am the only person, besides the bride herself, to be present on both occasions. After the ceremony we adjourn to the Rembrandt Hotel just across the road, for the wedding breakfast, fifteen of us sitting around a round table. We have plenty of wine, and a very good spread, including a delicious pêche melba made with fresh peaches, but there is no wedding cake, owing to the difficulties with sugar rationing. Altogether it is a pleasant wedding party, with not too many speeches or formalities. The couple drive off to spend their weekend honeymoon at the Cumberland Hotel, for the bride has not yet been released from her job as corset buyer in a West End store.

SUNDAY, 30 JUNE

Maggie Joy Blunt
News as follows: De Gaulle has been recognised by our Government. Lady Mosley and other society high-lights have been detained. Channel Islands, evacuated and disarmed, have been bombed by German raiders.

RAF are carrying out heavy raids on military objectives in Germany.

Chamberlain denies emphatically that Britain has the slightest intention of seeking peace. Chamberlain still believes that time is on our side and that Hitler will find us a tough nut.

Christopher Tomlin
I feel very sorry indeed for Chamberlain whose voice broke with sorrow. Father wonders if 'the fight for freedom' means 'freedom to take 40 years off your life at a job and drop you on the scrap heap without pension'.

The Nazis are using delayed-action bombs – very dangerous for they don't explode for hours. FH, volunteer reservist electrician, called to see me. He has 48 hours' leave. Says it is not just propaganda that the boys want another smack at Hitler: '80% are dying to go back.' Two or three boys I know say the officers put on a damned bad show at Dunkirk; they were the first to be aboard. Not all officers of course, just the yellow ones.

Pam Ashford
Today's demonstration of incendiary bombs was at Whiteinch, within ten minutes of the house. Last time I left at the fifth item because of the heavy rain. It turns out that there were two other items, both given by men from the Auxiliary Fire Service. The first demonstration was of stirrup pumps, then came the *pièce de résistance*, a large bonfire of straw and old furniture set on fire by several incendiary bombs. Policemen began to blow whistles. Two temporary fire engines entered the enclosure and drove round.

MONDAY, 1 JULY

Christopher Tomlin
Hitler said he would invade Britain on July 2nd. Tomorrow!

TUESDAY, 2 JULY

Christopher Tomlin
A plane flew over here at midnight, very low: one of ours? Nazi engines have a noise of their own I'm told; rhythm is like '1 (pause) 2 (pause) 3 (pause)' and a tinny sound. Father was up until 4 a.m. before he would go to bed. He takes air raids too seriously – I'm a Christian fatalist. Where oh where have the gas-masks gone? All the children wear one but one adult in 1,000 carries one of the clumsy things. I took mine with me in my attaché case today, first time for 6 months. It's hidden from view. I have no intention of being called – mentally or vocally – 'you sissy!'

Single-decker corporation buses now have camouflaged roofs.

Eileen Potter
I go to a joint meeting of the London Clubs for Business and Professional Women, arranged by the Ministry of Information. The

speaker tonight is Lady Snowden, the subject 'Anti-Gossip'. She gives some rather unfortunate examples of rumour-spreading, repeating herself the rumours she has heard on various occasions and not categorically denying them, and altogether her speech has rather a depressing and disheartening effect. But I reflect that this may have something to do with the fact that she takes the line that criticism of Chamberlain is an unkindness to an old, tired man.

Maggie Joy Blunt
Still nothing definite happens. Woman in antique shop in village today sounded panicky but prepared. Fanny told me of people she knew who had left coastal towns, their houses deserted and gardens planted with vegetables. The finest summer we have had for years, and instead of seaside resorts thronged with satisfied visitors – barbed wire and troops.

Bombs have fallen near Bournemouth, Ipswich and Cambridge. *News Chronicle* suggests that they will next try to occupy Iceland and Ireland and so have us surrounded. There is much agitation that the men of Munich should go.

Tilly Rice
E has abandoned the idea of a shelter in favour of a refuge room. He says that the war might be over before S got it built.

Pam Ashford
The glass roof at 21 Hope Street [the office] is to be replaced with wood.

WEDNESDAY, 3 JULY

Pam Ashford
Agnes reported that she had seen a Pole doing the goose step in Buchanan Street. Agnes is, of course, 'man-mad', and the Poles seem to be causing her thrills all over.

When taking my evening walk I bought a roll of cellophane, the only way I know to protect the glass front door, which consists of three large pieces of glass painted on one side with floral design. Mother said, 'You would be better to keep that job for the Saturday half-holiday,' and so I should, but I feel that every minute is precious.

I want to get the house as fully protected as possible before the trouble starts.

Tilly Rice

Went to see M and W last night. M takes a view of the war which is rather different from that of anyone else I've met. She looks upon it as the unavoidable result of man's having pursued the wrong things. She talked of people's intense pre-occupation with money.

'Money is only a means to an end,' M said, 'but the trouble is that people have made it an end in itself. How W and I have the laugh over them; having nothing, we are not afraid of the war. It's the people with money who are afraid.'

W being Swiss has had to have a Home Office permit to continue with his studies at the hospital. M said that he could not take his midwifery properly because the doctor refused to have any foreigners studying under him – another potential Nazi! The doctor, I mean.

I thought I could detect a certain nervousness on M's part. A constable had stationed himself on the pavement opposite the entrance to their flats. I commented on it. 'What a funny place for him to stand . . . '

'Yes,' said M, 'he has been there before, I don't know why.'

I said, 'If he's watching anyone he's doing it in a very inexpert manner, because anyone could guess what he was up to.'

Christopher Tomlin

'Let him that is without sin cast the first stone. Man's inhumanity to man makes countless thousands mourn' – a window poster written in ink on the house of a local counterfeiter's wife. He was caught and convicted some months ago. I am sorry for her but not for him; he didn't care who was defrauded and would be at the game yet if the police hadn't spreadeagled his stumps. According to a customer there is now an income of £4 a week from the prisoners' aid society. 'She owes £90 to a Blackpool shop and is still owing for the Xmas dinner.'

25 German aircrews won't bomb any more! 25 machines destroyed in a fortnight is grand news when you consider that Nazi bombers cost approx. £500,000 each (that's judging from the cost of ours). Good old Winston!

THURSDAY, 4 JULY

Christopher Tomlin
The building society allows us to pay interest-only on the mortgage until August 30th, when our circumstances will be reviewed. The interest is £1.12 a month. There is £3 owing to my local wholesale stationer: it is in hand bar 10/-. Water rate and the first half of the general rate are due. My income is £3. My pocket money is 6/- a week. We have two meals a day, breakfast and high tea. Supper – cup of tea and biscuit.

Pam Ashford
Mr Hutchison was telling me about his experiences with the parashots. He said, 'You have no idea what a wonderful camouflage khaki is. Soldiers practise with us: they creep across the short grass, taking advantage of the undulations in the ground. They try to get up to us undetected. I saw two and pointed my gun at them. They said, "You would not do that if we were Germans, you would shoot." Our instructions are to shoot. If a German put up both arms as if to surrender, we would still shoot. That is a common trick. They may have a hand grenade in both hands. You have to be quick – it is them or you. We stop everything on the road. Last night we stopped two ambulances, and they were annoyed when we examined their papers. But they might have been Jerries.

'There are a lot of Poles out our way. They are supposed to be in at 10 but they aren't. We put them in the lock-up. Most of them know some French.' (He wrote out some French phrases: 'Quick March', 'Attention', 'Halt', 'Correct – pass friend', 'Approach and be recognised', 'Identity card or disc'.)

FRIDAY, 5 JULY

Tilly Rice
At last the rain, lovely steady summer rain. I've never felt the slightest desire to go and live in the Southern countries where the sun always shines, for I'm sure the incessant glare and clash of continual sunshine would so get on my nerves that I should soon be a nervous wreck.

I have also lately been feeling some secret satisfaction (very unkind of me no doubt, but I offer no excuse for myself) at the plight of all those people who with a blind disdain for the real beauties of England had taken up residencies in the South of France. They are going to inveigh against their fate now that they have had to return to Britain, and it is a pity we have to have them. Still no news of Somerset Maugham.

No eggs here this weekend. One of my suppliers says that it is owing to transport difficulties, but two other sources say that it is because none are coming from the Continent and because shops have to buy them at the same price as which they sell them – 2/6 per dozen. The proprietor of one shop told me that he wouldn't buy them to sell at no profit, rather an unpatriotic action I thought.

I'm so glad that I live in 1940. I should have hated to miss it all, even though I may get a bomb on me. I think people attach too much importance to getting killed. Human beings have been getting killed and maimed right from the beginning of the world, and I do think we should keep a sense of proportion about these things, and certainly not get jittery about it. If one is going to come to a violent end one way or another (and that might just as easily happen in peacetime, judging by the numbers of people killed on the roads), surely it is best to make the most of the time left to you rather than to waste it in apprehension. Life is as easily produced as it is destroyed.

SUNDAY, 7 JULY

Maggie Joy Blunt
The war seems as fantastic and far away as ever. Successful air attacks by the RAF on enemy objectives continue. The Italians show up poorly as fighters. Several of their submarines have been sunk. The *Andora Star* carrying 1,500 German and Italian internees has been torpedoed and we have fought and disabled the French fleet. A great demonstration followed Mr Churchill's statement of this terrible action – he was in tears at the end of it. The rage of Germany at this move is unequalled.

I can still get as much good food as I need. London, except for the balloons and sandbags, ARP notices and black-out, seems as normal as ever. Shops are in full summer sale array. Went to the bank, the dressmaker, and attended a family lunch party. Bought new grey slacks at Peter Bobs. Bank manager said to me, 'They will never get London.'

The only paper I have seen who quoted Morrison – 'The Germans have never yet beaten a country which they had not first weakened and eaten away from within' – is the local *Windsor, Slough and Eton Express*. The Editor's article says:

'The 1930/31 crisis taught the nations nothing . . . Hitler could never have obtained his power and might in a healthy Europe which recognised that nations could live unto themselves alone. We made no effective efforts to tackle the three main questions of England – unemployment, waste and agriculture. We have at last come to realise under pressure of war that what a man does with his own life is the concern of the community as well as himself.

'Hitler saw that a nation became strong through co-ordinated effort. The uses to which he applied his wisdom are abominable and wicked but we cannot deny that he had vision and an understanding we lacked. We hope and believe we have seen it now and are working together for one end. It is the only way we can win this war, and tackle the problems after the war. If we do not take this to heart . . . the war will have been in vain.'

There has been an improvement recently in *BBC Postscripts*, with another good one tonight by Priestley. This is a war between despair and hope. Nazism is an expression of despair, a death worship. People were watching the other night a brood of ducklings on Whitestone Pond [Hampstead]. A symbol of hope.

Christopher Tomlin

9 o'clock communion, the first 9 a.m. one I've been to since I became a Catholic. I kept a voluntary fast all day and it's the first time I've done it and I went to special evening benediction where the priest told us, 'It was excellent to see the numbers who received communion this morning. You have made a grand start but there's 17 more days to go. I advise you to tackle one day at a time and be faithful to the utmost of your ability.'

MONDAY, 8 JULY

Pam Ashford

Mr Hutchison has a card which he says authorises him to look at anyone's identity card. I said, 'Only when you are on duty as a parashot.' He says not.

He had a book in about using rifles, which he is reading with enthusiasm. I looked at it and it seemed ghastly. He says that the parashots are there to kill the parachutists and if they save thousands of lives in this country thereby, it is all to the good. He does not mind being killed in the process. I once said I would not mind shooting a rifle in the circumstances, but now I feel that to throw an ornament at someone's head is about my limit. Miss Bousie, of course, would limit herself to a hard smack.

At the Soroptimist Club today, dug-outs in gardens were spoken of. One lady's was built by a brother who camouflaged it. Someone came along and unknowingly planted a row of lettuces on the top, which help to camouflage it still further.

TUESDAY, 9 JULY

Christopher Tomlin

I changed books at the county library. Took in *The Oxford Book of Light Verse*, *European Jungle* by Yeats Brown, and *The Wonder of Life* by Professor Arthur Thomson. Took out *Story of San Michele* by Axel Munthe, *Orientations* by Sir Ronald Storrs, and *Ways and Byways in Diplomacy* by W.J. Oudendyk. Wrote a letter or petite lecture to Dick who'd criticised religion and prayer scathingly. He's supposed to be an atheist or pretends he is, yet he goes to church in the RAF and receives communion. (All my relations are C of E.) He is now 1st class aircraftman, wireless and electrical mechanic at 4/6 per diem. I'm working like a private soldier in this week of prayer and penance. Church twice a day and no wireless entertainment, cinema or tobacco.

Pam Ashford

At teatime I said to Mother how strangely the war has affected people's work and incomes. Certain women, e.g. at Rolls Royce, are working very hard and getting it is said as much as £5 a week. These conductresses on our trams and buses get £3 rising to £3.10/- a week. A beggar came to the door, and I said, 'No,' but returning to Mother I said, 'It beats me how a man of twenty can be out of work today.' I thought perhaps he was physically unfit and gave him three slices of bread and butter, which he ate ravenously on the stair.

Tilly Rice

On Saturday night while out for a stroll E and I discovered that there have been various dumps arranged about the neighbourhood for old iron. There are several, including one outside Mrs C's house, who told me that after the stuff had been dumped various people came to take what took their fancy and that her husband had to chase after one man who was making off with a particular choice piece.

My *News Chronicle* tells me that Somerset Maugham is safe, so that's all right.

WEDNESDAY, 10 JULY

Pam Ashford

When I was attending to the black-out, I was surprised to see a rainbow from the kitchen window, rising from the Cripple School. Not a complete bow, but about a quarter bow. It was 9.30 a.m., and I watched it till it faded at 10. Mother got very biblical about it, taking it as a sign of better times to come.

For a long time this morning the telephone communication with Cardiff was cut. We presumed it was a raid and in the afternoon our Cardiff friends said that six bombs had fallen beside their offices. It is wonderful the nonchalance with which people accept this state of affairs. The 1 p.m. news was made interesting by a talk by Somerset Maugham on his experiences coming from Cannes to this country.

In the afternoon spies were discussed again. Mr Mitchell was relating a story of a motorist who gave a soldier a lift. The man was interested in Greenock and Oban, and then the motorist saw that his uniform was not right. He realised the man was a spy, called a policeman, and the man was taken off.

THURSDAY, 11 JULY

Pam Ashford

I feel very low-spirited today. I read in the *Record* at lunch that they are suggesting that Hitler thinks it will be easy to capture Ireland and then to throw forces on Lancashire and Glasgow.

Christopher Tomlin

I am white-hot with fury at recent price increases which mean our purchases must be cut down. We can't afford to pay the extras on milk and eggs. It's a good thing for munitions workers who earn £5 a week – many families have an income of £14. They've caused and can afford the increases but it's a bloody disgrace for families in circumstances like mine.

The ranting humbug written about the 12-hour day! My father worked a 12-hour day for 20 years without pay for overtime. Munitions workers are on a bloody good thing. They are out for themselves. They would be serving the nation nobly if they earned 2/- a day like the servicemen.

Benediction. Church packed.

Chapter Thirteen

THE COST OF LIVING

IF IT'S CHOCOLATE THEN IT'S FOOD

Chocolate to celebrate our survival:
Cadbury's does its bit for the war effort.

'Within a few days of the outbreak of war, I was consulted by a powerful-looking man who, although over forty, was anxious to join up and, as he rather shyly put it, "play some part in fighting for freedom".

"But," he added, "I'm beginning to think I'm not the stuff of which soldiers are made."

It seems that the day before he had been seized with a sudden panic at an unexpected burst of gunfire from an anti-aircraft battery. Running a few paces he was mortified to discover that the noise was due to a next-door neighbour vigorously beating carpets in the back garden. In short, he was afraid of being afraid. I had little difficulty in reassuring him. Knowledge, a common purpose and preparedness for action: these are the remedies for faintness of heart in the face of danger.'

A medical psychologist cures the jitters. The Home Service, 25 July 1940

* * *

12 July German aircraft raid Aberdeen and Cardiff, while RAF destroy four bombers off the Suffolk coast. **14 July** In Vichy, France, Bastille Day is officially declared 'a day of national mourning'. **23 July** Soviet forces take Lithuania, Latvia and Estonia. **25 July** United States places embargo on strategic materials to Japan. **3–19 August** Italians occupy British Somaliland in East Africa.

FRIDAY, 12 JULY

Christopher Tomlin

Up till now this week is a nightmare – weather wretched. Canvassing consequently v. hard, my little consolations voluntarily forgone – but in spite of some mental irritability, I offer it to God in a spirit of penance: no tobacco, no wireless entertainment, no cinema. Just books.

Of the vile things I think the treatment of John Florey, Oxfordshire farmer, the vilest [Florey was fined for spreading gloom and disillusionment]. He wasn't even allowed to enter a defence for himself. If I was the farmer, I would demand considerably more than an apology! Blasted bureaucracy! It makes me vomit to read of the stupid blunders made by those with a little brief authority. Is this England? The blunders are clear evidence of half-suppressed panic. They must cease. There is nothing to prevent a spiteful person lying to the police about something you never said. The whole thing is a nightmare, a conspiracy of Beelzebub. 9/- repeat orders.

Pam Ashford

I am now at Helensburgh, complete with notebook. We are staying at the house of Miss Carson, 124 West Princes Street. We spent the morning on the front, the afternoon in the Hermitage Park and the evening on the banks of the Gareloch.

Miss Carson at once asked after Cardross, a small village 5 miles east of Helensburgh. She had been told that bombs had been dropped there, and she says crowds are going down to Cardross to collect souvenirs. Believe it or not, people are getting immense amusement from the perils that surround us. And the postponement of the invasion is becoming a first class joke.

SATURDAY, 13 JULY

Eileen Potter

Our family business has recently paid a dividend on the ordinary shares (for only the third time since my father's death in 1922!) This practically doubles my income for the year, so I decide to take the H family out to celebrate. First we go and have a drink, and then to the cinema at Shepherds Bush, as my favourite film star, Brian Aherne, is appearing there in *Vigil in the Night*. It consists very largely of scenes in which children die from meningitis.

SUNDAY, 14 JULY

Maggie Joy Blunt

A week of showers and cool wind, of chores and letters and ARP lectures, of garden and books and restlessness. I came across a notice of the Fabian Society and wrote for particulars. Today I am sending a subscription and offer of my services. They are asking for research helpers, and there might be some donkey work I can do.

Tea is now rationed to 2 ozs. Next week total allowance of butter and marg to be 7 ozs. This really will touch me. I do like my little bit of butter to my bread. Apples (imported) are 10d a lb. Lemons 4d each. Cherries and berries of the season are plentiful.

Green line and country buses are to have women conductors. Bevin is to present a scheme for women, including the middle-classes, to relieve hard-pressed regulars in factories, and if this comes about I might volunteer. I have started the Home Nursing course and begin more First Aid on Monday.

The South Bucks anti-gas instructress is a terrifyingly efficient person. She is slim, trim and precise with a very upper-class manner. Her complexion is shocking – she looks as though she is worked to death. Some of our First Aid unit are going in for their anti-gas exam and were put through their gas drill the other night. When everyone's gas-mask had been properly fitted and tested we were shepherded into a gas-filled cell. The masks are certainly good, even the civilian one I have that has been dumped and bumped about enough this past year and not once cleaned. We tested for gas, i.e. took a deep breath, thrust two fingers into the side of our mask and 'pecked' thrice. Eyeballs began to prick at once. Just before we came out we ripped off our masks and took a lungfull – and rushed out weeping. It was a harmless experience.

Interesting to listen to the German version of the news. The Bremen station reported last week that the *Hood* and the *Ark Royal* had been hit in the Mediterranean, denied today by the Admiralty. German air attacks on Britain apparently highly successful.

A man fined for having expressed the opinion that Hitler would win said that it might not be too bad in this country if Hitler were ruler and that £1 notes would be worth 1/- a cwt.

RAF is doing magnificent work. British Union of Fascists has been made illegal.

Pam Ashford

In the morning we walked along to near Rhu. The Sunday papers must be having good sales; on every seat practically everyone was buried behind one. An article by the *Observer*'s military correspondent says, 'Perhaps Hitler will postpone the invasion as long as next Friday.' But we are here in Helensburgh and mean to do our utmost to get as much pleasure as we can. We used always to do a lot of sightseeing, but frankly my zest is weak this year. For one thing I am dead tired and for another nowadays I never feel happy in lonely places far from shelters. I expect the invasion to come with suddenness.

Mr Churchill is to speak on the wireless tonight. Miss Carson said, 'He will be giving us good news.' I said, 'I think he will be confident, but he will be giving us directions of some sort; it is plain that the crisis is intensifying.'

8.30. Interest is rising as to what Mr Churchill is going to say. I think he is going to tell us that the hour is nigh. Mother says, 'We have heard that so many times that it is just like the boy crying wolf now. No one believes it.' I said, 'Hitler has promised the Germans that we shall be defeated by 15th August and if he has not moved by then, the Germans will want to know why.' Today I feel that the invasion will break before the date we are due to return, the 22nd. What shall we do – stop here or go home?

9.30. Comments on the speech. Miss Carson: 'My, that was fine stuff.' Mother: 'Does that not give you confidence?' I: 'We are going to defend London street by street, we shall fight for every village. That is what the nation wants.'

Christopher Tomlin

It is splendid to know so many buggering Nazis are down. Fast today. As I fasted I could smoke, thank goodness!

9 p.m. News. A grand enervating rag-chew from Winston Churchill who disappointed me when he said we would attack in 1942 (not before). Will this war last two more years? Charles Gardner's recorded description of the RAF fight over the Channel was an unexpected delight. More please! I must confess I'm nervous

of this diary being in authorities' hands. It might get me a year or at least 6 months. Are the authorities aware and agreeable to M-O keeping war-diaries going?

MONDAY, 15 JULY

Christopher Tomlin

I take 5 or 6 months to cover my round usually, but on looking at my order books I see Preston has just been done in 4 months, a record which makes me despondent. Sales have fallen since the 2½d stamp was introduced. Consequently, I have to make more calls per day to reach my daily quota of 26/-. Therefore each district is quickly done. The terrible winter killed 8 good elderly clients of mine. On top of all I understand a young man is a new agent, for Messrs Swaffer, in my best district, Penwortham. With those thoughts in mind I decided to discover the damage done by my rival: I couldn't find any.

Our gas-masks were fitted with the new filters this evening.

Pam Ashford

On the banks of Gareloch was a board giving its name. This surprises us, for during the past three days we have kept on being 'surprised' to find name plates removed or names covered with wood (on war memorials) or painted over – railway stations, parks, signposts. The vendors of Helensburgh toffee have had to dispense with the name 'Helensburgh', though the stationers may still exhibit postcards with the name.

In the morning we read that the axis powers promise that the invasion will start in four or five days' time. The evening papers say Hitler is arranging a triumphant march in Berlin for Saturday 27th to celebrate the defeat of Britain. These are no doubt ominous signs, but nevertheless they amuse us immensely.

TUESDAY, 16 JULY

Christopher Tomlin

A German reconnaissance plane flew over here at 1.30 a.m. People near could tell by the engine. I thought it would not be long before the north-west was for it.

I must be very careful what I say and remember to see all, hear all and say 'nowt' to anybody but MO. The silly little things said thoughtlessly can easily lead to jail. The only brake on the actions of officialdom is broken and petty tyrants can do with us as they will. Sentences are left to the 'discretion' of a JP, otherwise why would one man be sentenced to 3 months and another to a year for the same offence? I have no room for defeatists, Communists and Fascists, but neither have I room for those who twist the thoughtless and innocent remarks of a man. If it's his first lapse he should be warned, not handled like putrid fish.

To the Empress for *I Stole a Million*. Rotten!

Maggie Joy Blunt

Lack of imports have made our fresh fruit in season very dear. Raspberries 1/9d, blackcurrants 1/4d, tomatoes still 1/-. Meat and fish are dear too in this district. Should like to know the prices in, say, Camden Town.

Experimental smoke barrages are being held in Slough, covering a radius of 5 miles. Rain began yesterday (St Swithins) and has scarcely left off. Air round here like a tropical mist, steamy damp.

Am grateful for what I have now. I thank God sincerely for my cottage comforts, the garden, the cats, my books and food and clothes and health and the long, quiet nights. But how can I sit in my solitary peace writing *The Confessions of an Old Maid* when the world is being shaken and shattered around me? I want to be in contact with life when the old order crumbles, I want to be in at death, part of suffering, growing humanity, not a dry isolated speck in security.

WEDNESDAY, 17 JULY

Christopher Tomlin

Germany will invade us on Friday!

Pam Ashford

In Plato's *Republic* there is a passage that says a person who has been released from pain thinks he is experiencing pleasure; actually, of course, he is only experiencing release from pain. So it is now. Life seems quite pleasant, though what has really happened is that here on holiday our nerves are spared the talk of rumour mongers and despondent people.

THURSDAY, 18 JULY

Christopher Tomlin
Am anxious to see if we resist invasion. In fact I wish it was Christmas now so that I could know what's happened. Father is very nervous, a little panicky. Thinks our leaders are too full of bluff. Really worries most about the fate of our home, lest 40 years' work is blasted by a bomb.

Sydney, my printer, 27, goes for his medical on Wednesday, and is hoping for 3 months' grace.

FRIDAY, 19 JULY

Christopher Tomlin
No invasion yet! Little Tich likes to invade in the early hours, and though I heard the cats caterwauling I didn't hear any of his crew – no bombs, no women and children screaming, just the soft chuckling of a couple in the street.

For the first time I am using hair pomade regularly – never before have I used anything on my hair. I don't know why I use it now; I pride myself on not caring two hoots what I wear or look like. Mother is responsible for whatever neatness speaks from my dress. I'm bohemian.

Pam Ashford
Hitler is to speak on the wireless tonight. I feel that the invasion cannot be delayed much longer. At the present moment, 7.45, it seems to me that Hitler's speech will be the signal to go. Perhaps they will come tonight, perhaps tomorrow, perhaps Sunday.

SATURDAY, 20 JULY

Eileen Potter
Go to the Cecil Sharp House for the weekly party, to which I have not been for some time. The big man whom I call 'The Tank' is there, throwing his very considerable weight about as usual. He even succeeds in kicking off his shoes in one of the dances and hops around waving his bare foot about, as he is not wearing socks. He plays the fool to such an extent that one begins to harbour fantastic

ideas about him. He has a high-pitched voice and a slightly Germanic accent – can he possibly be a Nazi agent posing as a fool? He offers me a lift part way home in his car, and as he lives in Putney, I go with him as far as Hammersmith Broadway. He begins talking about politics almost at once. He appears to be a strong anti-Nazi, but suspects the Government of being about to 'do a deal with the Germans' and murmurs something about this being really a class war. Again I wonder if he is deliberately trying to spread 'alarm and despondency' or something, but no doubt such ideas are too fantastic to be true.

Pam Ashford

In the afternoon Mother and I took the train to Arrochar and Tarbert and sat on the banks of Loch Lomond. It seems so quiet now. The 'eternal hills' have a new meaning today; how unchanging they are, at a time when every village is having its face deranged by barricades.

When we go home, Miss Carson has news about a raid on Glasgow yesterday. The picture in this morning's paper of the wrecked tenement was painfully reminiscent of a building scheme about a mile from us in Hyndland Road, but I have been saying, 'There must be hundreds of houses with that pattern.' However, it is so: a Helensburgh gentleman who lives next door visited an old gentleman in bed in this tenement. Soon after leaving, the bomb fell. He went back and found the tenement wrecked.

Christopher Tomlin

Hitler's speech is remarkable. He is evidently colour blind, unable to tell white from black. The stupid things he says about neutral countries to excuse his vile attacks on them! Baron Munchausen is Hitler's great-great grandfather!

I am afraid of the change in leadership in Britain. It's redolent of the swapping around before the collapse of France.

396 killed in air raids in a month is a bloody disgrace – far more than I expected. What is wrong with our air-raid defence and shelters?

SUNDAY, 21 JULY

Eileen Potter

Have rather a hurried lunch as I am going to the Emergency
Conference convened by the National Council of Civil Liberties to
deal with recent proposals to restrict the freedom of the press, etc. I
have arranged to meet my colleague, Miss B, outside the Conway
Hall, where the meeting is to be held. The hour is 2.30 p.m. on a
Sunday, surely the time in all the week when the British Public is in its
most supine state, and it occurs to me that not many people will turn
out at such a time.

On the contrary, however, as soon as I leave the Underground at
Holborn I see people streaming towards the Conway Hall. Miss B is
waiting for me, and informs me that delegates from Trade Unions,
Societies, etc., are being given the preference in admission, and
'visitors' such as ourselves must obtain special tickets and wait. As I
am elbowing my way towards the table where the tickets are being
given out, someone calls out: 'Visitors this way!' and we hastily
follow the crowd to a small hall in the basement, where there is to be
an overflow meeting. A chairman appears from somewhere. The
secretary of the National Council comes in and makes a general
introductory speech. Then there is a pause and people are asked if
they would like to ask questions. They are rather a 'prickly' lot –
certainly liberty-loving and individualistic – and plenty of questions
are asked, amongst them being a demand for a continuous flow of
speakers in view of the fact that the meeting is already very late in
starting. Two very pertinent questions are asked, one as to whether
the same liberties would be claimed for Mosley and his followers as
for those of other political complexions, and the other about whether
it is any worse to be told what to think by the Government than by a
commercialised press.

Presently the Chairman announces that there is another large
overflow meeting in the Holborn Hall and that there is room for
everybody there – would we like to join that meeting, or would we
prefer to stay where we are? It appears that the only speaker that we
shall have missed is Gollancz, whom I have heard several times
before [Victor Gollancz, humanitarian, publisher and co-founder of
the Left Book Club]. We troop along the streets to the Holborn Hall
in a straggling procession. The editor of the *Evening Standard* is just

about to begin his speech in defence of the liberty of the press. He is a fluent and forceful speaker, and his general approach to the subject is much more 'left-wing' than one might have expected from previous perusals of the *Standard*. He has occasion in the course of his speech to refer to Soviet Russia, the International Brigade and the *Daily Worker*, and there is evidently a strong near-Communist element in the body of the hall, for whenever these subjects are referred to they bust out into automatic applause, almost a reflex action. Lord Strabolgi is the next speaker. He complains that the present government, whilst not complacent like the Chamberlain government, has been more addicted to 'panic executive action', e.g. in the wholesale internment of aliens, the new Bill for special emergency courts, etc. We decide to leave after this speech, without waiting for the resolutions. A collection is being taken at the door for expenses, so we put into the plate the shillings that we should have paid for admission. We have to walk some distance down Holborn before we find a Lyons that is open.

Christopher Tomlin

Sydney my printer: 'The opinion is 10 to 1 on Hitler winning the war, though we daren't say so openly.' He is now labouring at a munitions works. He registered with the 27s and goes for his medical on Wednesday this week. His surname begins with F so there's some time to pass before they come to the 28s and me.

Father thinks Churchill and his ministers are bluffing: 'They know we can't win.' He expects Hitler's invasion this week. Of course Dad's opinion is a purely private one, but I wonder how we can succeed when our air force is outnumbered ten to one, and Germany, Italy, Spain and Russia are against us? Our leaders have little faith in the outcome when they imprison people who criticise the conduct of the Battle of Britain. The only hope for us is in attack not defence.

MONDAY, 22 JULY

Christopher Tomlin

'Gossip if you like,' says Harold Nicholson! Is the fellow mad or merely trying to impress other countries with his fatuous remarks? When I heard the resume of his talk I would dearly have thrown a brick at the simpering fool! Doesn't he read the accounts of innocent folk being sent to jail because of a foolish phrase or two? There is no freedom of speech, even gossiping to neighbours and friends is dangerous, you don't know what elephant-eared police spy is listening in. There is a policeman next door to us now who is panting to seize some poor bugger who may be too free with his tongue. It is a marvellous opportunity for those police who are yellow, as it needs no bravery to charge a woman who honestly thinks we may lose the war. The system of informers and arrests reflects the hidden but powerful panic in the hearts of our leaders.

God grant a place of refreshment, light and peace to the crew of HM submarine *Salmon* – the bravest of the brave, yet Christian enough to refrain from sinking the Bremen. The recent wireless programme about the *Salmon* was stirring and fine! Customers ask 'what do you think the end of the war will be?' and when I say 'we'll win OK' and explain why I think so, I feel as though I'm betraying their trust.

Maggie Joy Blunt

Last Friday, it was said, Hitler was to have swooped on us. Air raids have increased round the coast but that is all. Yesterday I heard neighbours saying, 'He's two days late . . . schedule not working out well . . . '

My first duty at the FAP [First Aid Post/Point] last night. The point is in the gym of a boys' prep school on the edge of the Common. We sleep on camp beds which we have to erect and make with our stock blankets and of course clear away in the morning. I should have worn uniform but it had never occurred to me and no one had told me. Did not sleep very well but night was without incident. Returned home by 7 a.m.

TUESDAY, 23 JULY

Christopher Tomlin

It was too much to hope the RAF's luck would continue. 11 of their machines went west on Sunday and 4 yesterday. It is a boon for me to express my anger and joy in my diary; if I had no medium of expression I'd burst.

Mother made raspberry jam on Saturday, the first since last war. Raspberries came from next-door's allotment and cost 1/6 for two pounds. The jam is lovely and pure, not turnip and vegetable mash. Cakes are hard to buy so mother bakes her own (rock buns, bakewell tarts, egg and bacon tarts). Damned sight better than those sold by shops. We do know how ours are made!

Eileen Potter

The Budget. I am afraid I must confess to a feeling of relief to hear that the burdens on people of about my own income are not to be *too* heavy (though I know that on principle the Budget is inadequate). Now I can decide to put a large proportion of my dividends into voluntary National Savings. The rest of the news seems to me to be all satisfactory (though it is all a matter of remedying past mistakes or omissions). First comes the news of our recognition of the Czecho-Slovak Government, then that of the revision of sentences for 'Despondency and Alarm', the abolition of the 'Silent Column', the release of some of the interned aliens. I wonder if the conference on Sunday has had anything to do with some of these decisions on the part of the Government.

Pam Ashford

I went to work. The talk was all about raids. Miss Smith said, 'When people returned from holidays it used to be romances they had had, but now it is the bombs they have had.'

Agnes has also returned today from Gourock. Agnes can be trusted to get the full dramatic effect of the raids down that way. She said that a German plane was brought down on the Greenock golf course on the 13th. On the 20th the Greenock torpedo works were bombed. While the German plane was sowing the magnetic mines, Agnes lay in bed. She heard the mines falling into the water, splash, splash, splash. The anti-aircraft firing was deafening and the sky was lit with the searchlights. Agnes was terrified to move lest she wake her mother. On Saturday morning crowds watched the mine sweeping from the esplanade. The minesweepers captured one mine and exploded another. The noise was terrific.

WEDNESDAY, 24 JULY

Maggie Joy Blunt

'The Die Is Cast.' 'Britain Has Chosen Her Fate.' These are the headings in recent Berlin papers commenting on Halifax's speech ('We never wanted war; certainly no one here wants the war to go on for a day longer than is necessary. But we shall not stop fighting till freedom for ourselves and others is secure.')

Rain again. Ella and Aunt A have a mother and two young children evacuees from Southend.

The new Budget: Income tax 8/6d. 1d per pint on beer; ½d on ten cigarettes, 1½d on 1 oz tobacco. A tax on entertainments.

Christopher Tomlin

I see the cost of living is up 30% on 1939. Is the Government pleased with the hardship caused to servicemen's families? How can wives and mothers live on the meagre dependants' allowance?

I am wholly satisfied with Mr Churchill, who is a leader worth following. His broom sweeps away the vile tittle-tattler, over-zealous constable, panic-soaked spinster and other vermin.

The Budget! I cannot afford cigarettes now. I much prefer a pipe, it's more satisfying, and an ounce of Tom Long tobacco now lasts a week. A week's cigarettes would cost 3/-. As my spending money is 5/- to 7/-, varying with sales, the saving is worth while.

Pam Ashford

At 6.30 a.m. I was awakened by noises that I concluded were (1) thunder, (2) bombs, (3) guns, (4) the cleansing department, after which I went to sleep again.

On reaching work I found that everyone (no exceptions) had been awakened. The Bousies had dressed at once. Mr Mitchell, on reaching the office at 9.30, told us that 4 bombs had been dropped on Hillington. Rolls Royce have a large aeroplane engine works there. Agnes knows someone who saw four planes (hers are always complete with Swastika on the tail). Miss Bousie says that a father in Kenmure Street was pointing the German planes out to his children all gathered round a window.

Home to tea. Charlie returned at 6.30, and fairly took our breath away by saying that his soup factory was hit this morning! He is chairman of Jean McGregor Ltd, Hillington. A bomb fell on either side. All the glass is broken and the roof damaged; the day's 'boiling' was lost, and a number of tins of soup perforated. The printing works next door was blown to bits. The damage done to the aeroplane works was trifling. There were no personal injuries. For some reason we have all been laughing heartily about the raid having touched the Oakley household. Just why, I don't know.

THURSDAY, 25 JULY

Pam Ashford
1 p.m. Wireless said that last night there was no raid anywhere, the first time for more than a month. Perhaps this affected conversation, for in the office there was talk about the moderation of the attacks so far, everyone having expected things to be on a much bigger scale long before this. Miss Bousie said, 'There is a clearing in the air. One feels the improved atmosphere. Hitler wants to give us another chance to do the right thing.'

Mr Mitchell said, 'There is a man in our road, Mr Nevin. I often travel in the train with him; he takes a serious view of the war. His boy was at Dunkirk. The other evening one of the neighbours stopped me and said, "Is it not terrible the way Mr Nevin talks? He thinks we are going to be defeated. He says a major told him." Mr Mitchell said, 'We are not going to be defeated, not with a Navy like ours. Don't take the man seriously.' However, this woman and a number of others in the road have reported Mr Nevin to the police. He has been arrested. They let him out on £20 bail. He has employed a solicitor to defend him. He was despondent, they say. One of the women says he distressed her so much she had to be revived with brandy.

FRIDAY, 26 JULY

Christopher Tomlin
The increasingly heavy raids on our convoys are chords of doom: the Nazis will soon tire and in their anger and frustration try to bomb us to make us cry, 'No, not that! We give in!' They will try but by the eye tooth of the Great God Kang we'll swipe the floor with the conceited German. Not the Isle of Elba, nor the castle of Doorn, but a thick rope and a six foot drop!

It is my duty to praise Air Chief Marshal Philip Joubert who, with his cool, calm, wise talk, soothes us and puts our minds at ease. I can't rest without showing appreciation.

SATURDAY, 27 JULY

Pam Ashford

I said to Mr Mitchell, 'If Hitler does not have his Blitzkrieg soon, he won't be able to have it at all. The summer is now so far on.'

Mr Mitchell said, 'Hitler has already lost the war, and he knows it. He cannot defeat this country. We shall have a state of deadlock, each side sending a few machines over each day.'

Maggie Joy Blunt

We are beginning to think now, 'Perhaps the threatened invasion will not take place, not perhaps immediately, perhaps never . . . Hitler is evidently having to change his plans and he will have to hurry to be here by August 18th.'

London Philharmonic Orchestra is to tour music halls instead of being disbanded as was feared through lack of financial support. This happened through the publicity given to the matter by Priestley and the *News Chronicle*, which roused Jack Hylton, 'whose personal enthusiasms go far beyond dance music', to act as sponsor. A curious situation, but results may be excellent.

Military activity in and around the Beeches. Lorries parked. Troops marching.

Christopher Tomlin

A heavy thunderstorm. I'm in the 7th heaven when the wind is fierce, the rain is drenching down, the thunder is roaring, the seawaves are wild and high. I would love to exult, throwing my arms high, and dance alone to the rhythm of the elements. It's the only time I am really contented and happy.

SUNDAY, 28 JULY

Maggie Joy Blunt

This afternoon I began to read John Strachey's *Why You Should Become a Socialist*, which I have had since 1938.

These figures stick in my mind, and in my throat: approximately 90% of the population earns £250 and under per annum, a large proportion of which are families of four living on £2 a week. 'With individual exceptions, the employing class cares nothing about the conditions which the existing economic system imposes upon the working class,' he writes. I'd say rather that the major part of the employing class (if he means the middle classes as a whole) do not know the conditions. How can you live nearly all your life in this sort of area of some suburb or provincial town and never pass through or by a slum? Only by desultory reading have I become conscious of the magnitude of social inequalities and injustices. At one time I honestly and happily believed that the working classes were a minority of the total population.

The *Canadian Geographical Journal* is publishing my article in the August issue. Think of it – it must be in print and in circulation now!

Christopher Tomlin

Father and mother say the public's treatment of Gracie Fields is damnable. [Fields was accused of being a traitor when she went abroad in 1940 in an attempt to avoid the internment of her Italian husband.] Me: 'It's not the people, it's the newspaper.' Mother: 'Nothing of the kind – it's the socialist MPs.'

I'm disgusted at the so-called remissions of 'chatter bug crimes'. People must receive compensation for wrongful sentencing to jail or the government's mad fit of 5th columnitis will rock the high heaven. Is this Britain – a land of free adults – or a place of slaves whipped and controlled by lunatics?

My attitude to the war: 1. To carry on my job until I'm called up. 2. To do all I'm told. 3. To work like a fiend for promotion. 4. To leave the rest to the government.

I'm no longer ready to listen to 'we will win' optimists or 'we are bound to lose' damned fools. I refuse to be destroyed spiritually. If I do all I am told and the worst happens, it's the government's blasted idiocy to blame, not me. The politicians knew what they would have to face; they knew if we were prepared; they chose to fight on; therefore victory or unjust peace depends on them.

MONDAY, 29 JULY

Pam Ashford

At the Soroptimist lunch the talk was all about being 'all dressed up for the Blitzkrieg and nowhere to go'. The talk turned on bombs. The newest type, it is said, are sent down by parachute; they don't bury themselves in such big craters and spread their destructive powers over a wider area. They have much thinner shells. The bomb splinters found at Hillington proved this. Everyone knew that the printing works had been blown to bits and sympathy was expressed with the owner who had put everything into it. Christmas cards were scattered all over the neighbourhood.

TUESDAY, 30 JULY

Christopher Tomlin

My sister's birthday. Pile trouble worse than ever. Have been OK for weeks and now a nasty do. It is because I took too much Epsom salts. It is delightful to read of the battle of Dover. The RAF is indeed grand. Oh yes, a customer mentioned that her son (Army) says, 'The RAF boys are the darlings of the nation – they get everything they want.' Why shouldn't they?

I cannot afford to buy cigarettes so am making my own with a 'Rizla jiffy machine' and Rizla papers purchased before the war. The tobacco I use, Three Castles, costs 1/1 an ounce. I've made 20 cigarettes so far and have enough tobacco left for three times as many. I noticed a soldier using a Jiffy machine in town.

WEDNESDAY, 31 JULY

Maggie Joy Blunt

It is exciting to ride off late at night, through the dark woods and along the edge of the mist-hidden common as mysterious as the sea, with bright beams of light searching for an aeroplane and a pale moon edging its way between low clouds. No signs of life. In nursing frock and apron with gas-mask swinging from one's shoulder one feels original and important. But the night spent on a hard strange camp bed in the unfamiliar darkness is more oppressive than too many blankets. The pillow is bumpy and too low. One sleeps lightly, with one ear open. One turns and sighs, conscious of strange and vivid dreams, hearing one's companion stir in the next bed. An owl seems to be crooning all night on the doorstep. One wonders if daylight will ever dawn again. Then suddenly one wakes to see gaps in window coverings and under the door – it is a relief to be up early to put the blankets and beds away. Riding home in the young morning one is tired. Supposing one had been up all night attending to casualties – would one feel as tired as this? I don't think so.

Mr Morrison is making determined efforts to have our salvage collected properly. He broadcast an appeal on Sunday and gave us the slogan, 'Up, housewives, and at 'em.' All the housewives I know are only too willing to co-operate.

Days are drawing in. I am not looking forward to the winter. I hope to have some coal sorted. But what will the food supply be like? Each meal I have now, I think how rich and good it is. Plenty of wholemeal bread, mixed butter and marg, plenty of fresh greenstuff from the garden, marmalade, figs, sultanas, prunes, honey . . . fresh fruit is expensive but English apples and plums are just coming in. The other night I had half of a steamed mackerel (3d) with new potatoes (2d or 3d a lb), spinach from the garden, and parsley sauce made from lard, wholemeal flour, water and home-grown parsley, and stewed fruit and bread and butter. Black treacle, important for my health, is difficult to get but I have managed so far and hope that Aunt A will be able to order me some from the stores. Every shop has only a limited supply in once a month so you have to book an order if you can.

And then the long black nights, the awful business of blacking-out. For six weeks or more I've had to black out scarcely at all, simply by gong to bed when it was dark and getting up early. No, I am not looking forward to the winter, particularly when going on Red Cross duty.

Priestley's broadcasts are excellent. I am astonished that the BBC allow them. He says insistently that this war is not to restore the old order, that we must not return to the old muddle and injustices. It is in our order to commence a period of reconstruction and new activity, so exciting and absorbing that Hitler and his Nazis will be forgotten in a few years. Already, he says, he has had letters telling him to get off the air before the government puts him where he belongs.

A film called *Grapes of Wrath* has just been released and has had startlingly good criticisms in every paper. It tells a story of American life that is not often mentioned, of unemployed and down-and-outs trekking across the continent in search of work, 'The sort of film,' writes the *New Statesman*, 'that the Bolsheviks might have made before the revolution burst.' There are no stars in the cast –

characters are all played by ordinary men and women. It is being shown at the Leicester Square Odeon.

Tilly Rice

I have heard of an air raid warning in Cornwall. The village possesses no siren. The vicar's sister is Air Raid Warden and the other day she received the 'red' signal. Instantly she donned her tin hat and trousers and started to run down the village street blowing her whistle. The village had always thought she was half mad, and thought she had gone completely, and took no notice of her when she tried to push the people into their houses. Bombs were dropped near, with the customary inaccuracy.

The piano tuner today was quite eager to discuss the pros and cons of the situation. (Why do piano tuners always have pursed lips, protruding chins and a precise manner?) He said, 'They'll have a smack at London. They'll send over so many that some of them are bound to get through.' I said, 'But London is very well protected.' He nodded his head. 'One or two will manage it. But I think it is terrible that the cream of our young men are being killed, and if they're not killed they'll never be the same again because their nerves can't keep up to it.'

Had a refreshing evening at Studio One on Monday seeing a cinema programme which scarcely mentioned the war. It's sad to think that we shan't get any more amusing French films.

THURSDAY, 1 AUGUST

Pam Ashford

There is an ARP trade exhibition on at the Scottish Building Centre and I manipulated my lunch hour so as to go in for 10 minutes, which was a quite inadequate length of time. There was a good deal of glass exhibited, showing the effect that blast has upon glass treated with various preparations. There is no doubt that net, varnished over, is the best method. Several firms were exhibiting lighting installations for black-outs.

Miss Bousie came to work very angry about Mr Duff Cooper [who announced a public survey ostensibly concerned with morale]. Heaven help the canvasser who calls on her. Miss Bousie maintains that no one in their senses would give a total stranger information, but I replied that the investigators whom I used to know very seldom received a refusal. I have since remembered that someone once called at the Bousie's with a questionnaire dealing with radio, and one question asked about the constitution of the family. Miss Bousie was convinced that the party was acting for a burglar who was trying to get at the movements of the house, and she complained to the police, who assured her that it was a genuine venture. I think, but I am not sure, that the BBC had something to do with it.

Mother is most uncertain as to what she would do if a canvasser called, but when I said that Miss Bousie thoroughly disapproved of Mr Duff Cooper, Mother pealed with laughter. 'Has the Government ever done anything of which Miss Bousie did approve?' she asked. I am amused too, but my amusement is more as to what this lady who so much objects to being made the object of study would say if she realised that she is in point of fact being studied so closely.

Tilly Rice

As I came in the gate this morning a voice said softly from the branches of a tree above my head, 'Cuckoo! Cuckoo!' and I looked up to see a Canadian nestling among the leaves (of course I looked away again quickly – it doesn't do to look at Canadians long). A party of them had descended on the lane to hang a field telephone wire in the trees and all the morning there was a great to-do while they scrambled up and down, lopped bits off, unrolled yards of wire and kept the kids in a fever of high delight. After a while they all moved off, and I didn't see mine for the rest of the morning. Dick came back before Bob and when I asked him where he was he said Bob had gone off with the Canadians. I sent Dick after him and he found him quite a distance away.

'I *had* to follow the soldiers with their lorry Mummy,' Bob said when I protested. Then later he remarked, 'I liked all those nice soldiers.' 'They were Canadians,' I told him. 'I know,' he said, 'you don't need to tell me.'

The Canadians are apparently causing some trouble in some places. Mr J's shoe man said: 'In a little village near Woking all the men of the village got out one night and barred the road to stop them coming in. All the women were after them.' It is said round here that the married women run after the soldiers more than the single girls.

FRIDAY, 2 AUGUST

Tilly Rice
The Germans have now started leaflet raids. I was hoping that they would do something like that; I thought it would be interesting to see if their stuff was any good. But to my disappointment all they've dropped is extracts from Hitler's speech. We don't want our streets littered up with stale news. Can't they think up something more amusing than that? And they are supposed to be an efficient race.

SATURDAY, 3 AUGUST

Christopher Tomlin
A heavy delivery. On my return, I picked up an envelope addressed to me and marked OHMS. At last! My medical exam! Saturday, August 10th at 10.30 am.

SUNDAY, 4 AUGUST

Pam Ashford
There have been times when I have thought that perhaps Hitler would like to choose the anniversary of the outbreak of the last war to launch his Blitzkrieg; however, now today has come, I feel I don't care much. I'm awfully fed up with the war. One day last week I wrote in this diary and then crossed out, 'For the sake of public morale, it is to be hoped that the invasion will come soon.' I crossed it out because of course we don't want the invasion at all, and we do want as much time as we can to build up our war effort in case it does come.

MONDAY, 5 AUGUST

Eileen Potter
The first day of my holidays. We have been warned not to go too far away from London, in case we have to be recalled at short notice, so I have decided to stay at home for the first week and go to a place on the borders of Surrey and Sussex for the second week, Hitler permitting. I set off to Golders Green for tennis as usual. Miss Y

comes tonight. The staff at her hostel have had to help looking after refugees from Gibraltar who have not yet been de-loused.
(This is Eileen Potter's last entry.)

Pam Ashford

Today the Soroptimists met again. Three quarters of an hour elapsed before any real good war talk was introduced. Miss Cheetham began it. She is a paid ARP organiser and said that on Saturday a warden came into HQ. He lay about the benches, complaining of drowsiness and feeling ill. He alleged he was gassed. They disbelieved him and advised him to go away and see his panel doctor.

Dr Marshall of the Royal Infirmary said that on Saturday morning four cases of suspected poison gas presented themselves. A warden, who has studied gases so much that he has lost his sense of proportion, began to cough after the all-clear had sounded. Then he sniffed the air and thought it smelt of musty hay. Just then a working man passed and coughed. The warden questioned him, and the man, not appreciating the point, said, 'What the h*** has that to do with you? Can't I cough now?'

The warden found three other people who were ready to believe that they were gassed and the party was taken to the Infirmary. There was nothing the matter with them, just imagination.

Christopher Tomlin

Bugle-blowing newspapers and the BBC make me doubt their sagacity: 'When victory is ours we will restore Europe ... we will win, no doubt of that ... that evil thing will be crushed' etc. are boasts. Not empty ones but still boasts. Have we failed to realise the lesson of France – the trumped-up Maginot line, the 'victory is certain, can't those damn fool Germans see it' attitude? Boasting is babyish; action not talking is what we sorely need. I am so despondent when I see Britain waiting for invasion. Why do we wait? Why don't we harry Germany's long coastline and give her a bloody good tossing. Has the Viking fire forsaken our bones?

The war will be lost by us in a month or two – three at the outside. That is my secret thought, not for the world would I tell it to anybody but you. It doesn't prevent me doing my duty for Britain, as I prefer to go down fighting. Sydney asked for 6 months' exemption – he gets two. It looks as if I'll have to do with two, too.

Maggie Joy Blunt

'The Prime Minister wishes it to be known that the possibility of German attempts at invasion has by no means passed away.' We are ready for it.

I travelled up from London the other day with a Tommy in the Tank Corps returning from leave. He was a plump, comfortable, typically satisfied and humorous Englishman who gave out to all and sundry that our defences were now excellent. A month or so ago they were not. If Hitler had attacked then . . . But now we are ready. His admiration for the Air Force was generous. Stories of their marvellous prowess and courage are universal. Also from another source I heard that the Navy is tremendously satisfied with their preparation. Altogether we are in better heart.

Chapter Fourteen

COAL, DUSTBIN AND DRAIN

Homes destroyed, death to hundreds: the Blitz on London begins.

'What you are taught at Osterley is not pretty. You are taught, for example, how to stab a tank crew sentry in the back so that he will die without making any noise. And you are then told how to deal with the sleeping crew with about eighteen inches of lead piping.

We were told a lot about guerrilla fighting: how to immobilise cars by putting sugar in the petrol tank, how to stop trains from getting very far by filling the lubricating boxes with a few handfuls of sand or grit. I learnt a lot about street fighting and defending houses from a man who got his experience from the Spanish Civil War, and in the afternoon the students were put through practical exercises which must have reminded them of playing Red Indians when they were children.'

Edward Ward attends a two-day course for the Home Guard. Home Service, 8 August 1940

* * *

13 August German bombing offensive against airfields and factories in England. **15 August** Air battles and daylight raids over Britain, with more than 1,000 German planes in action. **17 August** Hitler declares a blockade of the British Isles. **23–24 August** First German air raids on central London. **25–26 August** First British air raid on Berlin.

TUESDAY, 6 AUGUST

Tilly Rice
The BBC is making painful efforts to spin out their bulletins with meticulous descriptions of RAF exploits and repetitions of 'reports' from their observers. Rather foolish I think; surely if they have no new war news there are other things happening. I sometimes feel that anytime now I may turn on the radio to hear an announcer say in a shaky voice, 'The Germans made an attempted landing at so-and-so today . . . ' It would bound to be an 'attempted' landing.

WEDNESDAY, 7 AUGUST

Christopher Tomlin
I began today in hope and finished in despair. An awful struggle to sell 17/- of stationery. I clenched my teeth and carried on. I booked 'nowt' the first hour and orders came in a tiny trickle. I canvassed for 7 hours non-stop.

Tilly Rice
At the present moment the war has apparently moved to other parts of the globe for the Italians are reported to have invaded British Somaliland and Egypt has been warned to expect an attack at any time.

Our local LDVs are coming out in their uniforms. I think they look a bit funny-peculiar, rather like something Mother has run up on the machine for Sonny so that he shall be like Daddy. Still, they are doing fine work these chaps, spending their nights keeping a look-out for old Nasty. I only hope though that thought is being given to the winter and that they won't be expected to keep guard in their rompers during chill and frosty nights but will be provided with something more adequate.

V on the phone this morning with a lovely story of how the Nazis get these photographs of 'loyal' French subjects doing the Nazi salute. They get a crowd together, call out 'Hands up all those who don't speak German!' and then snap 'em quickly.

Went swimming at Reigate baths today amidst many Canadians.

Pam Ashford
With a suggestion of humour, Miss Bousie said, 'So we are going to

have snoopers coming into our houses now, to see if we are wasting food.' Personally I feel appalled at the way that our freedom to choose between right and wrong is being controlled by government regulations, and not to be able to choose means you become a robot. Many people give away food that is unfit for their own use to their cleaners, so apparently what is fit for human consumption varies with class.

In the afternoon Miss Bousie saw a bill with 'No invasion' on it. Everyone seems convinced on this point. I wonder. In the afternoon, however, there was definitely a rising interest in Egypt, and the general view is that the war is to be fought in Africa now, and accompanying it is a feeling that our skins are safe for the time being. I feel that way too and I hate myself for it.

THURSDAY, 8 AUGUST

Christopher Tomlin
Had a bath, ready for my medical at 10.30 on Saturday.

Pam Ashford
I don't understand things. In July we were all keyed up for an invasion, intense aerial bombardment, attacks on the ports, and 'public morale was wonderful', but when we found ourselves in August with nothing having happened, we seemed to subside like a balloon that had had the air let out. In myself I recognise the same psychological condition that I have always experienced after an examination, finding that the intense mental effort lowered the reservoir of nervous energy and that it was days, or even weeks before I could take any interest at all in anything whatsoever. Looking at other people I sometimes think their frame of mind is that, 'We have been "had", whether by Hitler or the British government.'

Miss Bousie then pointed out that the 15th is next week, the day Hitler booked for his triumphant march through London. Clearly no one expects anything to happen between now and the 15th. I said, 'It is no use counting on the German people to rebel for a long while yet, though I do wonder how Hitler is going to explain what has happened to his plan.'

FRIDAY, 9 AUGUST

Christopher Tomlin

4 to 1: a bloody fine show! I am proud to be a Briton; now I know we can't lose. A day of apprehension, expecting the worst at my medical examination tomorrow. This evening father was in a 'gaseous state': we had no right to rescue German airmen from the sea, they were better off dead. They machine-gunned women and children and said the only race fit to live is the German. We should kill them all.

SATURDAY, 10 AUGUST

Pam Ashford

Last night at 9.20 an American gave a talk about Lord Haw Haw and I sat up when he said that Lord Haw Haw was William Joyce and that Eduard Dietze frequently deputised for him. Roderich Eduard Dietze, born at Broomhill, Glasgow! Mr Mitchell's surmise last autumn was right. I might say that the *Daily Record* never paid him for giving them that material; what happened instead was that they gave his name to the police as a possible Fifth Columnist.

My clearest recollection of yesterday was the delivery of a government leaflet telling us to 'stay put' if the invader comes. Charlie and Mother also read this closely, and I am sure it is the first time Mother has ever paid any heed at all to a government leaflet. Believing firmly that the attempt at invasion *will* come, I ought to have been stirred by that leaflet, and I was, but one cannot stay keyed up all the time! What we are going through now is just like what we go through in a dentist's waiting room.

Christopher Tomlin

Medical exam: one doctor was puzzled because I couldn't touch my toes. He tried other exercises on me which I did easily. He appealed to a colleague, 'How is it he can't touch his toes?' The opinion was 'stiffness'. At the end, I was informed that if it hadn't been for my eyes I would be grade 1; but through my eyes I am grade 3. I interviewed the RAF officer and I am asking for 3 months' redemption.

Christopher Tomlin

I am accepted for the RAF and not the Army. The battle dress never appealed to me and I feel one cannot do enough for the boys who fly our machines. I mean to give every ounce of assistance I possibly can. I'm doing bending exercises.

MONDAY, 12 AUGUST

Tilly Rice

The Germans announce that the attack on Britain has already begun. Certainly these last days there has been plenty of battle in the air, with more than 131 German aeroplanes bagged by the RAF. I get a great thrill out of listening to the BBC accounts of these battles.

The war in Africa goes on and there is much uneasiness in other parts. I often feel that at any moment now this may develop into a real world war, a general dog-fight of *all* the nations, and I picture a horrible mix-up in the end when nobody is quite clear who is fighting whom.

Said Dick at lunch the other day, full of valour, 'I'd like to kill old Hitler.' 'Oh, you shouldn't do that,' said Bob gravely, 'that might make the war worster.' 'Why do you think that Bob?' I asked him. 'Because,' he explained, 'the people in Germany might wonder where he was.'

Tomorrow I'm going to make some plum jam – this week I get my next jam ration of sugar.

Pam Ashford

The most wonderful thing happened today at 12. We are to get a second week's holiday! The first week of September has been allotted to me. Mother and I both have the same desire, viz. Ayr. Mrs Stewart is there this month and we think she might be able to find us rooms. Mother means to get her address from Mr Stewart tonight, but as I had seen four Polish officers entering the house we think that Mr Stewart must have company. Today we are so happy, so happy, so happy.

My mind is rapidly becoming adjusted to the 'failure' to materialise of the July Blitzkrieg. The war is really interesting again today. It would be very strange if one did not find it so. Miss Bousie was distressed about the air battles yesterday saying, 'It is terrible.' I said, 'We have driven them from our shores; that is what matters.'

At the Soroptimist luncheon housekeeping cropped up again and again. Mrs Allan: 'And eggs at 3d!' There was talk of Australian eggs, eggs produced by fowls on unnatural diets, American eggs that are to be here in October, eggs fit for cakes only, disagreeable tasting eggs with pale yokes.

Miss Wilson called in the evening. Her neighbours are Portsmouth people and are worried about relatives there. She says that the authorities are warning the inhabitants that they may have to go and that they would get only a few hours' notice. Then half-an-hour later the 9 o'clock news came on reporting an attack on Portsmouth today.

TUESDAY, 13 AUGUST

Christopher Tomlin
Customers wish me God-speed. More buggering machines come down. I am delighted but worried: my brother's on an island off the south coast. There have been fatal casualties at one aerodrome on the south-east coast.

Maggie Joy Blunt
Sirens, I have just been told, went for this district about half-an-hour ago and the all-clear a little later. And me on Point duty again tonight. I didn't hear the sirens – I never seem to, even when awake. But I did hear shots the other night: the LDV, or Home Guard as they are called now, have been active for some obscure and whispered reason. Last night Commandant JM was agitated because two Germans were at the first-aid lecture. Their husbands have been interned and they are suspects.

Saw an excellent and well produced MOI film this weekend: Mary Clare and Martita Hunt deal with a dead German parachutist and a German spy in an English officer's uniform.

Tilly Rice
The egg difficulty persists in this district. Occasionally the United Dairy allows me three in a week. I asked the milkman if he had any this morning. He shook his head and said, 'I haven't any today, but

they have given me a pamphlet to explain to the customers why we haven't got any.' 'I can't give that to the baby for her dinner,' I said. 'It would take you about half an hour to read it,' returned the milkman.

Pam Ashford

All day I have been thinking of Portsmouth and there are three trends in my thoughts. It does seem as if the Battle for Britain has begun now. This is no false alarm. Glasgow remains quiet and peaceful and normal, and our interest in the war, though quickening, remains pretty much detached. However, it is clear that this phase of detachment is rapidly nearing its close. Secondly, of course, I think again and again of our various relatives and friends in Hampshire, although most of them live a sufficiently far distance from the dockyard to make us think they are safe.

I had no idea that Portsmouth meant so much to me. I was only 18 months when I left, and my knowledge was gleaned in three holidays there at 5, 9 and 10 years of age. I had a weekend at 19, but it is the childish recollections that are stirring in my mind.

In the afternoon people kept on coming in saying that the Germans are shelling the south coast of England from France. I said, 'That is easy to do, but the point is, are they aiming straight on the military objectives they want to hit?' Most people commented thus: 'The war is getting under way now.' Miss Bousie: 'We are in an unholy mess.'

WEDNESDAY, 14 AUGUST

Pam Ashford

Yesterday we shot down 78 German planes. This is good news, at any rate to the way of thinking of Mother, Charlie, Mr Mitchell and me. Miss Bousie is miserable about it. While she is reconciled to the possibility of our winning the war, she is very sensitive about the loss of life. All the same she is hardening and said today, 'I do not see how we can just accept everything the Germans do.' I almost think that the time is coming when she will fail to rebuke someone who expresses the view that it is right to resist force by force.

There are reports of revolts in France, and that is the straw Miss Bousie grasps nowadays. Mr Mitchell and I think that for a long while yet Germany will hold the Continent. Military adventures by this country are out of the question until the Battle for Britain is won.

The business of our own affairs is, however, putting the war into the background. All these small cargoes don't amount to much profit but they keep us busy. An historian reading this diary in 100 years' time might think it daft but the fact is that smaller things that touch you personally absorb your attention more than bigger things in which you can only take an abstract interest.

Christopher Tomlin

Father is dubious about RAF claims. Thinks reported German losses are hot air. It is easy for a pilot to think he's sent a machine down; the authorities have only the pilot's figures to rely on. If the figures are true, Germany will soon stop sending bombers here, as she can't afford to lose them at that rate. 'Unless she's hundreds to chuck away.' I believe our figures are true. But when 400 or 500 Nazis come across and 60 are forced down, there still remain 340 or 440 to bomb. They aren't all forced to return and, I believe, considerable damage is done which our authorities are loath to tell. Therefore I look forward to hearing the truth about Germany's bombing raids and losses from my brother who comes home on 10 days' leave on the 30th of this month.

Tilly Rice

I feel more oppressed by the war this evening than I have for a long time, and this is partly through reading the scare-headlines of that noxious rag the *Daily Express* while visiting J and partly due to the visit itself. There is such a feeling of suspended animation about J and her husband. Their life has been completely swept away by the war (formerly he was a tea-broker, now he is serving in the WRP), and all the things they used to talk about – going to parties, visiting friends, going away for weekends – just don't happen. Their life is just the bare routine of existence and their conversation, from lack of events to recount, is stilted. It must be hellish for young people like them. Everything is taken away and with nothing in reserve to replace it. They are not despondent, they are just stopped.

I have lately been struck by the light-hearted way in which boys will overstay their leave home, quite cheerfully accepting the consequent CB. I cannot remember there being such a disregard of the regulations in the last war; the Army seemed to have been taken much more seriously. J's husband said the Canadians never care what time they get back. Their passes are always made out for midnight, but they say providing they get back in the morning in time for roll call that's all that matters.

THURSDAY, 15 AUGUST

Pam Ashford

Undoubtedly the topic of the day is the parachutes. Last evening both the wireless and the newspapers mentioned finding some in Scotland, at Fenwick Manor. Miss Crawford was full of it. 'I was telling Mother last night that even if our bell rang during the night she was not to open the door.' This produced a chorus of 'Certainly not!' and 'Good Gracious, no!' I asked Mr Mitchell what was the source of his information. This was a LDV man who got it from a policeman. I said, 'He should not say such things.' Mr Mitchell: 'But they did.'

I endeavoured to show the office that the parachutes might have been a hoax, but Mr Roxburgh said 'No. They would not have come down if there had not been a man attached, and since there are no dead bodies lying around there must be live men walking about.'

Soon after, I saw a chalked notice, 'Bloodhounds to track parachutists.' Later I read in the papers that the bloodhounds are in the midlands of England.

Today is the 15th, for which Hitler announced his triumphant procession. We have had many laughs at Hitler's expense. All the same, Miss Bousie has been looking for bad omens.

Tilly Rice

PW brought a carload of women and babies to call on me this afternoon. One young woman amused us very much by recounting sayings of a cockney woman who works for her. She is a devout Catholic and is perfectly satisfied that she will be safe because she has hidden her rosary. She came into work the other day saying blithely, 'Quarter to four next week – the invasion ma'am!' Then she added in an awestruck voice, 'Ere, wot do you think he'll do when he gets 'ere?' 'Do?' echoed my friend. 'Why he'll come straight out to Epsom to rape you, Mrs Thing!' 'Wot me!' She shook her head. 'Oh no, no man's touched me for fifteen years, and *he*'s not going to start!'

337

FRIDAY, 16 AUGUST

Christopher Tomlin

Or should I say Thursday 12 a.m. Father listens in and calls us upstairs. 'Did you hear that? The Air Ministry say that final reports are not in, but the Nazi losses are known to exceed the figure given very considerably!' Later: 144 down – shades of Don Bradman! I wondered how long it would take us to score a century. Father says the Germans have many more planes than us. 'They produce 2,000 a week, and we admit that fact. They must have thousands hidden somewhere. In spite of over 1,000 British raids on Germany they can still come across with 500 planes a day. In spite of their losses there can be only one end to the struggle: they've 10 times our planes, we bring 4 of theirs down for the loss of one, but they are bound to win because of their numbers.'

People must not be condemned for wondering if RAF reports are true. For months we watched in stupefaction as Hitler overcame the defences of every country, even boastful France. We heard about his dreadful dive bombers and we thought his army and air force supreme. Perfect and invisible. We secretly thought the war was lost when France caved in and that it was a matter of a few weeks before Britain was done. To know the RAF can wallop the Lufthansa is mightily encouraging.

What do I feel about the losses? 1. The best Nazi pilots have yet to be in action. 2. The best German planes have yet to come.

Pam Ashford

Mother is enthusiastic about the big battle yesterday, and Miss Bousie is aghast at the loss of life. Charlie was in the air raid on London yesterday. He slept in the train two nights running. When the 9 p.m. news last night mentioned 'Croydon', I sat up and said 'London at last', but I never gave a thought to Charlie, knowing Croydon is many miles from Whitehall. Mother, however, had a disturbed night thinking of him. Charlie turned up at 8 a.m., full of beans.

SATURDAY, 17 AUGUST

Pam Ashford
Yesterday south-west London was bombed. The Battle for Britain is indeed started. This is no isolated occurrence, but the real thing. What are my feelings? I am neither elated nor depressed. I am perfectly normal. Indeed the degree of normality would seem abnormal if it were not that most other people seem just the same.

SUNDAY, 18 AUGUST

Maggie Joy Blunt
This was the date, it was said, that Hitler was to have been in London. He was to have had Britain on her knees by the 15th. An attack on London attempted this afternoon, two or three local warnings these last few days. German air losses, if our figures are correct, are tremendous. Is this the beginning of the big attack? Perhaps there is worse to come but we are not defeated yet.

MONDAY, 19 AUGUST

Pam Ashford
Miss Bousie and I had an argument as to the effect of the air raids on the population. She said they must be terror-stricken, while I said that I thought the bulk of the population would be quite calm. While a raid is on and bombs are falling around you, naturally you experience fear, but I don't think people go about all day and all night in a panic in case something might happen to them.

Yesterday the 1 p.m. news was broken by two minutes' silence, then the announcer's voice came on again. I think the local transmission failed. It turns out that Miss Bousie and Agnes regarded it as an ominous sign. It means enemy aircraft were about. Miss Bousie definitely heard the planes overhead.

Christopher Tomlin
I strongly wish it was August 30th, when Dick comes home. I fear something may happen to him. No answer to my application for postponement. 27/- sales. To my amusement customers wish me *bon voyage* and *au revoir* and finish with, 'I'm glad you are in the Air

Force if that's what you want,' as if to say, 'It's the last thing I would have chosen.' One customer thinks the Battle of Britain will end in six weeks and then we will attack the Continent. Her view (my view too) is common, and I do hope it's not wishful thinking. There is a feeling that the war will go on for a year or two, and that every part of Britain will be bombed. One customer holds an unusual view: 'There will be no need to attack Hitler on the Continent. Germany will collapse if the Battle of Britain should fail. They won't last the winter.' A view which I strongly oppose; too good to be true.

Tilly Rice

J tells me he has become an LDV and goes up to spend nights guarding the local telephone exchange. 'I've got a uniform,' he says proudly. 'What, a pair of rompers?' 'No. An armlet.'

While we were playing Monopoly, the kids were laughing and chattering, but I could hear thuds and explosions in the distance and I felt frightened, underneath. For a moment everything seemed to lose its stability. But my fear wasn't unpleasant, it had a thrill like daring something, and when next day came with no further raids I found myself wishing for the warning to sound so that I could feel we were getting on with the job. This morning Dick said to me, 'I feel bored now on the days when there is no warning.'

E took upon himself to tell a man off in the train for 'chatter-bugging', a crime with which he has no patience at all. One said to the other after they had settled down the other day, 'You see! We've only just got the news about the sinking of the *** and it went down in July!' Then E butted in: 'I don't suppose it has occurred to you that all the relatives of the men lost have to be found and informed before the news is made public? How would you like to hear of the death of a relative of yours by radio or newspaper?' 'I wasn't talking to you,' snorted the man. 'No, but I'm talking to *you*,' retorted E, and proceeded to give him a good telling off about careless talk. There wasn't another word uttered by anyone for the rest of the journey.

Listened to Haw Haw yesterday who is really getting sillier and sillier. I like his way of announcing that the German aeroplanes are about to attack London (although they might be a little delayed, owing to the strong west wind . . .) Just as though they were coming to tea.

340

TUESDAY, 20 AUGUST

Christopher Tomlin

Rained off. A notice from the authorities re my postponement: it is referred to the hardship committee. So my appeal for 3 months' grace appears to be useless. I don't know the date my case is to be heard. The surrender – for the euphemistically titled 'evacuation' of Somaliland is nothing more – is just what I expected. To give way to Blackshirt scum is terrible. Since the war began we have left everywhere in a bloody hurry. Only in Britain do we dig in our heels and make a stand, because we have to.

Letter from Dick: they have been in hell. The strain is terrific. A hangar was burnt out. 3 bombers burned too.

WEDNESDAY, 21 AUGUST

Maggie Joy Blunt

A lull in air activity since Sunday. I continue with Red Cross work. Went last Thursday afternoon to Slough centre where I lunched and padded splints and returned home to a comfortable tea on the lawn with Stella. On Saturday Paul and friends drove down and we all went on the river. A heavenly day. No sign or sound of war. At Cookham hotel (small and unimpressive) we tried to get a meal. Set dinner 4/6d. Grilled steak 3/-. Nothing cheaper but bread and cheese and sausages. We protested. Woman grew testy, and said didn't we know there was a war on? Waiter told us later that guests paying 16 guineas a week wanted privacy and that was why prices were high. 16 guineas!

Ventured to London, and a journey to London is an adventure. Ella and Aunt A have evacuee mother and two children from Southend. Mother is bone-lazy and has no control over small boy aged 2. His hands perpetually sticky. Loves coal, dustbin and drain. Mother does minimum of housework. Baby lies in pram on pillow always wet. Stories of other evacuees in neighbourhood with disgusting habits. Our own people. It is shocking. And to think that the Belgians they housed (with a not too sanitary reputation from last war) were clean, industrious, grateful.

Troops in the Beeches today: they seem to come and picnic every midday and go off again. One day a machine gun in a lorry trained skywards just outside the cottages.

An astonishing growth of feeling towards a new order is manifest everywhere. I am beginning to believe in it.

Christopher Tomlin
Started to work today with an anxious mind. There was a vile gale, one or two showers and it was very cold. I sold 23/- worth of paper and through a little hole in my mackintosh pocket lost a 2/- piece. The district I canvassed is an unlucky one for me: a few months ago, ordering goods for the above district, the money was stolen. I felt depressed all day. So many reports of attacks on our aerodromes . . . Dick might not return. I wish it was the 30th.

Mr Churchill's speech was pessimistic: 'If victory comes,' not 'victory is sure'. This is the first time a statesman faced reality and tried to tell the truth. It is an encouragement to me.

At 10 o'clock there was a rat-a-tat-tat on the door and to my joy Dick stood there, home on 11 days' leave! On Sunday night, 20 delay-action bombs fell on his aerodrome, and they haven't exploded yet. He hasn't had a full night's sleep for two weeks. Every squadron of German planes flies over his aerodrome, and the sirens always go at meal times and just as the men are falling asleep. Dick described the red tape, 'six men to a one-man job and scrimshanking'. Obviously I cannot write all he said, but it has made us very pessimistic. The men and officers are grand but the Whitehall, red tape, jack-in office, organisation is rotten. There is a crying – nay shrieking – for efficiency experts up there.

Again I meet my fat old friend 'slight damage' who isn't slight at all. Whoever is responsible for judging between 'some damage', 'slight damage' and 'little damage' has a warped sense of values. But it wouldn't do for us to know too much – witness the hushed-up zeppelin attacks on the east end in the last war. The casual way in which the BBC announcer reads '. . . there was little damage to property, some civilians were killed . . .' blisters my soul.

THURSDAY, 22 AUGUST

Pam Ashford
Miss Bousie has been attacking the Home Guard. 'What is the use of shooting at parachutists? Some of them are altogether too ready with their guns. A policeman should be quite sufficient.' Miss Crawford

agrees with Miss Bousie. Mr Mitchell: 'The Germans cannot land forces here in any numbers. Their Blitzkrieg is a fizzle-out.' I said, 'The reduced intensity of their attacks during the last day or two may mean that their heavy losses have caused them to feel they must evolve new airplane types, or what is more likely, a new technique.'

FRIDAY, 23 AUGUST

Tilly Rice
I awoke at 4 a.m. this morning sensing that something was wrong and the next moment I heard the sound of AA fire. I went into E's room and saw the searchlights all caught up in a bunch, gossamer pale in the brilliant moonlight, and in the core of their light what appeared to be a tiny gold aeroplane. The whole scene struck me as rather lovely, like some impressionistic picture. I watched the plane for some minutes until it disappeared over in the direction of London.

Report has it on good authority that Dick's school received a bomb last Tuesday. Dick was in high fettle about it at first ('Now we shan't be able to go back after the holidays!') until he discovered that it fell in the school grounds, and now he is consumed with anxiety over the fate of the tuck shop.

SATURDAY, 24 AUGUST

Christopher Tomlin
An old customer invited me in to drink a cognac and soda and eat a cream cake. Wasn't it good! One customer told me that neither the Forces nor the Home programmes were on between 3 and 4 today. The news is very bad. I wouldn't live in the south. Are the southerners really calm, confident and free from panic?

Pam Ashford
There was talk about Hitler's refusal to say he will respect British children being evacuated overseas, since we don't respect their children in our raids over Germany. (Is it not the case that we bomb only military objectives?) Mr Mitchell says Hitler is right. This is total war and everyone is in it. He says 'We are going to win the war. I put it at autumn next year.' Miss Bousie was aghast at this long delay.

Miss Bousie was in Lewis's when a loudspeaker said, 'Stand by.' She was distressed, believing an air raid was at hand. However, the speaker went on to say that the Director of Lewis's had given money to buy a Spitfire. There is plenty of talk about buying Spitfires. Some people want to have Spitfires bought by all the 'Davids', all the 'Margarets', etc.

SUNDAY, 25 AUGUST

Pam Ashford

Today has been a day of more than usual rest. Even my customary laundry work did not proceed very far, for I was just starting when Margaret McEwan called. This is the friend who went to Netley Hospital, Southampton, last November as a sister. She has seven days' leave, her first break, and does not know when she will get more. During her first months she was constantly pressing her desire to go to France to a Casualty Clearing Station, little thinking that Netley would become one. Netley had the French wounded from Dunkirk. She has had all sorts of foreigners in there as, besides the French, just before France capitulated, Czechs and Poles poured into Southampton.

Talk turned to air raids. In Netley the bed patients just stay where they are and they put mattresses around them. The patients who can rise have the option of going under the bed or down to the shelter. The nurses go on with their work. They cannot spare the time to do otherwise. They like to peep out of the windows (though this is forbidden, naturally) and to see the air battles going on. They have 4 or 6 raids a day, and night after night.

'You get used to raids,' Margaret said. 'People are going to bed earlier to make up for it. When bombs drop near the hospital, people make faces at the Germans and say, "You missed us that time."'

Maggie Joy Blunt

Yesterday I received a telegram from brother Pooh in the Suez to say that he and family were well but mails were badly delayed and he wanted news. I cabled a message back and have today sent a letter. I parted with it with a pang of fear. What is to be its route, its adventures, and will it ever arrive at its destination?

It is sometimes difficult to believe in this war. This afternoon it was so quiet in the garden. From the sultry sky came the sound of one far-off plane. Churchill has made another impressive speech this week. He is undoubtedly a figure in our history. Trotsky has been murdered in Mexico. Our belated account of recent air battles has impressed America who had been given the impression by swift German reports of a shattered and demoralised Britain.

Animals must be suffering more than we are from this war. Proper food for them is difficult to get. Ginger Tom has been looking wretched for weeks, and in desperation at the sores around his head and his thinness I took him to the vet yesterday. I was told he was not being fed adequately. He needs quantities of raw, red meat. Raw red meat. I wheedled some pieces from the butcher but he told me we were liable to two years' imprisonment! I wonder what Lady A does for her Alsatian. He used to be given 1 lb of meat a day.

I stepped from a Red Cross lecture in Slough the other night at 9.30 into a darkness that was pitch, and without a torch stumbled my way from bus to bus to get home. I had forgotten how medieval our nights are now. And as I stepped out into the darkness I was touched with a premonition of terror I've never experienced before. It had returned each night, is with me now. Over a cloudy sky searchlights are moving restlessly. A plane has passed and disappeared. I am sure I heard thuds just now which might have been gunfire or bombs a long way off. I do not want to go to bed although it is stupid to sit up getting jittery like this.

Tonight and last night the wireless began to play tricks about 10 o'clock. The programme on the usual north regional wavelength suddenly died out. Last night it was cut into by a foreign station playing dance music. Tonight it just stopped. From 9 p.m. it has been wavering and scratchy. I found it again on the Scottish regional. Last night when I twiddled the dial the air was full of strange voices, dance music, light music. English was being spoken from Athlone, but everywhere else was music or voices speaking French, German, or languages I didn't know. It was like an old fairy tale, the voice of Goodness surrounded and threatened by demon laughter. This being alone at night with a fey wireless scares me. If my link with the BBC is broken I shall feel adrift, alone in an ocean with no one to guide me. That will seem silly in daylight, reassured by the homely sounds of near neighbours. But that's how I feel at night now.

Christopher Tomlin

I paid the last £1.

Careless talking has increased. Now the silent column is gone the pendulum swings too far to the other extreme. I've been guilty recently of showing off, though I never mention names or places, and there are thousands worse than me. During Duff Cooper's terrorist campaign everybody was silent as the grave. Now the terror is over an unwanted reaction has set in. Yesterday I learned from idle chatter: 1. How many, and at what time, British bombers went to bomb Germany from Hull. 2. That there is a poison gas factory in Lancashire (the place is near W***). 3. That admiralty officials are at the local docks. 4. That damage done by Nazis is very heavy.

MONDAY, 26 AUGUST

Pam Ashford

We have bombed Berlin and one person after another expressed satisfaction as they came into the office. I reiterated my view that I don't wish this country to bomb civilians; let us keep to military objectives. This is not a common view (though from the 6 p.m. news it seems to be the official one). Reprisals for the attack on London seems to be the general desire – an eye for an eye.

Miss Carswell in her shelter wonders all the time whether she is dressed neatly and what other people are like. I say, 'If I am killed, it does not worry me whether I am killed with all my clothes on or in my night dress.' They think this foolhardy.

Behind me on the bus two ladies (say 60 and 35) discussed the war. The younger lady said she wanted a siren suit and the elder responded with enthusiasm to this subject. These two might have been discussing a dress show of Norman Hartnell's. There are siren suits in nigger brown and navy blue; wool and serge; piped and plain; with buttons and with zips; at 19/6 and 29/6; at Lewis's, at Copland's. Stocks are coming in now; most shops were sold out immediately following the first Glasgow warning. There are one-piece and two-piece garments. The lady's husband is 'very strict and detests beach pyjamas', but he thinks his wife should have a siren suit for use at night in raids. It is much better than catching her death from cold.

Maggie Joy Blunt

As exhausted this morning as though I had been up half the night. London was twice raided. Screaming bombs were dropped on a south-west district, with little damage and a few casualties reported. But fire in the city on a Saturday night has disorganised that area and workers this morning 'may find it difficult to get to their work'. Berlin has been raided in return.

No names of damaged places are published. I hear that bombs have dropped at Datchet and Chertsey, only a few miles from here. I wonder if such suppression of information is a good thing. Wildest rumours will be circulating as they did when Croydon was hit. Ronald Walker in the *News Chronicle* says that the enemy has changed his tactics from mass attacks to small formations and single bombers and we must expect raids nightly now. 'This change of tactics,' he says, 'is clear evidence that Britain as an intended victim has proved to be unwilling and surprisingly difficult.'

Am reading Walter de la Mare's *Memoirs of a Midget*. Fascinating: a picture of life from a great distance. It has the clarity and precision of a fine miniature. Familiar things glow suddenly with bright, unfamiliar colour. 'Alone I would sit sometimes in a luxurious trance, like a lily in a pot . . . Only seven yards or so of dusky air divided us . . .'

My home nursing exam is on the 6th. I have asked my commandant to tea and am in a twitter about it. Don't know whether it is 'done', whether I'm not being too impulsive. But after all I was at school with her and I have been wanting to make a friendly gesture as she has been so kind and is now offering to coach me for the exam.

TUESDAY, 27 AUGUST

Christopher Tomlin

Weather beautiful. Dick's leave is singularly free from rain, he couldn't have chosen better days. Facts noted recently: 1. Our fighters are losing their ratio of five-for-one. The ratio fell to three-for-one on Sunday and two-for-one yesterday. Maybe some of the RAF aerodromes are badly damaged and fighters cannot land and take off as they could a fortnight ago. 2. Aerodromes are the object of attack. This is to be expected, but what precautions have we taken to prevent machines being destroyed on the ground? We should have learned a wholesome lesson from events in France, where hundreds of machines were bombed and set on fire before they could take to the air. 3. Are enough commonsense measures taken for the safety of RAF ground staff personnel? One aerodrome has shelters just outside the barracks, and as the barrack buildings are three storeys high and could easily fall on the shelters the risk of injury is great. And it is still greater, when we realise that the Nazis will naturally attempt to blow the barracks to blazes. Why aren't the shelters farther away? There is no excuse for muddling through in this war with two dictators who are efficiency experts. We don't require campaigns to make us do our bit for our country; but there's an urgent need for a campaign to show us how to do that bit efficiently. Our idiotic pride in muddling along must be ruthlessly swept away.

Pam Ashford

Jackie left this afternoon to go into the Air Force. He is a junior in our subsidiary concern, C.F. Dunlop and Sons, and the first of us to go (probably the only one too). He is very quiet, shy and girlish, and there is no one who does not think the training will do him a world of good (i.e. no one except Miss Bousie).

Last night the wireless gave a long statement from the Government pointing out that more intense air raids should be expected at night and that the danger of invasion was not over yet, and would not be for five weeks.

WEDNESDAY, 28 AUGUST

Christopher Tomlin

At 12.30 a.m. I heard a bomber fly by and instinctively knew it was a boche. I drew Dick's attention to the row. We listened and heard the Nazi fly around for just a little while. At times, we heard nowt, and then it came again. I saw a blue light in the sky and heard a peal of 'thunder', which Dick says was bursting bombs. We are on a hill and have a grand view. The sirens didn't go. And far from feeling windy, I wished I could take a shot at the blasted thing. I was tickled at an unexpected thrill.

THURSDAY, 29 AUGUST

Christopher Tomlin

I looked forward to canvassing for I knew there would be umpteen versions of last night's affair.

In order, these are the things I was told: 1. 'A bomb fell near Uncle Tom's Cabin in Fulwood and two fell in Fishwick Bottoms. Children were collecting the shrapnel.' 2. 'It wasn't a bomb but a flare that fell in Fulwood. Marks and Spencer's shop was on fire too.' 3. 'The manager of the Co-Op in Frenchwood came to work with a white face because a bomb fell near his home there.' 4 . 'Is it true that Marks and Spencer's and Woolworth's were burned out?' 5. 'The plane was very low, I thought it would knock the chimney off.' 6. 'It is Talbot's fishmongers shop that is burnt out, not Marks and Spencer's.' 7. 'The bomber was bombed down I think, because my husband saw a German "bomber" on a lorry in North Road.'

To me it is clear bombs dropped and that the Nazis circled around Preston for two hours because their attention was drawn to the fire. Tonight's *Post* says no damage or casualties were effected by the bombing plane. Morale: excited interest and relief that there is a war on up here too.

Tilly Rice

Today we had the car out for a drive and had a lovely afternoon cruising round: Guildford, Frensham Ponds, Devil's Punchbowl, Milford, Newlands Corner, Box Hill – a good dose of Surrey's spacious and lovely vistas coming as a fine antidote to air-raid nights. Looking out over those hills and planes, aeroplanes and bombs seemed something very small. And sitting after tea, alone on a sunlit veranda while the family went off to explore, comfortably smoking a cigarette, looking at the white cupola on top of the granary, I thought what a stupidly impossible task the Germans had taken on. To fight to Nazify Britain . . . why, they'd have to destroy the whole country and start from the very soil up.

FRIDAY, 30 AUGUST

Christopher Tomlin

Two free bucketfuls of sand have been supplied to every house in

Fulwood and Broughton by our urban district council. In spite of many public shelters we have no Anderson shelters at all. Midnight. Spewing Syd same over very quickly. There was a terrific barrage of AA fire from Southport and Liverpool.

Tilly Rice

I telephoned M and was in the midst of it when 'Wallop!' – the unmistakable sound of bombs dropping, and before you could say 'Pussy' there was a fine dog fight going on over Dorking way. Rumour has it that three were brought down. After it was all quiet, the siren starts wailing as usual. We are unlucky here: we get Surrey's air raids and London's warning, which practically always means that the things have gone over before we are warned.

Siren after siren. Four I think it was today, but one loses count. Everyone taking things more and more for granted as the days go by. E took the children yesterday, and I spent most of the day in the kitchen (the shelter room) with Jan. I have now evolved a new technique: I've started a 'siren' story and every time the siren goes I down tools and turn to my typewriter. I find that my brain works better with danger in the offing and ideas flow to the accompaniment of distant wallops. I told E of my new plan with great enthusiasm, but he was not so keen. 'Now you'll spend the whole day writing stories – what about my socks?'

SATURDAY, 31 AUGUST

Christopher Tomlin

A heavy day. Last night's ack-ack fire in the north west sent a hun bomber to its doom. Morale: people determined to carry on with a laugh and a smile. No wonder the RAF ratio is now two boche for one: for every German bomber now has a fighter plane and the fighters fly in a layer above the bomber planes. Our fellows get in between the two to break up the bomber formation and the Nazi divers try to dive on top of them. And surprisingly enough many of the RAF pilots are OK even if their planes do go down.

Dick says Hitler is moving around Britain's coastline probing for a weak spot: from Scotland he went to the south coast, next south and Midlands, then south and London, now round here. May try to invade us from the Irish Free State, and he will stop at nowt, not even an attempt to fox us with Red Cross boats and planes. We must bomb Berlin, we must punch at Germany. It's high time the Prussian Junker swallowed his own medicine! The general opinion up here: damage done to Britain is severe. The papers and radio daren't tell us the truth.

Pam Ashford

Mother and I got the 1.06 train to Ayr. The rule that names must be removed from stations would not matter if the porters called out the names, but that is never done. We stopped at a number of stations without knowing what they were. Mother was anxious lest we were carried too far, though I knew we would see the Old Bridge just before Ayr station, and a lady in the carriage said she was getting out at Ayr too, which was reassuring. There were obviously many people returning from holidays, and a fair number going.

Ayr is a good sized town with other livelihoods besides catering for holidaymakers. We are staying with Mrs Dempster, 21 Dalbair Road.

After lunch we went along the front a little and then back through the town shopping. Everywhere was very crowded. Both the RAF and the Army are here in large numbers. I am giving away no secret in saying that Prestwick is an RAF training centre, three miles down the coast. We have seen quite a number of places where the military are based, in halls and under canvas. Many of the soldiers look like raw beginners.

Chapter Fifteen

TRUTH, JOURNALISM AND
THE SKY DESCENDING

"........ but for Heaven's sake
don't say I told you!"

CARELESS TALK
COSTS LIVES

A great service to mankind: the Fougasse posters stir paranoia and
button lips.

'In the Research and Experiments Department we have a very wholesome respect for flying glass. It is true that so far only one case of a person being killed by it has been reported, but of all air-raid casualties, where bombs have fallen among houses, one in five is caused by glass. Yet I have seen people standing, during air-raid alarms, in shop doorways.

Don't trust too much to your curtains and blinds; they will do very little to stop glass flying, though they may do something. Screens made of wire netting will stop all but a few small pieces of glass. Then there are what we call adhesive treatments – that is, materials to stick on glass. When people tell you that windows have been saved by some treatment or other they're just talking nonsense. The fact that unprotected windows next door have been broken merely means that the blast on the two windows was different.'

A technical expert from the Ministry of Home Security berates charlatan domestic products. Home Service, 10 September 1940

* * *

3 September Hitler plans the invasion of Britain (Operation Sealion). **7 September** Start of London Blitz: between 7 September and 12 November, 13,000 tons of high explosives and about 1 million shells fell on the city, killing 13,000 and injuring 20,000 more. **13 September** Italians invade Egypt. **15 September** Massive German air raids on London, Southampton, Bristol, Cardiff, Liverpool and Manchester. **16 September** United States military conscription bill passed. **23 September** Operation Menace: attack of English naval forces at Dakar, ahead of a failed landing of Gaullist troops.

SUNDAY, 1 SEPTEMBER

Pam Ashford

We spent the morning on the Low Green. The RAF were putting in practice today, planes of various types flying all over the sky, singly, several abreast and one behind the other. Since the outbreak of hostilities we have seen comparatively few planes in Glasgow, and the general activity here is a distinct novelty.

The papers are full of the air raids on SE England. How different is our experience. In Glasgow we escaped bombs, but we got plenty of war talk. Here you don't even get that. There are signs of the war, of course – barricades, poles on open spaces, soldiers, early black-outs, smashed Italian shops – but one gets used to these things.

Christopher Tomlin

Saturday midnight. Mother again saw yellow flashes in the sky and called our attention to them. We heard bombs explode in the distance. Mother thought it was 2 miles away and we knew there would be a bad night again. A few minutes after the explosions, police combed this district for black-out offenders. I heard the police say, 'The chief has given orders that from now on there will be no warnings, only summonses!'

I went to bed unwillingly and couldn't sleep, for planes circled about until 3. I strained my ears listening for local AA fire and there wasn't any. I did hear bombs explode and gunfire a long way off. I worked myself into a jelly of unuttered fears.

My brother slept calmly and I would have loved to chat to him if it hadn't been his last night at home (he returned by the 8.45 train today). It is the irony of fate that Dick should come home for peace and quiet for just 11 days and find bloody swines flying up here. Wednesday was the first time Nazi bombers came to Preston. I felt as if my home was the only one in the centre of a field; that the Germans could see only me and that they were after me. I felt so defenceless; I worried because our local defences did not operate. Experiences like this are easier to bear if you have someone to talk to; they are rotten when alone. I snapped back into line, into my commonsense self with the reflection 'they will go now' – it was 3 a.m. 'They won't wait to be trapped at dawn and as France is two hours away and dawn is at

4.30 the buggers will skidaddle.' They did. But unfortunately I then heard the refrigerator from the dairy next door and mistook it for a hovering plane.

Maggie Joy Blunt

Just back from a heavenly weekend to Stratford and Warwick with Paul and Stella. I get on with them so well. We sat by the river on Saturday morning and I practised home-nursing bandages on her. I enjoy discovering buildings of architectural interest with Paul. We saw *Measure for Measure* at the Shakespeare Theatre. Could not find rooms for the night at Stratford so drove on to Warwick. Horizon a-flicker with lights and flashes from some distant raided city and in the air echoes of distant gunfire.

Now that I am home again and they have gone on to London my conscience is troubled. Their interest in everything is so superficial. They never see humanity as living, different persons, but only as types. They speak of members of the working classes as though they were zoological specimens. They speak of tradition and cultures as though they belonged exclusively to one class and had no roots or movement and as though in the hands of our present socialists and Communists they'll be destroyed. They mimic the people they affect to despise and I laugh at their mimicry (they do it very well). I laugh at their comments in all the right places. And I feel I am betraying something in myself, that I become as superficial and trivial in outlook as they are. It is such an effort to watch out for their trickery. I could cry now. I feel I have dirty hands.

Every night and many days there have been raids over London and the provinces. This weekend has been particularly bad. I seem to sleep through everything and will, I suspect, only wake when a bomb falls in the garden.

MONDAY, 2 SEPTEMBER

Christopher Tomlin

Went to bed yesterday at 10 p.m. with cotton wool in my ears. I was determined to sleep 'no matter what happens'. I slept like a top after making sure the dairy refrigerator wasn't the bomber back again. I had two or three queasy moments when I heard voices outside and car doors banging – the local ARP services and Home Guard ready to take up position. There's a new moon tonight. Will it assist the raiders or the defence?

WEDNESDAY, 4 SEPTEMBER

Pam Ashford

After lunch we went on a motor coach tour described as the Scottish Highlands, though 'Uplands' would be a more suitable word. We went via Hollybush to Patna, thence to Dalmellington. Here they mine coal and iron and I was delighted to see the source of origin of some of the fuels that I have corresponded about at times. The bus then dropped into the lovely Galloway pastoral district, and soon we reached our objective for tea, New Galloway.

But here the tone of the story must change, for when you stop to look you find in New Galloway a degree of war consciousness that is almost overwhelming. On reaching the village we went into an ice-cream shop which had as interior decorations two Fougasse pictures ['Walls have ears . . .'], and a card headed 'Morale'. Subsequently we saw this card again outside the town hall and the post office, and inside most of the shops. It is a reprint from the *Galloway News* and, over the signatures of leading civic officials of Wigtown and Kirkcudbright, contained about 20 lines of reading matter, such as the need to help others, the avoidance of rumours, and trusting God (it sounded a little moral-rearmamentish).

The town hall also displayed a poster announcing the first of weekly winter whist drives to raise money for the comfort of the troops, and the post office had outside an advertisement of the WVS appealing for the services of all women. It goes without saying that volunteers for ARP had their allegiance placarded outside their homes.

It was left to the police station to provide the *pièce de résistance*. This was a conspicuous poster in French which turned out to be a message from General de Gaulle to all Frenchmen. We gasped and looked at one another. 'Where do the Frenchmen lurk to whom this message is addressed?' we asked. But perhaps it was really put there to fill an empty space, for clearly the representatives of the law here are one with nature in abhorring a vacuum. Every scrap of wall space is plastered with public notices dealing with the meaning of sirens, care of gas masks, production of identity cards, control of noise, and rationing of food. We are not sure which this village anticipates the more – aerial warfare or an invasion, they are so well prepared against both. The windows must rank among the best protected in Scotland and the local defences are no mere barricades but are supplemented with wooden erections covered with barbed wire all ready to be swung across the road. Mother suggested that perhaps it is their proximity to the dams that makes the villagers apprehensive.

THURSDAY, 5 SEPTEMBER

Pam Ashford

The sixth day of our holiday and this is the first day that there has been no wind, and we could sit in exposed sites without being tuzzled.

We had a chat with the lady who owns the motor coaches. She said that last season was the bad one. Last September no one would go on tours, and all through 1939 people were afraid to spend money. She then evinced a violent hatred towards the German nation, demanding that every man jack of them should be exterminated, this being the only way to get rid of their evil bloody ways. She also wanted them torn to pieces. She did say that her son was at Ramsgate, which was of course badly bombed the other day.

Mrs Dempster then said, 'In the last war I never saw my husband for five years. He went away as a despatch rider at the outset and did not return till six months after the war. He was in the East, at Salonika and in Russia. I had a terrible time. He is above the age now, but when this war broke out he wanted to enlist. I said, 'No. I am not going to spend five more years weeping by the fireside. If you go I shall spend this war enjoying myself.'

SATURDAY, 7 SEPTEMBER

Pam Ashford

All good things must come to a close and now the holiday is over. In the morning we went to Prestwick. It goes without saying that there were many flying men about.

We got the 4.30 train home and reached Hyndland about 6.30. We did not get an emergency food card and had arranged with the butcher to leave our Sunday joint in a sweet shop that stays open until 9. The 9 o'clock news reported that the worst raid of the war was on London.

SUNDAY, 8 SEPTEMBER

Maggie Joy Blunt

Am reading L.A.G. Strong's *The Open Sky*. Interesting, but the principal character (David) and his problems seem just a shade too theoretical. They aren't drawn with that convincing quality Somerset Maugham gets into his characters. But with the fisherman Donough I am madly in love! As David says of him, 'He is simple, all of a piece, he doesn't have to wrestle with himself. There would be no wars if there were people like him, though he would fight to the death if he had to fight. It's men like me who make wars, though we have ten times the sensitiveness and hate war.' If I had ever met a man like Donough I'd have married long ago. Or so I like to think. But in the over-civilised diseased strata of society in which I move there are no such men.

Pam Ashford

The reports on last night's raids on London are serious. Perhaps similar blows are coming here. The *Sunday Chronicle* has an article showing the German State Railways office in London was a spy organisation. I wonder if this is truth or journalism.

MONDAY, 9 SEPTEMBER

Maggie Joy Blunt

Raids over London are incessant and of increasing intensity. Damage and death over the docks and East End have been terrible. But Hitler won't win. Rash perhaps to prophesy, but I believe I can feel a spirit awake and moving among our people. We will not be subdued. We will have a better world. Confound German arrogance. Damnation to them who machine-gun our women and children, and they do. Only last week a hundred or more factory girls were killed in this way during their lunch-hour at Weybridge. There are people in the village who once knew the dead. One girl escaped by diving under a hedge.

We have had our adventures too. Bombs at Burnham and Farnham Royal. Cows killed and property damaged. German planes are over every night. The cottage has been shaken by explosions. Shrapnel has fallen over the village. Our voluntary services are on the *qui vive* every night. So far we have had no casualties at the FAP but one never knows when one goes on duty what the night will bring. June has been wondering whether she should take G out of London to stay with me but has decided to keep him at Hampstead for the time being. There seems to be little to choose in risk between the two places though I think we hear less noise here.

Life goes on. That is what amazes and thrills me. In spite of this increasing terror and destruction over London and the constant rumours of invasion, we get our food, our papers and letters. Buses and trains run fairly well to time. Work in factories and offices and shops continues. I have a great feeling that this is the death and birth of ages . . . the old order passing . . . and life in fire from the sky descending.

Christopher Tomlin

Quite an effort to canvass. About 2 p.m. I heard the unmistakable sound of Hun aeroplane engines, a stressed note followed by an unstressed one – Pumph-er, Pumph-er – and saw two bombers cross a short distance away. There was no siren. I felt a little windy but kept on.

Most of my customers are calm, though mildly cursing that 'He couldn't leave us alone.' We are still numbed by events on Saturday night and customers want to know why local AA guns didn't fire and why the siren didn't go. At last I realise there's a war on and that I must take my chances with the fighting men. I read the article 'Don't be a Siren Casualty' in the *Lancashire Daily Post* and profited thereby. The advice that 'the chances are 1,000 to 1 against a direct hit' doesn't cheer me. I might be the one.

10.45 p.m. Preston sirens go for the first time. Mother and I take cover under the stairs, she wears a hat and gives me a mac to cover my head in case of splinters. Dad peeps through the curtains upstairs. The all-clear went at 11. We could see the flames and hear the noise of guns in the far distance. It was a false alarm.

Has the attention of the Ministry of Home Security been drawn to the fact that it's almost impossible to hear a siren when the radio is on full blare? People should be advised to have their sets on as low as possible, or not on at all after a certain time.

Pam Ashford

People are, of course, looking at the pictures in the newspapers closely and expressing such sentiments as, 'London has had a bad time!' If the raid was meant to appal the British nation it has completely failed so far as Clydeside is concerned. I said, 'I wonder what people who kept their children in London think now!', expecting everyone would say, 'Now they will wish they took the Government's advice,' which is my way of thinking. I was surprised to find Agnes saying, 'They will be glad they kept them at home. If your house is bombed you will want your children with you.' Miss Smith: 'It must be terrible to think that if you are killed your children are with strangers in the country. There was general agreement that country people don't want evacuees, excepting Guernsey children who are reported to be nicely-mannered.

The Soroptimists met again today. Last week the lunch was followed by a talk on Blood Transfusion and in the near future we are to have one on Poison Gases and their Treatment. It was a business meeting today. Miss Allan says that the streets are thronged with soldiers at night who are getting into bad company, and wants us to run a dance hall under respectable conditions. But the idea that seemed to meet with most favour was a hostel for bed and breakfast. The papers are now full of stories of men on leave wandering the streets all night looking for somewhere to sleep.

On the way to work I saw chalked notices saying 'Poison warnings in Glasgow'. Mrs Allan said, 'There are some queer stories about.' She had heard that German planes were dropping poisoned sweets to tempt children. What the evening paper reports is that children stole tablets of a poisonous nature from a doctor's cart; a policeman chased them, but some tablets were not found.

Miss Cheetham (Organiser, ARP Casualty Services) said that in the last seven weeks Newcastle-on-Tyne has had only eight nights without bombs falling. I said, 'I sometimes wish they did come here; if they came here they might give Newcastle-on-Tyne a rest. It is a pity that the sleepless nights cannot be spread a little more evenly.' This was not a popular view.

Miss Murray spoke of a London business house with which she deals. They evacuated to the country but one member (and only one) refused to leave London and travelled into the country each day. She was killed on Saturday.

Christopher Tomlin

Reports of damage done around here show that 99% of the 'stuff' has been dropped on fields and roads. Though feeling a little queasy because of a bomber suddenly zooming very low while I was in town, and after reading about the effects of a high-explosive bomb, I cheered customers with the above reflection. I hope it proves true, but we do feel defenceless. What terrors Dick is going through!

Pam Ashford

The nation is approaching a 'colossal' point in its history. Mr Mitchell thinks that Hitler's idea is, win or lose, he will erase London.

The bombing of the London maternity hospital shocked us more than anything. At the Exchange Mr Mitchell learnt details about the severity of the attack. Liverpool Street and Euston Stations are damaged. The corner has been blown off a building facing the Bank of England. During the afternoon he met a naval man just up from Devonport and he said that up till now 200 people have been killed there, and no military objectives of importance hit.

Home to the 6 o'clock news. Mr Malcolm MacDonald's speech on billeting the homeless brought the war home to us more than the news bulletins. Soon after there was a talk on flying glass. Charlie has suddenly decided that the whole house must be netted as soon as possible. He wants the finest mesh and the best quality (what a bill). Mother never said a word during the conversation, which we took to indicate consent, but it has since transpired that being a little deaf, she did not grasp what we were talking about. It was only when I began to measure the windows that the awful truth dawned, and so we are at the old point that she does not want any light cut off. However, Charlie and I are firm.

Since this is a truthful diary I will record that without being in the slightest degree in the condition called 'getting the wind up', I feel we are approaching dangerous times. What a great thing it is to have been born in the 20th Century. This supreme moment in the nation's history did not come in my great grandparents' time, it is not something lying in wait for my great-grandchildren, but it is here in *my* time. When the victory comes what a day for those who are here, and for what a cause to have gone out, for those who are not here.

WEDNESDAY, 11 SEPTEMBER

Pam Ashford

The bombing of London has changed from being unpleasant news to a source of indignation. Reports that damage has been done in Berlin are received with satisfaction. I don't know what has become of the text 'love thy enemies' – it must have been packed away till the end of the war.

In the afternoon Mr Mitchell came back to say that a time-bomb had exploded at Buckingham Palace. At 6 Mr Churchill spoke on the wireless. He makes articulate what the nation thinks and feels. It was as most of us had expected, a warning that the invasion is very near.

Christopher Tomlin

Took mother to the Empress to see *Destry Rides Again*. I would have enjoyed it if I hadn't felt apprehensive.

It is very open in Fulwood, not crowded, so is perhaps very much safer than Liverpool and Manchester. But why attack Southport of all places? I am most afraid of indiscriminate bombing.

THURSDAY, 12 SEPTEMBER

Maggie Joy Blunt

Raids on London every night. Homes destroyed, death to hundreds. The city in flames. June writes that the fires seen from Parliament Hill 'have been terrible but oh so beautiful. Bombs have fallen near Haverstock Hill, noise has been shattering, but somehow I don't mind half so much as I thought I would before it all began, and there is something almost exhilarating about people's new comradeliness.'

It makes me wish I could be with them. But I'm hard at work on the Fabian job and a good thing too as I have no time to speculate and wonder and worry. Newspapers are late every morning, letters badly delayed. Am told that no trains are running from Slough direct to Paddington now. Some London telephone lines are unobtainable. Our nights here are still relatively peaceful. We heard more gunfire last night than we have before, but it did not prevent me from sleeping. Bombs have fallen in Farnham Park (belonging I think to Lord Kemsley). Fanny tells me the owners are known here as 'friends of Hitler', having visited him before the war. (I'm trying to write this and listen to the broadcast *Hippodrome Memories*.)

There is something in the Britisher when his life, his heritage or whatever is threatened which refuses to be beaten, or perhaps it's a refusal to accept the idea of defeat. How dare the Germans think they can conquer us! We are not as effete as Nazi propaganda made out. I think the Nazis have miscalculated – they do not understand British psychology. I don't think anyone does, least of all ourselves. I am thrilled to be here, a Britisher in England. I am willing, ready and waiting to take my place in the fighting line when necessary.

I must also note this: that I cannot believe life as I know and am living it will stop or be destroyed. I feel that no-one I know in London will be lost, and that in a little while I shall see them all again. June and Kassim, Stella and Paul . . . Jules, Mavis, Marie . . . we are living through a dramatic, a vital moment in history, but the threads which hold me to each of my friends will not be broken, whatever drastic changes we have to endure.

9 p.m. News: Bombs have fallen on Mme Tussaud's, Regent Street and on some newspaper offices.

10.30 p.m. Local sirens have just wailed their dread warning. Usually when that happens a deep silence follows. A thought: German resources must be great, perhaps greater than we are allowed to know. Suppose the Nazis do go on and on attacking – really, how long can our little island stand it? Granted we are better equipped than we ever were, but the Nazis have the whole continent at their disposal. Suppose the rumours and reports we hear of the troubles and dissatisfaction in occupied territories are exaggerated? Suppose the majority of the people in Europe are for Hitler? Suppose the Nazis do win and we are dominated? My thoughts touch on these things often, particularly when the sirens wail at night.

But only when all communications with the capital are broken and war civil defence services worked to exhaustion (I in my place with the Red Cross) – then and only then shall I grow a little discouraged and afraid.

And there is the all-clear!

Pam Ashford

Miss Bousie's holiday starts this Saturday and she has decided to limit herself to day trips. Mr Mitchell and Mr Roxburgh have gone fishing today on Loch Lomond. It is Mr Mitchell's first day's holiday this year. Mr Ferguson has gone to Ayr today for his annual holiday. Three people go for their week on Saturday.

Miss Bousie asked in seriousness, 'When the war is over, what shall we do with Hitler, Goering, Goebbels, Himmler, and Hess?' Everyone said, 'We should not be bothered with that issue as they would all commit suicide when they saw they were defeated.'

The King and Queen are tremendously admired for their visits to the East End. If any harm came to them, the country would be swept by a rage the intensity of which exceeds my imagination.

FRIDAY, 13 SEPTEMBER

Pam Ashford

I often wonder at our immunity. Can it be that Hitler so misjudges the Scots as to have in his mind the detachment of them from the Union to his advantage? Or if the invasion is to be via Eire, perhaps he is waiting till he gets (which Heaven forbid!) jumping-off grounds in Northern Ireland.

Mr Mitchell has met a naval man who says there was an attempt at invasion off Yorkshire recently. Barges propelled by aeroplane engines for speed were encircled by our naval vessels. We dropped depth charges and the explosion so agitated the waters that the barges were capsized and the Germans drowned.

SUNDAY, 15 SEPTEMBER

Pam Ashford

I got up at 10.30 and worked till 5.30 putting up net. All that remains to be done are the upper portions of the three drawing room windows. Earlier in the week I said that people did not seem to take the invasion with gravity, but the realisation is growing rapidly; Mr Churchill's speech has sunk in by now. No one has the slightest doubt that we shall come out top. The sooner they come the sooner they will be defeated. The hatred against the Germans is intense, and the parachutists or seaborne invaders would receive a terrible manhandling.

For weeks I have been saying to Mother that net pasted on should not obscure light more than net curtains hanging at the windows. Now the deed is done she is delighted and says, 'Look how much time I shall save in not having to wash curtains.'

Christopher Tomlin

I want to live but through the 'Grace of God' am not afraid to die.

My people can't afford to buy stuff to make a refuge room. We have no Anderson shelter. We must rely on bricks and mortar on the pantry under the stairs and unfortunately it is not safe there for one wall is an outside one. The other is thin board.

Am scared by the indiscriminate night bombing of London and rest of England. It is obvious to anybody that the RAF and AA people cannot do much about it. We can beat off the swines in daylight but not when it's dark. How can I or anyone go to sleep under such conditions? If sirens, or gunfire was heard, each time the enemy came I could fall to sleep with a calm mind knowing that if danger was near I would hear either the siren or 'ack-ack' reports. As it is, I am continually straining my ears for Jerry and falling to sleep with ears cocked. Any unusual sound is sure to wake me. My ears have become twice as sensitive.

V. tired. I dread going to bed.

MONDAY, 16 SEPTEMBER

Pam Ashford

The idea that the invasion is off is growing. I still think he will try if he possibly can, though it will be a wild gamble. The bomb that was removed from St Paul's is also spoken of. Mr Mitchell thinks these men should get VCs. Agnes's view is that it would be better to let St Paul's blow up and not risk lives. 'They should have remembered what Mr Churchill said, that he does not mind if every street in London is destroyed. It is the lives that matter.'

The Soroptimist Club was very pleasant. Talk at the table turned again and again to the siren last night. I believe the Ashfords are the only people in Glasgow who treated it with indifference. Everyone else appears to have got up hastily, believing we were going to get the same as London. It was even said that some people went into hysterics at the sound. Most people have warm clothes beside their beds; one lady puts on the best of everything, so that if all else is lost, she is still respectably dressed.

It turns out that quite a number of people at the table don't expect to live long enough to see the peace, which they envisage as being decades ahead.

WEDNESDAY, 18 SEPTEMBER

Pam Ashford

The real thing at last! At 1.45 I was awakened by the siren and between then and 5.15 we had three warnings and three all-clears, and quite a considerable number of dull thuds which I had no doubt represented bombs. Mother slept peacefully through. I slept fitfully throughout, and Charlie says he was much the same. At 8 Glasgow was mentioned on the news.

Every morning our Granton Office sends through by train a bag of papers which the office girl collects at 9 a.m. This week Lottie is on holiday and I am calling at Queen Street Station before work. Not knowing that George Square had been the scene of damage, I left by the Dundas Street exit and had reached the junction of Buchanan Street and St Vincent Street before I got wise. There in the street was a mass of masonry. I could see nowhere on the building that had been hit and asked a man. He was excited and said, 'A house has been knocked down on George Square. You should go along before you go to work before the debris has been removed.' I was afraid to start wandering about when I was supposed to be walking to the office with the bag, but I could not resist the temptation of slipping along to the corner of George Square, but failed to see anything. There were dense crowds in Queen Street, however, so I made my way to the office by that route. The corner facing the Royal Exchange must have every pane of glass smashed.

The raids are the subject of conversation, of course. Miss Carswell got tired of getting up and going into the shelter and just stayed in bed when the last warning went. Mr Mitchell went to the decontamination centre the first time but stayed in bed thereafter (Bridge of Weir had four warnings against our three). Agnes and her Mother (under Agnes's orders) remained up all night. They have a large oriel window and neighbours came in to watch the progress of the raids therefrom. They and the neighbours had two tea parties in the MacPhails' house during the night. Mr Ferguson phoned from Ayr eager for news. Miss Smith bought us chocolate to celebrate our survival.

In the course of the morning Cathedral Street, Merkland Street subway, a cruiser in Yorkhill Dock, and King's Park have been mentioned as being hit. The raid has been a stimulating and exciting novelty and we feel that we are in the war at last. And our morale? It's splendid.

Entering the house for lunch I found Mother better informed than I had anticipated. The grocer's boy who called for orders at 8.45 had said five bombs fell (I presume this is Partick he refers to, for 43 fell on Glasgow). One had knocked the end off Peel Street. The district had been evacuated. An incendiary bomb had set fire to a house in Dumbarton Road. A munitions ship had been struck in the river. 23 persons have been injured. Mr Hutchison met a girl who drives an ambulance and she says a man had his leg blown off.

THURSDAY, 19 SEPTEMBER

Pam Ashford

At 1 a.m. a terrific din of gunfire threw me violently from blissful sleep to this war-ridden world. Mother who had slept through 3 hours of air raid was shaken up this time. I thought the gun was at the ARP headquarters in the cripple school playground adjoining our back green.

In the evening I went to the Commercial College. My mind has been torn between the advantages of oral classes (meeting other students has given rise to many friendships and one need not work unless one wants) as against correspondence courses (they tempt you to overwork and are lonely, but they do surmount the black-out difficulties). We had just entered the classroom when the sirens sounded and the whole body descended into the basement. The shelter was filled entirely by women students (surely the sexes are not deliberately segregated but things happened thus). It was like feminine gatherings always are, chatter, chatter, chatter. One had to shout to make oneself heard.

I had expected that Mother would hear nothing. What happened was that she heard the all-clear and supposed it to be the warning. She said to herself that she must work while the raid was on, and when I got in had just blacked-out, put the bird to bed, laid the supper, wound up the clocks and put the hot water bottles in the beds.

At the Soroptimist Club a neighbour was telling me that a soldier friend wants milk chocolate and she visited 6 shops before locating any. Margaret has the same story. Her dog has been accustomed to a bar of Cadbury's milk chocolate a day and declines to accept any other make or flavour. Dandy has always had his dog biscuits spread thickly with butter and now has Margaret's rations. He takes six fresh eggs a week and has his helpings of liver daily. Catering for Dandy's needs is becoming an issue.

FRIDAY, 20 SEPTEMBER

Pam Ashford

Last night Miss Carswell's sister was at the Alhambra where Richard Tauber is playing in *The Land of Smiles*. The warning was announced thus. Tauber approached the leading lady with emotion, but instead of saying, 'I love you,' he said, 'The siren has just sounded.' The house roared with laughter.

At 2 Mr Mitchell saw a notice at the Central Station reading, 'All troops except those on leave to report to the Railway Transport Board.' Is it that troops are to be rushed to the coast as an invasion is imminent? Or is it a clumsily worded notice associated with the blockage of the line due to the railway accident in Glasgow today?

MONDAY, 23 SEPTEMBER

Maggie Joy Blunt

Artist friend Ruth was killed on Friday week ago. June wrote and told me. This has brought the war into sharper perspective. Ruth was visiting friends two doors down from her own house in Adelaide Road. A direct hit. Her own house untouched. June has taken G to a school in Cornwall. M and I are convinced that we and our friends will survive this war. She thinks that everyone caught by a bomb was fated to be so.

How endless this war seems. On neither side are resources or courage exhausted or full force of attack released. Destruction in London terrible: churches, hospitals, schools, Buckingham Palace, big stores in Oxford Street, Regent Street and the Strand have been hit. Raiders creep through singly at night and do this damage. Mass raids in the daytime are a conspicuous failure. 187 enemy planes shot down a week ago.

I have heard of several cases of lynching of fallen Nazi airmen. This seems to me barbaric, horrible in the extreme. Whose fault? Our cheaper press? But what do the Germans do to our men? It's all such a ghastly futile business. Last week a ship carrying evacuee children to Canada was torpedoed and many children and adults drowned in a stormy sea at night.

The Archbishop of York (Dr Temple) has begun a series of broadcasts.

Pam Ashford

Mr Roxburgh met a man who travelled up from Nottingham and a woman in the train said she had not had her clothes off for six weeks.

Mr Roxburgh expressed his view on [Home Office minister, former Jarrow crusader] Ellen Wilkinson's broadcast yesterday to Miss Bousie who approved of every word, viz. 'An evil little creature all her days! You heard the way she said, "And now I am in a Government department . . ." What a change over! The most evil little creature that ever went on a platform. She talked under the auspices of the League of Nations Union and used her opportunity to put over Labour propaganda.'

Mr Roxburgh has heard that a German airman shot down demanded to be taken to the nearest German quarters. He had been told that all Scotland and most of England were already in German hands and London alone remained.

Miss Bousie is indignant about people being photographed dancing the Lambeth Walk among the debris in Lambeth Walk. 'It does no good!'

TUESDAY, 24 SEPTEMBER

Christopher Tomlin

Am convinced it was a grave mistake to describe London's terror raids by press and radio and particularly to publish pictures. Everybody here in Preston had the wind up thinking London's fate might be ours. Now we hope for the best and try to carry on with a smile. The siren here has gone three times since raids commenced on the north-west and the Nazis to date have just littered our fields. I understand that Preston is hard to find because it is in a valley surrounded by hills and at night is covered with a heavy ground mist: it may be true. Am sorry to say I am a coward because I rush for shelter the moment I hear the siren go. Mother and father laugh at me, they just stay put: of course if bombs dropped they would immediately move to a 'safe' place.

Father is very angry with the Government's lack of foresight. 'We began night bombing (of German objectives) in May and all through the Government knew what might happen. They haven't provided deep shelters for the civilian population!'

It's a pity Randolph Churchill is MP for Preston; we will lose our peace and quiet. The name Churchill is like a red rag to that bull Hitler.

Pam Ashford

Another quiet day from every angle. The rush of Irish business has subsided, and we are thankful that our Faroese and Icelandic connections are still giving us something to do, but that cannot last long.

In the evening I walked to Jordanhill by way of a new housing estate (Beechwood Drive). The sun was setting, and everything was pink, a beautiful scene. On the way back I passed the birthplace of Eduard Roderich Dietze, Lord Haw Haw's assistant, and I wondered how anyone could be hostile to our dear and lovely land who had been born in a house from which such a lovely sunset could be viewed.

Chapter Sixteen

NEW WORLD ORDER

One boy took a scarf from a dead German pilot's neck: a crashed
Messerschmitt in the grounds of Windsor Castle.

'The streets have all been instantly and neatly swept, so that there is no look of demoralisation. The broken glass is all in tidy piles. Men go down the street sweeping it up into the gutters as if it were ice. The roping off is as firm as the roping off of a boxing ring. You stare at the wreck of a house or a roped round crater in the road, and, wanton as the damage is, you do feel that somebody has already taken charge. London was never as efficient as this in peace time.'

Clemence Dane surveys the damage of the Blitz. BBC Overseas Service, 24 September 1940

* * *

27 September Tripartite Axis Pact signed by Germany, Italy and Japan. **30 September** Last major daylight raid on Britain. **3 October** Chamberlain resigns from the War Cabinet; more than 170,000 people spend the night in London Underground stations. **5 October** RAF continues to thwart Messerschmitt raids over London, forcing Luftwaffe to drop its bombs over Hastings. **7 October** German troops enter Romania. **9 October** Churchill becomes new leader of the Conservative Party.

WEDNESDAY, 25 SEPTEMBER

Pam Ashford

Mother went to All Saints whist drive this afternoon and says her friend, Mrs Bridge, is in a distressing state of fear; she imagines she hears sirens, bombs, guns all the time. Quite a number of other ladies expressed themselves as terribly anxious. Mother goes out so little that she does not realise that the indifference of the Ashford household is an extreme attitude. It seems to me that the people who are nervous are the people who see things in degrees. By that I mean, they say 'if things get very bad we shall have to yield'.

THURSDAY, 26 SEPTEMBER

Pam Ashford

The Dakar incident is, of course, today's news [the failure of the British attempt to assist Gaullist forces to invade]. Mr Roxburgh has been scoffing at the Air Force for long enough and the Dakar affair has given him an occasion to scoff at the Army instead. Miss Bousie is contemptuous at 'us' for allowing the French battleships to pass Gibraltar. Mr Mitchell and I, without much spirit, have been philosophising. I still insist on the British 'keeping their hands clean', whereas he thinks, 'It is no good keeping your hands clean and losing the war. We should not have let the Italians and Germans get such a grip on Dakar.' What dilemmas confront our nation. A scrupulous observation of international law seems again and again to be turned to the detriment of its practitioners.

After work I purchased an ostrich skin handbag. This is Charlie's birthday present to me, bought now so as to avoid the tax. I have only one respectable umbrella, a black one with red handle, which clashes with every garment I possess. So I have decided tomorrow night to get a brown one before the tax is on.

FRIDAY, 27 SEPTEMBER

Pam Ashford

Bad news at 1, viz. Jap Alliance with Italy and Germany. Also talk of Hitler besieging Gibraltar. It cast a gloom over both Mr Mitchell and me. At 9 I nearly shot out of my chair to hear that John Hannah, 18, Glasgow boy, had the VC. I know a boy of that name and age, and of course supposed it was the same, but from the photos in the papers he is not the same. Never mind, it is a wonderful story of courage.

SATURDAY, 28 SEPTEMBER

Pam Ashford
Last night when I heard of the intense air activity over England I felt, 'They will come tonight,' and sure enough about midnight I heard them taking their motor vehicles out of the ARP garage adjoining the back green. In the morning Mr Ferguson was told on the phone by friends in Edinburgh that they had been bombed at 8 last night, two bombs fell in the playing grounds of Heriot Watt College, two near Bruce Peebles (electrical engineers), and 3 or 4 near Holyrood. I pointed out that there is a barracks beside Holyrood, but it was felt by others that the Germans don't care what they throw their bombs at. Personally I still think when they come as far as Scotland they try to give their journey some purpose.

It is said that grocers are to be rationed for biscuits.

SUNDAY, 29 SEPTEMBER

Pam Ashford
The papers report that it was all a rumour about the Purchase Tax to start on 1st October, and that the shopping boom last week had little point.

MONDAY, 30 SEPTEMBER

Pam Ashford
Today is the Autumn Holiday and practically all the shops and offices are shut, though one does not see much evidence of hilarity or high spirits. Mother and I took a motor coach tour run by Lawson, the only company here that still tours. For the morning they advertised five long and expensive trips and for the afternoon two, the Three Lochs and the Ochil Hills. We booked yesterday by phone, which was lucky for everything was gone by today.

On Saturday I had said to Mr Mitchell that I should take a map but he said that it was illegal to own one – even mine, which is out of a Ward Lock guidebook – and that they should have been surrendered. I have my doubts, but I did not take the map, for I am sure I don't want the military to take it away. The absence of signposts is a nuisance for one has only the vaguest idea where one is.

The motor stopped at a number of hotels, all of which refused to serve tea. At one they said they had not enough food for the officers and their wives billeted there, let alone passing trade. At Blackford the driver suggested we should look for ourselves and about 14 or 15 people got food at various cafés.

The coach went on to Stirling. It was 8 before everyone was back in the coach and 9.30 before we were in Glasgow. When one pays for a coach tour to see the country it is a rum thing to go through in the black-out. This is the first time I have been in the country in the dark. I marvelled at the ease with which the driver negotiated the country roads, passed the barricades, etc. It was a contrast to the appalling driving that we had on the Glasgow Corporation bus coming back to Hyndland.

Mother was so annoyed about the late return that she goes about saying that she will never take one of Lawson's tours again.

TUESDAY, 1 OCTOBER

Tilly Rice

Yesterday Tadworth got into the *News Chronicle* by having a Messerschmitt 109 crash just outside Kingswood Church. The zooming and swooping was very loud and I heard the plane come down with a terrific wallop. This morning while out on my tour of the garden looking for delayed-action shells I came upon a cartridge clip, which I've no doubt will be eagerly pounced on by Dick for his collection, now growing apace.

Last week, on one daylight raid, Dad and I saw about fifty German aeroplanes approaching London in the distance, all in neat formation. They got up to a certain point but up went the barrages and one could see little black puffs of smoke in clusters in the sky, like currants. The Germans apparently made no attempt whatsoever to pass the barrage, but simply turned and made off in the opposite direction. Then we looked closer and saw the clouds just above the barrage were closely patrolled by our Hurricanes. One of the RAF's big days.

Last week Dad and I went for a walk across the Heath. We were just passing along the cinder track, which incidentally we had to ourselves, when suddenly out of nowhere, and seemingly right over our left shoulders, came an aeroplane flying as low as I have ever seen an aeroplane fly. At the same moment came the sound of exploding bombs, and I wasn't surprised when I saw swastikas and a cross on the plane. The moment the blighter saw us he let up his machine gun. Calling to Dad to come on, I pushed Jan behind a blackberry bush. But Dad stayed where he was, took his pipe out of his mouth and stared at the raider in indignation. He let up his machine gun at a school as he was passing, and then let down some more bombs when he was over Mogador way. I didn't see him rise into the air again and people say he crashed at Gatton Park. Maybe. Before coming on us he had circled over Tadworth, machine-gunning the station with no effect whatsoever and had, very inexpertly, dive-bombed the grandstand on the racecourse, one bomb falling on the paddock and damaging a stables, one falling in a field behind that and one falling in front of the stand itself, all very wide of the mark. And of course he didn't hit us. When Dad and I resumed our walk he gave voice to his indignation. 'The impudence – when you're taking a walk with a lady!'

Coming back from the grocers we suddenly thought that perhaps one of his bombs might have hit the Rat, but it was still safe.

Went down to Epsom yesterday to see *Pinocchio*. The previous night Epsom had had some bombs, but the Capitol was full, and when the announcement was made of an air-raid warning, only two people got up and went out, one a girl with a tin hat who probably had to be on duty and the other a woman with a tiny baby who ought not to have been there. V came with us. I said, 'Look at all the panic-stricken population creeping about the streets!' 'Look bad, don't they,' she grinned.

Rang Mother to see how she was getting on and found her as calm as ever. 'We've had three bombs', she told me, 'one on an air-raid shelter in the recreation ground that fell before the warning so there was no one in it. There's a moral there. I was in Sainsbury this morning when the warning went and that battle started. They drew the shutters of the shop down and made all the customers go under the bacon counter while the manager patrolled up and down keeping guard.'

Pam Ashford

During the morning I looked over old files and in the afternoon Miss Bousie gave me a job to sew one of the office curtains. The papers I looked over included shipping instructions from last year. I have grown indifferent to our 'Hamburg Friends', though they were one of the 'plums' in our collection, and while I suppose when the war is over we shall try to make contact again, at the moment I don't care twopence if a bomb knocks them out of existence. There is even indifference in my feelings for Duisburg and Dresden, though there real personal friendships existed. I am sure that the aluminium works that the RAF have been bombing lately near Dresden must be the place to which our Dresden friends sent the Scotch coke they bought from us.

WEDNESDAY, 2 OCTOBER

Maggie Joy Blunt

The noise of guns has increased in this area and we have had a few more bombs, but it is relatively quiet at night. We sleep in comfort and with thankfulness.

Have had a nice, encouraging letter from the secretary of the RIBA Education department *re* the Fabian work and he wants me to meet him for lunch on Friday. Am in a dither and a flap. He should be very helpful but I'm awfully scared and have the additional anxiety of getting up to and across bomb-bruised London.

M has been here for over a week. She went up again to London on Monday and has not yet returned but I have a feeling she is all right and will be back this evening. There is something tremendously likeable about M. She does all she does with such generosity. She is going to have a baby and has made June and me feel (we have never been enthusiastic) that perhaps there is something rather thrilling in the idea. The idea of it delights M. Her difficulties – that she is not married, has very little capital and negligible income, and that jobs are hard to find – do not daunt her at all. She just radiates happiness. Is trying now to wheedle from a family solicitor enough money to support her comfortably for the next 18 months. She'll probably get it – she always seems to get what she wants. In the meantime she knits and plans and beams and chatters. A heartening experience.

The number of new people I have met recently thinking and

talking on the same socialistic, New World Order lines. Am thinking particularly of JM who was on duty with me at the Point last night. Her liberal views, her tolerance, her sense of humour, her admiration of Wells and Priestley . . . She realises that politics must be a subject of interest to the people and talks of doing away with vested interests, nationalising public schools, pooling the brains of the world, establishing internationalism and so on. Again and again have I heard people saying these same things. There is no cause to fear.

5 p.m. Now I begin to get agitated. No M. Supposing she doesn't come this evening – shall I phone? But then it will be difficult to get through. I shall have to go to the call box. The guns will be firing. London, one hears, is a shambles. A friend of Lady A is driving an ambulance there. At night it is terrible, bomb craters in the roads which they cannot see. No time to pick up the dead or give first aid to the wounded. All they can do is move the living away from dangerous places as quickly as possible and stuff them into the ambulance. Horrible. No sleep. Perpetual tension.

Yet our letters and newspapers come. The BBC programmes continue with the utmost regularity. Food is still plentiful and reasonably cheap though prices are rising. Shall I have the courage to go to London on Friday? I wish M would come.

Pam Ashford

After work I called at the School of Accountancy and enrolled for their Advanced German course. So the die is cast. I said to the gentleman there, 'You won't get much demand for German now,' to which he said, 'You would be surprised at the number who take German at the Preliminaries; it may be that they think that German will be known all over Europe in the future as a result of the German occupation of so many countries.'

Ethel and her husband are here on a week's leave from the I of W and this afternoon she paid the office a visit. She has been sunbathing for three months and looked tremendously fit. The perils with which we saw her surrounded have sat lightly upon her. In fact she is not distressed at all: 'You get used to raids.' She does not get up for a warning and sleeps through all that is going on overhead.

The German planes fly over the I of W and concentrate on Portsmouth. Her outstanding impression is one big raid on Portsmouth when 200 planes (Germans) were involved. It was the dive-bombing that fascinated her, as the planes swooped down almost vertically just above the house tops. (There is a considerable difference between my Portsmouth relatives' dislike for being dive-bombed and Ethel's attitude that it was a thrilling spectacle.)

THURSDAY, 3 OCTOBER

Tilly Rice

I see from the *News Chronicle* that the Germans are now admitting that the 'Blitz' has failed. I could have told them that. They are so silly these Germans, so lacking in understanding. They think that by systematic pounding they can beat Britons down, forgetting how quickly we can adapt ourselves to anything systematic. They should have tried the uncertainty tactics – coming early one night, late another – but it's too late now. I believe I know Goering's job better than he does.

And so Herbert Morrison is to be Home Secretary and Minister of Home Security; I would rather see him in Information. I do wish though that the Foreign Secretary could be changed, as I feel that he may undo so much of the good work we are doing on the home front. We want someone daring with imagination; that's what is wanted nearly all the way along the line nowadays: daring, daring, daring! We've got it among the people. We dared Hitler to do his damnedest and he did, or some of his damnedest, and like so many threatened things, found that realisation was in no way as bad as apprehension. Still, I think Churchill is gradually moulding the Government he wants. He has brains and a fine determination, so I think we should be all right. He'll have his way. I'm a great believer in faces, and it's heartening to compare Churchill's to Hitler's.

Pam Ashford

During the day Mr Chamberlain's resignation has been announced. No one troubled to comment upon this, which surprised me in view of the bitter things they have said in the past. I drew Agnes on, and she thinks he should have been shot two years ago and she would have liked to be in the shooting party. I approached Miss Bousie and she expressed satisfaction that her lifelong foe was out of it. I cannot see for the life of me what they hate Mr Chamberlain for.

After work I bought a grey striped umbrella with a bright blue handle to be stored till next summer. It matches both my summer coat, costume and blue frock. The wireless was poor tonight, so I had an evening of gramophone records. I have the three discs making up Elgar's *Enigma Variations*, and it never fails to transform me.

FRIDAY, 4 OCTOBER

Christopher Tomlin
It is more than I'm able to do to keep this diary every day.

I feel more cheerful and am ready to serve my country, or, to be frank, to defend my own bit of Britain. I have great faith in the RAF but very little in the Army authority or whoever was responsible for the Dakar fiasco. After the bloomers made in the past I hoped the Government had learned its lesson but No! How can we win the war if such bungling continues?

Father, Mother and I are white hot with anger that the Government has made no real protection for civilians. Where are the deep air raid shelters? It's not a case of fighting for freedom but being murdered because the government hasn't the bloody sense to provide proper care for its people.

SATURDAY, 5 OCTOBER

Pam Ashford
In the afternoon Mrs Fraser and I went to see *Pastor Hall* at the Cosmo, 'the most damning indictment of the Nazi regime ever presented.' The house was crowded at 2.30 and the film is being retained. Mother who saw it earlier in the week could not sleep at night for thinking of the concentration camp scenes, and Mr Mitchell said to me not to go, but Lil had made up her mind. I am glad I went. We entered the house as they were arresting the pastor so we started off with the 15 minutes in the concentration camp, which was lucky for we knew that the other 2 hours in the cinema would not be as harassing. When the show came round to the concentration camp again Lil wanted to clear out. There was a kind of exodus at this point.

Mrs Robinson's son has returned from Portsmouth with two broken ribs caused by falling over his gun in the black-out. He wired at 8 a.m. yesterday morning to say he was coming and arrived at

3 a.m. today. The wire was delivered by the postman this morning. His arrival gave his mother a great shock, she apparently believing him dead and that it was his ghost.

SUNDAY, 6 OCTOBER

Christopher Tomlin
The explanation for the RAF's change of leaders is satisfactory. 'Defence over: attack begun!' Sir Cyril Newall has the gratitude of the nation, his job was magnificently done.

Feeling is rising against all the French since the flop at Dakar. I've heard some uncomplimentary remarks about de Gaulle. In a recent letter my brother writes, 'I think de Gaulle is just out for an easy living.' We have been betrayed so often since war began that we don't trust anyone. We even wonder if some of our allies in Britain may be fifth columnists or spies, and we distrust the cheerful things written in our newspapers. We are in deadly fear that the spirit of complacency, or the 'Maginot mind', will rise again. The French will have to do something spectacular if they want to gain Britain's confidence.

I've been granted 3 months' exemption by the Military Hardship Committee Board.

MONDAY, 7 OCTOBER

Pam Ashford
On the tram coming in Mr Roxburgh sat beside a 'wee soldier' with 'Royal Engineers' on his shoulder. Mr Roxburgh said, 'You are all "Royal" nowadays. RAF, Royal Navy, etc., and how is the war going on?' This man was a territorial and joined the regular army two years ago. He is fed up with it. He has been on leave and should have returned on Saturday night but when he reached the station he said, 'Nae, I'll jist take the weekend at hame.' He will get 14 days' CB for it, and his pay will be docked. It is the docking of the pay that the soldiers don't like, not the confinement to barracks. When he was gone Mr Roxburgh was annoyed with himself for not giving the man some tips. 'Old soldiers got up tales before. They were all lees. Their Mother was taken sick and they did not have the time to telegraph for an extension of leave. All lees. But they got away with it. You

have to adapt yourself to every situation. They are just little white lies.'

Agnes has been told by a friend that in Lewis's there is wholesale thieving by the public when the sirens sound. People lean over the counters helping themselves.

Germany entered Romania today. Mr Hutchison and Mr Mitchell want us to bomb the Romanian oil wells now. I think it is perfectly awful to bomb the Romanians. Mr H and Mr M say the time for kindness and soft feelings is over. I say the time for kindness is never over. They think the whole world has gone mad, and that is just what it looks like.

When I was in Political Philosophy at the University (1930) I was top with an essay inspired by Bernard Bosanquet on the World State, but I imagined a world peopled by philosophers. Looking into the future, may it be that some of the young folk who are not killed in the war may live to see the World State some stages further forward? But is that World State to be inspired by British/American or German conceptions? That is the issue of this war.

TUESDAY, 8 OCTOBER

Christopher Tomlin
Father says the new Nazi tactic of sending 10 bombers escorted with 40 fighters (and variations) has the RAF beaten for the time being. 'It always takes the RAF a week or two to find a way and in the meantime great damage is done.'

6 p.m. News: Extracts from Churchill's speech. Father: 'Every time the bugger speaks he gets worse. According to his speech, Germany has as good as won the war!' I feel bewildered and sick too. His attempt to excuse the passing of 6 French ships to Dakar ('Neither the Admiralty nor the Government knew until it was too late . . . ') makes me shed tears of blood. His concluding remarks are really terrible. If this is how he feels it is high time to end this bloody blundering war! 'If Poland is attacked, we fight!' And how!

Mother believes Morrison will be Prime Minister before the war is over and though I admire Lord Halifax, the confounded stumblings of the Foreign Office has probably lost us the war.

Pam Ashford

Charlie has an additional appointment. Besides being officer for the Scotland Ministry of Aircraft Production, he has now to see to the rebuilding of bombed factories that contribute to aircraft production. His secretiveness is complete.

Mother went to a whist drive in aid of the seamen today and says the gathering was full of stories of hundreds of dead Germans floating about the Seven Seas. One single torpedo from a British submarine had sent more to the bottom than the total killed in the London air raids so far.

Tilly Rice

M came over last Sunday, the first time since the Blitz started. Dick gave her a bit of Messerschmitt and she told us of a policeman she was speaking to whose job it is to watch for falling aeroplanes. He has to immediately jump on his cycle and go to the spot and he says that he has never yet beaten the boys to a wreck. They are always there first and the other day he got to a crashed aeroplane to find the little devils inside it. One boy took a scarf from a dead German pilot's neck.

She and her mother have now settled down into the air-raid routine and since they all turned out to help deal with a Molotov bread-basket her mother seems to have lost her nervousness. M said she heard a hissing sound, and with four movements was out of bed, into her trousers, coat and sandals and went outside. There were bombs all over the place, all flickering as bright as day and sending up lovely coloured flames. M called out to a stirrup party, 'Want any help?' 'Rather!' came the reply and soon she was busily running backwards and forwards with buckets of water. She said it is an awkward business going into strange houses in the dark. You bump into things.

She has been suffering a great poverty of work owing to the bombing. Her job is fashion-drawing. I pointed out to her that it was probably only a temporary set-back, for with the intensification of bombing postal shopping would increase, and some catalogues were sure to get printed.

Maggie Joy Blunt

Waiting for M again. She turned up last Wednesday all right, as I hope she will tonight.

A crowded weekend. Lunch appointment on Friday most

successful, all my questions answered and much help given. Nights were fairly quiet. London looked remarkably tidy and in form. I was surprised that the damage showed so little; it hasn't disturbed the essence of London at all. People looked tired and strained but on the whole cheerful, going about their work in buses, tubes and streets as usual. Feeding at snack bars and cafés, like a colony of ants who build and continue their life as they build.

I attended the first of the Fabian Autumn lectures (Harold Laski on 'The Need for a European Revolution'). The optimism of people is very encouraging.

Red Cross activities in abeyance, and I have withdrawn from duty at the Slough centre. There is never anything to do there, we never get any practice and the people bore me. JM has just called to say the local Point is closed for the time being. There is infantile paralysis in the neighbourhood and the headmaster of the prep school where we had our Point has put the school in quarantine.

7.30 p.m. Still no M. I was a short-sighted fool not to have a phone installed earlier. Just to know she is all right is all I want. Perhaps got some money yesterday and decided to spend it today and has been delayed again. But the 6 o'clock news said a bus caught on fire today, and a train was hit and shops damaged in London. They never say officially exactly where. It is maddening.

The sirens are going again. Wail upon wail. How agonising not to know can be.

WEDNESDAY, 9 OCTOBER

Christopher Tomlin

Mother, Father and I think Churchill's confidence has gone. Father: 'Never had any time for him,' after reading how he escaped in the Boer War. 'He hid under a tarpaulin and said the Boers prodded with their bayonets between his legs and hands and left thinking he wasn't there. What a tale to tell! He has always been too theatrical.'

We asked for encouragement and received a stone.

The poor devils in London sought sanctuary in the Underground, although the Government didn't advise them to. It expected them to stay for hours in cold, miserable, windy, waterlogged Anderson shelters, or at best sit inside public trench shelters from dusk until dawn. Londoners moved first.

On reading Winston's speech in full in the *Daily Mail* my attitude changed a lot. I like his frankness and strength but deplore the way he ends. It is hard to judge from bits on the air.

I booked 20/- worth of orders in one hour, most for Christmas cards, on which I make a trifle over 50%.

My certificate of exemption came this morning. I will be called up on on Armistice Day!

What with delay on the railway through ruddy air raids and anxiety to get the goods I order, plus risks to myself and people, the war has made me feel 10 years older. A selfish view? Perhaps it is, but nobody but me will look after my family.

Farewell Neville: you strove magnificently to preserve peace but a child would beat you at making war. In your marrow you're a man of rectitude and honour with a passionate longing to live in harmony with each fellow man. I am very sad to see you go.

Chapter Seventeen

HISTORY OF THE PEOPLE

A credit to the people who have trained her: Princess Elizabeth addresses the Empire as her sister looks on.

'Thousands of you in this country have had to leave your homes and be separated from your fathers and mothers. My sister, Margaret Rose, and I feel so much for you as we know from experience what it means to be away from those we love most of all. To you, living in new surroundings, we send a message of true sympathy and at the same time we should like to thank the kind people who have welcomed you to their homes in the country . . .

We know, every one of us, that in the end all will be well; for God will care for us and give us victory and peace. And when peace comes, remember it will be for us, the children of today, to make the world of tomorrow a better and happier place.

My sister is by my side and we are both going to say goodnight to you. Come on, Margaret!'

Margaret: 'Goodnight children.'

'Goodnight, and good luck to you all.'

Princess Elizabeth speaks to the children of the Empire, a broadcast which inaugurated the BBC's North American service for those evacuated to the United States and Canada, 13 October 1940

* * *

12 October Germans postpone British invasion plans to spring 1941. **15 October** RAF raid Berlin as Luftwaffe conducts night attack on London. Oxford Street and Broadcasting House are hit, and 600 are trapped at Balham Underground station. About 400 people are killed and 900 injured. **17 October** Waterloo station is bombed, and London Transport appeals for replacement buses from other parts of the country. **21 October** Purchase Tax introduced, a forerunner of VAT. **24 October** Significant civilian casualties caused by British raids on Berlin and Hamburg. **28 October** Italy invades Greece from Albania. **29 October** The first American draftees are selected by lottery.

THURSDAY, 10 OCTOBER

Christopher Tomlin
Almost a cloudless sky. 35/- sales in 4 hours! In Ashton too! Possibly because it is my last time round.

After tea I went to confession, the first time for 6 weeks, and while I was in church the 'alert' sounded. I walked to a town cinema where *Rebecca* was shown. 10 minutes after I sat down, a public address announcement was broadcast from the stage. 'The all-clear is just going. There is no need for anxiety.'

Pam Ashford
What has dismayed me today is the official report that St Paul's Cathedral has suffered the loss of its High Altar.

Mother is taking the aerial warfare more seriously now and is declining invitations to all evening whist drives. Her objection is the black-out, though I assure her that the 'starlight' street lighting makes this less troublesome now. However, I don't want her out at night for the same reason I don't want myself out: you might get stuck in a shelter longer than you would wish.

However, the outstanding experience in my day has nothing to do with the war at all. At lunchtime I picked up the minutes of the Corporation of Glasgow. Yes, gentle reader, the minutes of the Corporation of Glasgow, in an envelope bearing Councillor Carmichael's name. I took them back to the City Chambers – in business hours too, not in my own time at 5.30, for Miss Smith thought they would be awfully worried. The Commissionaire was most appreciative and took my name and address so that I can get a letter of thanks. I was amused by the Commissionaire who said, 'That man is always in a hurry. Rushing here, and rushing there all the time. Must have jerked the envelope out of his pocket.' No man is a hero to his valet, and it is clear that these mighty individuals who rule our local destinies command little respect from their commissionaires.

FRIDAY, 11 OCTOBER

Tilly Rice
A letter from Port Isaac says that the village is filling up. One large hotel there has been taken for evacuees and many houses are full. It

should add much to the life of that little community and it will be interesting to see (Raiders Passed!) if this enforced mixing up will do anything to cure the Cornish of their intense clannishness.

We are not being unduly troubled by raids. The children are completely impervious to them and don't even jump when we have bombs fairly near. Bob is convinced that nothing is going to happen to him and he assured me the other day that I need not worry, no bombs were going to fall on this house. Everyone I have spoken to here has accepted the nightly conditions as part of their lives and one scarcely hears the raids mentioned now.

G the butcher is chafing because he hasn't been called up yet. S the grocer hasn't even been called for a medical.

SATURDAY, 12 OCTOBER

Pam Ashford
According to the public notices in the *Herald* there are no end of bodies holding their meetings on Saturday afternoons, for example the Geographical Society on 'Turkey as a Modern State' by Prof (not a local name), and the Historical Association of Scotland has a tour of a department of the Museum for its people. For years (1935–37) I used to wonder what to do with myself on Saturday mornings. (The Exhibition, the Cosmo, and the Bookkeeping Class solved the problem subsequently.) Now the goods to be had are so many that they compete with one another.

This afternoon has been one of the happiest ever. I went to the first of the WEA lectures on 'The Appreciation of Music' at the Scottish National Academy of Music. These WEA lectures lack formality and Mr Mackie throws in many asides. Three today bore on the war:

1) 'There are people who go about saying that they have no use for music in these times. Music is a spiritual experience that we need, but what we don't want is for music to be a drug against reality. We don't want to build up a world of our own detached from the world outside.'

2) Putting on a record of *Rosamunda* conducted by Bruno Walter, he said, 'Does anyone know where Bruno Walter is? I heard he was safe in America. Perhaps he is. He was in Vienna, then he went to Berlin, then back to Vienna. Then he went to France and became a naturalised Frenchman. I have heard he is safe in America now. Does

anyone know if he is?' Going home to Mother I said how extraordinary it is that an international figure like that could be apparently 'lost'.

3) Mr Mackie said the following in a hesitant manner; he was really begging for someone else and feeling it painful: 'Last year we got Dr Whittaker to come and play the clavichord to us. I think I will ask him again this year. We might get Lamont too. He is a very nice gentleman. Very interesting. He would be very interested in you folks coming week after week to listen to music. We would need to give him something simply because he needs it. Twice in his lifetime he has lost everything (1914 and 1939). A man with international fame to come down! We would need to pay 1/- or 1/6 for an evening with Lamont – just ourselves and our friends.'

Going home to Mother I said how ironical it was that Germany should be the ruin of the man who is universally held to be the greatest living exponent of the pianoforte works of their Beethoven.

SUNDAY, 13 OCTOBER

Christopher Tomlin

For the first time in 2 months I went to my parish church instead of St Austin's. (At the latter place there is an 11.30 a.m. mass: 11 a.m. is the last mass at my own.) I enjoy an extra hour in bed on Sunday now the weary Wilhelms are around.

A few days ago evacuees – mothers and children from London – were billeted on householders in a neighbouring suburb. It is bad enough to disturb the privacy of the family, to force strangers into a home. But to expect housewives to bed, feed and serve evacuees gratis in these times is too bloody much. These evacuees have arrived without food and without money. It is difficult to make ends meet for your own family, without catering for strangers. I am aware that allowances will come through in a week or two but it is sheer thoughtless injustice to expect a housewife to buy-in until it does. Many couldn't do it. MO knows the state of *my* mother's exchequer, and how the income is a ⅓ of what it once was. Well, it would be impossible for us to buy-in for two families like the people have to a mile away. As Mother says, 'Since the war began, the onus of every damned thing has been pushed on to the people by the Government.'

I dread the knowledge that strangers may occupy my bed, *my* home, while I am away. When my brother and I come home on leave we want to sleep in our own bed and rest in the privacy of our own home. We aren't fighting for the mythical object 'Freedom' but for the sanctity and preservation of HOME!

Am glad that most BBC speakers no longer say, 'We are fighting for Freedom,' or 'for Liberty.' I used to hear these clichés with an ironic grin, asking, 'Whose freedom and liberty do they mean?' Father, in irascible mood, said, 'The Government treated ordinary people like dogs before the war and now "we are all soldiers", fighting for the right to be free. It's a wonder the ordinary man doesn't rise up and tell the Government what he really thinks of them.' We are, however, loyal and long-suffering.

The young people love Britain but they haven't forgotten that their Fathers died in vain to make Britain a land fit for us, their children, to live in. If politicians break their word again it will put despair in our hearts. But in the meantime we must hold back the Goths from our lovely land.

I am sorry our leaders merit more blame than praise. The only politicians I admire are the Labour men, co-opted into the Government to satisfy working men. I am supposed to be a Conservative, but as John Gordon says in the *Sunday Express*, what do party labels matter when we are fighting for our lives?

Pam Ashford
At 5.15 we heard Princess Elizabeth's first broadcast. Her voice is very much like her mother's. We thought she was a credit to the people who had trained her. Princess Margaret's voice at the end amused us immensely.

MONDAY, 14 OCTOBER

Christopher Tomlin
We tuned in for *High Gang* on the Focus Programme last night, but West Regional was off the air, so was North Regional. We knew that heavy raids were in progress.

Dick writes to tell us he will be home this Thursday. A few days ago while cycling along the aerodrome he was attacked by a Jerry who dived from a low cloud, machine guns blazing. Dick jumped from the bike and crawled on his belly behind a lorry which was providentially near. He writes, 'I was quite cool while I was in danger but afterwards I shook like a leaf.'

There will be two brick surface shelters in my street. One already has its foundation laid outside the front door – easy access.

Pam Ashford
Today the office has been getting down to the protection against flying glass. A man has been putting up net on some partitions, another man has been scraping the paper strips off the windows, two others have been cleaning the windows. The net man had the accent of Northern Ireland and did some gassing about the extensive damage due to raids thereabouts. There would seem to be a German prisoners' camp there and he was talking about having seen the things removed from their pockets – German newspapers, cigarettes, chocolates, etc. Some are quite decent fellows, he says, and others are real Nazis.

TUESDAY, 15 OCTOBER

Christopher Tomlin
On the way home a woman stopped me. 'I hope you don't mind me stopping you, but we are having trouble to move a bed. Munitions workers are coming in tonight. Could you give us a hand?' Naturally I went with her to a house in a suburb and took the bed to pieces, carted it into another bedroom and erected it again. I tested it and found it OK. Her mistress, a stranger to me, 'made' me accept 2/6. I wouldn't have taken a penny, but munitions work pays pretty well. Anyway, it was hard work.

WEDNESDAY, 16 OCTOBER

Tilly Rice
Today I have been feeling depressed again. I'm tired and am beginning to feel the need for a rest very badly. I find that I jump at bangs much more than I used to do. My heart seems to be taken over and thereafter my breathing apparatus doesn't appear to work so well. But all this would pass I feel if only I could let up for a little.

We had a nice little pond down here called Priests Mere. It was quite an ancient little place, and now it has been drained and shifted twenty feet or so to the left by a delayed-action bomb. Strangely I felt more angry with this unrequested change of our landscape than I have over any destruction of buildings. It was such a nice little pond with a smooth grass verge, and now it is all ploughed up with great clods of earth just as though a giant child had started to dig a pool and then had tired in the middle of the task.

One bomb brought the ceiling down in the Rat, blew its windows out and knocked all the glasses out of the customers' hands.

Later: The alert went fairly early tonight, and in spite of the low thick clouds, the Nazis are buzzing about everywhere. They can't do anything on nights like this other than just scatter their bombs any old how. I expect E to be rather late home again tonight for it is said that they got all the London stations last night on one of the heaviest raids yet. Dad came in with a story of seven hundred people drowned in the tube at Kennington – which seems a bit tall to me, particularly as Kennington is one of the underground stations to be cleared during air raids.

Whilst listening to the nine o'clock news last night I'm sure we heard a bomb fall near the studio. Bruce Belfrage was reading the news and had just got as far as 'this is the Home Service . . . ' when there was a terrific crumping wallop. He paused for a minute – one could hear him take breath and imagined him looking backward over his shoulder to see a lump of studio gone – and then he continued with the news, though one could hear the sound of voices in the background and someone calling out, 'All right!' E said afterwards that perhaps it was a drum falling over in the studio, but I pointed out that when there was any extraneous noise like that they always explained it afterwards, but if it was a bomb they would obviously say nothing about it. They didn't mention it, and neither was it mentioned in the papers today. No doubt it will come out in a few days' time. One had to admire the coolness of the announcer. [The bomb killed seven people at Broadcasting House.]

The other day, while there was rather a noisy air battle going on overhead, I suddenly heard the sound of bagpipes. Now I love street-music in general and bagpipes in particular. I thought, 'I must give them a penny for having the guts to go on piping with all this row going on.' So I picked up my purse and went to the front door to find a troop of Scottish Canadians out on a route march headed by a piper.

My parents seem to have thoroughly settled down here and aren't worrying a bit about their flat left locked up at Clapham. I asked Dad today if he was worrying about it, and what about his letters. He said, 'Why worry? After all, what does it matter!' And I was talking to KT and she said, 'We get snug in our dugout at night and don't worry any further!' 'But supposing an incendiary device falls on the house?' I asked her. 'We don't worry about that. After all, what does it matter if you still have your life!' Surely a sign of that disregard of the importance of material things from which I hope so much.

One point has struck me: in this war, up to the present, there has been a much more even destruction of population. It isn't all the young men who are going this time but an even distribution of the population, young and old, men and women alike.

Maggie Joy Blunt

How quickly the year passes. October. Long nights.

Each time I go to London I am astonished at its indestructibility. One can walk down Regent Street in full October sunshine, buy a hat at Dickens and Jones, lunch at Lyon's Corner House while sirens wail. Crowds throng the pavements, familiar traffic lines the roads. What is this talk of air raids, devastation, death, and crumbling empire? But we have heard of the massacre in the East End, people made homeless in a night, districts without water, gas rationed, and millions sleeping for safety in the stuffy bowels of London's Underground. Trains are delayed, telephone lines are unobtainable, letters take days to be delivered. Nor does London alone suffer. East, west, north and south the raiders pass over our country, Bristol, Birmingham, Liverpool and Brighton. Last week a string of bombs fell across the common, a land mine exploded in the Beeches not very far from the cottage, cracking one window pane. Our first war scar of which we are very proud.

Dinah has two adorable black and ginger kittens. They are not 3 weeks old yet but climbed from their box last night and waddled about at the top of the stairs with great confidence and determination.

Pam Ashford

After work I went to the Royal Philosophical Society's lecture on 'Nutrition in Wartime', by Dr Cuthbertson of the University's

Physiological Department. There was a large attendance and the many questions asked showed how keen was the attention paid.

Miss Andross, a dietician of the Dough School, had arranged an exhibition of wartime foods. We saw a loaf baked with potato flour, a substitute for wheaten flour that they seem anxious to introduce. This loaf smelt very nice but it does not seem popular. Potato flour is more likely to make its hit in scones. Several platefuls of scones were displayed with various substitutes for wheaten flour – barley, rye, oats, potato, chocolate-potato, and 'black-bread', which is a mixture of rye, oats and barley.

There were two dishes displayed as contrasts, one was macaroni and cheese, accompanied by a piece of plain bread, it being impossible to spare the butter; the other was meant to do without bread and butter as an accompaniment, so that you now would not need the plain bread. I think it was macaroni and cheese with potato added, but I got a little mixed. Miss Andross has made preparations from most of the wild fruits (sloe conserve, wild raspberry jam, crab apple jelly, etc.) and had a soup made from pulped rosehips, which was supposed to be highly nutritious and very tasty. There were bottles containing all sorts of vegetables preserved in brine; there were dried vegetables to be soaked in water, and dried mint and dried parsley chopped small; also French beans preserved by being buried in a jar of salt.

I just came home in time to hear the Archbishop of York on 'Justice'. He puts so much into 15 minutes that you can't retain it all.

THURSDAY, 17 OCTOBER

Pam Ashford

Mr Ferguson has been told all about the death of the Russian princess in London recently. The bus was held up by traffic lights when the bomb fell, and 52 people were killed. Tarpaulins were taken from a passing vehicle to cover the mutilated bodies.

Somewhere in this diary there is reference to a neighbour of Mr Mitchell's who was prosecuted for causing dismay. He has now been tried and fined £15. Mr Mitchell thinks the case should never have been gone into, for it was just a 'lot of women's gossip' about him. However, witnesses testified that he had said 'he did not believe what was given out by the BBC', and he has to pay £15 for his disbelief.

Miss Bousie is full of praise for the Archbishop, 'who thinks of the people', and she is going to buy the *Listener* to read him in full.

FRIDAY, 18 OCTOBER

Christopher Tomlin
25/- sales. Oh heaven, I am so weary and sick and disappointed by those in power. Clumsy oafish antics (or lack of any movement at all) which plunge Britain further in the mire. Why can't we have a man to dictate over here, to say, 'Do this for the people,' and it's done? Too many cooks; too bloody much red tape, rules and regulations. Use form XYZ12345OL!

I will do everything possible for Britain but it now seems a waste of effort and time, for with the bloody Huns in charge of the nation Hitler is bound to win. We could win the war in Egypt *if* we had three times the servicemen out there, but 3,000,000 men are allowed to dry rot in England, ready for a mythical invasion which won't come. 2,000,000 should immediately be placed under General Wavell, otherwise Egypt will quickly belong to the Axis Powers. Neither of us can win outright. Hitler can't land an army here and we cannot invade the channel ports. It is madness to think we can land an army there in spring. There are 8,000,000 German troops in the channel ports.

SATURDAY, 19 OCTOBER

Christopher Tomlin
It is so easy for me to criticise. It is so simple to watch others and cuss them when they fail. Perhaps Mr Churchill and his ministers are afraid to do the exciting thing for fear they displease the people. Maybe if we encouraged and coaxed them to action they would do remarkably well. It's obviously impossible for them to take the initiative alone. Constructive criticism is needed, not the voice of Master Sneerwell. The trouble is that we foolishly expect our war ministers to be supermen.

My brother arrived at 4 p.m. yesterday. He left Portsmouth at noon on Thursday and the railway journey to Preston took 16 hours. He thinks the war will end inconclusively, a stalemate.

Pam Ashford

The Soroptimists had a lunch today. At the table I thought the conversation was full of 'mass observations' and how interesting today's entry would be. That phase of the lunch has, however, been completely swamped out by the speech that followed. In the Polish Army there is a woman doctor, Major Martha Korwin, and she spoke to us for 30 minutes on the siege of Warsaw.

She dealt with her subject chronologically. At first it was not so bad. They were bombed regularly at breakfast, lunch and teatime, but in between and at night their lives were not disturbed. Things grew worse, of course. Nothing I have ever heard could be set beside this ghastly tale of carnage. Wounded soldiers and air-raid casualties, bombs and artillery, fire, hunger, and at the end, no water.

Again and again she spoke of the courage of individual Poles; one of the nurses going on with her work after having been given her father's watch by a wounded soldier who had seen him killed; the matron continuing after learning that her only son was killed and buried in a common grave which she would never be able to locate. The 'morale' of the wounded depended on the confidence of the nurses.

Frequently people were killed on the way to the hospital with gifts. One boy brought in dying was brought in clutching a packet of tea 'for the wounded soldiers', and a girl died on the mattress that she was carrying there for the soldiers. One death scene followed another: a soldier dying from chest wounds refused morphine as he wanted to dedicate his death pangs to Poland; dying people giving nurses messages for relatives whom the nurses knew well were dead already; a dying child and the nurse pretending that her parents were on the way to visit her in the hospital, well knowing that the child was the last survivor in the home.

So the story went on, day after day getting grimmer. 'Our hands were covered with blood, our aprons all blood; we were literally wading in blood.'

The last few days were like scenes from Dante's *Inferno*. The air was filled with the stench from decomposing German bodies lying unburied in the suburbs, and they were almost suffocated from the smoke from fires that could not be put out through lack of water. These fires were kept from spreading by people tearing down the walls of buildings that lay in the path of the flames.

Then came the end. For days the noise of German artillery had been deafening, and the Polish replies to it grew weaker and weaker. Then came the point when there was no ammunition left. The next morning there was a silence, a deathly silence such as one had never experienced before. Warsaw had surrendered.

When the Major sat down there was a long pause, as the conventional applause would have been so completely out of place, and then Mrs Tebb, who looked deeply shocked, called on Mrs Tweedale to propose the vote of thanks.

SUNDAY, 20 OCTOBER

Christopher Tomlin

The time between the alert and the clear last night is the longest there's been. During the 5 hours we heard planes pass 10 times. It is more than Father can do to sit still and read a book. He's on the prowl, looking at the sky from the windows upstairs, listening for bombs, guns and aeroplanes. Whenever he hears anything he rushes down to tell us.

Yesterday, my mother, my niece (3) and I calmly listened to the radio and acted as usual. Once by accident we tuned in The Sniffling Humbug at Hamburg, who sneered at the Underground shelter accommodation. I hate the suave way he speaks on those things about which we are ashamed. The Underground *does* stink like a cesspool. My brother passed through there and says there will be terrible disease epidemics this winter.

7.45 p.m. – siren again.

8.05 p.m. – all clear.

We are very sorry J.B. Priestley has gone from the air and we wonder who has put his back up. He must return. His talks are confident and sane.

MONDAY, 21 OCTOBER

Christopher Tomlin

A note has just come: Compulsory Government Luxury Tax. As we are wholesale stationers and printers we are compelled to raise our prices of all lines to all agents by 33⅓% from 21st October. This luxury tax we have to pay to the Government. I must be a glorified tax collector and collect the tax for no pay. Should any further information be received about the same you will be notified accordingly.

Having had a belly-full of travelling in the train in war-time, Dick is returning on his motor bicycle. It will be a two-day trip, as he will not travel at night. His machine is a modern twin-engined Triumph.

Tonight he took me to town and I rode on the pillion. It was a little foggy and very dark. We went to two posh pubs, had a couple of beers and went to the cinema to see *Young Tom Edison*, a very enjoyable film which was in part reflective of Dick's own early days.

Dick is in the Coastal Command and says that whenever we hear 'Blenheim Machines of the Coastal Command' on the air we will know it's his aerodrome.

Tilly Rice

The purchase tax comes into force today. I've been wondering how many traders will try and take advantage of it by putting it on goods they already have in stock. The announcement *re* silk stockings has apparently caused a great rush in stocking sales. I had previously ordered two pairs of stockings from Ws. One pair had arrived but not the other so this afternoon I rang them about it and the girl said, 'I went in and spoke to her about it on Saturday Mrs R, but she was so rushed with people coming in to buy stockings that she had not time to send them in . . . '

Air raids continue. S the grocer is still un-called up, but my old UD milkman came on the round on Saturday and he was highly delighted to tell me that he had been accepted for the RAF after all. George the butcher continues to be impatient.

The possibility of our return to the West now grows nearer. E says it would give him a great sense of relief to get the children out of the way.

WEDNESDAY, 23 OCTOBER

Pam Ashford

I have been working all day, but not with orders coming in. We are circulating everyone we know in the Western Highlands and Islands on the off chance that some of the estate owners may prefer to live on their estates to remaining in London under the Blitzkrieg. As I looked through the filing cabinet I thought, 'Where are the old familiar faces?' Harry Jacob and the Blumenfelds (German), Carl Haasters (Dutch), Mr Riga (Belgian), Marcel Frick (Paris), Mr Hansen and Mr Thomasen (Copenhagen), and most painful of all, the Le Seurs of Jersey. I always thought exporting the cream of the trades – it introduced you to so many out-of-the-ordinary people, but now I feel in spirit bruised and wounded. Probably this depression is the aftermath of a cold and deranged digestion, but things look black today. I do not like the rumours that France might take up arms against us. The French are getting abused on all sides (which I don't like), except by certain people with a defeatist mentality (that I also loathe) and who go about saying that no one on earth can stand up to the German war machine, so why blame the French who took the only course open to them. What distrust and mistrust we are surrounded with nowadays in our foreign affairs!

THURSDAY, 24 OCTOBER

Maggie Joy Blunt

The wind has gone to the north. I sit by a coal fire alone. Raids have slackened a little but I heard planes passing earlier this evening.

The telephone was fixed and I spent the evening making out a phone numbers index and sent a telegram to brother Pooh.

Tilly Rice

Hitler and Co are hatching something again I believe, after a meeting in Paris with M Laval. Hitler has gone to meet General Franco. *Gone* to meet, we notice, which would almost make it appear as if commercial traveller Ribbentrop has not been thought a weighty enough personage for bargaining. And what bargain does he wish to strike I wonder? It has occurred to me that he may be trying to build up a United Europe against Britain.

It is all very interesting, but I wish I could feel that our own foreign policy was being pursued with a like quickness of wit and accomplishment. The war grows more and more like a gigantic game of poker, and there are our dear old boys settling down to a nice quiet game of whist.

Port Isaac is filling up. Dear old Port Isaac . . . I'll bet there'll be some storms before the winter's out.

FRIDAY, 25 OCTOBER

Christopher Tomlin

A letter from a finance company *re* Dick's motor bicycle. It threatened to take Father to court for the balance of £10 owing, as he gave his name as guarantor when Dick ordered the machine. It is too bad to be so brutal considering my brother has faithfully paid 7/8 of the purchase price. Last time the finance company wrote they threatened to increase the £10 by 2/6 a month so long as it remained unpaid. We took no notice. Now we have their latest move.

Dick returned on the motor-bike yesterday, leaving at 8 a.m. We received a telegram to say, 'Arrived at Oxford non-stop 1.30 p.m.'!

I changed books at the country library.

Pam Ashford

These people who get up at night and go about complaining of sleepiness by day . . . Miss Bousie (who has long hair) said after she let it down last night, she said, 'No, it is not safe.' So she put it up again, with a cap on top to keep it straight. She intends in future to always sleep in her hairpins, and remember for six weeks she has been sleeping (in so far as possible) fully dressed.

Mother met Mrs Wallace this afternoon. The siren is fixed on Hyndland School within 40 yards of her house and the noise is awful. (I always suspected it was there, for 12 months ago I saw them making some curious alterations to the roof.) That is why we don't hear it loudly, for we are quite a distance away and there are quite a lot of buildings in between to break the sound. I am thankful!

Mrs Wallace is getting fed up with it and last night stayed in bed. Mother is telling her that people who get up are 'Fifth Columnists', i.e. are playing Hitler's game, for the loss of sleep lowers their output next day and the war effort goes down. Mother has a gem that I have heard three times today, viz. 'She intends to die only once, she does not intend to die every day,' and, 'She intends to be blown up by a bomb only once, she does not intend to be blown up by a bomb every day.' I've since remembered that Julius Caesar (Shakespeare) expressed the same idea in more poetic language – 'Cowards die many times before their death, the valiant but once.' First prize for morale goes to Mother. Undoubtedly Glasgow is getting apprehensive. A friend was telling Mrs Wallace that women in

Glasgow have been going daft going into his shop and buying up things to escape the Purchase Tax. Mrs Wallace said, 'What about your own wife?' and it turns out that she was as bad as his customers. One woman bought 40 pairs of silk stockings. Mother said, 'It is hoped that a bomb will destroy them.' I said, 'It is to be hoped they all ladder when first put on!!!' I cannot understand these people, for they know very well the embargo on silk is because it is needed for parachutes.

SATURDAY, 26 OCTOBER

Christopher Tomlin

Kept awake by a plane between 1 a.m. and 2.

Father has a brain-wave: discovers 3,000 envelopes in stock here and decides to sell them on Monday for immediate delivery. They are scarce and dear locally. We can sell them boxed or in 25s, 50s or 100s. There is approximately 30/- worth. I popped out for half an hour this evening and sold 9/- worth.

Mother rather flushed and upset: 'They are going to start on Preston and its dock when they have finished with Liverpool! That's the latest!'

Pam Ashford

Miss Bousie looks as if she is near finished. People said, 'You should sleep this afternoon,' but she thinks sleeping in the afternoon is bad for the morale.

Siren suits for ladies – and fur coats for dogs! That's the latest. At least 'Simba' Carswell has had a fur coat made for him by his mistresses so that if his sleeping basket is destroyed in a raid, he won't catch cold. Simba is obviously noticing all the nocturnal activities of the Carswells and last night bolted straight up to the bedroom and got into the bed with Mrs Carswell, Isa and Miss Carswell, who are sleeping three in a double bed, so as to be all killed together.

Now it is being said that the German bombers are coming from Cherbourg, following the West Coastline of England (and Wales) and coming inland at Kilwinning.

King's College, Aberdeen, was struck last night. I do hope the chapel is all right. It is one of the few Scottish ecclesiastical buildings worth seeing.

In the early days of the war I often lamented the bad bus service. Mother says that 300 of our buses have gone to London and that is the trouble, but I have heard this from no other source and think she is confusing us with Halifax, Yorks. This afternoon I stood from 2.30 till 3, and at 5-minute intervals buses approached, and passed, only one stopping to let a passenger off and to take someone on. I gave things up as hopeless then and went into town by tram. I strongly object to paying for a bus season and not being able to use it, and I felt so rattled that I did not get as much good from the Music Lecture today as it deserved. There were nearly 50 enrolled. Mr Mackie is dealing with Schubert and said, 'How I wish Herr Hitler had listened to Schubert instead of Wagner. Listen to Schubert – there is nothing nasty, or evil, or wicked.' Then I went to the Cosmo (*The Nine Bachelors* with Sacha Guitry).

The bus service had 'vanished' altogether. I got on the fifth tram, a Botanic Gardens one. At Radnor Street the current was turned off. I cannot say I fancied being in a glass house in a raid; however, I thought, 'Life is full of experience, so here's a new one.' I had had to take a seat on the upper deck and I don't think there were any other women passengers. All over the car there were male voices murmuring, 'If your number is on it . . .'

MONDAY, 28 OCTOBER

Christopher Tomlin

Last night: Siren 6.30, all-clear 8.25. The raid was on the usual objective, a munitions works 9 miles from here. Said to be 2nd largest in Britain. We stayed indoors. The shelter in front of the house is completed, but who wants to starve to death?

We are afraid of the lone bomber about which we are not warned. It does as much harm through the unexpectedness of its attack as does a wave of bombers. A lone raider dived from a cloud to bomb a steel mill and killed and wounded a score of people a week ago, and yesterday at 6 p.m. a lone machine bombed the same object and killed 16 citizens. The German planes fly up the river here and do everything they please. It isn't surprising the local people are disgusted with the Government.

My insurance agent, a widow of 65, told me Italy invaded Greece. We both hoped Churchill knows how to help the Greeks and doesn't delay. Everybody I meet hopes the same. One thing is certain, Britain will *not* tolerate another fiasco. If the Government fails to assist Greece immediately I don't care if Hitler invades us tomorrow. I prefer a man who *rules*. I am desperately tired of red-taped, slumbering, hidebound bureaucrats. An evacuee from London was trapped for five hours in the raid on Sunday. As a consequence both his legs must be amputated. How long will this bloody murder continue? Evidently Britain is still short of fighters, guns and ministers with brains and second sight. Somewhere there is the man we need.

My bother says the Luftwaffe doesn't deliberately bomb private houses, and that both newspapers and radio are at the old game of hate propaganda – atrocity stories. Heinz tries to hit a military objective and through anti-aircraft fire from the RAF often misses. But his bombs always fall very near to the target. Working-class homes are bombed accidentally, probably because such houses are usually near a docks, railway, mill, workshop, power station, etc. All just military targets. From my brother's knowledge and from my own limited experience, Fritz has not deliberately bombed civilians. Dick includes London.

Mother repeats what Dick says: 'When one door shuts another one opens.' What I would have done without the money from the sale of the envelopes I don't know. Over 30/- has come in. Every time mother is in difficulties something good arrives from Heaven.

I have no illusions: whether we win or lose the war, the working class has precious little that can be taken away. But we love our own bit of Britain and, properly led, will fight like Hell. Like plants without water, we wither without action.

How I enjoy telling customers I will be called up on Armistice Day. I do it because I don't want my customers to think I am shirking.

Pam Ashford
From the 8 a.m. news it was obvious that Greece was the next country to suffer invasion, and while out at the bank Miss Bousie learnt that this had actually come to pass. Of course, it causes comment: one says, 'What a condition Europe has come to'; another, 'Will Turkey come in to help Greece?' Again, 'The best thing that could have happened; it will give us more scope to attack Italy.' To that I said, 'That depends. Mussolini reckons to step from Greece to

Egypt.' I cannot but compare the situation today with the invasion of Albania on Good Friday last year. That act of violence jolted us through and through, but now we have grown so used to invasions, that yet another scarcely causes us to raise an eyebrow.

The Soroptimists again. The speaker after lunch was Mr Walter Jamieson, BSc, on 'The Domestic Side of Bombing'. His talk fell into three parts: 1) the mechanism of a bomb, 2) the way blasts and vacuums travel through the air, 3) the protection of windows. He had a number of sheets of glass protected with cellophane strips, varnish etc., together with samples of net approved by the Home Office. (Ours was one.) I asked the speaker a question: how to get the varnish off after the war. This is simple. ICI have a chemical called Nicromore which clears the varnish off in flakes in about 5 minutes.

I have begun a job that I have had my eye on for 5 years, but never tackled owing to the layers of dust with which it was surrounded, namely tidying the old filing cabinet. This is an antique piece of furniture that has been passed on from one inhabitant of the room to the next. We put into it things that we have no immediate use for but don't want to throw out. As the war has progressed I have put in file after file dealing with customers, countries and commodities with which we can no longer negotiate, and by now it is completely filled.

Maggie Joy Blunt

We shall discover in time that history is made by people. It is not a series of reigns, battles, and party politics but an unending story of events created by living people, people moved by emotions, ideals, passions . . .

We shall learn not that the Duke of Marlborough won the Battle of Blenheim in 1704 and so saved Vienna from the Elector of Bavaria and the line of James II from being restored in England, but *why* this battle was fought. We shall ask questions back and back until we come to the motives that governed the actions of the people who were the instruments of these happenings. We shall find them – the people, crippled with jealousy and greed and fear. Empires were founded not because such-and-such a thing happened or a battle was fought, but because a man here and a woman there was restless, unhappy, wanted power or revenge. Trivial, personal reasons. We shall ask again why and go seeking further.

I can see that every record we now have – the treaties, the letters, the laws, the pictures, verse, books and songs, buildings, clothes, everything – each has its place in the pattern of time, and can be knit into one piece and solve many puzzles. A moving web leading always to tomorrow.

Epilogue

At a certain stage, the war became institutionalised. Perhaps it was at that point where we take leave of our diarists – those weeks when the bombs fell every night and a routine took hold. As several diaries record, in the autumn of 1940 the impact of the Blitz became both greater and less, and a system had developed that was to remain in place for the next four years: the sirens wailed; people sighed and grudgingly made their way to domestic or public shelters; the all-clear sounded; people surveyed the damage or talked about the destruction nearby. Then they cleaned up, and while they waited for the cycle to repeat they pursued normality in daily lives as best they could. The excitement of the bombs wore off very quickly, but the fear never left them, and nor did a special sort of drained, low-level grumbling.

The weariness and disillusion that may be detected in the latter half of this book became persistent themes until the end of the war: our diarists often fell ill, and did not display much of an inclination to pull together in the cause of freedom and democracy until the D-Day landings and other European offensives of 1944. In the third and final instalment of extracts from Mass-Observation, to be published in the autumn of 2006, we will see that the 'Dunkirk spirit' was not quite as prevalent as popular myth would have us believe. Similarly, Winston Churchill inspired so much disapproval that he is almost unrecognisable from the heroic figures of our postage stamps and anniversary tributes.

But it is always useful to remind ourselves of the source of these conclusions. A handful of self-selecting diarists, thrown together at an editor's whim, can never hope to represent an accurate portrait of Britain. Even as they write about their fellow workers and family and friends, they can only hope to the personal views of a fleeting moment, and these may change as soon as they are posted. This is, of course, also their strength. 'The mood of a nation' will never tell us much worth knowing, but what better way to engage in individual experience than through sudden details and immediate impressions? Hindsight can mess with history to a fatal degree, and we are lucky to have such passionately argued and reliably frank correctives as these.

* * *

Christopher Tomlin maintained his diary for two more months, noting frequent raids near his home but no direct hits. Most entries contain times of alerts followed by the times of the all-clear, and many record his latest analysis of the conflict. On Friday 1 November he told his customers that neither Germany nor Britain had experienced war at home before. 'Now their women and children are bombed; neither country will ever fight again – the civilians won't allow them to.' Nearby raids inspire a grudging respect for the German bomber 'who flies all this way alone, putting his head in the lion's mouth – it needs great courage.' But he is under no illusions about the havoc they wreak among his customers, 'who have the clammy touch of the grave on their souls. They are full of dread, of terror at the sound of an aeroplane. Children scream – they daren't got to bed.' Tomlin is also nervous, and rattled by lack of sleep, and he is increasingly disdainful of the lack of adequate warnings and shelters. He learns of the bombing of Coventry in mid-November 1940 on a delivery day. 'Some of my customers say, "If they mention 1,000 killed you can take it for granted there are lots more."' The following day he concludes, 'If we cannot stop the massacre of innocents we must ask for peace. It's the only way. A preventative must be found immediately for the night bomber or our towns and cities will very soon be in ruins. We keep up the pretence of cheerfulness but in reality are terrified.'

He is still eager to join up, but not entirely for patriotic reasons. On Tuesday 12 November he wonders 'what picture the future historian will draw of my family? Not one of absolute bliss I hope, for it isn't so. My father is too fond of nattering, or carping criticism, of making sarcastic remarks to all members of the family. He has always been the same. At times I feel I'm in Hell. Deliver me from an unbridled tongue!'

A few weeks later he travelled to Padgate for induction training into the RAF Volunteer Reserve. He described his camp as 'a miniature town with wooden huts instead of bricks and stone'. He was told he would be training to be an equipment assistant at the rate of 2/6 a day, rising to 3/9 when qualified, both rates including 6d cigarette money. He also got a pint cup, cutlery and a towel. His two-day stay contained one calamity (he missed dinner because he joined the wrong group on parade) and one moment of pride (a corporal complimented him on his blanket-folding technique – 'Wasn't I pleased!').

His service was deferred for between four to six weeks, and after his return to Fulwood he contemplates the Christmas presents he will give his family, and considers how they will cope in his absence. 'I am very worried,' he wrote on 16 December. 'For the first time I wonder if it's any use to pray. At the end of this month there will be the rates and rent to settle. I wonder how it will be done? There will be no Xmas dinner for Mother and Father and me.' Three days later, things were looking up again. His brother had sent £1, and an aunt 10 shillings and nine pints of Worthington. His last entry reads: '3 alerts today. Order not here. Exchanged presents with my aunts. To cinema, bought 10 Players – first since the increased tobacco tax. Only four weeks at the most before I'm in uniform.'

I have been unable to discover what happened to him next. It would have been easier to trace his progress through the war had Christopher Tomlin been his real name. His real name was very common, particularly in Lancashire, and in researching wartime and post-war death registrations I came across at least 25 people who almost matched his particular details of birth, parentage and locality, but none who match precisely. Over the Internet I have contacted people with his surname all over the world without luck. If any readers recognise a relative or neighbour from his diary I would be delighted to discover more about him for use in a future edition.

* * *

The same applies to Tilly Rice. The final image we have of her is distressing. On 15 December she writes of her growing friendship with several Port Isaac locals, and describes how one woman was worried about her husband in Coventry. 'On Saturday she got a letter. It had been a week coming, and in it he said that he couldn't wire as everything was bombed to blazes. He said, "You have to see the destruction to believe it . . . it's a job to get anywhere to stay . . . Jerry has been over a bit – he likes to come and machine-gun the workers as they come out of the factories . . . "'

She reports that her own affairs have been chaotic. Bob, her youngest son, and Janet, her year-old daughter, both had whooping cough. 'Jan is rather bad right now and I have been worrying about her – despite my front of not caring. Still, my good Scottish doctor assures me that *he* isn't worrying – and I shan't if he isn't.' Her next entry is two weeks later, at the very beginning of 1941. 'My anxiety over Jan must have been instinctive, for two days before Xmas she died suddenly of heart failure following the whooping cough. This horrid blow set me in a state of confusion, and for some days the war and all that was happening with regard to it simply didn't exist. Everyone was wonderfully kind and so sad over her death that she might have been a native of the place.'

In the grieving weeks that followed she hoped that 1941 would be a better year for her family and the country. She noted that food supplies were adequate, although cakes had been rationed locally. Her sons remark on every passing plane, and she wrote of a conversation with her children.

'After the war, Mummy, it might be worster.'

'Why Bob?'

'Because there won't be any houses left.'

'But we shall have new ones,' puts in Dick.

Bob claps his hands. 'Ooo! Lovely new white houses - won't that be lovely!'

On 14 January, two weeks before her last entry, she had a conversation with a local registrar about his experiences with evacuees. He said that many were considering returning to London and were keen for him to provide the train fare. She told him that she had heard there would soon be a fresh batch arriving in Port Isaac. 'Now what did you want to tell me that for?' he asked. 'You quite spoilt my day.'

* * *

In the spring of 2005 I drove past Pam Ashford's former home in Hyndland Road, a typical brownstone tenement subdivided into many flats and undergoing refurbishment. I also stopped at her office in Hope Street, where the Forth & Clyde Shipping Co. is now an office supply company and stands next to the Solid Rock Café. What would Pam Ashford have made of the new Glasgow? I think she would have loved it, and I doubt she would have borne much sentiment for the old.

She continued to write for Mass-Observation throughout the war. In October 1941 her colleagues consider what will happen when the war ends. They imagine 'gorging ices, chocolate and cakes . . . orgies of spending on clothes . . . dancing till the small hours. All the wishes were of a pleasure nature; all presumed victorious conclusion; all presumed a reversion to pre-war conditions.' Ashford predicts that there will be a 'titanic' crisis before the war ends. 'I am quite sure that if not on the armistice day, then some time in the following week, I shall go into hysterics and cry like a watering cart.'

Ashford changed jobs twice, moving first to the US War Shipping Administration in Glasgow and then to an accountancy firm, Moores, Carson and Watson in West George Street, but she keeps in touch with Mr Mitchell and Miss Bousie as best she can. Her American colleagues become observed in a familiar manner in her new job, and one of them, a certain Captain MacGowan, treats her as if she is a spy. The Americans introduced her to many novel phrases and practices, including the US legal system and the concept of Mother's Day. 'People send their mothers flowers, candy and telegrams,' she notes. 'In the States no one would think it odd to send a friendly telegram to a colleague's wife. I am not at all sure that I would not like British people to do the same.'

She continues to attend Soroptimist meetings throughout the war, but begins to question their purpose. In early 1944 one meeting includes a raffle of items sent from friends in California: 'Eight boxes of biscuits, six small cakes of chocolate, a large piece of chocolate and a box of tea. I got a box of vanilla wafers. Lucky me! Table talk was ordinary. Before I was a Soroptimist I thought that at such gatherings the conversation scintillated. What a mistake.'

Pam Ashford's last entries for Mass-Observation were written in September 1945, not long after VJ Day. Churchill has been defeated by Attlee. The soldiers are returning, crime levels are increasing, and the country is settling into its gloomy period of reconstruction and austerity. Meanwhile, a friend of hers has her hair done in an American style; she learns that her old colleagues Mr Hutchison and Mr Ferguson have quarrelled; and she is looking forward to going to the theatre and art exhibitions more often. In Queen Street, the *Daily Express* Reading Room is showing photographs of Belsen.

* * *

Eileen Potter contributed no further diaries to Mass-Observation following her last entry in August 1940, but she did write two pages in response to MO's specific request for observers' experiences of VE Day in May 1945. She was still employed by the London County Council, and reported as usual on 7 May to find everyone too excited to concentrate on work. The red flag is suspended from the window of the ladies' lavatory and she thinks an operation to have her teeth extracted may be postponed. She spends the morning of 8 May at Kew Gardens, and is tempted to remain all day rather than battle through the jubilant crowds in the West End. But she returns home at lunchtime, and sets off with eight friends to Piccadilly Circus. 'We see several sailors and girls sliding down the boarded-up part below the statue of Eros, and also several "Yanks" perched on top of lamp-posts etc.' They carry on to the Cenotaph, where they hear Churchill's speech, and then it's on to St James's Park and Buckingham Palace before returning home. In the evening Potter attends her local church. 'The service is normally very "high", but there is little of that sort of thing tonight. The vicar, who was leader of the local fire-guard, shakes hands with all of us as we come out, and seems pleased to see us all . . . ' She listens to the King's speech with friends, but is chastised for not putting down her knitting while he is speaking, and for not standing during 'God Save The King'. Then she goes out again for a shandy, and to admire the local bonfires and choruses of 'Knees Up Mother Brown'. Her last entry reads, 'After the others have gone to bed, I sit up for some time in my own rooms, listening to the dance music on the wireless.'

Eileen Potter died in 1974 at the age of 76. She was unmarried, and still lived in South London. Her cause of death was registered as bronchopneumonia and primary senile dementia.

***

Not long after *Our Hidden Lives* was published I was fortunate to meet the niece of Maggie Joy Blunt, who told me of her aunt's post-war authorship of a book about the eighteenth-century Irish actress Mary Woffington and about the small bookshop she ran near her home in Farnham. At a meeting of the Farnhams' Society a few months later I also met several people who remembered her in the village – the bun in her hair, her serious but kind demeanour, her specialisation in cat books that drew visitors from abroad. I was introduced to the present owners of Wee Cottage, a young professional couple who work in London, who told me that, apart from its value and a small extension added in the 1980s, it probably hasn't changed that much since she lived in it. I also met a dyslexic man who told me that he would be forever grateful to Maggie Joy for helping him learn to read.

She continued writing to Mass-Observation throughout the war. In April 1946, at the age of 36, she composed a brief biographical sketch. 'My mother was an accomplished pianist before she married and had intended for herself a musical career,' she wrote. Her father was an architect, and for a while she intended to pursue the same career. But she failed her exams at University College, London, and switched courses. 'At the end of five years I left UCL with a Journalism Diploma, many new ideas, high ambitions and several good friends.

'That was in 1935. I continued my independent existence with Bohemian friends in Charlotte Street, near Fitzroy Square . . . For a year I studied ballroom dancing with Gwen Silvester (brother of Victor), and then joined a friend in Malta for a year. When we came home in 1938, war seemed inevitable, but it was not for this reason that I decided to take a cottage in the country. The lease of my flat [in Hampstead] ended in June 1939 and I wanted a change of scenery.

'An article on Malta was accepted by the *Architectural Review* and I intended to settle down in my rural retreat to writing seriously. The war intervened. I did some research on the education of architects for the Fabian Society, housed bombed-out friends, surveyed the blitzed City and worked for a short period at the end of 1941 for *Architect & Building News* and then the Fabian Society. In Jan. 1942 I obtained a job with the light alloy aircraft firm, High Duty Alloys Ltd, in Slough, as a writer in their very small publicity department, where I stayed until Feb. 1946.

'I have not married. I have no children. But I have many friends. I have had four lovers. I have had a few articles published, all on Malta, and still cherish an ambition to have other articles in print. I still cherish, also, the hope that I shall marry. Whether these ambitions will ever be realised I do not know . . . '

Maggie Joy Blunt died from cancer in August 1986, at the age of seventy-six. She had remained single and childless.

* * *

Almost 70 years after it was formed, Mass-Observation has far exceeded the ambitions of its original founders. A few people maintained their diaries into the 1960s, but most stopped long before. In 1967 Tom Harrisson transferred the majority of M-O documents to the University of Sussex, and the huge job of cataloguing the hundreds of thousands of pages began.

By the time Maggie Joy Blunt passed away, Mass-Observation had a fresh purpose. A new Project was established in 1981, and today has a database of more than 400 correspondents answering questionnaires and keeping records of their lives (themes have included the death of the Princess of Wales, mobile phones, owning pets, Saturday afternoons and the war in Iraq). The Project is keen to recruit new members to its panel.

moa@sussex.ac.uk

Or write to:

The Mass-Observation Project
Special Collections
The Library
University of Sussex
Brighton
BN1 9QL
UK

Acknowledgements

I wish to thank all the people who have worked so enthusiastically on this book at Ebury and Random House. I am also grateful to Jules Churchill, Sam Carroll, Jenna Bailey and Jake Garfield for assistance with photocopying and transcripts, and to Babs Everett, John and Caroline Benge, and Martin Bright for providing valuable information about the diarists and the period. As ever, Pat Kavanagh and her associates at PFD have provided terrific guidance. I am particularly indebted to the Trustees of the Mass-Observation Archive and Dorothy Sheridan, head of Special Collections at the University of Sussex library. With the help of many colleagues they have ensured that the archive is a vibrant and stimulating place, and one which continues to delight all those who use it.

www.sussex.ac.uk/library/massobs
www.simongarfield.com

Index